CompTIA A+®
Complete Fast Pass™

CompTIA A+®
Complete Fast Pass™

Emmett Dulaney

Wiley Publishing, Inc.

Acquisitions and Development Editor: Jeff Kellum
Technical Editor: Bill Ferguson
Production Editors: Martine Dardignac and Rachel Meyers
Copy Editor: Tiffany Taylor
Production Manager: Tim Tate
Vice President and Executive Group Publisher: Richard Swadley
Vice President and Executive Publisher: Joseph B. Wikert
Vice President and Publisher: Neil Edde
Media Development Specialist: Kit Malone
Book Designers: Judy Fung and Bill Gibson
Compositor: Jeffrey Wilson, Happenstance Type-O-Rama
Proofreader: Candace English
Indexer: Nancy Guenther
Cover Designers: Richard Miller, Calyx Design; Ryan Sneed

for Karen

Acknowledgments

There are a great many people to thank but three are key; without them this book would not be possible. First and foremost is Jeff Kellum of Sybex, who does his job extremely well and pulls you along with him. Thanks must also go to Faithe Wempen and David Groth for their work on the previous edition.

I also thank the production editors, Martine Dardignac and Rachel Meyers; the technical editor, Bill Ferguson; and the copy editor, Tiffany Taylor. Without their hard work, I would have never completed this book.

Contents at a Glance

Contents

Introduction

The A+ certification program was developed by the Computing Technology Industry Association (CompTIA) to provide an industry-wide means of certifying the competency of computer service technicians. The A+ certification, which is granted to those who have attained the level of knowledge and troubleshooting skills that are needed to provide capable support in the filed of personal computers, is similar to other certifications in the computer industry. For example, Microsoft offers the Microsoft Certified Systems Administrator (MCSA) and Microsoft Certified Systems Engineer (MCSE) programs to provide recognition to those professionals who deal with their products, and Novell has the Certified Novell Administrator (CNA) and Certified Novell Engineer (CNE) programs. The theory behind these certifications is that if you needed to have service performed on any of their products, you would sooner call a technician who has been certified in one of the appropriate programs than you would just call the first so-called expert in the phone book.

CompTIA's A+ exam objectives are periodically updated to keep the certification applicable to the most recent hardware and software. This is necessary because a technician must be able to work on the latest equipment. The most recent revisions to the objectives—and to the whole program—were enacted in 2006 and are reflected in this book.

This book and the Sybex *CompTIA A+ Complete Study Guide* (both the Standard and Deluxe Editions) are tools to help you prepare for this certification—and for the new areas of focus of a modern computer technician's job.

What Is A+ Certification?

The A+ certification program was created to offer a wide-ranging certification, in the sense that it's intended to certify competence with personal computers from many different makers/vendors. For the first time in its existence, you have the ability to become certified through three different paths. Everyone must take and pass the A+ Essentials exam. You can then choose one of the following:

- The A+ 220-602 exam, which is targeted for those with a high level of face-to-face contact in a corporate environment (some of the roles are enterprise technician, IT administrator, field service technician, and PC technician). Once you have taken and passed both the Essentials and 220-602 exams, you'll be certified with the IT Technician designation.

- The A+ 220-603 exam, which is targeted for those who work in remote-based environments in which client interaction, client training, operating systems, and connectivity are emphasized (some of the roles are remote support technician, help desk technician, call center technician, specialist, and representative). Once you have taken and passed both the Essentials and 220-603 exams, you'll be certified with the Remote Support Technician designation.

- The A+ 220-604 exam, which is targeted for those who work in settings with limited customer interaction and where hardware-related activities are emphasized (some of the roles are depot technician and bench technician). Once you have taken and passed both the Essentials and 220-604 exams, you'll be certified with the Depot Technician designation.

 CompTIA has left the door open for possible additional exams and designations. For more information on the exams, visit CompTIA's website at www.comptia.org.

You don't have to take the Essentials exam and the technician exam at the same time; you have 90 days from the time you pass one exam to pass the second test. The A+ certification isn't awarded until you've passed both tests. For the latest pricing on the exams and updates to the registration procedures, call Thomson Prometric at 866-Prometric (776-6387) or 800-77-MICRO (776-4276) or Pearson VUE at (877) 551-7587. You can also go to either www.2test.com or www.prometric.com for Thomson Prometric or www.vue.com for Pearson VUE for additional information or to register online. If you have further questions about the scope of the exams or related CompTIA programs, refer to the CompTIA website at www.comptia.org.

Who Should Buy This Book?

If you want to acquire a solid foundation in personal computer basics, and your goal is to prepare for the exams by filling in any gaps in your knowledge, this book is for you. You'll find clear explanations of the concepts you need to grasp and plenty of help to achieve the high level of professional competency you need in order to succeed in your chosen field.

If you want to become certified as an A+ holder, this book is definitely what you need. However, if you just want to attempt to pass the exam without really understanding the basics of personal computers, this guide isn't for you. It's written for people who want to acquire skills and knowledge of personal computer basics.

How to Use This Book and the CD

We've included several testing features in the book and on the CD-ROM. These tools will help you retain vital exam content as well as prepare to sit for the actual exams:

Chapter review questions   To test your knowledge as you progress through the book, there are review questions at the end of each chapter. As you finish each chapter, answer the review questions and then check your answers—the correct answers appear on the page following the review questions. You can go back to reread the section that deals with each question you got wrong to ensure that you answer correctly the next time you're tested on the material.

Electronic flashcards   You'll find flashcard questions on the CD for on-the-go review. These are short question and answers, just like the flashcards you probably used to study in school. You can answer them on your PC or download them onto a Palm device for quick and convenient reviewing.

Test engine   The CD also contains the Sybex Test Engine. Using this custom test engine, you can identify weak areas up front and then develop a solid studying strategy using each of these robust testing features. Our thorough readme file will walk you through the quick, easy installation process.

In addition to taking the assessment test and answering the chapter review questions in the test engine, you'll find sample exams on the CD. Take these practice exams just as if you were taking the actual exam (without any reference material). When you've finished the first exam, move on to the next one to solidify your test-taking skills. If you get more than 90 percent of the answers correct, you're ready to take the certification exams.

Because you need to take only one of the Technician exams, the likelihood of taking all three should be nonexistent. Therefore, some of the questions in the three "Technician" exams are the same, since there is so much overlap between the exam objectives.

Glossary of Terms in PDF   The CD-ROM contains this a very useful Glossary of Terms in PDF (Adobe Acrobat) format so you can easily read it on any computer. If you have to travel and brush up on any Key Terms, and you have a laptop with a CD-ROM drive, you can do so with this useful resource.

Minimum System Requirements

You should have a minimum of 45MB of disk space, as well as Windows 98 or higher to use the Sybex Test Engine. You will also need Adobe Acrobat Reader (included) for the Glossary.

Tips for Taking the A+ Exams

Here are some general tips for taking your exams successfully:

- Bring two forms of ID with you. One must be a photo ID, such as a driver's license. The other can be a major credit card or a passport. Both forms must include a signature.

- Arrive early at the exam center so you can relax and review your study materials, particularly tables and lists of exam-related information.

- Read the questions carefully. Don't be tempted to jump to an early conclusion. Make sure you know exactly what the question is asking.

- Don't leave any unanswered questions. Unanswered questions are scored against you.

- There will be questions with multiple correct responses. When there is more than one correct answer, a message at the bottom of the screen will prompt you to either "Choose two" or "Choose all that apply." Be sure to read the messages displayed to know how many correct answers you must choose.

- When answering multiple-choice questions you're not sure about, use a process of elimination to get rid of the obviously incorrect answers first. Doing so will improve your odds if you need to make an educated guess.

- On form-based tests (nonadaptive), because the hard questions will eat up the most time, save them for last. You can move forward and backward through the exam.

- For the latest pricing on the exams and updates to the registration procedures, visit CompTIA's website at www.comptia.org.

Exam Objectives

CompTIA goes to great lengths to ensure that its certification programs accurately reflect the IT industry's best practices. The company does this by establishing Cornerstone Committees for each of its exam programs. Each committee comprises a small group of IT professionals, training providers, and publishers who are responsible for establishing the exam's baseline competency level and who determine the appropriate target audience level.

Once these factors are determined, CompTIA shares this information with a group of hand-selected Subject Matter Experts (SMEs). These folks are the true brainpower behind the certification program. They review the committee's findings, refine them, and shape them into the objectives you see before you. CompTIA calls this process a Job Task Analysis (JTA).

Finally, CompTIA conducts a survey to ensure that the objectives and weightings truly reflect the job requirements. Only then can the SMEs go to work writing the hundreds of questions needed for the exam. And, in many cases, they have to go back to the drawing board for further refinements before the exam is ready to go live in its final state. So, rest assured, the content you're about to learn will serve you long after you take the exam.

 Exam objectives are subject to change at any time without prior notice and at CompTIA's sole discretion. Please visit the certification page of CompTIA's website at www.comptia.org for the most current listing of exam objectives.

CompTIA also publishes relative weightings for each of the exam's objectives. The following tables list the objective domains and the extent to which they're represented on each exam. For example, expect to spend more time answering questions that pertain to operating systems on the Essentials exam than questions on professionalism.

Essentials Exam Domains	% of Exam
1.0 Personal Computer Components	21%
2.0 Laptops and Portable Devices	11%
3.0 Operating Systems	21%
4.0 Printers and Scanners	9%
5.0 Networks	12%
6.0 Security	11%
7.0 Safety and Environmental Issues	10%
8.0 Professionalism and Communication	5%
Total	**100%**

220-602 Exam Domains	% of Exam
1.0 Personal Computer Components	18%
2.0 Laptops and Portable Devices	9%
3.0 Operating Systems	20%
4.0 Printers and Scanners	14%
5.0 Networks	11%
6.0 Security	8%
7.0 Safety and Environmental Issues	5%
8.0 Professionalism and Communication	15%
Total	**100%**

220-603 Exam Domains	% of Exam
1.0 Personal Computer Components	15%
2.0 Operating Systems	29%
3.0 Printers and Scanners	10%
4.0 Networks	11%
5.0 Security	15%
6.0 Professionalism and Communication	20%
Total	**100%**

220-604 Exam Domains	% of Exam
1.0 Personal Computer Components	45%
2.0 Laptops and Portable Devices	20%
3.0 Printers and Scanners	20%
4.0 Security	5%
5.0 Safety and Environmental Issues	10%
Total	**100%**

The following sections look at the objectives beneath each of these in more detail.

A+ Essentials Exam Objectives

1.0 Personal Computer Components

1.1 Identify the fundamental principles of using personal computers

- Identify the names, purposes, and characteristics of storage devices
  - FDD
  - HDD
  - CD / DVD/ RW (e.g. drive speeds, media types)
  - Removable storage (e.g. tape drive, solid state such as thumb drive, flash and SD cards, USB, external CD-RW and hard drive)
- Identify the names, purposes and characteristics of motherboards
  - Form Factor (e.g. ATX / BTX, micro ATX / NLX)
  - Components
    - Integrated I/Os (e.g. sound, video, USB, serial, IEEE 1394 / firewire, parallel, NIC, modem)
    - Memory slots (e.g. RIMM, DIMM)
    - Processor sockets
    - External cache memory

- Bus architecture
- Bus slots (e.g. PCI, AGP, PCIE, AMR, CNR)
- EIDE/ PATA
- SATA
- SCSI Technology
- Chipsets
- BIOS/ CMOS / Firmware
- Riser card / daughter board
  - Identify the names, purposes and characteristics of power supplies, for example: AC adapter, ATX, proprietary, voltage
  - Identify the names purposes and characteristics of processor / CPUs
- CPU chips (e.g. AMD, Intel)
- CPU technologies
  - Hyperthreading
  - Dual core
  - Throttling
  - Micro code (MMX)
  - Overclocking
  - Cache
  - VRM
  - Speed (real vs. actual)
  - 32 vs. 64 bit
- Identify the names, purposes and characteristics of memory
  - Types of memory (e.g. DRAM, SRAM, SDRAM, DDR / DDR2, RAMBUS)
  - Operational characteristics
    - Memory chips (8, 16, 32)
    - Parity versus non-parity
    - ECC vs. non-ECC
    - Single-sided vs. double-sided
- Identify the names, purposes and characteristics of display devices, for example: projectors, CRT and LCD

- Connector types (e.g. VGA, DVI / HDMi, S-Video, Component / RGB)
  - Settings (e.g. V-hold, refresh rate, resolution)
- Identify the names, purposes and characteristics of input devices for example: mouse, keyboard, bar code reader, multimedia (e.g. web and digital cameras, MIDI, microphones), biometric devices, touch screen
- Identify the names, purposes and characteristics of adapter cards
  - Video including PCI / PCI-E and AGP
  - Multimedia
  - I/O (SCSI, serial, USB, Parallel)
  - Communications including network and modem
- Identify the names, purposes and characteristics of ports and cables for example: USB 1.1 and 2.0, parallel, serial, IEEE 1394 / firewire, RJ45 and RJ11, PS2 / MINI-DIN, centronics (e.g. mini, 36) multimedia (e.g. 1 / 8 connector, MIDSI COAX, SPDIF)
- Identify the names, purposes and characteristics of cooling systems for example heat sinks, CPU and case fans, liquid cooling systems, thermal compound

1.2 Install, configure, optimize and upgrade personal computer components

- Add, remove and configure internal and external storage devices
  - Drive preparation of internal storage devices including format / file systems and imaging technology
- Install display devices
- Add, remove and configure basic input and multimedia devices

1.3 Identify tools, diagnostic procedures and troubleshooting techniques for personal computer components

- Recognize the basic aspects of troubleshooting theory for example:
  - Perform backups before making changes
  - Assess a problem systematically and divide larger problems into smaller components to be analyzed individually
  - Verify even the obvious, determine whether the problem is something simple and make no assumptions
  - Research ideas and establish priorities
  - Document findings, actions and outcomes

- Identify and apply basic diagnostic procedures and troubleshooting techniques for example:
  - Identify the problem including questioning user and identifying user changes to computer
  - Analyze the problem including potential causes and make an initial determination of software and / or hardware problems
  - Test related components including inspection, connections, hardware / software configurations, device manager and consult vendor documentation
  - Evaluate results and take additional steps if needed such as consultation, use of alternate resources, manuals
  - Document activities and outcomes
- Recognize and isolate issues with display, power, basic input devices, storage, memory, thermal, POST errors (e.g. BIOS, hardware)
- Apply basic troubleshooting techniques to check for problems (e.g. thermal issues, error codes, power, connections including cables and / or pins, compatibility, functionality, software / drivers) with components for example:
  - Motherboards
  - Power supply
  - Processor/CPUs
  - Memory
  - Display devices
  - Input devices
  - Adapter cards
- Recognize the names, purposes, characteristics and appropriate application of tools for example: BIOS, self-test, hard drive self-test and software diagnostic test

1.4 Perform preventative maintenance on personal computer components

- Identify and apply basic aspects of preventative maintenance theory for example:
  - Visual / audio inspection
  - Driver / firmware updates
  - Scheduling preventative maintenance
  - Use of appropriate repair tools and cleaning materials
  - Ensuring proper environment
- Identify and apply common preventative maintenance techniques for devices such as input devices and batteries

2.0 Laptops and Portable Devices

2.1 Identify the fundamental principles of using laptops and portable devices

- Identify names, purposes and characteristics of laptop-specific:
  - Form factors such as memory and hard drives
  - Peripherals (e.g. docking station, port replicator and media / accessory bay)
  - Expansion slots (e.g. PCMCIA I, II, and III, card and express bus)
  - Ports (e.g. mini PCI slot)
  - Communication connections (e.g. Bluetooth, infrared, cellular, WAN, Ethernet)
  - Power and electrical input devices (e.g. auto-switching and fixed-input power supplies, batteries)
  - LCD technologies (e.g. active and passive matrix, resolution such as XGA, SXGA+, UXGA, WUXGA, contrast ratio, native resolution)
  - Input devices (e.g. stylus / digitizer, function (Fn) keys and pointing devices such as touch pad, point stick / track point)
- Identify and distinguish between mobile and desktop motherboards and processors including throttling, power management and WiFi

2.2 Install, configure, optimize and upgrade laptops and portable devices

- Configure power management
  - Identify the features of BIOS-ACPI
  - Identify the difference between suspend, hibernate and standby
- Demonstrate safe removal of laptop-specific hardware such as peripherals, hot-swappable devices and non-hot-swappable devices

2.3 Identify tools, basic diagnostic procedures and troubleshooting techniques for laptops and portable devices

- Use procedures and techniques to diagnose power conditions, video, keyboard, pointer and wireless card issues, for example:
  - Verify AC power (e.g. LEDs, swap AC adapter)
  - Verify DC power
  - Remove unneeded peripherals
  - Plug in external monitor
  - Toggle Fn keys
  - Check LCD cutoff switch
  - Verify backlight functionality and pixilation

- Stylus issues (e.g. digitizer problems)

- Unique laptop keypad issues

- Antenna wires

2.4 Perform preventative maintenance on laptops and portable devices

- Identify and apply common preventative maintenance techniques for laptops and portable devices, for example: cooling devices, hardware and video cleaning materials, operating environments including temperature and air quality, storage, transportation and shipping.

3.0 Operating Systems

3.1 Identify the fundamentals of using operating systems

- Identify differences between operating systems (e.g. Mac, Windows, Linux) and describe operating system revision levels including GUI, system requirements, application and hardware compatibility

- Identify names, purposes and characteristics of the primary operating system components including registry, virtual memory and file system

- Describe features of operating system interfaces, for example:

  - Windows Explorer

  - My Computer

  - Control Panel

  - Command Prompt

  - My Network Places

  - Task bar / systray

  - Start Menu

- Identify the names, locations, purposes and characteristics of operating system files for example:

  - BOOT.INI

  - NTLDR

  - NTDETECT.COM

  - NTBOOTDD.SYS

  - Registry data files

- Identify concepts and procedures for creating, viewing, managing disks, directories and files in operating systems for example:

  - Disks (e.g. active, primary, extended and logical partitions)

- File systems (e.g. FAT 32, NTFS)
- Directory structures (e.g. create folders, navigate directory structures)
- Files (e.g. creation, extensions, attributes, permissions)

3.2 Install, configure, optimize and upgrade operating systems—references to upgrading from Windows 95 and NT may be made

- Identify procedures for installing operating systems including:
  - Verification of hardware compatibility and minimum requirements
  - Installation methods (e.g. boot media such as CD, floppy or USB, network installation, drive imaging)
  - Operating system installation options (e.g. attended / unattended, file system type, network configuration)
  - Disk preparation order (e.g. start installation, partition and format drive)
  - Device driver configuration (e.g. install and upload device drivers)
  - Verification of installation
- Identify procedures for upgrading operating systems including:
  - Upgrade considerations (e.g. hardware, application and / or network compatibility)
  - Implementation (e.g. backup data, install additional Windows components)
- Install / add a device including loading, adding device drivers and required software including:
  - Determine whether permissions are adequate for performing the task
  - Device driver installation (e.g. automated and / or manual search and installation of device drivers)
  - Using unsigned drivers (e.g. driver signing)
  - Verify installation of the driver (e.g. device manager and functionality)
- Identify procedures and utilities used to optimize operating systems for example, virtual memory, hard drives, temporary files, service, startup and applications

3.3 Identify tools, diagnostic procedures and troubleshooting techniques for operating systems

- Identify basic boot sequences, methods and utilities for recovering operating systems
  - Boot methods (e.g. safe mode, recovery console, boot to restore point)
  - Automated System Recovery (ASR) (e.g. Emergency Repair Disk (ERD))
- Identify and apply diagnostic procedures and troubleshooting techniques for example:
  - Identify the problem by questioning the user and identifying user changes to the computer
  - Analyze problem including potential causes and initial determination of software and / or hardware problem

- Test related components including connections, hardware / software configurations, device manager and consulting vendor documentation
- Evaluate results and take additional steps if needed such as consultation, alternate resources and manuals
- Document activities and outcomes

- Recognize and resolve common operational issues such as bluescreen, system lock-up, input / output device, application install, start or load and Windows-specific printing problems (e.g. print spool stalled, incorrect / incompatible driver for print)
- Explain common error messages and codes for example:
  - Boot (e.g. invalid boot disk, inaccessible boot drive, missing NTLDR)
  - Startup (e.g. device / service failed to start, device / program in registry not found)
  - Event Viewer
  - Registry
  - Windows reporting
- Identify the names, locations, purposes and characteristics of operating system utilities for example:
  - Disk management tools (e.g. DEFRAG, NTBACKUP, CHKDSK, Format)
  - System management tools (e.g. device and task manager, MSCONFIG.EXE)
  - File management tools (e.g. Windows Explorer, ATTRIB.EXE)

3.4 Perform preventative maintenance on operating systems

- Describe common utilities for performing preventative maintenance on operating systems for example, software and Windows updates (e.g. service packs), scheduled backups / restore, restore points

4.0 Printers and Scanners

4.1 Identify the fundamental principles of using printers and scanners

- Identify differences between types of printer and scanner technologies (e.g. laser, inkjet, thermal, solid ink, impact)
- Identify names, purposes and characteristics of printer and scanner components (e.g. memory, driver, firmware) and consumables (e.g. toner, ink cartridge, paper)
- Identify the names, purposes and characteristics of interfaces used by printers and scanners including port and cable types for example:
  - Parallel

- Network (e.g. NIC, print servers)
- USB
- Serial
- IEEE 1394 / firewire
- Wireless (e.g. Bluetooth, 802.11, infrared)
- SCSI

4.2 Identify basic concepts of installing, configuring, optimizing and upgrading printers and scanners

- Install and configure printers / scanners
  - Power and connect the device using local or network port
  - Install and update device driver and calibrate the device
  - Configure options and default settings
  - Print a test page
- Optimize printer performance for example, printer settings such as tray switching, print spool settings, device calibration, media types and paper orientation

4.3 Identify tools, basic diagnostic procedures and troubleshooting techniques for printers and scanners

- Gather information about printer / scanner problems
  - Identify symptom
  - Review device error codes, computer error messages and history (e.g. event log, user reports)
  - Print or scan test page
  - Use appropriate generic or vendor-specific diagnostic tools including web-based utilities
- Review and analyze collected data
  - Establish probable causes
  - Review service documentation
  - Review knowledge base and define and isolate the problem (e.g. software vs. hardware, driver, connectivity, printer)
- Identify solutions to identified printer / scanner problems
  - Define specific cause and apply fix
  - Replace consumables as needed
  - Verify functionality and get user acceptance of problem fix

5.0 Networks

5.1 Identify the fundamental principles of networks

- Describe basic networking concepts
  - Addressing
  - Bandwidth
  - Status indicators
  - Protocols (e.g. TCP / IP including IP, classful subnet, IPX / SPX including NWLINK, NETBEUI / NETBIOS)
  - Full-duplex, half-duplex
  - Cabling (e.g. twisted pair, coaxial cable, fiber optic, RS-232)
  - Networking models including peer-to-peer and client / server
- Identify names, purposes and characteristics of the common network cables
  - Plenum / PVC
  - UTP (e.g. CAT3, CAT5 / 5e, CAT6)
  - STP
  - Fiber (e.g. single-mode and multi-mode)
- Identify names, purposes and characteristics of network cables (e.g. RJ45 and RJ11, ST / SC / LC, USB, IEEE 1394 / Firewire)
- Identify names, purposes and characteristics (e.g. definition, speed and connections) of technologies for establishing connectivity for example:
  - LAN / WAN
  - ISDN
  - Broadband (e.g. DSL, cable, satellite)
  - Dial-up
  - Wireless (all 802.11)
  - Infrared
  - Bluetooth
  - Cellular
  - VoIP

5.2 Install, configure, optimize and upgrade networks

- Install and configure network cards (physical address)
- Install, identify and obtain wired and wireless connection

5.3 Identify tools, diagnostic procedures and troubleshooting techniques for networks

- Explain status indicators, for example speed, connection and activity lights and wireless signal strength

6.0 Security

6.1 Identify the fundamental principles of security

- Identify names, purposes and characteristics of hardware and software security for example:
  - Hardware deconstruction / recycling
  - Smart cards / biometrics (e.g. key fobs, cards, chips and scans)
  - Authentication technologies (e.g. user name, password, biometrics, smart cards)
  - Malicious software protection (e.g. viruses, Trojans, worms, spam, spyware, adware, grayware)
  - Software firewalls
  - File system security (e.g. FAT32 and NTFS)
- Identify names, purposes and characteristics of wireless security for example:
  - Wireless encryption (e.g. WEP.x and WPA.x) and client configuration
  - Access points (e.g. disable DHCP / use static IP, change SSID from default, disable SSID broadcast, MAC filtering, change default username and password, update firmware, firewall)
- Identify names, purposes and characteristics of data and physical security
  - Data access (basic local security policy)
  - Encryption technologies
  - Backups
  - Data migration
  - Data / remnant removal
  - Password management
  - Locking workstation (e.g. hardware, operating system)
- Describe importance and process of incidence reporting
- Recognize and respond appropriately to social engineering situations

6.2 Install, configure, upgrade and optimize security

- Install, configure, upgrade and optimize hardware, software and data security for example:
  - BIOS

- Smart cards
- Authentication technologies
- Malicious software protection
- Data access (basic local security policy)
- Backup procedures and access to backups
- Data migration
- Data / remnant removal

6.3 Identify tools, diagnostic procedures and troubleshooting techniques for security

- Diagnose and troubleshoot hardware, software and data security issues for example:
  - BIOS
  - Smart cards, biometrics
  - Authentication technologies
  - Malicious software
  - File system (e.g. FAT32, NTFS)
  - Data access (e.g. basic local security policy)
  - Backup
  - Data migration

6.4 Perform preventative maintenance for computer security

- Implement software security preventative maintenance techniques such as installing service packs and patches and training users about malicious software prevention technologies

7.0 Safety and Environmental Issues

7.1 Describe the aspects and importance of safety and environmental issues

- Identify potential safety hazards and take preventative action
- Use Material Safety Data Sheets (MSDS) or equivalent documentation and appropriate equipment documentation
- Use appropriate repair tools
- Describe methods to handle environmental and human (e.g. electrical, chemical, physical) accidents including incident reporting

7.2 Identify potential hazards and implement proper safety procedures including ESD precautions and procedures, safe work environment and equipment handling

7.3 Identify proper disposal procedures for batteries, display devices and chemical solvents and cans

8.0 Professionalism and Communication

8.1 Use good communication skills including listening and tact / discretion, when communicating with customers and colleagues

- Use clear, concise and direct statements
- Allow the customer to complete statements—avoid interrupting
- Clarify customer statements—ask pertinent questions
- Avoid using jargon, abbreviations and acronyms
- Listen to customers

8.2 Use job-related professional behavior including notation of privacy, confidentiality and respect for the customer and customers' property

- Behavior
  - Maintain a positive attitude and tone of voice
  - Avoid arguing with customers and / or becoming defensive
  - Don't minimize customers' problems
  - Avoid being judgmental and / or insulting or calling the customer names
  - Avoid distractions and / or interruptions when talking with customers
- Property
  - Telephone, laptop, desktop computer, printer, monitor, etc.

A+ 220-602 Elective Exam Objectives

1.0 Personal Computer Components

1.1 Install, configure, optimize and upgrade personal computer components

- Add, remove and configure personal computer components including selection and installation of appropriate components for example:
  - Storage devices
  - Motherboards

- Power supplies
- Processors / CPUs
- Memory
- Display devices
- Input devices (e.g. basic, specialty and multimedia)
- Adapter cards
- Cooling systems

1.2 Identify tools, diagnostic procedures and troubleshooting techniques for personal computer components

- Identify and apply basic diagnostic procedures and troubleshooting techniques
  - Isolate and identify the problem using visual and audible inspection of components and minimum configuration
- Recognize and isolate issues with peripherals, multimedia, specialty input devices, internal and external storage and CPUs
- Identify the steps used to troubleshoot components (e.g. check proper seating, installation, appropriate components, settings and current driver) for example:
  - Power supply
  - Processor / CPUs and motherboards
  - Memory
  - Adapter cards
  - Display and input devices
- Recognize names, purposes, characteristics and appropriate application of tools for example:
  - Multi-meter
  - Anti-static pad and wrist strap
  - Specialty hardware / tools
  - Loop back plugs
  - Cleaning products (e.g. vacuum, cleaning pads)

1.3 Perform preventative maintenance of personal computer components

- Identify and apply common preventative maintenance techniques for personal computer components for example:
  - Display devices (e.g. cleaning, ventilation)

- Power devices (e.g. appropriate source such as power strip, surge protector, ventilation and cooling)
- Input devices (e.g. covers)
- Storage devices (e.g. software tools such as DEFRAG and cleaning of optics and tape heads)
- Thermally sensitive devices such as motherboards, CPU, adapter cards, memory (e.g. cleaning, air flow)

2.0 Laptops and Portable Devices

2.1 Identify fundamental principles of using laptops and portable devices

- Identify appropriate applications for laptop-specific communication connections such as Bluetooth, infrared, cellular WAN and Ethernet
- Identify appropriate laptop-specific power and electrical input devices and determine how amperage and voltage can affect performance
- Identify the major components of the LCD including inverter, screen and video card

2.2 Install, configure, optimize and upgrade laptops and portable devices

- Removal of laptop-specific hardware such as peripherals, hot-swappable and non-hot-swappable devices
- Describe how video sharing affects memory upgrades

2.3 Use tools, diagnostic procedures and troubleshooting techniques for laptops and portable devices

- Use procedures and techniques to diagnose power conditions, video, keyboard, pointer and wireless card issues for example:
  - Verify AC power (e.g. LEDs, swap AC adapter)
  - Verify DC power
  - Remove unneeded peripherals
  - Plug in external monitor
  - Toggle Fn keys
  - Check LCD cutoff switch
  - Verify backlight functionality and pixilation
  - Stylus issues (e.g. digitizer problems)
  - Unique laptop keypad issues
  - Antenna wires

3.0 Operating Systems

3.1 Identify the fundamental principles of operating systems

- Use command-line functions and utilities to manage operating systems, including proper syntax and switches for example:
  - CMD
  - HELP
  - DIR
  - ATTRIB
  - EDIT
  - COPY
  - XCOPY
  - FORMAT
  - IPCONFIG
  - PING
  - MD / CD / RD
- Identify concepts and procedures for creating, viewing and managing disks, directories and files on operating systems
  - Disks (e.g. active, primary, extended and logical partitions and file systems including FAT32 and NTFS)
  - Directory structures (e.g. create folders, navigate directory structures)
  - Files (e.g. creation, attributes, permissions)
- Locate and use operating system utilities and available switches for example:
  - Disk management tools (e.g. DEFRAG, NTBACKUP, CHKDSK, Format)
  - System management tools
  - Device and Task Manager
  - MSCONFIG.EXE
  - REGEDIT.EXE
  - REGEDT32.EXE
  - CMD
  - Event Viewer
  - System Restore
  - Remote Desktop
  - File management tools (e.g. Windows EXPLORER, ATTRIB.EXE)

3.2 Install, configure, optimize and upgrade operating systems—references to upgrading from Windows 95 and NT may be made

- Identify procedures and utilities used to optimize operating systems for example:
  - Virtual memory
  - Hard drives (e.g. disk defragmentation)
  - Temporary files
  - Services
  - Startup
  - Application

3.3 Identify tools, diagnostic procedures and troubleshooting techniques for operating systems

- Demonstrate the ability to recover operating systems (e.g. boot methods, recovery console, ASR, ERD)
- Recognize and resolve common operational problems for example:
  - Windows specific printing problems (e.g. print spool stalled, incorrect / incompatible driver form print)
  - Auto-restart errors
  - Bluescreen error
  - System lock-up
  - Device drivers failure (input / output devices)
  - Application install, start or load failure
- Recognize and resolve common error messages and codes for example:
  - Boot (e.g. invalid boot disk, inaccessible boot drive, missing NTLDR)
  - Startup (e.g. device / service failed to start, device / program in registry not found)
  - Event Viewer
  - Registry
  - Windows reporting
- Use diagnostic utilities and tools to resolve operational problems for example:
  - Bootable media
  - Startup modes (e.g. safe mode, safe mode with command prompt or networking, step-by-step / single step mode)
  - Documentation resources (e.g. user / installation manuals, internet / web based, training materials)

- Task and Device Manager
- Event Viewer
- MSCONFIG
- Recover CD / recovery partition
- Remote Desktop Connection and Assistance
- System File Checker (SFC)

3.4 Perform preventative maintenance for operating systems

- Demonstrate the ability to perform preventative maintenance on operating systems including software and Windows updates (e.g. service packs), scheduled backups / restore, restore points

4.0 Printers and Scanners

4.1 Identify the fundamental principles of using printers and scanners

- Describe processes used by printers and scanners including laser, ink dispersion, thermal, solid ink and impact printers and scanners

4.2 Install, configure, optimize and upgrade printers and scanners

- Install and configure printers / scanners
  - Power and connect the device using local or network port
  - Install and update device driver and calibrate the device
  - Configure options and default settings
  - Install and configure print drivers (e.g. PCL™, Postscript™, GDI)
  - Validate compatibility with operating system and applications
  - Educate user about basic functionality
- Install and configure printer upgrades including memory and firmware
- Optimize scanner performance including resolution, file format and default settings

4.3 Identify tools and diagnostic procedures to troubleshooting printers and scanners

- Gather information about printer / scanner problems
- Review and analyze collected data
- Isolate and resolve identified printer / scanner problem including defining the cause, applying the fix and verifying functionality
- Identify appropriate tools used for troubleshooting and repairing printer / scanner problems
  - Multi-meter
  - Screwdrivers

- Cleaning solutions
- Extension magnet
- Test patterns

4.4 Perform preventative maintenance of printers and scanners

- Perform scheduled maintenance according to vendor guidelines (e.g. install maintenance kits, reset page counts)
- Ensure a suitable environment
- Use recommended supplies

5.0 Networks

5.1 Identify the fundamental principles or networks

- Identify names, purposes and characteristics of basic network protocols and terminologies for example:
    - ISP
    - TCP / IP (e.g. gateway, subnet mask, DNS, WINS, static and automatic address assignment)
    - IPX / SPX (NWLink)
    - NETBEUI / NETBIOS
    - SMTP
    - IMAP
    - HTML
    - HTTP
    - HTTPS
    - SSL
    - Telnet
    - FTP
    - DNS
- Identify names, purposes and characteristics of technologies for establishing connectivity for example:
    - Dial-up networking
    - Broadband (e.g. DSL, cable, satellite)
    - ISDN networking

- Wireless (all 802.11)
- LAN / WAN
- Infrared
- Bluetooth
- Cellular
- VoIP

5.2 Install, configure, optimize and upgrade networks

- Install and configure browsers
  - Enable / disable script support
  - Configure proxy and security settings
- Establish network connectivity
  - Install and configure network cards
  - Obtain a connection
  - Configure client options (e.g. Microsoft, Novell) and network options (e.g. domain, workgroup, tree)
  - Configure network options
- Demonstrate the ability to share network resources
  - Models
  - Configure permissions
  - Capacities / limitations for sharing for each operating system

5.3 Use tools and diagnostic procedures to troubleshoot network problems

- Identify names, purposes and characteristics of tools for example:
  - Command line tools (e.g. IPCONFIG.EXE, PING.EXE, TRACERT.EXE, NSLOOKUP.EXE)
  - Cable testing device
- Diagnose and troubleshoot basic network issue for example:
  - Driver / network interface
  - Protocol configuration
  - TCP / IP (e.g. gateway, subnet mask, DNS, WINS, static and automatic address assignment)
  - IPX / SPX (NWLink)
  - Permissions

- Firewall configuration
- Electrical interference

5.4 Perform preventative maintenance of networks including securing and protecting network cabling

6.0 Security

6.1 Identify the fundamentals and principles of security

- Identify the purposes and characteristics of access control for example:

  - Access to operating system (e.g. accounts such as user, admin and guest. Groups, permission actions, types and levels), components, restricted spaces

- Identify the purposes and characteristics of auditing and event logging

6.2 Install, configure, upgrade and optimize security

- Install and configure software, wireless and data security for example:
  - Authentication technologies
  - Software firewalls
  - Auditing and event logging (enable / disable only)
  - Wireless client configuration
  - Unused wireless connections
  - Data access (e.g. permissions, basic local security policy)
  - File systems (converting from FAT32 to NTFS only)

6.3 Identify tools, diagnostic procedures and troubleshooting techniques for security

- Diagnose and troubleshoot software and data security issues for example:
  - Software firewall issues
  - Wireless client configuration issues
  - Data access issues (e.g. permissions, security policies)
  - Encryption and encryption technology issues

6.4 Perform preventative maintenance for security

- Recognize social engineering and address social engineering situations

7.0 Safety and Environmental Issues

7.1 Identify potential hazards and proper safety procedures including power supply, display devices and environment (e.g. trip, liquid, situational, atmospheric hazards and high-voltage and moving equipment)

8.0 Professionalism and Communication

8.1 Use good communication skills including listening and tact / discretion, when communicating with customers and colleagues

- Use clear, concise and direct statements
- Allow the customer to complete statements—avoid interrupting
- Clarify customer statements—ask pertinent questions
- Avoid using jargon, abbreviations and acronyms
- Listen to customers

8.2 Use job-related professional behavior including notation of privacy, confidentiality and respect for the customer and customers' property

- Behavior
  - Maintain a positive attitude and tone of voice
  - Avoid arguing with customers and / or becoming defensive
  - Don't minimize customers' problems
  - Avoid being judgmental and / or insulting or calling the customer names
  - Avoid distractions and / or interruptions when talking with customers
- Property
  - Telephone, laptop, desktop computer, printer, monitor, etc.

A+ 220-603 Elective Exam Objectives

1.0 Personal Computer Components

1.1 Install, configure, optimize, and upgrade personal computer components

- Add, remove, and configure display devices, input devices and adapter cards including basic input and multimedia devices.

1.2 Identify tools, diagnostic procedures, and troubleshooting techniques for personal computer components

- Identify and apply basic diagnostic procedures and troubleshooting techniques, for example:
  - Identify and analyze the problem/potential problem
  - Test related components and evaluate results
  - Identify additional steps to be taken if/when necessary
  - Document activities and outcomes

- Recognize and isolate issues with display, peripheral, multimedia, specialty input device and storage.

- Apply steps in troubleshooting techniques to identify problems (e.g. physical environment, functionality and software/driver settings) with components including display, input devices and adapter cards

1.3 Perform preventative maintenance on personal computer components

- Identify and apply common preventative maintenance techniques for storage devices, for example:
  - Software tools (e.g., Defrag, CHKDSK)
  - Cleaning (e.g., optics, tape heads)

2.0 Operating Systems

2.1 Identify the fundamental principles of using operating systems

- Use command-line functions and utilities to manage Windows 2000, XP Professional and XP Home, including proper syntax and switches, for example:
  - CMD
  - HELP
  - DIR
  - ATTRIB
  - EDIT
  - COPY
  - XCOPY
  - FORMAT
  - IPCONFIG
  - PING
  - MD / CD/ RD
- Identify concepts and procedures for creating, viewing, managing disks, directories and files in Windows 2000, XP Professional and XP Home, for example:
  - Disks (e.g. active, primary, extended and logical partitions)
  - File systems (e.g. FAT 32, NTFS)
  - Directory structures (e.g. create folders, navigate directory structures)
  - Files (e.g. creation, extensions, attributes, permissions)

- Locate and use Windows 2000, XP Professional and XP Home utilities and available switches
  - Disk Management Tools (e.g. DEFRAG, NTBACKUP, CHKDSK, Format)
  - System Management Tools
  - Device and Task Manager
  - MSCONFIG.EXE
  - REGEDIT.EXE
  - REGEDIT32.EXE
  - CMD
  - Event Viewer
  - System Restore
  - Remote Desktop
  - File Management Tool (e.g. Windows Explorer, ATTRIB.EXE)

2.2 Install, configure, optimize and upgrade operating systems

- Identify procedures and utilities used to optimize the performance of Windows 2000, XP Professional and XP Home, for example:
  - Virtual memory
  - Hard drives (e.g. disk defragmentation)
  - Temporary files
  - Services
  - Startup
  - Applications

2.3 Identify tools, diagnostic procedures and troubleshooting techniques for operating systems.

- Recognize and resolve common operational problems, for example:
  - Windows-specific printing problems (e.g. print spool stalled, incorrect/incompatible driver form print)
  - Auto-restart errors
  - Bluescreen error
  - System lock-up
  - Device drivers failure (input/output devices)
  - Application install, start or load failure
- Recognize and resolve common error messages and codes, for example:
  - Boot (e.g. invalid boot disk, inaccessible boot device, missing NTLDR)

- Startup (e.g. device/service has failed to start, device/program references in registry not found)
- Event viewer
- Registry
- Windows

- Use diagnostic utilities and tools to resolve operational problems, for example:

  - Bootable media
  - Startup Modes (e.g. safe mode, safe mode with command prompt or networking, step-by-step/single step mode)
  - Documentation resources (e.g. user/installation manuals, internet/web-based, training materials)
  - Task and Device Manager
  - Event Viewer
  - MSCONFIG
  - Recovery CD / Recovery partition
  - Remote Desktop Connection and Assistance
  - System File Checker (SFC)

2.4 Perform preventative maintenance for operating systems

- Perform preventative maintenance on Windows 2000, XP Professional and XP Home including software and Windows updates (e.g. service packs)

3.0 Printers and Scanners

3.1 Identify the fundamental principles of using printers and scanners

- Describe processes used by printers and scanners including laser, ink dispersion, impact, solid ink and thermal printers.

3.2 Install, configure, optimize and upgrade printers and scanners

- Install and configure printers and scanners

  - Power and connect the device using network or local port
  - Install/update the device driver and calibrate the device
  - Configure options and default settings
  - Install and configure print drivers (e.g. PCL™, Postscript™ and GDI)
  - Validate compatibility with OS and applications
  - Educate user about basic functionality

- Optimize scanner performance for example: resolution, file format and default settings

3.3 Identify tools, diagnostic procedures and troubleshooting techniques for printers and scanners

- Gather information required to troubleshoot printer/scanner problems
- Troubleshoot a print failure (e.g. lack of paper, clear queue, restart print spooler, recycle power on printer, inspect for jams, check for visual indicators)

4.0 Networks

4.1 Identify the fundamental principles of networks

- Identify names, purposes, and characteristics of the basic network protocols and terminologies, for example:
  - ISP
  - TCP/IP (e.g. Gateway, Subnet mask, DNS, WINS, Static and automatic address assignment)
  - IPX/SPX (NWLink)
  - NETBEUI/NETBIOS
  - SMTP
  - IMAP
  - HTML
  - HTTP
  - HTTPS
  - SSL
  - Telnet
  - FTP
  - DNS
- Identify names, purposes, and characteristics of technologies for establishing connectivity, for example:
  - Dial-up networking
  - Broadband (e.g. DSL, cable, satellite)
  - ISDN Networking
  - Wireless
  - LAN/WAN

4.2 Install, configure, optimize and upgrade networks

- Establish network connectivity and share network resources

4.3 Identify tools, diagnostic procedures and troubleshooting techniques for networks

- Identify the names, purposes, and characteristics of command line tools, for example:
  - IPCONFIG.EXE
  - PING.EXE
  - TRACERT.EXE
  - NSLOOKUP.EXE
- Diagnose and troubleshoot basic network issues, for example:
  - Driver/network interface
  - Protocol configuration
  - TCP/IP (e.g. Gateway, Subnet mask, DNS, WINS, static and automatic address assignment)
  - IPX/SPX (NWLink)
  - Permissions
  - Firewall configuration
  - Electrical interference

5.0 Security

5.1 Identify the fundamental principles of security

- Identify the names, purposes, and characteristics of access control and permissions
  - Accounts including user, admin and guest
  - Groups
  - Permission levels, types (e.g. file systems and shared) and actions (e.g. read, write, change and execute)

5.2 Install, configure, optimizing and upgrade security

- Install and configure hardware, software, wireless and data security, for example:
  - Smart card readers
  - Key fobs
  - Biometric devices
  - Authentication technologies
  - Software firewalls

- Auditing and event logging (enable/disable only)
- Wireless client configuration
- Unused wireless connections
- Data access (e.g. permissions, security policies)
- Encryption and encryption technologies

5.3 Identify tools, diagnostic procedures and troubleshooting techniques for security issues

- Diagnose and troubleshoot software and data security issues, for example:
  - Software firewall issues
  - Wireless client configuration issues
  - Data access issues (e.g. permissions, security policies)
  - Encryption and encryption technology issues

5.4 Perform preventative maintenance for security

- Recognize social engineering and address social engineering situations

6.0 Professionalism and Communication

6.1 Use good communication skills, including listening and tact / discretion, when communicating with customers and colleagues

- Use clear, concise and direct statements
- Allow the customer to complete statements—avoid interrupting
- Clarify customer statements—ask pertinent questions
- Avoid using jargon, abbreviations and acronyms
- Listen to customers

6.2 Use job-related professional behavior including notation of privacy, confidentiality and respect for the customer and customers' property

- Behavior
  - Maintain a positive attitude and tone of voice
  - Avoid arguing with customers and / or becoming defensive
  - Do not minimize customers' problems
  - Avoid being judgmental and / or insulting or calling the customer names
  - Avoid distractions and / or interruptions when talking with customers
- Property
  - Telephone, laptop, desktop computer, printer, monitor, etc.

A+ 220-604 Elective Exam Objectives

1.0 Personal Computer Components

1.1 Install, configure, optimize and upgrade personal computer components

- Add, remove and configure internal storage devices, motherboards, power supplies, processor/CPU's, memory and adapter cards, including:
  - Drive preparation
  - Jumper configuration
  - Storage device power and cabling
  - Selection and installation of appropriate motherboard
  - BIOS set-up and configuration
  - Selection and installation of appropriate CPU
  - Selection and installation of appropriate memory
  - Installation of adapter cards including hardware and software/drivers
  - Configuration and optimization of adapter cards including adjusting hardware settings and obtaining network card connection
- Add, remove and configure systems

1.2 Identify tools, diagnostic procedures and troubleshooting techniques for personal computer components

- Identify and apply diagnostic procedures and troubleshooting techniques, for example:
  - Identify and isolate the problem using visual and audible inspection of components and minimum configuration
- Identify the steps used to troubleshoot components (e.g. check proper seating, installation, appropriate component, settings, current driver), for example:
  - Power supply
  - Processor/CPU's and motherboards
  - Memory
  - Adapter cards
- Recognize names, purposes, characteristics and appropriate application of tools, for example:
  - Multi-meter
  - Anti-static pad and wrist strap

- Specialty hardware/tools
- Loop back plugs
- Cleaning products (e.g. vacuum, cleaning pads)

1.3 Perform preventative maintenance of personal computer components

- Identify and apply common preventative maintenance techniques, for example:
  - Thermally sensitive devices (e.g. motherboards, CPU's, adapter cards, memory)
  - Cleaning
  - Air flow (e.g. slot covers, cable routing)
  - Adapter cards (e.g. driver/firmware updates)

2.0 Laptops and Portable Devices

2.1 Identify the fundamental principles of using laptops and portable devices

- Identify appropriate applications for laptop-specific communication connections, for example:
  - Bluetooth
  - Infrared devices
  - Cellular WAN
  - Ethernet
- Identify appropriate laptop-specific power and electrical input devices, for example:
  - Output performance requirements for amperage and voltage
- Identify the major components of the LCD (e.g. inverter, screen, video card)

2.2 Install, configure, optimize and upgrade laptops and portable devices

- Demonstrate the safe removal of laptop-specific hardware including peripherals, hot-swappable and non hot-swappable devices
- Identify the affect of video sharing on memory upgrades

2.3 Identify tools, diagnostic procedures and troubleshooting techniques for laptops and portable devices.

- Use procedures and techniques to diagnose power conditions, video issues, keyboard and pointer issues and wireless card issues, for example:
  - Verify AC power (e.g. LED's, swap AC adapter)
  - Verify DC power
  - Remove unneeded peripherals

- Plug in external monitor
- Toggle Fn keys
- Check LCD cutoff switch
- Verify backlight functionality and pixilation
- Stylus issues (e.g. digitizer problems)
- Unique laptop keypad issues
- Antenna wires

3.0 Printers and Scanners

3.1 Identify the fundamental principles of using printers and scanners

- Describe the processes used by printers and scanners including laser, inkjet, thermal, solid ink, and impact printers

3.2 Install, configure, optimize and upgrade printers and scanners

- Identify the steps used in the installation and configuration processes for printers and scanners, for example:
  - Power and connect the device using network or local port
  - Install and update the device driver
  - Calibrate the device
  - Configure options and default settings
  - Print test page
- Install and configure printer/scanner upgrades including memory and firmware

3.3 Identify tools, diagnostic methods and troubleshooting procedures for printers and scanners

- Gather data about printer/scanner problem
- Review and analyze data collected about printer/scanner problems
- Implement solutions to solve identified printer/scanner problems
- Identify appropriate tools used for troubleshooting and repairing printer/scanner problems
  - Multi-meter
  - Screw drivers
  - Cleaning solutions
  - Extension magnet
  - Test patterns

3.4 Perform preventative maintenance of printer and scanner problems

- Perform scheduled maintenance according to vendor guidelines (e.g. install maintenance kits, reset page counts)

- Ensure a suitable environment

- Use recommended supplies

4.0 Security

4.1 Identify the names, purposes and characteristics of physical security devices and processes

- Control access to PC's, servers, laptops and restricted spaces

  - Hardware

  - Operating systems

4.2 Install hardware security

- Smart card readers

- Key fobs

- Biometric devices

5.0 Safety and Environmental Issues

5.1 Identify potential hazards & proper safety procedures including power supply, display devices and environment (e.g. trip, liquid, situational, atmospheric hazards, high-voltage and moving equipment)

About the Author

Emmett Dulaney holds or has held 18 vendor certifications and is the author of over 30 books. An assistant professor at Anderson University, he is the former director of training for Mercury Technical Solutions. He specializes in certification and cross-platform integration, and is a columnist for CertCities and UnixReview. Emmett can be reached at `edulaney@iquest.net`.

CompTIA A+®
Complete Fast Pass™

Chapter 1

Personal Computer Components

COMPTIA A+ ESSENTIALS EXAM OBJECTIVES COVERED IN THIS CHAPTER:

✓ **1.1 Identify the fundamental principles of using personal computers**

- Identify the names, purposes, and characteristics of storage devices
  - FDD
  - HDD
  - CD / DVD / RW (e.g., drive speeds, media types)
  - Removable storage (e.g., tape drive, solid state, such as thumb drive, flash and SD cards, USB, external CD-RW, and hard drive)
- Identify the names, purposes, and characteristics of motherboards
  - Form Factor (e.g., ATX / BTX, micro ATX / NLX)
  - Components
  - Integrated I/Os (e.g., sound, video, USB, serial, IEEE 1394 / firewire, parallel, NIC, modem)
  - Memory slots (e.g., RIMM, DIMM)
  - Processor sockets
  - External cache memory
  - Bus architecture
  - Bus slots (e.g., PCI, AGP, PCIE, AMR, CNR)
  - EIDE / PATA
  - SATA
  - SCSI Technology
  - Chipsets
  - BIOS / CMOS / Firmware
  - Riser card / daughter board

- Identify the names, purposes, and characteristics of power supplies, for example: AC adapter, ATX, proprietary, voltage
- Identify the names purposes and characteristics of processor / CPUs
  - CPU chips (e.g., AMD, Intel)
  - CPU technologies
  - Hyperthreading
  - Dual core
  - Throttling
  - Micro code (MMX)
  - Overclocking
  - Cache
  - VRM
  - Speed (real vs. actual)
  - 32 vs. 64 bit
- Identify the names, purposes, and characteristics of memory
  - Types of memory (e.g., DRAM, SRAM, SDRAM, DDR / DDR2, RAMBUS)
  - Operational characteristics
  - Memory chips (8, 16, 32)
  - Parity versus non-parity
  - ECC vs. non-ECC
  - Single-sided vs. double-sided
- Identify the names, purposes, and characteristics of display devices, for example: projectors, CRT, and LCD
  - Connector types (e.g., VGA, DVI / HDMi, S-Video, Component / RGB)
  - Settings (e.g., V-hold, refresh rate, resolution)
- Identify the names, purposes, and characteristics of input devices, for example: mouse, keyboard, bar code reader, multimedia (e.g., web and digital cameras, MIDI, microphones), biometric devices, touch screen
- Identify the names, purposes, and characteristics of adapter cards
  - Video, including PCI / PCI-E and AGP

- Multimedia
- I / O (SCSI, serial, USB, Parallel)
- Communications, including network and modem
- Identify the names, purposes, and characteristics of ports and cables, for example: USB 1.1 and 2.0, parallel, serial, IEEE 1394 / firewire, RJ45 and RJ11, PS2 / MINI-DIN, centronics (e.g., mini, 36) multimedia (e.g., 1/8 connector, MIDSI COAX, SPDIF)
- Identify the names, purposes, and characteristics of cooling systems, for example heat sinks, CPU and case fans, liquid cooling systems, thermal compound

✓ **1.2 Install, configure, optimize, and upgrade personal computer components**

- Add, remove, and configure internal and external storage devices
- Drive preparation of internal storage devices, including format / file systems and imaging technology
- Install display devices
- Add, remove, and configure basic input and multimedia devices

✓ **1.3 Identify tools, diagnostic procedures, and troubleshooting techniques for personal computer components**

- Recognize the basic aspects of troubleshooting theory, for example:
  - Perform backups before making changes
  - Assess a problem systematically and divide large problems into smaller components to be analyzed individually
  - Verify even the obvious, determine whether the problem is something simple and make no assumptions
  - Research ideas and establish priorities
  - Document findings, actions, and outcomes
- Identify and apply basic diagnostic procedures and troubleshooting techniques, for example:
  - Identify the problem, including questioning user and identifying user changes to computer
  - Analyze the problem, including potential causes and make an initial determination of software and / or hardware problems

- Test related components, including inspection, connections, hardware / software configurations, device manager, and consult vendor documentation
- Evaluate results and take additional steps if needed, such as consultation, use of alternate resources, manuals
- Document activities and outcomes
- Recognize and isolate issues with display, power, basic input devices, storage, memory, thermal, POST errors (e.g., BIOS, hardware)
- Apply basic troubleshooting techniques to check for problems (e.g., thermal issues, error codes, power, connections, including cables and / or pins, compatibility, functionality, software / drivers) with components, for example:
  - Motherboards
  - Power supply
  - Processor / CPUs
  - Memory
  - Display devices
  - Input devices
  - Adapter cards
- Recognize the names, purposes, characteristics, and appropriate application of tools, for example: BIOS, self-test, hard drive self-test, and software diagnostics test

✓ **1.4 Perform preventative maintenance on personal computer components**

- Identify and apply basic aspects of preventative maintenance theory, for example:
  - Visual / audio inspection
  - Driver / firmware updates
  - Scheduling preventative maintenance
  - Use of appropriate repair tools and cleaning materials
  - Ensuring proper environment
- Identify and apply common preventative maintenance techniques for devices, such as input devices and batteries

This chapter covers a lot of material—in fact, it could easily be a book in and of itself. One of the things that CompTIA is notorious for is having overlap between domains and exams, and the A+ is no exception. This domain is weighted at 21 percent (tied for highest) of the Essentials exam, and a great deal of the material covered here also appears in other domains (not to mention in the Technician exams).

Because of this, you'll want to make sure you're comfortable with the information presented in this chapter before going on to any others. As a doctor must be intimately acquainted with human anatomy, so a computer technician must understand the physical and functional structure of a personal computer.

Identify Principles of Personal Computers

Any PC is a complex machine. It could be described as a melting pot of various technologies and products, manufactured by a host of companies in many different countries. This diversity is a great advantage because it gives the PC its versatility. However, these components don't always "melt" together into a unified whole without the help of a technician. The different products—whether they're hard disks, modems, sound cards, or memory boards—must share one processor and one motherboard and therefore must be designed to work in harmony. For this reason, configuration of the computer components is especially emphasized on the A+ Essentials exam, and nearly one-third of the exam's question pool pertains to the objectives reviewed in this chapter.

Before sitting for the exam, you'll need to have a working knowledge of the components that make up a computer and their function within the system as a whole. The exam will test your knowledge of the types of components and their functions. The objective of this chapter is to review and identify the main components and their functions.

To pass the exam, you must be able to recognize these components and understand their relationship to one another.

Critical Information

This first objective blends together many diverse topic areas as they relate to PCs. Figure 1.1 shows a typical PC, its components, and their locations.

For this objective, you need to know about 10 key component categories: storage devices, motherboards, power supplies, processor/CPUs, memory, display devices, input devices, adapter cards, ports and cables, and cooling systems. Each of these is discussed in the sections that follow.

FIGURE 1.1   Typical PC components

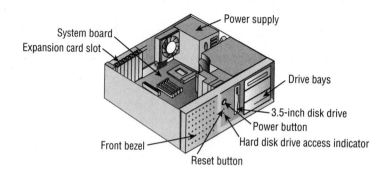

Storage Devices

Storage media hold the data being accessed, as well as the files the system needs to operate and data that needs to be saved. The various types of storage differ in terms of capacity, access time, and the physical type of media being used.

Hard-Disk Systems

Hard disks reside inside the computer (usually) and can hold more information than other forms of storage. The hard-disk system contains three critical components: the controller, the hard disk, and the host adapter. The controller controls the drive, the hard disk provides a physical medium to store the data, and the host adapter is the translator.

CompTIA favors the acronym HDD for *hard disk drive*.

Floppy Drives

A floppy disk drive (referred to by CompTIA as FDD) is a magnetic storage medium that uses a floppy disk made of thin plastic enclosed in a protective casing. The floppy disk itself (or *floppy*, as it's often called) enables the information to be transported from one computer to another easily. The downside of a floppy disk drive is its limited storage capacity. Floppy disks are limited to a maximum capacity of 2.88MB, but the most common type of floppy in use today holds only 1.44MB. Table 1.1 lists the various floppy disks and their capacity. All of these except the 1.44MB-capacity model are obsolete, and it isn't far behind.

CD-ROM Drives

CD-ROM stands for Compact Disc Read-Only Memory. The CD-ROM is used for long-term storage of data. CD-ROMs are read-only, meaning that once information is written to a CD, it can't be erased or changed. Access time for CD-ROMs is considerably slower than for a hard drive. CDs normally hold 650MB of data and use the ISO 9660 standard, which allows them to be used in multiple platforms.

TABLE 1.1   Floppy Disk Capacities

Floppy Drive Size	Common Designation	Number of Tracks	Capacity
5^1/$_4$″	Double-sided, Double-density	40	360KB
5^1/$_2$″	Double-sided, High-density	80	1.2MB
3^1/$_2$	Double-sided, Double-density	80	720KB
3^1/$_2$″	Double-sided, High-density	80	1.44MB
3^1/$_2$″	Double-sided, Ultra High Density	80	2.88MB

DVD-ROM Drives

Because DVD-ROMs use slightly different technology than CD-ROMs, they can store up to 1.6GB of data. This makes them a better choice for distributing large software bundles. Many software packages today are so huge that they take multiple CD-ROMs to hold all the installation and reference files. A single DVD-ROM, in a double-sided, double-layered configuration, can hold as much as 17GB (as much as 26 regular CD-ROMs).

Zip Drives and Jaz Drives

Iomega's Zip and Jaz drives are detachable, external hard disks that are used to store a large volume (around 100MB for the Zip, 1GB and 2GB for the Jaz) of data on a single, floppy-sized disk. The drives connect to either a parallel port or a special interface card. The major use of Zip and Jaz drives is to transport large amounts of data from place to place. This used to be accomplished with several floppies.

Tape Backup Devices

Another form of storage device is the tape backup. Tape backup devices can be installed internally or externally and use a magnetic tape medium instead of disks for storage. They hold much more data than any other medium but are also much slower. They're primarily used for archival storage.

Optical Drives

Optical drives work by using a laser rather than magnetism to change the characteristics of the storage medium.

Flash Drives (and SD Cards)

Flash drives have been growing in popularity for years and replacing floppy disks due to their capacity and small size. Flash is ideally suited for use not only with computers, but also with many other things—digital cameras, MP3 players, and so on.

Although the CompTIA objective lists flash and SecureDigital (SD) cards separately, in reality, SD cards are just one type of flash; there are many others. Figure 1.2 shows a CompactFlash card (larger of the two) and an SD card (the smaller of the two) along with an 8-in-1 card reader/writer. The reader shown connects to the USB port and then interacts with Compact-Flash, CompactFlash II, Memory Stick, Memory Stick PRO, SmartMedia, xD-Picture Cards, SD, and MultiMediaCards.

FIGURE 1.2   CompactFlash and SD cards together with a reader

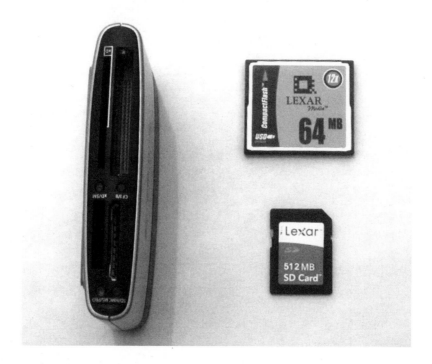

You can find flash cards in any of these formats available in a variety of sizes (16MB, 128MB, 256MB, and so on). The size of the flash card does place some limitation on the maximum capacity of the media, but most cards on the market are below that maximum. The maximum capacity for CompactFlash, for example, is 8GB, whereas for an SD card it's 1GB.

Thumb Drives

Thumb drives are USB flash drives that have become extremely popular for transporting files. Figure 1.3 shows three thumb drives (also known as *keychain drives*) next to a pack of gum for size comparison.

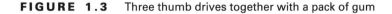

FIGURE 1.3   Three thumb drives together with a pack of gum

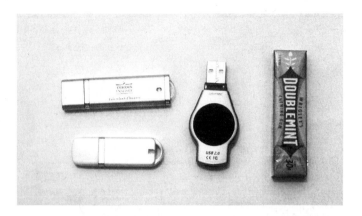

Like other flash drives, you can find these in a number of different size capacities. The maximum storage capacity for this media is 2GB. Many models include a write-protect switch to keep you from accidentally overwriting files stored on the drive. All include an LED to show when they're connected to the USB port. Other names for thumb drives include travel drives, flash drives, jump drives, and a host of others.

External Hard Drives

A number of vendors are now making external hard drives. These often connect to the computer through the USB port, but can also connect through the network (and be shared by other users) or other connections. While some are intended for expansion, many are marketed for the purpose of "mirroring" data on the internal drive(s) and often incorporate a push-button switch that starts a backup.

Motherboards

The motherboard is the backbone of a computer. The components of the motherboard provide basic services needed for the machine to operate and provide a platform for devices such as the processor, memory, disk drives, and expansion devices. For this objective, you should study the types of motherboards, their ports and memory, the types of CPU sockets, and the types of expansion slots.

System Board Form Factors

Form factor refers to the size and shape of a component. There are four popular motherboard form factors for desktop PCs: AT, ATX, BTX, and NLX.

AT   AT is an older style of motherboard. A slightly more modern variant of it is the baby AT, which is similar but smaller. Its key features are a two-piece power-supply connector, ribbon cables that connect the I/O ports to the board, and an AT-style keyboard connector. The expansion slots are parallel to the wide edge of the board. See Figure 1.4.

FIGURE 1.4   An AT-style motherboard

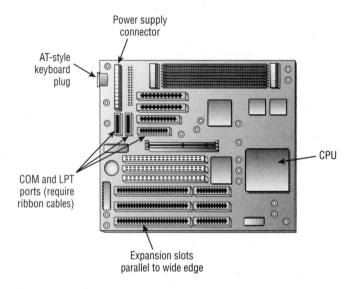

FIGURE 1.5   An ATX-style motherboard

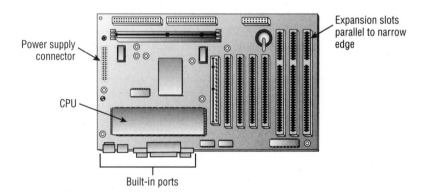

ATX   Most system boards today use the ATX form factor. It contains many design improvements over the AT, including I/O ports built directly into the side of the motherboard, the CPU positioned such that the power-supply fan helps cool it, and the ability for the PC to be turned on and off via software. It uses a PS/2 style-connector for the keyboard. The expansion slots are parallel to the narrow edge of the board. See Figure 1.5.

BTX   The Balanced Technology Extended (BTX) motherboard was designed by Intel to deal with issues surrounding ATX (heat, power consumption, and so on). The BTX motherboard is larger than ATX, so there is more room for integrated components; there is also an optimized airflow path and a low-profile option.

Although the standard has been around for a number of years, it isn't expected to become popular in the market until at least 2007.

NLX An acronym for New, Low profile eXtended, this form factor is used in low-profile case types. It incorporates expansion slots that are placed on a *riser board* to accommodate the reduction in case size. However, this design adds another component to troubleshoot.

Buses

A *bus* is a set of signal pathways that allows information and signals to travel between components inside or outside a computer. A motherboard has several buses, each with its own speed and width.

The *external data bus*, also called the *system bus*, connects the CPU to the chipset. On modern systems, it's 64-bit. The *address bus* connects the RAM to the CPU. On modern systems, it's 64-bit.

The *expansion bus* connects the I/O ports and expansion slots to the chipset. There are usually several different expansion buses on a motherboard. Expansion buses can be broken into two broad categories: internal and external. Internal expansion buses include Industry Standard Architecture (ISA), Peripheral Component Interconnect (PCI), and Accelerated Graphics Port (AGP); they're for circuit boards. External expansion buses include serial, parallel, Universal Serial Bus (USB), FireWire, and infrared. The following sections explain some of the most common buses.

 There are many obsolete bus types, including Video Electronics Standards Association Local Bus (VESA local bus, or VL-Bus), Microchannel Architecture (MCA), and enhanced ISA (EISA). These were not on the last iteration of the A+ test and should not appear on this one either.

ISA

This is a 16-bit bus (originally 8-bit on the oldest computers) that operates at 8MHz. Its slots are usually black. New motherboards may not have this type of slot, because the ISA bus is old technology and is being phased out.

Besides the slow speed and narrow width, another drawback of the ISA bus is that each ISA device requires separate system resources, including separate Interrupt Requests (IRQs). In a heavily loaded system, this can cause an IRQ shortage. (PCI slots, in contrast, can share some resources.)

PCI

The PCI bus is a fast (33MHz), wide (32-bit or 64-bit) expansion bus that is the modern standard in motherboards today for general-purpose expansion devices. Its slots are typically white. PCI devices can share IRQs and other system resources with one another in some cases. All modern motherboards have at least three PCI slots. Figure 1.6 shows some PCI slots.

FIGURE 1.6   PCI bus connectors

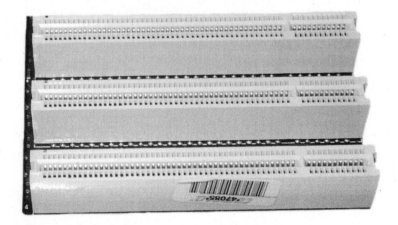

AGP

As systems got faster, PC game players wanted games that had better graphics, more realism, and more speed. However, as the computers got faster, the video technology couldn't seem to keep up, even with the PCI bus. The AGP bus was developed to meet this need.

The AGP slot is usually brown, and there is only one. It's a 32-bit or 64-bit bus, and it runs very fast (66MHz or faster). It's used exclusively for the video card. If you use a PCI video card, the AGP slot remains empty. See Figure 1.7.

FIGURE 1.7   An AGP slot on a motherboard

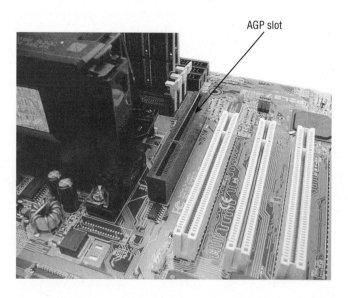

AGP slot

PCIE

PCI Express (PCIE , PCI-E, or PCIe) uses a network of serial interconnects that operate at high speed. It's based on the PCI system; most existing systems can be easily converted to PCIE. Intended as a replacement for AGP and PCI, PCIE has the capability of being faster than AGP, while maintaining the flexibility of PCI. There are currently six different speed levels and they correspond to AGP speeds: 1X, 2X, 4X, 8X, 16X, and 32X.

AMR AND CNR

Audio Modem Riser (AMR) was originally created to speed manufacturing (and certification) by separating the analog circuitry (modem and analog audio) onto its own card. Over time, this has been replaced by CNR (Communications Network Riser), which includes the capabilities of AMR and allows the motherboard chipset to be designed with additional integrated features.

LEGACY PARALLEL AND SERIAL

These buses are called *legacy* because they're old technology and are being phased out. The legacy serial port, also called an RS-232 port, is a 9-pin or 25-pin male connector. It sends data one bit at a time and is usually limited to about 115Kbps in speed.

The legacy parallel port transfers data 8 bits at a time. It's a 25-pin female connector. A system typically has only one parallel port, but because many printers are now coming with USB interfaces, this is no longer the inconvenience that it used to be.

USB

USB is a newer expansion bus type that is used almost exclusively for external devices. All motherboards today have at least two USB ports. Some of the advantages of USB include hot-plugging and the capability for up to 127 USB devices to share a single set of system resources. USB 1.1 runs at 12Mbps, and USB 2.0 runs at 480Mbps. Because USB is a serial interface, its width is 1 bit.

IEEE 1394/FIREWIRE

Some newer motherboards have a built-in IEEE 1394/FireWire port, although this port is more typically found on a PCI expansion board. It transfers data at 400Mbps and supports up to 63 chained devices on a single set of resources. It's hot-pluggable, like USB. Figure 1.8 shows the connections on a FireWire card.

FIGURE 1.8 FireWire connections

Motherboard RAM Slots

RAM is discussed extensively in the "Memory" section later in this chapter. For now, know that the RAM and the RAM slots on the motherboard must match.

Processor Sockets

Table 1.2 lists the various CPU slots and sockets you may find in a motherboard and explains which CPUs will fit into them. CPUs are covered in detail in the "Processor/CPUs" section of this chapter.

TABLE 1.2   Processor Sockets and Slots

Slot/Socket	CPU Used
Slot 1	Pentium II
Slot 2	Pentium III
Slot A	AMD Athlon
Socket A	AMD Athlon
Socket 7	Pentium (second and third generation), AMD K6
Socket 8	Pentium Pro
Socket 423	Pentium 4
Socket 478	Pentium 4
Socket 370	Pentium III

On-Motherboard Cache

On older motherboards, the L2 cache is on its own RAM-like stick made of very fast static random access memory (SRAM). It's known as *cache on a stick (COAST)*. On newer systems, the L2 cache is built into the CPU packaging.

Some newer systems also have an L3 cache, which is an external cache on the motherboard that sits between the CPU and RAM.

IDE and SCSI On-Motherboard Interfaces

Most motherboards include two Integrated Drive Electronics (IDE) channels but don't include built-in Small Computer System Interface (SCSI). A consideration when choosing a motherboard for IDE is that it needs to support the desired level of UltraDMA to match the capabilities of the hard drive you want to use.

Chipsets

The *chipset* is the set of controller chips that monitors and directs the traffic on the motherboard between the buses. It usually consists of two or more chips. Motherboards use two basic chipset designs: the *north/south bridge chipset* and the *hub chipset.*

North/south bridge is the older of the two. The north bridge connects the system bus to the other relatively fast buses (AGP and PCI). The south bridge connects ISA, IDE, and USB. A third chip, SuperIO, connects the legacy parallel and serial ports.

The hub chipset includes a memory controller hub (equivalent to the north bridge), an I/O controller hub (equivalent to the south bridge), and a SuperIO chip.

CMOS

You can adjust a computer's base-level settings through a Basic Input/Output System (BIOS) Setup program, which you access by pressing a certain key at startup, such as F1 or Delete (depending on the system). Another name for this setup program is CMOS Setup. The most common settings to adjust in CMOS include port settings (parallel, serial, USB), drive types, boot sequence, date and time, and virus/security protections.

ACCESSING CMOS SETUP

Your PC keeps these settings in a special memory chip called the Complementary Metallic Oxide Semiconductor (CMOS) chip. The CMOS chip must have a constant source of power to keep its settings. To prevent the loss of data, motherboard manufacturers include a small battery to power the CMOS memory. On modern systems, this is a coin-style battery, about the same diameter of a dime and about 1/4 inch thick.

You can press a certain key or group of keys to access the setup program during the power on self-test (POST). This utility allows you to change the configuration through a group of menus. There are many different CMOS Setup programs, depending on the BIOS make and manufacturer, so it's impossible to provide specifics here; instead, we'll look at capabilities.

LOAD SETUP DEFAULTS

The purpose of this setting is to configure the PC back to the default settings set by the factory. If you make changes to your settings and the machine becomes disabled, in most cases, selecting this menu item returns the machine to a usable state. You may then try different settings until you achieve your desired configuration. This is an important setting to know about before making any other changes.

DATE AND TIME

One of the most basic things you can change in CMOS Setup is the system date and time. You can also change this from within the operating system.

CPU SETTINGS

In most modern systems, the BIOS detects the CPU's type and speed automatically, so any CPU setting in CMOS Setup is likely to be read-only.

MEMORY SPEED/PARITY

Most systems today detect the RAM amount and speed automatically. Some motherboards can use different types of RAM, such as parity and nonparity, or different speeds, and the CMOS Setup program may provide the opportunity to change those settings. Increasingly, however, RAM is becoming a read-only part of CMOS Setup programs.

POWER MANAGEMENT

The Power Management settings determine the way the PC will act after it has been idle for certain time periods. For example, you may have choices like Minimum, Maximum, and User Defined. The Minimum and Maximum settings control the HDD Off After, Doze Mode, Standby Mode, and Suspend Mode settings with predefined parameters. If you select User Defined, you must manually configure these settings to your personal preferences.

 Laptops have even more power settings because of the need to conserve battery power. Chapter 2 focuses on laptops and portable devices.

PORTS AND PERIPHERALS

In CMOS Setup, you can enable or disable integrated components, such as built-in video cards, sound cards, or network cards. You may disable them in order to replace them with different models on expansion boards, for example.

You can also disable the on-board I/O ports for the motherboard, including parallel, serial, and USB. Depending on the utility, there may also be settings that enable or disable USB keyboard usage, Wake On LAN, or other special features.

In addition to enabling or disabling legacy parallel ports, you can also assign an operational mode to the port. Table 1.3 lists the common modes for a parallel port. When you're troubleshooting parallel port problems, sometimes trying a different mode will help.

TABLE 1.3 Printer or Parallel Port Settings

Setting	Description	Use
EPP (enhanced parallel port)	Supports bidirectional communication and high transfer rates	Newer ink-jet and laser printers that can utilize bidirectional communication, and scanners
ECP (enhanced capabilities port)	Supports bidirectional communication and high transfer rates	Newer ink-jet and laser printers that can utilize bidirectional communication, connectivity devices, and scanners
SPP (standard parallel port)	Supports bidirectional communication	Older ink-jet and laser printers and slower scanners

PASSWORDS

In most CMOS Setup programs, you can set a supervisor password. Doing so requires a password to be entered in order to use the CMOS Setup program, effectively locking out users from making changes to it. You may also be able to set a user password, which restricts the PC from booting unless the password is entered.

To reset a forgotten password, you can remove the CMOS battery to reset everything. There also may be a Reset jumper on the motherboard.

VIRUS PROTECTION

Some CMOS Setup programs have a rudimentary virus-protection mechanism that prevents applications from writing to the boot sector of a disk without your permission. If this setting is turned on, and you install a new operating system, a confirmation box may appear at some point, warning you that the operating system's Setup program is trying to write to the boot sector. Let it.

HDD AUTO DETECTION

Some CMOS Setup programs have a feature that polls the IDE channels and provides information about the IDE devices attached to them. You can use this feature to gather the settings for a hard disk. However, most hard disks these days are fully Plug and Play, so they automatically report themselves to the CMOS Setup.

DRIVE CONFIGURATION

You can specify how many floppy drives are installed and what types they are. Floppy drives aren't automatically detected. The settings needed for a floppy drive are size (3½-inch or 5¼-inch) and density (double-density or high-density). You can also set each floppy drive to be enabled or disabled from being bootable. Almost all floppy drives today are high-density 3½-inch.

Hard drives, on the other hand, can be auto-detected by most systems if the IDE setting is set to Auto. The settings detected may include the drive's capacity; its geometry (cylinders, heads, and sectors); and its preferred PIO (Programmed Input/Output), direct memory access (DMA), or UltraDMA operating mode. You can also configure a hard drive by entering its CHS values manually, but doing so is almost never necessary anymore.

CHS stands for *cylinders, heads, and sectors*. This is also called the *drive geometry*, because together these three numbers determine how much data the disk can hold. Most CMOS Setup programs are able to automatically detect the CHS values.

BOOT SEQUENCE

Each system has a default boot order, which is the order in which it checks the drives for a valid operating system to boot. Usually, this order is set for floppy first, then hard disk, and finally CD-ROM, but these components can be placed in any boot order. For example, you might set CD-ROM first to boot from a Windows XP Setup disk on a system that already contained an operating system.

EXITING THE CMOS SETUP

The CMOS Setup program includes an Exit command, with options including Save Changes and Discard Changes. In most programs, Esc is a shortcut for exiting and discarding changes, and F10 is a common shortcut for exiting and saving changes.

Firmware

Any software that is built into a hardware device is called *firmware*. Firmware is typically in flash ROM and can be updated as newer versions become available. An example of firmware is the software in a laser printer that controls it and allows you to interact with it at the console (usually through a limited menu of options).

Daughterboards

Any boards added to the motherboard to expand its capabilities are known as *daughterboards* ("daughters" of the "mother"). A common use is to insert one daughterboard (also called *daughter boards*) into the motherboard and allow expansion cards to then be inserted into it sideways, thus saving space.

Power Supplies

The device in the computer that provides the power is the *power supply*. A power supply converts 110-volt AC current into the voltages a computer needs to operate. On an AT motherboard, these are +5 volts DC, −5 volts DC, +12 volts DC, and −12 volts DC. Components in modern PCs don't use the negative voltages; they're provided for backward compatibility only. On an ATX motherboard, an additional voltage is provided: +3.3 volts DC.

Power-supply problems are usually easy to troubleshoot. The system doesn't respond in any way when the power is turned on. When this happens, open the case, remove the power supply, and replace it with a new one.

Be aware that different cases have different types of on/off switches. The process of replacing a power supply is a lot easier if you purchase a replacement with the same mechanism. Even so, remember to document exactly how the power supply was connected to the on/off switch before you remove it.

Power supplies contain transformers and capacitors that carry *lethal* amounts of current. They aren't meant to be serviced. *Do not* attempt to open them or do any work on them. Figure 1.9 shows a generic power supply.

A power supply has a rated output capacity in watts, and when you fill a system with power-hungry devices, you must make sure that maximum capacity isn't exceeded. Otherwise, problems with power can occur, creating lockups or spontaneous reboots.

To determine the wattage a device draws, multiply voltage by current. For example, if a device uses 5 amps of +3.3V and 0.7 amps of +12V, a total of 25 watts is consumed. Do this calculation for every device installed. Most devices have labels that state their power requirements. Some devices don't have power labels; for such devices, use the numbers in Table 1.4 for estimations.

FIGURE 1.9   A power supply

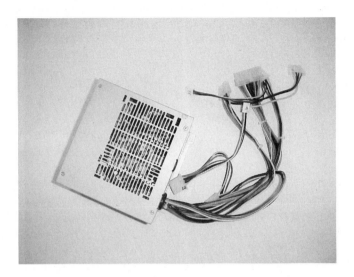

 As a general rule, you should have a large enough power supply for all the slots in the computer with the most likely devices that will be installed. In other words, you should calculate the power-supply capacity from what is possible and not just what is currently on the motherboard.

TABLE 1.4   Estimating Power Consumption

Component	Watts Consumed, for Estimating Purposes
Motherboard	20–30 watts
CPU	30–70 watts (faster CPU, more watts)
AGP video card	20–50 watts
PCI circuit boards	5 watts each
ISA circuit boards	10 watts each
Floppy drive	5 watts
CD drive	10–25 watts

TABLE 1.4   Estimating Power Consumption *(continued)*

Component	Watts Consumed, for Estimating Purposes
RAM	8 watts per 128MB
IDE hard drive	5–15 watts
SCSI hard drive	10–40 watts

Processor/CPUs

The *central processing unit (CPU)* is a processor chip consisting of an array of millions of integrated circuits. Its purpose is to accept, perform calculations on, and eject numeric data. It's considered the "brain" of the computer because it's the part that performs the mathematical operations required for all other activity.

There are two form factors for CPU chips: pin grid array (PGA) and single edge contact cartridge (SECC). The PGA style is a flat square or rectangular ceramic chip with an array of pins in the bottom. The actual CPU is a tiny silicon wafer embedded inside that ceramic chip. The SECC style is a circuit board with the silicon wafer mounted on it. The circuit board is then surrounded by a plastic cartridge for protection; the circuit board sticks out of the cartridge along one edge. This edge fits into a slot in the motherboard.

All CPUs today require cooling because they generate heat as they operate. The cooling can be either active or passive. A *passive heat sink* is a block of heat-conductive material that sits close to the CPU and wicks away the heat into the air. An *active heat sink* contains a fan that pulls the hot air away from the CPU.

One way to determine which CPU your computer is using is to open the case and view the numbers stamped on the CPU. However, some passive heat sinks are glued to the CPU, so the numbers may not be visible without removing it. Another way to determine a computer's CPU is to save your work, exit any open programs, and restart the computer. Watch closely as the computer returns to its normal state. You should see a notation that tells you what chip you're using. The General tab of the System Properties in Windows may also report the CPU speed. Later versions of Windows will also report the CPU speed in the System Information tool.

External Speed (Clock Speed)

The *clock speed*, or *external speed*, is the speed at which the motherboard communicates with the CPU. It's determined by the motherboard, and its cadence is set by a quartz crystal (the system crystal) that generates regular electrical pulses.

Internal Speed

The *internal speed* is the maximum speed at which the CPU can perform its internal operations. This may be the same as the motherboard's speed (the external speed), but it's more likely to be a multiple of it. For example, a CPU may have an internal speed of 1.3GHz but an external speed of 133MHz. That means for every tick of the system crystal's clock, the CPU has 10 internal ticks of its own clock.

Cache Memory

A *cache* is an area of extremely fast memory used to store data that is waiting to enter or exit the CPU. The *Level 1 cache*, also known as the *L1* or *front-side cache*, holds data that is waiting to enter the CPU. On modern systems, the L1 cache is built into the CPU. The *Level 2 cache*, also known as the *L2* or *back-side cache*, holds data that is exiting the CPU and is waiting to return to RAM. On modern systems, the L2 cache is in the same packaging as the CPU but on a separate chip. On older systems, the L2 cache was on a separate circuit board installed in the motherboard, and was sometimes called COAST.

The Bus

The processor's ability to communicate with the rest of the system's components relies on the supporting circuitry. The system board's underlying circuitry is called the *bus*. The computer's bus moves information into and out of the processor and other devices. A bus allows all devices to communicate with each other. The motherboard has several buses. The *external data bus* carries information to and from the CPU and is the fastest bus on the system. The *address bus* typically runs at the same speed as the external data bus and carries data to and from RAM. The PCI, AGP, and ISA interfaces also have their own buses with their own widths and speeds.

The CPU must be compatible with the motherboard in the following ways:

Physical connectivity The CPU must be in the right kind of package to fit into the motherboard.

Speed The motherboard's chipset dictates its external data-bus speed; the CPU must be capable of operating at that external speed.

Instruction set The motherboard's chipset contains an instruction set for communicating with the CPU; the CPU must understand the commands in that set. For example, a motherboard designed for an AMD Athlon CPU can't accept an Intel Pentium CPU, because the instruction set is different.

Voltage The CPU requires that a certain voltage of power be supplied to it via the motherboard's interface. This can be anywhere from +5V for a very old CPU down to around +2.1V for a modern one. The wrong voltage can ruin the CPU.

There are several ways of differentiating one CPU from another. The following sections explain specifications according to type, speed, voltage, and cache memory.

CPU Speed

The CPU's speed is the frequency at which it executes instructions. This frequency is measured in millions of cycles per second, or megahertz (MHz); or billions of cycles per second, or gigahertz (GHz).

The CPU has an internal and an external speed. The external speed corresponds with the motherboard's speed, based on its system crystal. The system crystal pulses, generating a cadence at which operations occur on the motherboard. Each pulse is called a clock tick. The CPU's internal speed is usually a multiple of that, so that multiple operations occur internally per clock tick. A CPU's speed as described in its specifications is its internal speed.

CPU Cache

Each CPU has at least two caches: L1 and L2. The L1 cache is built into the CPU on modern systems. It's the front-side cache, where data waits to enter the CPU. The L2 cache, or backside cache, is where data exiting the CPU waits. On modern systems, the L2 cache is within the CPU's packaging but not integrated into the CPU's die. On older systems, the L2 cache was on a separate set of chips on the motherboard. You can compare one CPU to another according to the size of its L1 and L2 caches.

On some CPUs, the L2 cache operates at the same speed as the CPU; on others, the cache speed is only half the CPU speed. Chips with full-speed L2 caches have better performance.

Some newer systems also have an *L3 cache*, which is external to the CPU. It sits between the CPU and RAM to optimize data transfer between them.

CPU Voltage

A CPU's voltage is the amount of electricity provided to it by the motherboard. Older CPUs have higher voltages (around +5V); newer ones have lower voltages (less than +2V in some cases).

One reason a given motherboard can't support many different CPUs is that it must provide the correct voltage. To get around this issue, some motherboards have *voltage regulator modules (VRMs)* that are able to change the voltage based on the CPU.

CPU Manufacturers

The market leader in the manufacture of chips is Intel Corporation, with Advanced Micro Devices (AMD) gaining market share in the home PC market. Other competitors include Motorola and IBM.

INTEL PROCESSORS

The first commercially successful Intel CPU was the 8086, developed in the late 1970s. It was used in the IBM XT, one of the early home and business personal computers. Other early Intel CPUs included the 80286, 80386, and 80486. You may find it useful to learn about the specifications of these CPUs for your own knowledge, but they aren't covered on the current A+ exam.

PENTIUM

Intel introduced the Pentium processor in 1993. This processor has 3.1 million transistors using a 64-bit data path, a 32-bit address bus, and a 16KB on-chip cache, and it comes in speeds from 60MHz to 200MHz. With the release of the Pentium chips, *dual pipelining* was introduced (also called *superscalar architecture*), allowing the chip to process two operations at once.

The term *Pentium* refers to three separate CPUs: first-generation, second-generation, and MMX. First-generation Pentiums were 273-pin PGA CPUs (Socket 4) drawing +5V. They ran at 60MHz or 66MHz. The second-generation Pentiums were 296-pin models (Socket 5 or Socket 7) drawing +3.3V. They ran at between 75Mhz and 200MHz. Third-generation (MMX) Pentiums, released in 1997, added multimedia extensions (MMX) to help the CPU work with graphic-intensive games. They used Socket 7 sockets, drew +2.8V, and ran at 166MHz to 233MHz. Due to the voltage difference between the Pentium MMX CPU and other Socket 7 CPUs, the MMX CPU required a motherboard that either was specifically for that CPU or had a VRM that could take the voltage down to that level.

PENTIUM PRO

The Pentium Pro, released in 1995, came between the second- and third-generation Pentiums. Physically, the Pentium Pro was a PGA-style, rectangular chip with 387 pins, using a Socket 8 socket drawing +3V. It was designed primarily for server usage, and was optimized for 32-bit operating systems. On a 16-bit OS like Windows 3.1, the Pentium Pro ran more slowly than a Pentium, so it failed to gain widespread consumer support.

The Pentium Pro included *quad pipelining*, which processed four operations at once. It was also the first CPU to include an on-chip L2 cache. Another advantage of the Pentium Pro was *dynamic processing*, which allowed it to run instructions out of order whenever it was waiting for something else to happen.

 Throttling is a term CompTIA expects you to know for the exam. With throttling, you artificially reduce the amount of resource available. Although commonly used with bandwidth to prevent one user from absorbing all the resources on a network, it can also be applied to processors and applications. In many senses, throttling in this manner is the opposite of *overclocking*— where you attempt to get the processor to run at a speed higher than it's marked by using a faster bus speed or some other trick.

PENTIUM II

Intel next released the Pentium II: This chip's speeds ranged from 233MHz to over 400MHz. It was introduced in 1997 and was designed to be a multimedia chip with special on-chip multimedia instructions and high-speed cache memory. It has 32KB of L1 cache, dynamic execution, and MMX technology. The Pentium II uses an SECC to attach to the motherboard instead of the standard PGA package used with the earlier processor types.

When released, the Pentium II was designed for single-processor-only applications. Intel also released a separate processor, known as the Pentium II Xeon, to fill the need for multi-processor applications such as servers. The Xeon's primary advantage is a huge L2 cache (up to 2MB) that runs at the same speed as the CPU. The Xeon uses a special size of SECC-style slot called Slot 2.

Different voltages have been used for the Pentium II over its lifespan, ranging from +2.8V to +2.0V. When you're using a Pentium II, it's important that the motherboard provide the correct voltage to it. This can be achieved with a VRM on the motherboard that detects the CPU's needs and adjusts the voltage provided.

CELERON

To offer a less-costly alternative and to keep its large market share, Intel released the Celeron. In some cases, the Celeron was priced as low as half the retail price of the Pentium II. Because it was developed after the Pentium II, it benefited from some advancements and in certain aspects outperformed its more expensive counterpart. Intel has also named its low-budget Pentium III CPUs Celeron.

The Celeron CPU has come in several package types, including a 370-pin PGA socket (Socket 370) and an SECC variant called single edge processor (SEP) that is similar to the circuit board inside an SECC cartridge but without the plastic outer shell.

PENTIUM III

The Pentium III was released in 1999 and uses the same SECC connector as its predecessor, the Pentium II. It included 70 new instructions and a processor serial number (PSN), a unique number electronically encoded into the processor. This number can be used to uniquely identify a system during Internet transactions.

The Pentium III has two styles: an SECC-style cartridge called SECC2, and a PGA-style chip with 370 pins. The Pentium III PGA chip has the CPU chip mounted on the top rather than the bottom of the ceramic square; it's called a flip chip (FC), or FC-PGA.

 Like the Pentium II, the Pentium III has a multiprocessor Xeon version as well.

PENTIUM 4

The Pentium 4 was released in 2002. It runs on a motherboard with a fast system bus (between 400MHz and 800MHz) and provides some incremental improvements over the Pentium III. It's a PGA-style CPU.

One of the improvements the Pentium 4 offers is *hyperthreading* technology. This feature enables the computer to multitask more efficiently between CPU-demanding applications.

 Dual-core processors, available from Intel as well as AMD, essentially combine two processors into one chip. Instead of adding two processors to a machine (making it a multiprocessor system), you have one chip splitting operations and essentially performing as if it's two processors in order to get better performance.

SUMMARY OF INTEL PROCESSORS

Table 1.5 provides a summary of the history of the Intel processors. Table 1.6 shows the physical characteristics of Pentium-class (and higher-class) processors.

TABLE 1.5   The Intel Family of Processors

Chip	Year Added	Data Bus Width (in Bits)	Address Bus Width (in Bits)	Speed (in MHz)
8080	1974	8	8	2
8086	1978	16	20	5–10
8088	1979	8	20	4.77
80286	1982	16	24	8–12
386DX	1985	32	32	16–33
386SX	1988	32	24	16–20
486DX	1989	32	32	25–50
486SX	1991	32	32	16–33
487SX	1991	32	32	16–33
486DX2	1991	32	32	33–66
486DX4	1992	32	32	75–100
Pentium	1993	32	32	60–166
Pentium Pro	1995	64	32	150–200
Pentium II	1997	64	64	233–300
Pentium II Xeon	1998	64	64	400–600
Celeron	1999	64	64	400–600
Pentium III	1999	64	64	350–1000
Pentium III Xeon	1999	64	64	350–1000
Pentium 4	2002	64	64	1000–3000

NOTE A Pentium 4 Extreme Edition was released in 2003. Featuring a dual-core processor as its biggest modification over the Pentium 4, it's targeted for the gaming user.

TABLE 1.6   Physical Characteristics of Pentium-Class Processors

Processor	Speeds (MHz)	Socket	Pins	Voltage
Pentium-P5 (first generation)	60–66	4	273	+5V
Pentium-P54C (second generation)	75–200	5 or 7	296	+3.3V
Pentium-P55C (third generation)	166–233	7	321	+2.8V
Pentium Pro	150–200	8	387	+3V
Pentium II	233–450	SECC	N/A	+2.0V–+2.8V
Pentium III	450–1130	SECC2 or Socket 370	370	+2.0V
Pentium 4	1300–3000 (at this writing)	Socket 423 or Socket 478	423 or 478	+1.53V– +1.75V

INTEL CLONES AND OTHERS

Intel *clones* are processors that are based on the *x*86 architecture and are produced by other vendors; the most notable is AMD. AMD's competitor to the Pentium II is the K6. The original K6 ran at between 166MHz and 300MHz. The K6-2, at 266MHz to 475MHz, added 3DNow! Technology for improved multimedia. The K6-3, at 400MHz to 450MHz, adds a full-speed L2 cache. Because all the K6 chips are PGA, whereas Pentiums are SECC, you need a special motherboard for the K6 chips designed specifically for them.

AMD's competitor to the Pentium III is the Athlon. It uses an SECC-style slot called Slot A that is physically the same but not pin-compatible with Intel-style Slot 1 SECC. AMD also has a low-budget version called the Duron that has less L2 cache.

Memory

To pass the A+ exam and be a productive computer technician, you must be familiar with memory. Not only will you be tested on this subject, but one of the most common upgrades performed on a PC is adding memory. Adding memory is a simple task, but before you can add memory you must have the correct type. When we say *memory*, we are most often referring to Random Access Memory (RAM). However, there are other types of memory. We'll discuss them all in this section. Be familiar with the various types and their usage.

Physical Memory

Physically, memory is a collection of integrated circuits that store data and program information as patterns of 1s and 0s (on and off states) in the chip. Most memory chips require constant power (also called a constant *refresh*) to maintain those patterns of 1s and 0s. If power is lost, all those tiny switches revert back to the off position, effectively erasing the data from memory. Some memory types, however, don't require a refresh.

There are many types of RAM. In this section, we examine each type in detail.

SRAM

Static RAM (SRAM) stores whatever is placed in it until it's changed. Unlike dynamic RAM (DRAM), it doesn't require constant electrical refreshing. Another name for it is nonvolatile RAM (NVRAM). It's expensive, so it isn't typically used for the main memory in a system.

DRAM

DRAM is an improvement over SRAM. DRAM uses a different approach to storing the 1s and 0s. Instead of using transistors, DRAM stores information as charges in very small capacitors. If a charge exists in a capacitor, it's interpreted as a 1. The absence of a charge is interpreted as a 0.

Because DRAM uses capacitors instead of switches, it needs to use a constant refresh signal to keep the information in memory. DRAM requires more power than SRAM for refresh signals and, therefore, is mostly found in desktop computers.

DRAM technology allows several memory units, called *cells*, to be packed to a high density. Therefore, these chips can hold very large amounts of information. Most PCs today use DRAM of one type or another.

Let's take a brief look at some of the different types of DRAM:

Fast page mode (FPM)   An older type of RAM (almost always 72-pin SIMM packaging) that isn't synchronized in speed with the motherboard. It's rated in nanoseconds of delay, with lower numbers being better (for example, 60ns). FPM is now obsolete.

Extended data out (EDO)   Like FPM, an older type of RAM, usually in 72-pin SIMM form. It performs a bit better than normal FPM RAM because it needs to be refreshed less frequently. Like FPM, it's now obsolete.

Synchronous DRAM (SDRAM)   Synchronized to the speed of the motherboard's system bus. Synchronizing the speed of the systems prevents the address bus from having to wait for the memory because of different clock speeds. SDRAM typically comes in the form of 168-pin DIMMs or 184-pin RIMMs.

Double data rate (DDR) SDRAM/DDR2   Essentially, clock-doubled SDRAM. The memory chip can perform reads and writes on both sides of any clock cycle (the up, or start, and the down, or ending), thus doubling the effective memory executions per second. So, if you're using DDR SDRAM with a 100MHz memory bus, the memory will execute reads and writes at 200MHz and transfer the data to the processor at 100MHz. The advantage of DDR over regular SDRAM is increased throughput and thus increased overall system speed.

The next generation of DDR SDRAM is DDR2 (double data rate 2). This allows for two accesses per clock cycle and effectively doubles the speed of the memory.

RAMBUS   A relatively new and extremely fast (up to 800MHz) technology that uses, for the most part, a new methodology in memory system design. RAMBUS (also known as direct Rambus) is a memory bus that transfers data at 800MHz. RAMBUS memory models (often called Rambus inline memory modules [RIMMs]), like DDR SDRAM, can transfer data on both the rising and falling edges of a clock cycle. That feature, combined with the 16-bit bus for efficient transfer of data, results in the ultra-high memory transfer rate (800MHz) and the high bandwidth of up to 1.6GBps.

Memory Chip Package Types

Memory chips come in many different types of packages. The ones most frequently encountered are discussed in the following sections.

DUAL INLINE PACKAGE (DIP)

Dual inline package (DIP) memory is so named because the individual RAM chips use the DIP-style package for the memory module. Older computers, such as the IBM AT, arranged these small chips like rows of caskets in a small memory "graveyard." This type of memory has long been obsolete.

SIMMS

Single inline memory modules (SIMMs) were developed because DIPs took up too much real estate on the logic board. Someone got the idea to put several DIP chips on a small circuit board and then make that board easily removable.

Each of these RAM circuit boards is a *stick* of RAM. There are two sizes of SIMMs: 30-pin and 72-pin. The 30-pin are older, 8-bit sticks. The 72-pin are 32-bit sticks. Figure 1.10 shows one of each. SIMMs are called *single* because they're single-sided. When you count the number of pins (the metal tabs) along the bottom, there are 30 or 72 of them. In contrast, DIMMs (dual inline memory modules) are double-sided; for example, a 168-pin DIMM has 84 pins on each side.

FIGURE 1.10   Single inline memory modules (SIMMs)

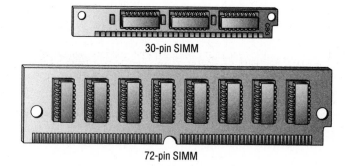

30-pin SIMM

72-pin SIMM

DIMMS AND RIMMS

DIMMs are double-sided memory chips used in modern systems (Pentium and higher). They typically have 168 pins and are 64 bits in width. Figure 1.11 shows a DIMM.

A RIMM is just like a DIMM, except it's a Rambus DRAM stick, has 184 pins, and is slightly longer in size.

SODIMMS AND MICRODIMMS

Portable computers (notebooks and subnotebooks) require smaller sticks of RAM because of their smaller size. Two types are small outline DIMM (SoDIMM) and MicroDIMM.

Parity and Nonparity RAM

Some sticks of RAM have a parity bit on them for error correction. The parity bit works by adding up the number of 1s in a particular row of data in RAM (for example, 32-bit RAM has 32 individual binary digits). It then adds either 1 or 0 to that total to make it come out even. When retrieving the data from RAM, it re-adds the 1s again, and if the parity bit doesn't come out the same, it knows an error has occurred.

You can identify a parity SIMM by counting the number of chips on the stick. If there are nine, it's parity RAM. If there are eight, it's nonparity.

When do you choose parity RAM? Usually the motherboard requires either parity or nonparity; a few motherboards will accept either. Nowadays parity RAM is rarely needed because advances in RAM technology have created reliable RAM that seldom makes errors.

One type of parity RAM is error correction code (ECC). This is a now-obsolete type of parity RAM. Most RAM today is non-ECC.

RAM Banks and Bit Width

As explained earlier, 30-pin SIMMs are 8-bit, 72-pin SIMMs are 32-bit, and DIMMs are 64-bit. The motherboard has an address bus that carries data from the RAM to the CPU and chipset. It has a certain width. On Pentium and higher systems, it's 64-bit; on earlier systems, it's 32-bit (386 and 486) or less (286 and below). A bank of RAM is a single stick or a group of sticks where the collective bit width adds up to the width of the address bus.

For example, on a Pentium motherboard, a single bank consists of a single 64-bit DIMM or a pair of two 32-bit SIMMs. For a 486 motherboard, a single bank is a single 32-bit SIMM or four 8-bit SIMMs.

FIGURE 1.11   Dual inline memory module (DIMM)

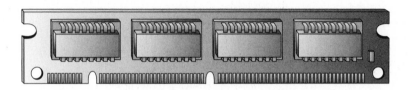

Video RAM

Video memory (also called *video RAM [VRAM]*) is used to store image data for processing by the video adapter. The more video memory an adapter has, the better the quality of image that it can display. Also, more VRAM allows the adapter to display a higher resolution of image.

Display Devices

Display systems convert computer signals into text and pictures and display them on a television-like screen. Several different types of computer displays are used today, including the TV. All of them use either the same *cathode ray tube* (*CRT*) technology found in television sets or the *liquid crystal display* (*LCD*) technology found on all laptop, notebook, and palmtop computers.

In a CRT, a device called an *electron gun* shoots electrons toward the back of the monitor screen (see Figure 1.12). The back of the screen is coated with special chemicals (called *phosphors*) that glow when electrons strike them. This beam of electrons scans the monitor from left to right and top to bottom to create the image.

FIGURE 1.12   How a CRT monitor works

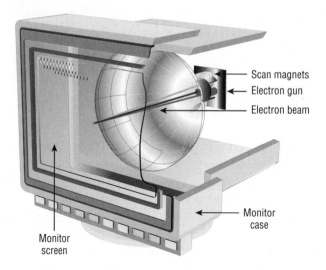

Scan magnets
Electron gun
Electron beam
Monitor case
Monitor screen

There are two ways of measuring a monitor's image quality: dot pitch and refresh (scan) rate. A monitor's *dot pitch* is the distance between two dots of the same color on the monitor. Usually given in fractions of a millimeter (mm), it tells how sharp the picture is. The lower the number, the closer together the pixels are, and thus the sharper the image. An average dot pitch is 0.28mm.

A monitor's *refresh rate* specifies how many times in one second the scanning beam of electrons redraws the screen. The phosphors stay bright for only a fraction of a second, so they must constantly be hit with electrons to stay lit. Given in draws per second, or hertz (Hz), the refresh rate specifies how much energy is being put into keeping the screen lit. Most people notice a flicker in the display at refresh rates of 75Hz or lower because the phosphors begin to decay to black before they're revived; increasing the refresh rate can help reduce eyestrain by reducing the flickering.

The *resolution* of a monitor is the number of horizontal and vertical pixels that are displayed. Most monitors allow for two or more resolutions, and you can pick the one to use in the desktop settings of the operating system. The vertical hold (V-hold) settings can be tweaked to make the image appear properly in the monitor. Connectors commonly used to connect the display device include the following:

VGA   This is the traditional connector, which is shaped like a D and has three rows of five pins each, for a total of 15 pins. This is also often called the DB-15 connector.

A 9-pin VGA connector does exist, but it's very uncommon.

Digital video interface (DVI)   There are several types of DVI pin configurations, but all connectors are D-shaped. The wiring differs based on whether the connector is single linked or dual linked (extra pins are used for the dual link). DVI differs from everything else in that it includes both digital and analog signals at the same time, which makes it popular for LCD and plasma TVs. Figure 1.13 shows a DVI connector.

FIGURE 1.13   One of several possible DVI connectors

High definition multimedia interface (HDMi)   These connectors are used to connect compatible digital items (DVD players, for example). The Type A connector has 19 pins and is backward compatible with DVI. Type B connectors have 29 pins and aren't backward compatible with DVI, but they support greater resolutions.

S-Video   The S-Video connector looks much like a PS/2 connector, except that it has four conductors. These are also known as Y/C connectors; they break the signal into two components (luminance and chrominance) instead of carrying them in a single signal.

Component/RGB   Component connectors are similar to what you use to connect video recorders and other items to televisions. They have RCA jacks and use red, green, and blue signals.

Liquid Crystal Displays

Two major types of LCDs are used in laptops today: *active matrix* screens and *passive matrix* screens. Their main differences lie in the quality of the image. Both types use some kind of lighting behind the LCD panel to make the screen easier to view.

Passive matrix   A passive matrix screen uses a row of transistors across the top of the screen and a column of them down the side. It sends pulses to each pixel at the intersections of each row and column combination, telling it what to display.

Passive matrix displays are becoming obsolete because they're less bright and have poorer refresh rates and image quality than active matrix displays. However, they use less power than active matrix displays do.

Active matrix   An active matrix screen uses a separate transistor for each individual pixel in the display, resulting in higher refresh rates and brighter display quality. These screens use more power, however, because of the increased number of transistors that must be powered. Almost all notebook PCs today use active matrix. A variant called thin-film transistor (TFT) uses multiple transistors per pixel, resulting in even better display quality.

Display System Problems

There are two types of video problems: no video and bad video. *No video* means no image appears on the screen when the computer is powered up. *Bad video* means the quality is substandard for the type of display system being used.

NO VIDEO

Any number of things can cause a blank screen. The first three are the most common: the power is off, the monitor's cable is unplugged, or the contrast or brightness is turned down.

If you've checked the power as well as the brightness and contrast settings, then the problem could be a bad video card or a bad monitor. Most monitors these days display a *Working* message briefly when you turn them on, so you can ascertain that the monitor is working and that an amber light appears on the front. When the PC starts up, the light on the front of the monitor changes from amber to green, indicating that the monitor is receiving a signal.

If the monitor is working but not receiving a signal from the PC, the video card may be bad. However, no video can also mean a problem with the motherboard, RAM, or CPU, so it isn't a given that the video card is at fault when no video appears.

Malfunctioning monitors are usually not worth fixing, because the cost of the labor involved exceeds the cost of a brand-new monitor. In addition, it may be difficult to find a technician to work on a monitor, because it isn't part of most standard PC technician training programs (due to the risk of electric shock from the high-voltage capacitor inside the monitor).

BAD VIDEO

A monitor that doesn't display one of the three basic colors (red, green, or blue) probably has a bad cable, a bent or broken pin, or a loose connection at either the PC or the monitor. This is the case because different pins on the connectors—and wires in the cable—control different colors.

Color problems may also result from the monitor being out of adjustment. With most new monitors, this is an easy problem to fix. Old monitors had to be partially disassembled to change these settings; new monitors have push-button control panels for changing these settings.

Exposure to a magnetic field can cause swirls and fuzziness even in high-quality monitors. The Earth generates magnetic fields, as do unshielded speakers and power surges. Most monitors have metal shields that can protect against magnetic fields. But eventually these shields can become polluted by taking on the same magnetic field as the Earth, so they becomes useless. To solve this problem, these monitors have a built-in feature known as *Degauss*; it removes the effects of the magnetic field by creating a stronger magnetic field with opposite polarity that gradually fades to a field of zero. A special Degauss button or feature in the monitor's on-screen software activates it. You need only press it when the picture starts to deteriorate. The image will shake momentarily during the Degauss cycle and then return to normal.

> If you have a monitor that shows bad distortion, and changing the settings or Degaussing has no effect, then look for magnetic interference caused by nearby florescent lights or large power sources.

Input Devices

A virtually unlimited number of types of input devices can be connected to a PC. In addition to the standard keyboard and mouse, there are bar-code readers, digital cameras, microphones, biometric devices, touch screens, and a plethora of others. Many today connect through the USB or FireWire port, using instructions from the vendor. However, you must know about other types of connections for the A+ exam.

Keyboard connectors allow for the direct connection of the keyboard to the motherboard. There are now essentially three types of keyboard connectors: AT, PS/2, and USB.

AT connectors are round, about ½ inch in diameter, and have five sockets in the DIN-5 configuration. They're found on AT motherboards. The second style, PS/2 connectors, are smaller and look just like a PS/2 mouse connector; these are found on ATX motherboards. USB keyboards are rapidly growing in popularity and allow you to connect to any available USB port (front, back, side, etc.).

A mouse connector is a PS/2-style connector; on an ATX it's built into the side of the motherboard, and on an AT a small ribbon cable connects a back-mountable port to the motherboard.

Peripheral Ports and Connectors

PCs were developed to perform calculations on data. In order for the PC to be useful, there must be a way to get the data into and out of the computer. To accomplish this, several ports are available. The four most common types of ports are the serial, parallel, USB, and game ports. Figure 1.14 shows some typical ports built into an ATX motherboard.

FIGURE 1.14   Built-in ports on a motherboard

These ports are connected to the motherboard using small ribbon cables on an AT system, or they're built directly into the side of the motherboard on an ATX system.

Adapter Cards

Adapter cards are also known by many other names, including *circuit boards/cards* and *expansion boards/cards*. In all cases, adapter cards are circuit boards that fit into expansion slots in the motherboard. They can include modems, network interface cards, sound cards, and many other types of devices.

Adapter cards are purchased to match an available expansion slot in the motherboard. PCI is the most common type of expansion slot for an adapter card in today's PCs. ISA slots are nearly obsolete, and AGP slots are used only for video cards.

Expansion slots are used to install various devices in the computer to expand its capabilities. Some expansion devices that may be installed in these slots include video, network, sound, and disk interface cards.

Expansion slots come in three main types: ISA, PCI, and AGP. Each type is different in appearance and function, as you'll learn in future chapters. You should be able to visually identify the different expansion slots on the motherboard:

ISA expansion slots   If you're repairing a computer made before 1997, chances are the motherboard in your computer has a few ISA slots. These slots are usually brown and are separated into two unequal lengths. Computers made after 1997 generally include a few ISA slots for backward compatibility with old expansion cards.

PCI expansion slots   Most computers made today contain primarily PCI slots. They're easily recognizable, because they're short (around 3 inches long) and are usually white. PCI slots can usually be found in any computer that has a Pentium-class processor or higher.

AGP expansion slots   AGP slots are becoming more popular. In the past, if you wanted to use a high-speed, accelerated 3D graphics video card, you had to install the card into an existing PCI or ISA slot. AGP slots were designed to be a direct connection between the video circuitry and the PC's memory. They're also easily recognizable because they're usually brown and located right next to the PCI slots on the motherboard. Figure 1.15 shows an example of an AGP slot, along with a PCI slot for comparison. Notice the difference in length between the two.

PCIE expansion slots   PCIE combines the functionality of PCI with AGP and was discussed earlier in this chapter.

Ports and Cables

A computer's peripheral ports are the physical connectors found outside the computer. Cables of various types are designed to plug into these ports and create a connection between the PC and the external devices that may be attached to it. A successful IT technician should have an in-depth knowledge of ports and cables.

Because the peripheral components need to be upgraded frequently, either to keep pace with technological change or to replace broken devices, the test requires a well-rounded familiarity with the ports and their associated cabling.

FIGURE 1.15   An AGP slot compared to a PCI slot

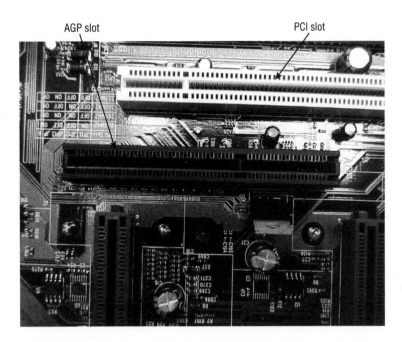

Unless a peripheral device connects directly to the motherboard, it must use a port. Ports can be distinguished from one another by three factors:

Bits of data simultaneously conveyed   A s*erial cable* carries only one bit at a time. A *parallel cable* carries multiple bits at a time (usually eight).

Data transmission speed   This is expressed in kilobits or megabits per second and refers to the overall data throughput.

Type of connector   A wide variety of connectors are used in PCs today, including the DB-style (as with legacy parallel and serial ports and VGA monitors), Centronics style (as with printers and some SCSI devices), and USB.

Parallel vs. Serial

A cable (and its port) can be either parallel or serial, and it isn't always immediately obvious from looking which is which. For example, both parallel and serial cables can use the DB-25 style of connector.

Both parallel and serial cables have multiple wires inside them, but they use them for different purposes. A parallel cable uses eight wires to carry bits of data in each direction, plus extra wires for signaling and traffic control. A serial cable uses only one wire to carry data in each direction; all the rest of its wires are for signaling and traffic control.

Transmission Speed

Neither parallel nor serial is intrinsically faster than the other. There are both fast and slow parallel and serial connections. For example, a legacy serial port such as for an external modem carries data fairly slowly (about 115Kbps), but a USB cable (also serial) carries data very quickly (up to 12Mbps for USB 1.1, and even faster for USB 2.0).

Connector Types

The following are common connector types:

DB   A D-shaped connector with a metal ring around a set of pins. Named for the number of pins/holes used: DB-25, DB-9, DB-15, and so on. Can be either parallel or serial. Common uses: VGA video, legacy serial devices such as external modems, and parallel printer cables (the connector on the PC only; the printer end uses Centronics).

RJ   Registered jack; a plastic plug with small metal tabs, like a telephone cord plug. Numbering is used in the naming: RJ-11 has two metal tabs, and RJ-14 has four. Both are used for telephone systems. RJ-45 has eight tabs and is used for Ethernet 10BaseT/100BaseT networking. Always serial.

BNC   Stands for Bayonet-Neill Connector or British Naval Connector. A metal wire surrounded by shielding, like a cable television connector. Used for 10Base2 Ethernet networking. Always serial.

Centronics   A plastic block with metal tabs flat against it, surrounded by a D-shaped metal ring. Used to connect a parallel printer cable to the printer, and also for some SCSI devices. Always parallel.

Ribbon connector   A rectangular block consisting of a set of square holes that connect to pins on a circuit board. Used to connect floppy drives, IDE drives, and some SCSI devices to their controllers. Always parallel.

PS/2 (mini-DIN)   A round connector with six small pins inside, commonly used to connect keyboards on ATX motherboards or PS/2 style mice.

DIN   A larger round connector with five rather large pins inside, used for connecting the keyboard on an AT motherboard.

USB   A flat rectangular connector, used with USB interfaces.

Cabling

Cables are used to connect two or more entities together. They're usually constructed of several wires encased in a rubberized outer coating. The wires are soldered to modular connectors at both ends. These connectors allow the cables to be quickly attached to the devices they connect.

Cables may be either shielded or unshielded. This refers to shielding against electromagnetic interference (EMI); it has nothing to do with whether the cable is shielded against dirt or water.

A list of common cable types used in PCs, their descriptions, their maximum effective lengths, and their most common uses is given in Table 1.7. The F or M in a connector's designation is for female (holes) or male (pins).

TABLE 1.7 Common PC Cable Descriptions

Application	1st Connector	2nd Connector	Max. Length
Null modem	DB-9F	DB-9F	25 feet
Null modem	DB-25F	DB-25F	25 feet
RS-232 (modem cable)	DB-9F	DB-25M	25 feet
RS-232 (modem cable)	DB-25F	DB-25M	25 feet
Parallel printer	DB-25M	Centronics 36M	10 feet
External SCSI cable	Centronics 50M	Centronics 50M	10 feet (total SCSI bus length)
VGA extension cable	DB-15M	DB-15M	3 feet
UTP Ethernet cable	RJ-45M	RJ-45M	100 meters
Thinnet Ethernet cable	BNC-M	BNC-M	100 meters
Telephone wall cable	RJ-11M or RJ-14M	RJ-11M or RJ-14M	N/A

One cable that deserves special mention is the null modem cable. It allows two computers to communicate with each other without using a modem. This cable has its transmit and receive wires crossed at both ends, so when one entity transmits on its TD line, the other entity receives it on its RD line.

Unshielded twisted pair (UTP) is the most common type of cable used for network cabling. There are various categories of network cabling; the category required for 10BaseT/100BaseT networking is Category 5, often shortened to Cat 5. There is also a Cat 5e cable type, which is used for higher-speed Ethernet such as Gigabit Ethernet.

Cooling Systems

The cooling system consists of the fan in the power supply, the fan or heat sink on the CPU, and any additional heat sinks or fans in the case. If a system is inadequately cooled, lockups and spontaneous reboots may occur.

Liquid-cooled cases are now available that use circulating water rather than fans to keep components cool. These cases are typically more expensive than standard ones and may be more difficult for an untrained technician to work on, but they result in an almost completely silent system.

Air cooling is the most common cooling method used in PCs. CPUs typically have *active heat sinks*, which are heat sinks that include an electric fan that constantly channels heat away.

A CPU that is running too hot may benefit from a better cooling fan. The heat sink portion is a block of spikes that channel heat away from the CPU.

Most *passive heat sinks* (that is, heat sinks that don't include a fan) are attached to the CPU using a glue-like thermal compound. This makes the connection between the heat sink and the CPU more seamless and direct. Thermal compound can be used on active heat sinks too, but generally it isn't because of the possibility that the fan may stop working and need to be replaced.

In addition to the main fan in the power supply, you can also install additional cooling fans in a case to help circulate air through the case.

Exam Essentials

Know what the BIOS does.   This is a ROM chip on the motherboard. It contains the BIOS software that tells the processor how to interact with the hardware in the computer. The BIOS chip tells the motherboard how to start up, check itself and its components, and pass off control to the operating system.

Know the different types of memory.   DRAM is dynamic random access memory. SRAM is static random access memory. ROM stands for read-only memory, and it's normally used to store the computer's BIOS. CMOS is a special kind of memory that holds the BIOS configuration settings.

Know the CPU package types.   Pin grid array (PGA) is a square or rectangular ceramic chip with pins in the bottom. Single edge contact cartridge (SECC) is a plastic cartridge that fits into a slot in the motherboard.

Know what RJ-45 connectors are used for.   You're likely to be asked what type of connector would be used to attach a network connector to a wall jack.

Know what PS2/mini-DIN connectors are used for.   You're likely to be asked what type of connector would be used to connect a keyboard or mouse to the back of a PC.

Know what RJ-11 connectors are used for.   You're likely to be asked what type of connector would be used to connect a modem to a telephone jack.

Understand parallel versus serial.   Parallel cables carry data eight bits at a time; serial cables carry it one bit at a time.

Understand the differences between PCI, ISA, and AGP.   Know the bus widths and speeds, and be able to select the best bus type for a given device.

Know what factors go into making memory compatible with a PC.   These factors can include physical size, capacity, technology, speed, and compatibility with existing RAM in the system.

Be able to calculate the wattage requirements of power supplies.   Given the voltage and amperage draws for a group of devices, determine the wattage of a power supply required to support them.

Understand the processor's job. The processor is the brain of the PC. Most actions performed by the PC require use of the processor to accomplish their task.

Understand the differences between the classes of Pentium chips. The Intel Pentium has gone through several changes since its release. You'll need to understand the differences between the various classes in terms of their physical packaging, speeds, voltages, and caches.

Know what a VRM is. A voltage regulator module (VRM) on a motherboard allows it to change the voltage that it provides to the CPU to accommodate a wider range of CPUs.

Know the differences between RAM types. Make sure you can differentiate between all the acronyms, such as SRAM, DRAM, SDRAM, DDR SDRAM, EDO DRAM, and so on.

Understand the different RAM packaging. Be able to differentiate between SIMMs and DIMMs, including the number of pins each has and their bit widths.

Know the purpose of parity in RAM. Understand how a parity bit is used for error correction.

Know the motherboard form factors. Understand the differences between AT, ATX, and NLX.

Distinguish between ISA, PCI, and AGP. Know their bus widths and maximum speeds, and that they're all used for expansion boards inside the PC.

Distinguish between I/O ports on a motherboard. Know the different types of ports, such as USB, IEEE 1394, legacy parallel, and legacy serial.

Know the sizes and shapes of CPU slots/sockets. Be able to specify what type of socket or slot various CPUs require.

Know what the CMOS Setup utility does. The CMOS Setup utility allows you to configure the characteristics of certain portions of the PC.

Be familiar with the common menu items listed. Knowing these common menu items and their function can greatly aid troubleshooting.

Understand the different printer port settings. Although there is no good rule of thumb on which of these settings will fix a communication error, in most cases you can resolve the issue by systematically trying the different settings.

Install, Configure, and Optimize PC Components

Knowing about personal computer components is only part of the requirements for this exam. You must also know how to install, configure, and optimize them. The components in question for this part of the exam are storage devices (internal and external), display devices, and input/multimedia devices.

Critical Information

To know how to interact with the components in question, you must understand something about system modules not already covered, as well as IDE and SCSI. Although these two acronyms popped up on occasion earlier, we didn't dwell on them because it wouldn't have done them justice to discuss them in only a sentence or two.

This section looks at some system modules that didn't fit in to the discussion earlier, as well as the differences between IDE and SCSI, and focuses on these two technologies.

 There is a great deal of overlap between this objective and its counterpart in Chapter 9. You're strongly encouraged to read Chapter 9 (this domain is a requirement on every technician exam) as you study for this part of the exam.

Concepts and Modules

The system modules described in this section are either essential computer components or available on the market as optional equipment. Each has a distinct and practical function. To troubleshoot and repair computers, you must be familiar with the components and their function when operating. Each component provides a specific function to the operation of the computer.

System Board

The spine of the computer is the *system board,* or *motherboard.* This component is made of green or brown fiberglass and is placed in the bottom or side of the case. It's the most important component in the computer because it connects all the other components of a PC together. Figure 1.16 shows a typical PC system board, as seen from above. On the system board you'll find the CPU, underlying circuitry, expansion slots, video components, RAM slots, and a variety of other chips.

FIGURE 1.16   A typical system board

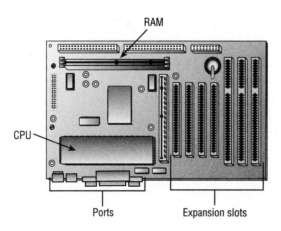

INTEGRATED COMPONENTS

Some motherboards have some of the peripheral devices built in, such as video, sound, and/or networking. These are referred to as *integrated system boards*. Such boards are cost-effective because they don't require a separate video card, sound card, and so on. The built-in components can be disabled through BIOS Setup if they should ever malfunction or need to be replaced by newer models.

SYSTEM BOARD COMPONENTS

Motherboards include components that provide basic functionality to the computer. The following components are found on a typical motherboard:

- Expansion slots
- Memory (RAM) slots
- CPU slot or socket
- Power connector
- Floppy and IDE drive connectors
- Keyboard and mouse connectors
- Peripheral port connectors (COM, LPT, USB)
- BIOS chip
- Battery

Figure 1.17 illustrates many of the components found on a typical motherboard.

FIGURE 1.17   Components on a motherboard

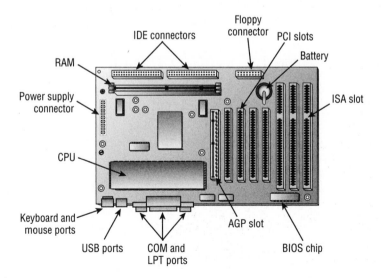

Many of these components were discussed previously. Those that were not include the following:

Memory slots   Memory, or RAM, slots contain the memory chips. There are many and varied types of memory for PCs today. We'll further discuss memory later in this chapter. PCs use memory chips arranged on a small circuit board. These circuit boards are called *single inline memory modules (SIMMs)* or *dual inline memory modules (DIMMs)*. DIMMs utilize memory chips on both sides of the circuit board, whereas SIMMs utilize memory chips on a single side. There is also a high-speed type of RAM called *Rambus dynamic RAM (RDRAM),* which comes on circuit boards called *RIMMs*.

Along with chip placement, memory modules also differ in the number of conductors, or pins, that the particular module uses. The number of pins used directly affects the overall size of the memory slot. Slot sizes include 30-pin, 72-pin, 168-pin, and 184-pin. Laptop memory comes in smaller form factors known as *small outline DIMMs (SoDIMMs)*. Figure 1.18 shows the form factors for the most popular memory chips. Notice that they basically look the same, but the memory module sizes are different.

FIGURE 1.18   Various memory module form factors

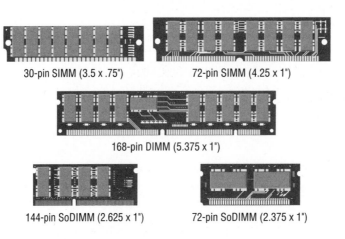

30-pin SIMM (3.5 x .75")   72-pin SIMM (4.25 x 1")

168-pin DIMM (5.375 x 1")

144-pin SoDIMM (2.625 x 1")   72-pin SoDIMM (2.375 x 1")

Memory slots are easy to identify on a motherboard. They're usually white and placed very close together. The number of memory slots varies from motherboard to motherboard, but the appearance of the different slots is similar. Metal pins in the bottom make contact with the soldered tabs on each memory module. Small metal or plastic tabs on each side of the slot keep the memory module securely in its slot.

Central processing unit (CPU) and processor slots   The CPU slot permits the attachment of the CPU to the motherboard, allowing the CPU to use the other components of the system. There are many different types of processors, which means many types of CPU slots.

The CPU slot can take on several different forms. In the past, the CPU slot was a rectangular box called a PGA socket, with many small holes to accommodate the pins on the bottom of the chip. With the release of new and more-powerful chips, additional holes were added, changing the configuration of the slot and its designator or number. Figure 1.19 shows a typical PGA-type CPU socket.

With the release of the Pentium II, the architecture of the slot went from a rectangle to more of an expansion-slot style of interface called an SECC. This style of CPU slot includes Slot 1 and Slot 2 for Intel CPUs, and Slot A for Athlon (AMD) CPUs. This type of slot looks much like an expansion slot, but it's located in a different place on the motherboard than the other expansion slots.

To see which socket type is used for which processors, examine Table 1.8.

FIGURE 1.19   A PGA CPU socket

TABLE 1.8   Socket Types and the Processors They Support

Connector Type	Processor
Socket 1	486 SX/SX2, 486 DX/DX2, 486 DX4 Overdrive
Socket 2	486 SX/SX2, 486 DX/DX2, 486 DX4 Overdrive, 486 Pentium Overdrive
Socket 3	486 SX/SX2, 486 DX/DX2, 486 DX4 486 Pentium Overdrive
Socket 4	Pentium 60/66, Pentium 60/66 Overdrive
Socket 5	Pentium 75-133, Pentium 75+ Overdrive
Socket 6	DX4, 486 Pentium Overdrive
Socket 7	Pentium 75-200, Pentium 75+ Overdrive

TABLE 1.8 Socket Types and the Processors They Support *(continued)*

Connector Type	Processor
Socket 8	Pentium Pro
Socket 370	Pentium III
Socket 423	Pentium 4
SECC (Type I), Slot 1	Pentium II
SECC2 (Type II), Slot 2	Pentium III
Slot A	Athlon

Power connectors   A power connector allows the motherboard to be connected to the power supply. As you saw in Figures 1.4 and 1.5, the power supply connector is different for AT versus ATX systems. On an ATX, there is a single power connector consisting of a block of 20 holes (in two rows). On an AT, there is a block consisting of 12 pins sticking up; these pins are covered by two connectors with six holes each.

Figure 1.20 shows a very versatile motherboard that happens to have both kinds, so you can compare. The upper connector is for ATX, and the lower one is for AT.

FIGURE 1.20   Power connectors on a motherboard

On-board floppy and IDE connectors   With the exception of diskless workstations, every PC made today uses some type of disk drive to store data and programs until they're needed. Disk drives need a connection to the motherboard in order for the computer to utilize the disk drive. These connections are known as *drive interfaces*. There are two primary types: *floppy drive interfaces* and *IDE interfaces*. Floppy drive interfaces allow floppy disk drives to be connected to the motherboard, and, similarly, IDE interfaces do the same for hard disks, CD drives, and other IDE-based drives. When you see them on the motherboard, these interfaces are said to be *on board*, as opposed to being on an expansion card, known as *off board*. The interfaces consist of circuitry and a port. A few motherboards also have SCSI interfaces that can be used for connecting drives.

Battery   Your PC has to keep certain settings when it's turned off and its power cord is unplugged. These settings include the date, time, hard-drive configuration, and memory.

Your PC stores the settings in a special memory chip called the CMOS chip. To retain these settings, the CMOS chip requires power constantly. To prevent the CMOS chip from losing its charge, a small battery is located on the motherboard.

SYSTEM BOARD FORM FACTORS
Form factor refers to the size and shape of a component. Most system boards today use the ATX form factor (refer back to Figure 1.5). Some of its key features are its orientation of the expansion slots parallel to the narrow edge of the board, a one-piece power connector from the power supply, the built-in I/O ports on the side, and the orientation of the CPU in such a position that the power-supply fan helps to cool it.

An older, alternative form factor for a system board is the baby AT style (refer back to Figure 1.4). This type uses a two-piece power supply connector, uses ribbon cables to connect ports to the board, and orients the expansion slots parallel to the wide edge of the board.

A case is generally designed to hold one or the other of these motherboard form factors, and a power supply is designed to work with one or the other; therefore those three components must be chosen as a group.

JUMPERS AND DIP SWITCHES
Jumpers and DIP switches are used to configure various hardware options on the motherboard. Processors use different voltages and multipliers to achieve their target voltage and frequency. You must set these parameters on the motherboard by changing the jumper or DIP-switch settings. Figure 1.21 shows a jumper and two types of DIP switches. Individual jumpers are often labeled with the moniker *JPx* (where *x* is the number of the jumper).

FIGURE 1.21   A jumper set and DIP switches

Jumper   "Rocker-type" DIP switch   "Slide-type" DIP switch

Cases

The *case* is the metal or plastic box in which the motherboard, power supply, disk drives, and other internal components are installed. A case is typically—but not always—purchased with a power supply already installed.

Choosing the right case for the motherboard is important. Recall from the preceding sections that motherboards come in two form factors: ATX and AT. Each requires a different style of case and a different type of power supply.

One case may also be distinguished from another in terms of its orientation. A desktop case lies with its widest side flat on the desk; a tower case stands up on end.

Finally, one case differs from another in terms of the number of drive bays it has. For example, within the broad category of *tower* cases are mini-towers (typically with two large and two small drive bays), mid-towers, and full towers (typically with four large and three small drive bays). However, there is little standardization of the number of drive bays that constitute a particular size; one manufacturer's full tower may have more or fewer bays than another's.

Although it isn't common, you may occasionally encounter a slim-line case, which is a desktop-orientation case that is shorter and thinner than a normal one—so short that normal expansion boards won't fit perpendicular to the motherboard. In such cases a *riser card* is installed, which sits perpendicular to the motherboard and contains expansion slots. The expansion cards can then be oriented parallel to the motherboard when installed.

IDE Devices

IDE drives are the most common type of hard drive found in computers. But IDE is much more than a hard drive interface; it's also a popular interface for many other drive types, including CD-ROM, DVD, and Zip. IDE drives are the most prevalent in the industry today. IDE drives are easy to install and configure, and they provide acceptable performance for most applications. Their ease of use relates to their most identifiable feature—the controller is located on the drive itself.

IDE TECHNOLOGIES

The design of the IDE is simple: Put the controller right on the drive, and use a relatively short ribbon cable to connect the drive/controller to the IDE interface. This offers the benefits of decreasing signal loss (thus increasing reliability) and making the drive easier to install. The IDE interface can be an expansion board, or it can be built into the motherboard, as is the case on almost all systems today.

IDE generically refers to any drive that has a built-in controller. The IDE we know today is more properly called AT IDE; two previous types of IDE (MCA IDE and XT IDE) are obsolete and incompatible with it.

There have been many revisions of the IDE standard over the years, and each one is designated with a certain AT attachment (ATA) number—ATA-1 through ATA-8. Drives that support ATA-2 and higher are generically referred to as enhanced IDE (EIDE).

With ATA-3, a technology called ATA Packet Interface (ATAPI) was introduced to help deal with IDE devices other than hard disks. ATAPI enables the BIOS to recognize an IDE CD-ROM drive, for example, or a tape backup or Zip drive.

Starting with ATA-4, a new technology was introduced called UltraDMA, supporting transfer modes of up to 33MBps.

ATA-5 supports UltraDMA/66, with transfer modes of up to 66MBps. To achieve this high rate, the drive must have a special 80-wire ribbon cable, and the motherboard or IDE controller card must support ATA-5.

ATA-6 supports UltraDMA/100, with transfer modes of up to 100MBps.

 If an ATA-5 or ATA-6 drive is used with a normal 40-wire cable or is used on a system that doesn't support the higher modes, it reverts to the ATA-4 performance level.

ATA-7 supports UltraDMA/133, with transfer modes of up to 150MBps and serial ATA (discussed later).

ATA-8 made only minor revisions to ATA-7 and also supports UltraDMA/133, with transfer modes of up to 150MBps and serial ATA.

IDE PROS AND CONS

The primary benefit of IDE is that it's nearly universally supported. Almost every motherboard has IDE connectors. In addition, IDE devices are typically the cheapest and most readily available type.

A typical motherboard has two IDE connectors, and each connector can support up to two drives on the same cable. That means you're limited to four IDE devices per system unless you add an expansion board containing another IDE interface. In contrast, with SCSI you can have up to seven drives per interface (or even more on some types of SCSI).

Performance also may suffer when IDE devices share an interface. When you're burning CDs, for example, if the reading and writing CD drives are both on the same cable, errors may occur. SCSI drives are much more efficient with this type of transfer.

INSTALLATION AND CONFIGURATION

To install an IDE drive, do the following:

1. Set the master/slave jumper on the drive.

2. Install the drive in the drive bay.

3. Connect the power-supply cable.

4. Connect the ribbon cable to the drive and to the motherboard or IDE expansion board.

5. Configure the drive in BIOS Setup if it isn't automatically detected.

6. Partition and format the drive using the operating system.

Each IDE interface can have only one *master* drive on it. If there are two drives on a single cable, one of them must be the *slave* drive. This setting is accomplished via a jumper on the drive. Some drives have a separate setting for Single (that is, master with no slave) and Master (that is, master with a slave); others use the Master setting generically to refer to either case. Figure 1.22 shows a typical master/slave jumper scenario, but different drives may have different jumper positions to represent each state.

FIGURE 1.22 Master/slave jumpers

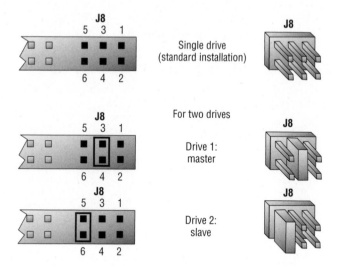

Most BIOS Setup programs today support Plug and Play, so they detect the new drive automatically at startup. If this doesn't work, the drive may not be installed correctly, the jumper settings may be wrong, or the BIOS Setup may have the IDE interface set to None rather than Auto. Enter BIOS Setup, and find out. Setting the IDE interface to Auto and then allowing the BIOS to detect the drive is usually all that is required.

In BIOS Setup for the drive, you might have the option of selecting a DMA or programmed input/output (PIO) setting for the drive. Both are methods for improving drive performance by allowing the drive to write directly to RAM, bypassing the CPU when possible. For modern drives that support UltraDMA, neither of these settings is necessary or desirable.

Now that your drive is installed, you can proceed to partition and format it for the operating system you've chosen. Then, finally, you can install your operating system of choice.

For a Windows 2000 or XP system, allow the Windows Setup program to partition and format the drive, or use the Disk Management utility in Windows to perform those tasks. To access Disk Management, from the Control Panel, choose Administrative Tools and then choose Computer Management.

SATA and PATA

Serial ATA (SATA) came out as a standard recently and was first adopted in desktops and then laptops. Whereas ATA had always been an interface that sends 16 bits at a time, SATA sends only one bit at a time. The benefit is that the cable used can be much smaller, and faster cycling can actually increase performance.

Parallel ATA (PATA) is the name retroactively given to the ATA/IDE standards when SATA became available. PATA uses a normal 40-pin connector, whereas SATA uses a 7-pin connector.

SCSI Devices

The *Small Computer System Interface* (*SCSI*) is a type of subsystem that is both highly flexible and robust. The range of devices that can use SCSI technology includes hard disk drives, scanners, tape drives, and CD-ROM drives. This is why it's so flexible, but also why its standards are so complex.

SCSI (pronounced "scuzzy") is a technology developed and standardized by the American National Standards Institute (ANSI). The standard specifies a universal, parallel, system-level interface for connecting up to eight devices (including the controller) on a single shared cable, called the *SCSI bus*. One of the many benefits of SCSI is that it's a very fast, flexible interface. You can buy a SCSI disk and install it in a Mac, a PC, or virtually any computer if a SCSI adapter is available.

SCSI is used for more than just drives. There are also SCSI scanners, tape backup units, and even printers.

SCSI CONNECTORS

SCSI devices can be either internal or external to the computer. Eight-bit SCSI-1 and SCSI-2 internal devices use a SCSI A cable, a 50-pin ribbon cable similar to that of an IDE drive. Sixteen-bit SCSI uses a SCSI P cable, with 68 wires and a DB-style connector. There is also an 80-pin internal connector called SCA used for some high-end SCSI devices.

External SCSI connectors depend on the type. SCSI-1 uses a 50-pin Centronics connector, as with a parallel printer. SCSI-2 uses a 25-, 50-, or 68-pin female DB-style connector. SCSI-3 uses a 68- or 80-pin female DB-style connector.

IDS AND TERMINATION

To configure SCSI, you must assign a unique device number (often called a *SCSI address*) to each device on the SCSI bus. These numbers are configured through either jumpers or DIP switches. When the computer needs to send data to the device, it sends a signal on the wire addressed to that number.

A device called a *terminator* (technically a *terminating resistor pack*) must be installed at both ends of the bus to keep the signals "on the bus." The device then responds with a signal that contains the device number that sent the information and the data itself. The terminator can be built into the device and activated/deactivated with a jumper, or it can be a separate block or connector hooked onto the device when termination is required.

Termination can be either active or passive. A *passive terminator* works with resistors driven by the small amount of electricity that travels through the SCSI bus. *Active termination* uses voltage regulators inside the terminator. Active termination is much better, and you should use it whenever you have fast, wide, or Ultra SCSI devices on the chain and/or more than two SCSI devices on the chain. It may not be obvious from looking at a terminator whether it's active or passive.

TYPES OF SCSI

The original implementation of SCSI was just called "SCSI" at its inception. However, as new implementations came out, the original was referred to as *SCSI-1*. This implementation is characterized by its 5Mbps transfer rate, its Centronics 50 or DB-25 female connectors, and its 8-bit bus width. SCSI-1 had some problems, however. Some devices wouldn't operate correctly when they were on the same SCSI bus as other devices. The main problem was that the ANSI SCSI standard was so new, vendors chose to implement it differently. These differences were the primary source of conflicts.

The first improvement that was designed into *SCSI-2* was a wider bus. The new specification specified both 8-bit and 16-bit buses. The larger of the two specifications is known as *Wide SCSI-2*. It improved data throughput for large data transfers. Another important change was to improve upon the now-limiting 5Mbps transfer rate. The *Fast SCSI-2* specification allowed for a 10Mbps transfer rate, thus allowing transfers twice as fast as SCSI-1. So, Wide SCSI-2 transfers data 16 bits at a time, and Fast SCSI-2 transfers data 8 bits at a time but twice as fast (at 10Mbps).

SCSI-3, also known as *Ultra SCSI*, comes in two widths: 8-bit (narrow) and 16-bit (wide), and three speeds: 20Mbps, 40Mbps, and 80Mbps. See Table 1.9.

T A B L E 1 . 9   SCSI-3 Speeds

SCSI-3 Type	Narrow (8-Bit)	Wide (16-Bit)
Ultra 1	20MBps	40MBps
Ultra 2	40MBps	80MBps
Ultra 3	80MBps	160MBps

SCSI-3 also provides ways to increase the maximum distance for the chain. Standard SCSI is also known as single-ended (SE) SCSI, and it can go about 10 feet. Low-voltage differential (LVD) SCSI is a variant with higher speeds and longer maximum distances, up to 39 feet. LVD and SE can work together on the same chain, but all will revert to SE limitations in that case.

High-voltage differential (HVD) is a special type of SCSI incompatible with the other two types. It has a maximum distance of 82 feet and must have a special HVD terminator.

SCSI DEVICE INSTALLATION AND CONFIGURATION

Installing SCSI devices is more complex than installing an IDE drive. The main issues with installing SCSI devices are cabling, termination, and addressing.

We'll discuss termination and cabling together because they're closely tied. There are two types of cabling:

- *Internal cabling* uses a 50-wire ribbon cable with several keyed connectors on them. These connectors are attached to the devices in the computer (the order is unimportant), with one connector connecting to the adapter.

- *External cabling* uses thick, shielded cables that run from adapter to device to device in a fashion known as *daisy-chaining*. Each device has two ports on it (most of the time). When hooking up external SCSI devices, you run a cable from the adapter to the first device. Then, you run a cable from the first device to the second device, from the second to the third, and so on.

Because there are two types of cabling devices, you have three ways to connect them. The methods differ by where the devices are located and whether the adapter has the terminator installed. The guide to remember here is that *both ends* of the bus must be terminated. Let's look briefly at the three connection methods:

Internal devices only   When you have only internal SCSI devices, you connect the cable to the adapter and to every SCSI device in the computer. You then install the terminating resistors on the adapter and terminate the last drive in the chain. All other devices are unterminated. This is demonstrated in Figure 1.23.

FIGURE 1.23   Cabling internal SCSI devices only

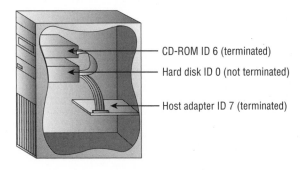

CD-ROM ID 6 (terminated)

Hard disk ID 0 (not terminated)

Host adapter ID 7 (terminated)

Some devices and adapters don't use terminating resistor packs; instead, you use a jumper or DIP switch to activate or deactivate SCSI termination on such devices. Check the documentation to find out what type your device uses.

External devices only   In the next situation, you have external devices only, as shown in Figure 1.24. By external devices, we mean that each has its own power supply. You connect the devices in the same manner in which you connected internal devices, but in this method you use several very short (less than 0.5 meters) *stub* cables to run between the devices in a daisy chain (rather than one long cable with several connectors). The effect is the same. The adapter and the last device in the chain (which has only one stub cable attached to it) must be terminated.

FIGURE 1.24   Cabling external SCSI devices only

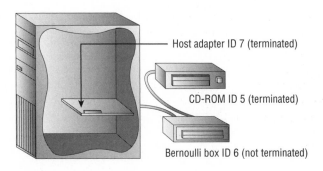

Host adapter ID 7 (terminated)

CD-ROM ID 5 (terminated)

Bernoulli box ID 6 (not terminated)

Both internal and external devices Finally, there's the hybrid situation in which you have both internal and external devices (Figure 1.25). Most adapters have connectors for both internal and external SCSI devices—if yours doesn't have both, you'll need to see if anybody makes one that will work with your devices. For adapters that do have both types of connectors, you connect your internal devices to the ribbon cable and attach the cable to the adapter. Then, you daisy-chain your external devices off the external port. You terminate the last device on each chain, leaving the adapter unterminated.

FIGURE 1.25 Cabling internal and external SCSI devices together

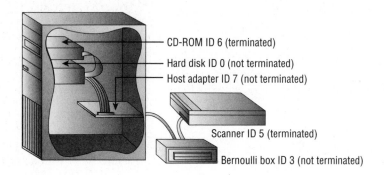

CD-ROM ID 6 (terminated)
Hard disk ID 0 (not terminated)
Host adapter ID 7 (not terminated)

Scanner ID 5 (terminated)

Bernoulli box ID 3 (not terminated)

Even though the third technique described is the technically correct way to install termination for the hybrid situation (in which you have both internal and external devices), some adapter cards still need to have terminators installed.

Each device must also have a unique SCSI ID number. This number can be assigned by the jumper (with internal devices) or with a rotary switch (on external devices). You start by assigning your adapter an address. This can be any number from 0 to 7 on an 8-bit bus, 0 to 15 on a 16-bit bus, and 0 to 31 on a 32-bit bus, as long as no other device is using that ID.

Here are some recommendations that are commonly accepted by the PC community. Remember that these are guidelines, not rules:

- Generally speaking, give slower devices higher priority so they can access the bus whenever they need it. Lower numbers are higher priority.
- Set the bootable (or first) hard disk to ID 0.
- Set the CD-ROM to ID 3.

After the devices are cabled and terminated, you have to get the PC to recognize the SCSI adapter and its devices. The SCSI adapter manages all SCSI device resource allocation, so generally all that is required is to make sure the operating system is able to see the SCSI adapter. This involves installing a Windows driver for the adapter in Windows, for example, or a real-mode driver in `CONFIG.SYS` for MS-DOS.

However, if you want to boot from a SCSI drive, the system must be able to read from that drive in order to load the operating system; you must enable the SCSI adapter's own BIOS extension so that the PC can read from it at startup without a driver. Check the documentation for the adapter; sometimes the BIOS Setup program for the SCSI adapter is activated via a function key at startup.

Once the drive is installed and talking to the computer, you can high-level-format the media and install the operating system.

If there are problems, double-check the termination and ID numbers. If everything looks correct, try changing the ID numbers one at a time. SCSI addressing is a gray area where many problems arise.

RAID

RAID stands for Redundant Array of Independent Disks. It's a way of combining the storage power of more than one hard disk for a special purpose such as increased performance or fault tolerance. RAID is more commonly done with SCSI drives, but it can be done with IDE drives.

There are several types of RAID:

RAID 0   Also known as *disk striping*. This is technically not RAID, because it doesn't provide fault tolerance. Data is written across multiple drives, so one drive can be reading or writing while the next drive's read-write head is moving. This makes for faster data access. However, if any one of the drives fails, all content is lost.

RAID 1   Also known as *disk mirroring*. This is a method of producing fault tolerance by writing all data simultaneously to two separate drives. If one drive fails, the other contains all the data and can be switched to. However, disk mirroring doesn't help access speed, and the cost is double that of a single drive.

RAID 5   Combines the benefits of both RAID 0 and RAID 1. It uses a parity block distributed across all the drives in the array, in addition to striping the data across them. That way, if one drive fails, the parity information can be used to recover what was on the failed drive. A minimum of three drives is required.

RAID works the same with SCSI as it does with IDE drives.

Upgrading Storage Devices

There are three major topic areas beneath objective 1.2: storage devices, display devices, and input/multimedia devices. The information given thus far covers all you should need to know to work with storage devices.

Upgrading Display Devices

Before connecting or disconnecting a monitor, ensure that the power to both the PC and the monitor is off. Then, connect a VGA (DB-15) cable from the monitor to the PC's video card, and connect the monitor's power cord to an AC outlet.

Other than the power supply, one of the most dangerous components to try to repair is the monitor, or CRT monitor. We recommend that you *not* try to repair monitors. To avoid the extremely hazardous environment contained inside the monitor—it can retain a high-voltage charge for hours after it's been turned off—take it to a certified monitor technician or television repair shop. The repair shop or certified technician will know and understand the proper procedures to discharge the monitor, which involves attaching a resistor to the flyback transformer's charging capacitor to release the high-voltage electrical charge that builds up during use. They will also be able to determine whether the monitor can be repaired or needs to be replaced. Remember, the monitor works in its own extremely protective environment (the monitor case) and may not respond well to your desire to try to open it. The CRT is vacuum-sealed. Be extremely careful when handling it—if you break the glass, the CRT will implode, which can send glass in any direction.

Even though we recommend not repairing monitors, the A+ exam does test your knowledge of the safety practices to use when you need to do so. If you have to open a monitor, you must first discharge the high-voltage charge on it using a high-voltage probe. This probe has a very large needle, a gauge that indicates volts, and a wire with an alligator clip. Attach the alligator clip to a ground (usually the round pin on the power cord). Slip the probe needle under the high-voltage cup on the monitor. You'll see the gauge spike to around 15,000 volts and slowly reduce to zero. When it reaches zero, you may remove the high-voltage probe and service the high-voltage components of the monitor.

Upgrading Input/Multimedia Devices

Input devices (of which multimedia devices are a subset) were discussed earlier in this chapter. Aside from following the manufacturer's instructions and the material already covered, there is nothing additional you need to know for this objective.

Exam Essentials

Know how many pins an IDE cable has.   An IDE cable has 40 pins. You're likely to be asked to choose a cable in a scenario question simply by knowing how many pins the drive requires.

Know how a controller works in a master/slave environment.   When you have a master and a slave, only one of the two controllers controls data transfers. You're likely to be asked a scenario question that relates to this environment.

Know what devices besides hard drives use IDE interfaces.   With the popularity of IDE technology, manufacturers have introduced tape drives and CD-ROMs that use IDE interfaces.

Know the transfer rates of the different types of SCSI architectures.   The different types of SCSI controllers and their supporting devices support throughput ranging from 5Mbps to 160Mbps. You should be familiar with these types and their throughput.

Understand SCSI IDs.   SCSI IDs are a critical concept to understand. Not only is this information necessary for the exam, but you also must be able to configure SCSI ID numbers in order to install a SCSI device.

Understand termination.   You must not only understand what termination does, but also know how to implement it for the exam and know how to install a SCSI device.

Know the difference between SE, LVD, and HVD.   Make sure you know which will coexist (SE and LVD) and what benefits LVD and HVD offer over SE.

Understand RAID levels.   Know that RAID 0 is performance enhancement with no fault tolerance, RAID 1 is fault tolerance with no performance enhancement, and RAID 5 offers fault tolerance and enhances performance.

Identify Tools and Diagnostics for PC Components

When you're troubleshooting hardware, there are a few common problems that any experienced technician should know about. These common issues usually have simple solutions. Knowing these problems and their solutions will make you a more efficient troubleshooter.

Critical Information

Most computer technicians spend a great deal of time troubleshooting and repairing systems. This objective tests your knowledge of basic troubleshooting procedures. To study for it, you'll need to familiarize yourself with common problems and solutions related to motherboards, hard disks, RAM, cooling, and the other major system components.

Basic Aspects of Troubleshooting

Although everyone approaches troubleshooting from a different perspective, a few things should remain constant. Among them is a basic appreciation for data. Any hardware component can be replaced, but data often can't be. For that reason, it's important to always perform backups before making any changes.

It's important to assess every problem systematically and try to isolate the root cause. You always start out with an issue and whittle away at it until you can get down to the point where you can pinpoint the problem—this often means eliminating, or verifying, the obvious.

You must establish priorities—one user being unable to print to the printer of their choice isn't as important as a floor full of accountants unable to run payroll. Prioritize every job and escalate it (or de-escalate it) as you need to.

Last, but perhaps most important, document everything—not just that there was a problem, but also the solution you found, the actions you tried, and the outcomes of each.

Basic Diagnostic Procedures

Just as all artists have their own style, all technicians have their own way to troubleshoot. Some people use their instincts; others rely on advice from other people. The most common troubleshooting tips can be condensed into a step-by-step process. You try each step, in order. If the first step doesn't narrow down the problem, you move on to the next step.

In this section, we'll look at each step in the troubleshooting process.

Step 1: Define the Problem

If you can't define the problem, you can't begin to solve it. You can define the problem by asking questions of the user. Here are a few questions to ask the user to aid in determining what the problem is, exactly:

Can you show me the problem?   This question is one of the best. It allows the user to show you exactly where and when they experience the problem.

How often does this happen?   This question establishes whether this problem is a one-time occurrence that can be solved with a reboot, or whether a specific sequence of events causes the problem to happen. The latter usually indicates a more serious problem that may require software installation or hardware replacement.

Has any new hardware been installed recently?   New hardware can mean compatibility problems with existing devices. Some Plug and Play devices install with the same resource settings as an existing device. This can cause both devices to become disabled.

Have any other changes been made to the computer recently?   If the answer is "Yes," ask if the user can remember approximately when the change was made. Then ask them approximately when the problem started. If the two dates seem related, then there's a good chance that the problem is related to the change. If it's a new hardware component, check to see that the hardware component was installed correctly.

Step 2: Check the Simple Stuff First

This step is the one that most experienced technicians overlook. Often, computer problems are the result of something simple. Technicians overlook these problems because they're so simple that the technicians assume they *couldn't* be the problem. Some examples of simple problems are shown here:

Is it plugged in?   And plugged in on both ends? Cables must be plugged in on *both ends* in order to function correctly. Cables can easily be tripped over and inadvertently pulled from their sockets.

Is it turned on?   This one seems the most obvious, but we've all fallen victim to it at one point or another. Computers and their peripherals must be turned on in order to function. Most have power switches with LEDs that glow when the power is turned on.

Is the system ready?   Computers must be ready before they can be used. *Ready* means the system is ready to accept commands from the user. An indication that a computer is ready is when the operating system screens come up and the computer presents you with a menu or a command prompt. If that computer uses a graphical interface, the computer is ready when the mouse pointer appears. Printers are ready when the On Line or Ready light on the front panel is lit.

Do the chips and cables need to be reseated?   You can solve some of the strangest problems (random hang-ups or errors) by opening the case and pressing down on each socketed chip. This remedies the chip-creep problem discussed later in this chapter. In addition, you should reseat any cables to make sure that they're making good contact.

Step 3: Check to See If It's User Error

This error is common but preventable. The indication that a problem is due to user error is when a user says they can't perform some very common computer task, such as printing or saving a file. As soon you hear these words, you should begin asking questions to determine if it's simply a matter of teaching the user the correct procedure. A good question to ask following their statement of the problem is, "Were you *ever* able to perform that task?" If they answer "No" to this question, it means they're probably doing the procedure wrong. If they answer "Yes," you must move on to another set of questions.

THE SOCIAL SIDE OF TROUBLESHOOTING

When you're looking for clues as to the nature of a problem, no one can give you more information than the person who was there when it happened. They can tell you what led up to the problem, what software was running, and the exact nature of the problem ("It happened when I tried to print"), and they can help you re-create the problem, if possible.

Use questioning techniques that are neutral in nature. Instead of saying, "What were you doing when it broke?" be more compassionate and say, "What was going on when the computer decided not to work?" It sounds silly, but these types of changes can make your job a lot easier!

Step 4: Restart the Computer

It's amazing how often a simple computer restart can solve a problem. Restarting the computer clears the memory and starts the computer with a clean slate. Whenever we perform phone support, we always ask the customer to restart the computer and try again. If restarting doesn't work, try powering down the system completely and then powering it up again (rebooting). More often than not, that will solve the problem.

Step 5: Determine If the Problem Is Hardware- or Software-Related

This step is important because it determines what part of the computer you should focus your troubleshooting skills on. Each part requires different skills and different tools.

To determine if a problem is hardware- or software-related, you can do a few things to narrow down the issue. For instance, does the problem manifest itself when the user uses a particular piece of hardware (a modem, for example)? If it does, the problem is more than likely hardware-related.

This step relies on personal experience more than any of the other steps do. You'll without a doubt run into strange software problems. Each one has a particular solution. Some may even require reinstallation of the software or the entire operating system.

Step 6: If the Problem Is Hardware-Related, Determine Which Component Is Failing

Hardware problems are pretty easy to figure out. If the modem doesn't work, and you know it isn't a software problem, the modem is probably the piece of hardware that needs to be replaced.

With some of the newer computers, several components are integrated into the motherboard. If you troubleshoot the computer and find a hardware component to be bad, there's a good chance that the bad component is integrated into the motherboard (for example, the parallel port circuitry) and the whole motherboard must be replaced—an expensive proposition, to be sure.

Step 7: Check Service Information Sources

As you may (or may not) have figured out by now, we're fond of old sayings. Another old saying applies here: "If all else fails, read the instructions." The service manuals are your instructions for troubleshooting and service information. Almost every computer and peripheral made today has service documentation in the form of books, service CD-ROMs, and websites. The latter of the three is growing in popularity as more and more service centers get connections to the Internet.

Step 8: If It Ain't Broke...

When doctors take the Hippocratic oath, they promise to not make their patients any sicker than they already were. Technicians should take a similar oath. It all boils down to, "If it ain't broke, don't fix it." When you troubleshoot, make one change at a time. If the change doesn't solve the problem, revert the computer to its previous state before making a different change.

Step 9: Ask for Help

If you don't know the answer, ask one of your fellow technicians. They may have run across the problem you're having and know the solution.

This solution does involve a little humility. You must admit that you don't know the answer. It's said that the beginning of wisdom is "I don't know." If you ask questions, you'll get answers, and you'll learn from the answers. Making mistakes is valuable as well, as long as you learn from them.

Throughout my career in the computer business, the reluctance to share information has been the thing that most concerns me about this industry. As computer professionals, we are valued due to the extent of our knowledge. Some of us intend to keep our value high by limiting the flow of knowledge to others. My position is different than that of those tight-lipped people. I like to help and to teach. This factor has been my best asset as I climbed from the help desk to become an IS manager. The most amusing thing is that despite my impressive title, many certifications, and two published technical books, I still ask for advice and help on a daily basis. If I don't know the answer, I ask, and it doesn't bother me a bit. If I know, and I'm asked, I share and try to bring the other person to the understanding that I have of that particular subject. One of the greatest assets you can have is another opinion or another person to bounce ideas off.

Recognizing and Isolating Issues

Your value as a technician increases as you gain experience, because of the reduced time it takes you to accomplish common repairs. Your ability to troubleshoot by past experiences and gut feelings will make you more efficient and more valuable, which in turn will allow you to advance and earn a better income. This section will give you some guidelines you can use to evaluate common hardware issues that you're sure to face.

POST Routines

Every computer has a diagnostic program built into its BIOS called the *power on self-test* (*POST*). When you turn on the computer, it executes this set of diagnostics. Many steps are involved the POST, but they happen very quickly, they're invisible to the user, and they vary among BIOS versions. The steps include checking the CPU, checking the RAM, checking for the presence of a video card, and so on. The main reason to be aware of the POST's existence is that if it encounters a problem, the boot process stops. Being able to determine at what point the problem occurred can help you troubleshoot.

One way to determine the source of a problem is to listen for a *beep code*. This is a series of beeps from the computer's speaker. The number, duration, and pattern of the beeps can sometimes tell you what component is causing the problem. However, the beeps differ depending on the BIOS manufacturer and version, so you must look up the beep code in a chart for your particular BIOS. Different BIOS manufacturers use the beeping differently. AMI BIOS, for example, relies on a raw number of beeps, and uses patterns of short and long beeps.

Another way to determine a problem during the POST routine is to use a *POST card*. This is a circuit board that fits into an ISA or PCI expansion slot in the motherboard and reports numeric codes as the boot process progresses. Each of those codes corresponds to a particular component being checked. If the POST card stops at a certain number, you can look up that number in the manual that came with the card to determine the problem.

 BIOS Central is a website containing charts detailing the beep codes and POST error codes for many different BIOS manufacturers: www.bioscentral.com/.

Applying Basic Troubleshooting Techniques

The following sections offer discussions of the basic items to check for common problems.

Motherboard and CPU Problems

Most motherboard and CPU problems manifest themselves by the system appearing completely dead. However, "completely dead" can be a symptom of a wide variety of problems, not only with the CPU or motherboard but also with the RAM or the power supply. So, a POST card (described in the preceding section) may be helpful in narrowing down the exact component that is faulty.

When a motherboard fails, it's usually because it has been damaged. Most technicians can't repair motherboard damage; the motherboard must be replaced. Motherboards can become damaged due to physical trauma, exposure to electrostatic discharge (ESD), or short-circuiting. To minimize the risk of these damages, observe the following rules:

- Handle a motherboard as little as possible, and keep it in an antistatic bag whenever it's removed from the PC case.

- Keep all liquids well away from the motherboard, because water can cause a short circuit.

- Wear an antistatic wrist strap when handling or touching a motherboard.

- When installing a motherboard in a case, make sure you use brass stand-offs with paper washers to prevent any stray solder around the screw holes from causing a short circuit with the metal of the screw.

A CPU may fail because of physical trauma or short-circuiting, but the most common cause for a CPU not to work is failure to install it properly. With a PGA-style CPU, ensure that the CPU is oriented correctly in the socket. With an SECC-style CPU, make sure the CPU is completely inserted into its slot.

I/O Ports and Cables

I/O ports include legacy parallel and serial, USB, and FireWire ports, all of which are used to connect external peripherals to the motherboard. When a port doesn't appear to be functioning, check the following:

- Cables are snugly connected.

- The port has not been disabled in BIOS Setup.

- The port has not been disabled in Device Manager in Windows.

- No pins are broken or bent on the male end of the port or of the cable being plugged into it.

If you suspect that the cable, rather than the port, may be the problem, swap out the cable with a known-good one. If you don't have an extra cable, you can test the existing cable with a multimeter by setting it to ohms and checking the resistance between one end of the cable and the other.

Use a pin-out diagram, if available, to determine which pin matches up to which at the other end. There is often—but not always—an inverse relationship between the ends. In other words, at one end pin 1 is at the left, and at the other end it's at the right on the same row of pins.

Cooling Issues

A PC that works for a few minutes and then locks up is probably experiencing overheating due to a heat sink or fan not functioning properly. To troubleshoot overheating, first check all fans inside the PC to ensure they're operating, and make sure any heat sinks are firmly attached to their chips.

In a properly designed, properly assembled PC case, air flows in a specific path from the power-supply fan through the vent holes. Cases are designed to cool by making the air flow in a certain way. Therefore, operating a PC with the cover removed can make a PC more susceptible to overheating, even though it's "getting more air."

Similarly, operating a PC with empty expansion-slot backplates removed can inhibit a PC's ability to cool itself properly because the extra holes change the airflow pattern from what was intended by its design.

Although CPUs are the most common component to overheat, occasionally chips on other devices, particularly video cards, may also overheat. Extra heat sinks or fans may be installed to cool these chips.

Case Issues

A PC case holds the drives in its bays, holds the power supply, and has lights and buttons on the front. For the first two of those functions, make sure that the drives and the power supply are tightly fastened in the case with screws.

If one of the lights or buttons on the front of the PC isn't functioning, remove the cover and check the wires that run from the back of that button/light to the motherboard. If the wire has become detached, reattach it. Refer to the motherboard manual or the writing on the motherboard itself to determine what goes where.

Hard-Disk System Problems

Hard-disk system problems usually stem from one of three causes:

- The adapter (that is, the IDE or SCSI interface) is bad.
- The disk is bad.
- The adapter and disk are connected incorrectly.

The first and last causes are easy to identify, because in either case the symptom will be obvious: The drive won't work. You won't be able to get the computer to communicate with the disk drive.

However, if the problem is a bad disk drive, the symptoms aren't as obvious. As long as the BIOS POST routines can communicate with the disk drive, they're usually satisfied. But the POST routines may not uncover problems related to storing information. Even with healthy POST results, you may find that you're permitted to save information to a bad disk, but when you try to read it back, you get errors. Or the computer may not boot as quickly as it used to, because the disk drive can't read the boot information successfully every time.

In some cases, reformatting the drive can solve the problems described in the preceding paragraph. In other cases, reformatting brings the drive back to life only for a short while. The bottom line is that read and write problems usually indicate that the drive is malfunctioning and should be replaced soon.

WARNING   Never low-level-format IDE or SCSI drives! They're low-level-formatted from the factory, and you may cause problems by using low-level utilities on these types of drives.

Modem Problems

The most common peripheral problems are those related to modem communications. The symptoms of these problems include the following:

- The modem won't dial.
- The modem keeps hanging up in the middle of the communications session.
- The modem spits out strange characters to the terminal screen.

If the modem won't dial, first check that it has been configured correctly in Windows, including its resource assignments.

Some modems work only under Windows because some of their functions rely on Windows software; these are called *Winmodems* or *software modems*. If such a modem doesn't work immediately upon installation, try running the Setup software that came with the modem.

If the configuration is correct, and Windows recognizes the modem, it should work for dial-up networking connections.

AT COMMANDS

When you're using a terminal application such as HyperTerminal, it's important to use the correct initialization commands. These are the commands sent to the modem by the communications program to initialize it. These commands tell the modem such things as how many rings to wait before answering, how long to wait after the last keystroke was detected for it to disconnect, and at what speed to communicate.

Modem initialization commands are known as the *Hayes command set* or the *AT command set*, because each Hayes modem command starts with the letters AT (presumably calling the modem to ATtention).

Each AT command does something different. The letters AT by themselves ask the modem if it's ready to receive commands. If it returns *OK*, the modem is ready to communicate. If you receive *Error*, there is an internal modem problem that may need to be resolved before communication can take place.

Table 1.10 lists a few of the most common AT commands, their functions, and the problems they can solve. You can send these commands to the modem by opening a terminal program like Windows Terminal or HyperTerminal and typing them in. All commands should return *OK* if they're successful.

TABLE 1.10   Common AT Commands

Command	Function	Usage
AT	Tells the modem that what follows the letters AT is a command that should be interpreted	Used to precede most commands.
ATDT *nnnnnnn*	Dials the number *nnnnnnn* as a tone-dialed number	Used to dial the number of another modem if the phone line is set up for tone dialing.
ATDP *nnnnnnn*	Dials the number *nnnnnnn* as a pulse-dialed number	Used to dial the number of another modem if the phone line is set up for rotary dialing.
ATA	Answers an incoming call manually	Places the line off-hook and starts to negotiate communication with the modem on the other end.

TABLE 1.10   Common AT Commands *(continued)*

Command	Function	Usage
ATH0 (or +++ and then ATH0)	Tells the modem to hang up immediately	Places the line on-hook and stops communication. (Note: The 0 in this command is a zero, not the letter *O*.)
AT&F	Resets the modem to factory default settings	This setting works as the initialization string when others don't. If you have problems with modems hanging up in the middle of a session or failing to establish connections, use this string by itself to initialize the modem.
ATZ	Resets the modem to power-up defaults	Almost as good as AT&F, but may not work if power-up defaults have been changed with S-registers.
ATS0-n	Waits n rings before answering a call	Sets the default number of rings that the modem will detect before taking the modem off-hook and negotiating a connection. (Note: The 0 in this command is a zero, not the letter *O*.)
ATS6-n	Waits n seconds for a dial tone before dialing	If the phone line is slow to give a dial tone, you may have to set this register to a number higher than 2.
,	Pauses briefly	When placed in a string of AT commands, the comma causes a pause to occur. Used to separate the number for an outside line (many businesses use 9 to connect to an outside line) and the real phone number (for example, 9,555-1234).
*70 or 1170	Turns off call waiting	The click you hear when you have call waiting (a feature offered by the phone company) will interrupt modem communication and cause the connection to be lost. To disable call waiting for a modem call, place these commands in the dialing string like so: *70,555-1234. Call waiting will resume after the call is hung up.

TABLE 1.10   Common AT Commands *(continued)*

Command	Function	Usage
CONNECT	Displays when a successful connection has been made	You may have to wait some time before this message is displayed. If this message isn't displayed, the modem couldn't negotiate a connection with the modem on the other end of the line, possibly due to line noise.
BUSY	Displays when the number dialed is busy	If this message is displayed, some programs wait a certain amount of time and try again to dial.
RING	Displays when the modem has detected a ringing line	When someone is calling your modem, the modem displays this message in the communications program. You type **ATA** to answer the call.

If two computers can connect, but they both receive garbage on their screens, there's a good chance that the computers don't agree on the communications settings. Settings such as data bits, parity, stop bits, and compression must all agree in order for communication to take place.

Keyboard and Mouse Problems

Usually, keyboard problems are environmental. Keyboards get dirty, and the keys start to stick.

If a keyboard is malfunctioning (for example, sending the wrong characters to the display), it's most cost effective to replace it rather than spend hours attempting to fix it, because keyboards are fairly inexpensive.

One way to clean a keyboard is with the keyboard cleaner sold by electronics supply stores. This cleaner foams up quickly and doesn't leave a residue behind. Spray it liberally on the keyboard and keys. Work the cleaner in between the keys with a stiff toothbrush. Blow away the excess with a strong blast of compressed air. Repeat until the keyboard functions properly. If you have to clean a keyboard that's had a soft drink spilled on it, remove the key caps before you perform the cleaning procedure; doing so makes it easier to reach the sticky plungers.

Remember that most of the dollars spent on systems are for labor. If you spend an hour cleaning a $12.00 keyboard, then you have probably just cost your company $20.00. Knowing how to fix certain things doesn't necessarily mean that you *should* fix them. Always evaluate your workload, the cost of replacement, and the estimated cost of the repair before deciding on a course of action.

Similarly, most mouse problems, such as the pointer failing to move in one direction or the other, or the pointer jumping around onscreen, are due to dirt building up inside the mouse. To clean a standard mouse, remove the plate on the bottom of the mouse that holds the ball in place; then, remove the ball, and clean the inside chamber with an alcohol-dipped cotton swab. Clean the ball itself with mild soap and water. Don't use alcohol on the ball, because it tends to dry out the rubber.

Display-System Problems

Display problems were discussed earlier in this chapter. As a general rule, there are two types of video problems: no video and bad video, both of which were previously discussed.

Floppy and Other Removable Disk-Drive Problems

Most floppy-drive problems result from bad media. Your first troubleshooting technique with floppy-drive issues should be to try a new disk.

One of the most common problems that develops with floppy drives is misaligned read/write heads. The symptoms are fairly easy to recognize—you can read and write to a floppy on one machine but not on any others. This is normally caused by the mechanical arm in the floppy drive becoming misaligned. When the disk was formatted, it wasn't properly positioned on the drive, thus preventing other floppy drives from reading it.

Numerous commercial tools are available to realign floppy drive read/write heads. They use a floppy drive that has been preformatted to reposition the mechanical arm. In most cases, though, this fix is temporary—the arm will move out of place again fairly soon. Given the inexpensive nature of the problem, the best solution is to spend a few dollars and replace the drive.

Another problem you may encounter is a phantom directory listing. For example, suppose you display the contents of a floppy disk, and then you swap to another floppy disk but the listing stays the same. This is almost always a result of a faulty ribbon cable; a particular wire in the ribbon cable signals when a disk swap has taken place, and when that wire breaks, this error occurs.

Sound-Card Problems

Sound cards are traditionally one of the most problem-ridden components in a PC. They demand a lot of PC resources and are notorious for being inflexible in their configuration. The most common problems related to sound cards involve resource conflicts (IRQ, DMA, or I/O address). The problem is much less pronounced on PCI than on ISA cards.

Luckily, most sound-card vendors are aware of the problems and ship very good diagnostic utilities to help resolve them. Use your PC troubleshooting skills to determine the conflict, and then reconfigure until you find an acceptable set of resources that aren't in use.

Some sound cards aren't completely Plug and Play–compatible. Windows may detect that new hardware has been installed but be unable to identify the new hardware as a working sound card. To fix this problem, run the Setup software that came with the sound card.

CD-ROM/DVD Issues

CD-ROM and DVD problems are normally media-related. Although compact disc technology is much more reliable than floppy disks, it's not perfect. Another factor to consider is the cleanliness of the disc. On many occasions, if a disc is unreadable, cleaning it with an approved cleaner and a lint-free cleaning towel will fix the problem.

If the operating system doesn't see the drive, start troubleshooting by determining whether the drive is receiving power. If the tray will eject, you can assume there is power to it. Next, check BIOS Setup (for IDE drives) to make sure the drive has been detected. If not, check the master/slave jumper on the drive, and make sure the IDE adapter is set to Auto, CD-ROM, or ATAPI in BIOS Setup.

In order to play movies, a DVD drive must have MPEG-decoding capability. This is usually accomplished via an expansion board, but it may be built into the video card or sound card, or it may be a software decoder. If DVD data discs will play but movies won't, suspect a problem with the MPEG decoding.

If a CD-RW or DVD drive works normally as a regular CD-ROM drive but doesn't perform its special capability (doesn't read DVD discs, or doesn't write to blank CDs), perhaps software needs to be installed to work with it. For example, with CD-RW drives, unless you're using an operating system such as Windows XP that supports CD writing, you must install CD-writing software in order to write to CDs.

Network Interface Card Problems

In general, network interface cards (NICs) are added to a PC via an expansion slot. The most common issue that prevents network connectivity is a bad or unplugged patch cable.

Cleaning crews and the rollers on the bottoms of chairs are the most common threats to a patch cable. In most cases, wall jacks are placed 4 to 10 feet away from the desktop. The patch cables are normally lying exposed under the user's desk, and from time to time damage is done to the cable, or it's inadvertently snagged and unplugged. When you troubleshoot a network adapter, start with the most rudimentary explanations first. Make sure the patch cable is tightly plugged in, and then look at the card and see if any lights are on. If there are lights on, use the NIC's documentation to help troubleshoot. More often than not, shutting down the machine, unplugging the patch and power cables for a moment, and then reattaching them and rebooting the PC will fix an unresponsive NIC.

Although this isn't on the test, it's useful information: Wake On LAN cards have more problems than standard network cards. In our opinion, this is because they're always on. In some cases, you'll be unable to get the card working again unless you unplug the PC's power supply and reset the card.

BIOS Issues

Computer BIOSes don't go bad; they just become out-of-date. This isn't necessarily a critical issue—they will continue to support the hardware that came with the box. It *does*, however, become an issue when the BIOS doesn't support some component that you would like to install—a larger hard drive, for instance.

Most of today's BIOSes are written to an EEPROM and can be updated through the use of software. Each manufacturer has its own method for accomplishing this. Check out the documentation for complete details.

WARNING   If you make a mistake in the upgrade process, the computer can become unbootable. If this happens, your only option may be to ship the box to a manufacturer-approved service center. Be careful!

Power-Supply Problems

Power-supply problems are usually easy to troubleshoot. The system doesn't respond in any way when the power is turned on. When this happens, open the case, remove the power supply, and replace it with a new one.

Be aware that different cases have different types of on/off switches. The process of replacing a power supply is a lot easier if you purchase a replacement with the same mechanism. Even so, remember to document exactly how the power supply was connected to the on/off switch before you remove it.

Miscellaneous Problems

Some common problems don't fit well into categories. This section lists some common hardware issues you'll be faced with.

DISLODGED CHIPS AND CARDS

The inside of a computer is a harsh environment. The temperature inside the case of some Pentium computers is well over 100° F! When you turn on your computer, it heats up. Turn it off, and it cools down. After several hundred such cycles, some components can't handle the stress and begin to move out of their sockets. This phenomenon is known as *chip creep*, and it can be really frustrating.

Chip creep can affect any socketed device, including ICs, RAM chips, and expansion cards. The solution to chip creep is simple: open the case, and reseat the devices. It's surprising how often this is the solution to phantom problems of all sorts.

Another important item worth mentioning is an unresponsive but freshly unboxed PC. With the introduction of the Type II and Type II-style of processors, the number of dead boxes increased dramatically. In fact, at that time I was leading a 2,000-unit migration for a large financial institution. As with any large migration, time and manpower were in short supply. The average dead PC ratio was about 1 out of every 20. When about 10 DOAs had stacked up, I stayed after work one night to assess the problem. After checking the power supply, RAM, and cables on these integrated systems, an examination of the chip provided me with the fix. These large, top-heavy processors can become dislodged during shipment. Shortly thereafter, manufacturers began using a heavier attachment point for the slot style of processor, which has helped tremendously.

ENVIRONMENTAL PROBLEMS

Computers are like human beings. They have similar tolerances to heat and cold. In general, anything comfortable to us is comfortable to computers. They need lots of clean, moving air to keep them functioning.

Dirt, grime, paint, smoke, and other airborne particles can become caked on the inside of the components. This is most common in automotive and manufacturing environments. The contaminants create a film that coats the components, causing them to overheat and/or conduct electricity on their surface. Blowing out these exposed systems with a can of condensed air from time to time can prevent damage to the components. While you're cleaning the components, be sure to clean any cooling fans in the power supply or on the heat sink.

 To clean the power-supply fan, blow the air from the inside of the case. When you do this, the fan will blow the contaminants out the cooling vents. If you spray from the vents toward the inside of the box, you'll be blowing the dust and grime inside the case or back into the fan motor.

One way to ensure that the environment has the least possible effect on your computer is to always leave the *blanks* in the empty slots on the back of your box. These pieces of metal are designed to keep dirt, dust, and other foreign matter from the inside of the computer. They also maintain proper airflow within the case to ensure that the computer doesn't overheat.

Applying the Appropriate Tools

Just as a mechanic must have the appropriate tools in their toolbox to be able to fix an automobile, you must have the right tools in your arsenal to be able to fix computer problems. Fortunately, many of the tools are included with the computer; you just need to know which ones to turn to. If there is a problem with the boot process, check the BIOS. If there is a problem with the hard drive, run diagnostic utilities on it.

The most important tool you have in your toolbox is common sense. Not only should you use it to determine which tool to use while working on a personal computer, but you should also use it to pick the correct answers on the A+ exam.

Exam Essentials

Be familiar with the purpose of POST routines.   The POST routines perform entry-level hardware troubleshooting as a PC starts. Be familiar with the abilities of the POST and its use.

Be able to diagnose port problems.   When a port isn't functioning, make sure you know the steps to take to ensure that it's physically connected, enabled in BIOS, and recognized in Windows.

Know how to troubleshoot hard-disk system problems.   Be aware of the common causes of hard-disk problems, including improper jumper configuration, BIOS Setup, and formatting/partitioning issues.

Identify problems that can result from overheating.   Overheating can cause spontaneous rebooting or shutdown. It's often caused by nonfunctioning cooling fans or improper airflow through the PC.

Be able to determine the cause of display-system problems.   The most common display problems relate to power, brightness, or contrast. Adjusting the monitor controls should be your first step when troubleshooting.

Recognize the symptoms of floppy-drive problems.   Most floppy-drive problems result from bad media. Your first troubleshooting technique with floppy-drive issues should be to try a new disk.

Know how to troubleshoot sound-card problems.   Sound cards demand a lot of PC resources and are notorious for being inflexible in their configuration. The most common problems related to sound cards involve resource conflicts (IRQ, DMA, or I/O address).

Learn to identify BIOS issues.   BIOS issues are related to the inability to support hardware. In most cases, a program or flash upgrade is available to update the BIOS so that components can be supported.

Recognize power-supply problems.   Become familiar with the symptoms of a dead, failing, or overloaded power supply.

Know the symptoms of dislodged chips and cards.   Dislodged components are the most common issues you'll face. Become familiar with the symptoms and their fixes.

Know the basic steps of troubleshooting.   Troubleshooting is a process of trial and error. For the exam and your career, use this system to diagnose and repair hardware-related issues.

Check your information sources.   Service manuals are your instructions for troubleshooting and service information. Almost every computer and peripheral made today has service documentation in the form of books, service CD-ROMs, and websites.

Ask for help.   If you don't know the answer, ask one of your fellow technicians. They may have run across the problem you're having and know the solution. This is one thing we feel very strongly about. Don't be embarrassed to ask, and don't be too tight-lipped to help others.

Perform Preventative Maintenance on Personal Computers

This section outlines some preventive maintenance products and procedures. Preventive maintenance is one of the most overlooked ways to reduce the cost of ownership in any environment.

Critical Information

Cleaning a computer system is the most important part of maintaining it. Computer components get dirty. Dirt reduces their operating efficiency and, ultimately, their life. Cleaning them is definitely important. But cleaning them with the right cleaning compounds is equally important. Using the wrong compounds can leave residue behind that is more harmful than the dirt you're trying to remove!

Most computer cases and monitor cases can be cleaned using mild soap and water on a clean, lint-free cloth. Make sure the power is off before you put anything wet near a computer. Dampen (don't soak) a cloth with a mild soap solution, and wipe the dirt and dust from the case. Then, wipe the moisture from the case with a dry, lint-free cloth. Anything with a plastic or metal case can be cleaned in this manner.

 WARNING   Don't drip liquid into any vent holes on equipment. CRTs in particular have vent holes in the top.

To clean a monitor screen, use glass cleaner designed specifically for monitors, and a soft cloth. Don't use commercial window cleaner, because the chemicals in it can ruin the antiglare coating on some monitors.

To clean a keyboard, use canned air to blow debris out from under keys, and use towelettes designed for use with computers to keep the key tops clean. If you spill anything on a keyboard, you can clean it by soaking it in distilled, *demineralized water*. The minerals and impurities have been removed from this type of water, so it won't leave any traces of residue that might interfere with the proper operation of the keyboard after cleaning. Make sure you let the keyboard dry for at least 48 hours before using it.

The electronic connectors of computer equipment, on the other hand, should never touch water. Instead, use a swab moistened in distilled, *denatured isopropyl alcohol* (also known as electronics cleaner and found in electronics stores) to clean contacts. Doing so will take the oxidation off the copper contacts.

A good way to remove dust and dirt from the inside of the computer is to use compressed air. Blow the dust from inside the computer using a stream of compressed air. However, be sure you do this outdoors, so you don't blow dust all over your work area or yourself. You can also use a vacuum, but it must be designed specifically for electronics—such models don't generate ESD, and have a finer filter than normal.

To prevent a computer from becoming dirty in the first place, control its environment. Make sure there is adequate ventilation in the work area and that the dust level isn't excessive. To avoid ESD, you should maintain 50 to 80 percent humidity in the room where the computer is operating.

One unique challenge when cleaning printers is spilled toner. It sticks to everything and should not be breathed. Use a vacuum designed specifically for electronics. A normal vacuum's filter isn't fine enough to catch all the particles, so the toner may be circulated into the air.

 TIP   If you get toner on your clothes, use a magnet to get it out (toner is half iron).

Removable media devices such as floppy and CD drives don't usually need to be cleaned during preventive maintenance. Clean one only if you're experiencing problems with it. Cleaning kits sold in computer stores provide the needed supplies. Usually, cleaning a floppy drive involves a dummy floppy disk made of semi-abrasive material. When you insert the disk in the drive, the drive spins it, and the abrasive action on the read-write head removes any debris.

An uninterruptible power supply (UPS) should be checked periodically as part of the preventive maintenance routine to make sure that its battery is operational. Most UPSs have a Test button you can press to simulate a power outage.

Remember, preventive maintenance is more than just manipulating hardware; it also encompasses running software utilities on a regular basis to keep the filesystem fit. These utilities can include Disk Defragmenter, ScanDisk, Check Disk, and Disk Cleanup.

Exam Essentials

Know what can be used to clean computer components.   Many types of cleaning solutions can be used to perform these procedures. Be familiar with which option is best for each component. Which ones can be cleaned with water? Which ones require alcohol? Which ones need canned air?

Know why the proper cleaning solutions should be used.   Using the wrong cleaning solution can damage components. Along with choosing the right cleaning solution, understand why the unchosen solutions are inappropriate for a particular component.

Review Questions

1. What two types of expansion slots are found on all modern motherboards? What is a third, older type that might or might not also be present?

2. Name three features that distinguish an ATX motherboard from an AT motherboard.

3. What are PGA and SECC? Which of those types is the Socket 423 used with the Pentium 4?

4. What voltages does a typical power supply provide to the motherboard?

5. On modern systems, what is the relationship between a CPU's internal and external speeds?

6. Which cache is also known as the back-side cache?

7. What is the purpose of a VRM on a motherboard?

8. What is the purpose of a parity bit on a SIMM?

9. Would the POST test identify a problem with RAM?

10. If a legacy serial port is physically fine but does not show up in Windows' Device Manager, how might you enable it?

Answers to Review Questions

1. PCI and AGP. The third type is ISA.

2. Possible answers include: (1) position of CPU, (2) expansion slot orientation, (3) built-in ports on the side, (4) one-piece power supply connector, (5) physical size and shape of the motherboard, and (6) type of keyboard connector.

3. They are the two types of slots/sockets for CPUs in motherboards. PGA is the type with a grid of holes into which pins fit on a flat chip. SECC is the type that accepts a circuit board surrounded by a cartridge. Whenever you see *socket* in the name, it's always a PGA type. SECC types have *slot* in the name.

4. +5V, -5V, +12V, and -12V for all power supplies, plus +3.3V for an ATX power supply.

5. The internal speed is a multiple of the external speed.

6. The L2 cache

7. To provide different voltages for different CPUs

8. Error correction

9. Yes. One of the components the POST checks is the RAM.

10. It may be disabled in BIOS Setup; try enabling it there.

Chapter
2

Laptops and Portable Devices

COMPTIA A+ ESSENTIALS EXAM OBJECTIVES COVERED IN THIS CHAPTER:

✓ **2.1 Identify the fundamental principles of using laptops and portable devices**

- Identify names, purposes, and characteristics of laptop-specific:
  - Form factors, such as memory and hard drives
  - Peripherals (e.g., docking station, port replicator, and media / accessory bay)
  - Expansion slots (e.g., PCMCIA I, II and III, card, and express bus)
  - Ports (e.g., mini PCI slot)
  - Communication connections (e.g., Bluetooth, infrared, cellular WAN, Ethernet)
  - Power and electrical input devices (e.g., auto-switching and fixed-input power supplies, batteries)
  - LCD technologies (e.g., active and passive matrix, resolution, such as XGA, SXGA+, UXGA, WUXGA, contrast radio, native resolution)
  - Input devices (e.g., stylus / digitizer, function (Fn) keys and pointing devices, such as touch pad, point stick / track point)
- Identify and distinguish between mobile and desktop motherboards and processors, including throttling, power management, and WiFi

✓ **2.2 Install, configure, optimize, and upgrade laptops and portable devices**

- Configure power management
- Identify the features of BIOS-ACPI

- Identify the difference between suspend, hibernate, and standby
- Demonstrate safe removal of laptop-specific hardware, such as peripherals, hot-swappable devices, and non-hot-swappable devices

✓ **2.3 Identify tools, basic diagnostic procedures, and troubleshooting techniques for laptops and portable devices**

- Use procedures and techniques to diagnose power conditions, video, keyboard, pointer, and wireless card issues, for example:
    - Verify AC power (e.g., LEDs, swap AC adapter)
    - Verify DC power
    - Remove unneeded peripherals
    - Plug in external monitor
    - Toggle Fn keys
    - Check LCD cutoff switch
    - Verify backlight functionality and pixilation
    - Stylus issues (e.g., digitizer problems)
    - Unique laptop keypad issues
    - Antenna wires

✓ **2.4 Perform preventative maintenance on laptops and portable devices**

- Identify and apply common preventative maintenance techniques for laptops and portable devices, for example: cooling devices, hardware and video cleaning materials, operating environments, including temperature and air quality, storage, transportation, and shipping

This domain is weighted at 11 percent of the Essentials exam. It also appears on two of the three Technician exams. Fewer technicians work on portable systems than desktop systems, because most portable systems use proprietary parts that can be difficult to obtain unless you're working for an authorized service center. In addition, each portable computer must be opened a slightly different way for service, and some require special tools for entry.

Nevertheless, a professional technician will likely be called upon occasionally to perform basic repairs or maintenance on a notebook computer. The most common tasks are upgrading the RAM and replacing the hard disk, and both of those activities can be performed using widely available parts.

Principles of Laptops and Portable Devices

Whether you choose to call them laptops, portable devices, or something different is mostly a matter of semantics. This objective tests your knowledge of some of the basic operations of laptops. In many cases, the components are the same as in a desktop computer, and they were discussed in Chapter 1. Those that are different are focused on here.

Critical Information

A portable computer must provide all the functionality of a desktop counterpart yet be able to withstand travel, run in the absence of AC power, and be much smaller and more compact. When you get right down to it, there is not a great deal of difference between laptop and desktop computers, with the exception that laptops are more difficult to disassemble and form factors on items such as motherboards, memory, and hard drives become important. While they perform the same functions, size is critical.

Laptop-specific elements are discussed in the following sections.

LCD Displays

When converting a desktop machine to a portable, one of the biggest problems the engineers faced was how to supply enough current to power the monitor. The solution they arrived at was the liquid crystal display (LCD). Instead of using the traditional vacuum tube to create the display, liquid crystals are employed. This lowers power consumption and has the added benefit of reducing the size of the monitor to a flat panel (made from two polarized glass panes with liquid between them).

The panels are made of columns and rows called a *matrix*. Depending on the capability of the display, most panels fall into the categories of *active* matrix or *passive* matrix. With a passive matrix, the display is essentially created at one time, and changes are made to an entire column; with an active matrix, a single liquid crystal (pixel) can be changed.

Passive matrix displays include the following:

- Color super-twist nematic (CSTN)
- Dual scan
- Ferroelectric
- High-Performance Addressing (HPA)

Because of the way the screen is refreshed, you typically can't run LCD projectors, LCD panels, or other similar devices from passive-matrix laptops. Active-matrix displays include the following:

- Metal-insulator-metal (MIM)
- Plasma-addressed liquid crystal (PALC)
- Thin-film transistors (TFT)

Display resolutions include the following, which you must know for the A+ Essentials exam:

XGA   Extended graphics array has been around since 1990. It's a 1024×768 resolution that offers fixed-function hardware acceleration for 2D tasks.

SXGA+   Super extended graphics array is a 1400×1050 resolution commonly used on 14-inch or 15-inch laptops. It's typically considered the maximum resolution that video projectors will work with.

UXGA   Ultra extended graphics array is a 1600×1200 resolution and is the next step in the monitor-resolution evolution.

WUXGA   Widescreen ultra extended graphics array is a resolution of 1920×1200 with a 16:10 screen aspect ratio. It's also a standard for use with television sets, at a slightly different ratio.

Peripherals

A docking station essentially allows a laptop computer to be converted to a desktop computer. When plugged into a docking station, the laptop has access to things it doesn't have as a stand-alone—the network, a workgroup printer, and so on. The cheapest form of docking station (if it can be called that) is a *port replicator*. Typically, you slide a laptop into the port replicator, and the laptop can then use a full-sized monitor, keyboard (versus the standard 84 keys on a laptop), mouse, and so on. Extended, or enhanced, replicators add other ports not found on the laptop, such as PC slots, sound, and more. The most common division between port replicators and docking stations is whether the peripheral provides network access.

Laptops can support plug and play at three different levels, depending on how dynamically they're able to adapt to changes:

Cold docking   The laptop must be turned off and back on for the change to be recognized.

Warm docking   The laptop must be put in and out of suspended mode for the change to be recognized.

Hot docking   The change can be made and is recognized while running normal operations.

Auto-Switching and Fixed Input

Auto-switching power supplies allow you to use the same supply for more than one voltage. Most auto-switching power supplies can operate on voltages from 100 to 240, allowing them to be used in countries almost anywhere in the world. Fixed-input power supplies, on the other hand, regulate the voltage coming in to make certain is stays consistent.

Notebook Batteries

When you're shopping for notebook batteries, be aware not only of the physical size and shape (which vary depending on the notebook manufacturer's specifications) but also of the battery technology:

Nickel-cadmium (NiCad)   The least preferable. Must be recharged every 3 to 4 hours. A full recharge can take as long as 12 hours. These batteries tend to lose their ability to hold a charge unless they're fully discharged each time before being recharged. Leaving the notebook PC plugged in all the time and using the battery only occasionally for short periods can eventually ruin the battery.

     NiCad batteries are not likely to be on any new device these days.

Nickel-metal hydride (NiMH)   Better than NiCad because they don't use heavy metals with great toxicity. They can also store up to 50 percent more power and don't suffer loss of functionality from partial draining and recharging.

Lithium ion (LIon)   Lightweight and have a long life, plus they aren't subject to problems with partial draining and recharging. They tend to be more expensive than NiCad or NiMH, however.

Fuel cell   Casio has announced plans to produce a hydrogen fuel cell battery for notebook computers that promises to last 20 hours or more on a single charge. By the time you read this, it may be available, offering greatly increased performance at a much higher price than normal notebook batteries.

When dealing with batteries, you must be careful not to dispose of them in the normal way, for they may harm the environment. Here are some rules from the back of a typical battery:

- Don't put in fire or mutilate; may burst or release toxic materials
- Don't crush, puncture, incinerate, or short external circuits
- Don't short-circuit; may cause burns

PCMCIA Cards

PCMCIA cards (named after the Personal Computer Memory Card International Association) are the expansion cards for notebook PCs. Most notebook PCs have a PCMCIA bay that can accept one Type III device or two Type I or Type II devices:

Type I   Up to 3.3mm thick. Used mostly for memory. These are very rarely used in today's systems, since the new laptops have other means of increasing memory, such as SoDIMMs.

Type II   The most common type. Up to 5.5mm thick. Used for devices that would typically be expansion boards in a desktop PC, such as network interface cards.

Type III   Up to 10.5mm thick. Used for drives. Not common.

In addition to these types based on thickness, there are other types based on technology. The PCMCIA (PC Card) standard has recently been updated to a new standard called Card-Bus; look for CardBus in the specification when you're buying PC Card devices. CardBus devices are backward-compatible with older PCMCIA slots. Even newer is the Peripheral Component Interconnect (PCI) Express bus—a serial bus addition that uses low-voltage differential signaling (LVDS), allowing you to attach several devices at the same time (using serial communication instead of the parallel communication standard with most PC buses).

Ports and Communication Connections

Many laptops now include a Mini PCI slot for use with wireless adapters. Mini PCI slots are also common on docking stations. Mini PCI is a 32-bit bus that operates at 32MHz. It operates at only 3.3 volts and has three card configurations: Type I, Type II, and Type III. Whereas Types I and III provide support for an RJ-45 connector, Type II cards have an RJ-45 connector mounted on them.

Other connections/connectors common on laptops include Bluetooth, infrared, cellular WAN, WiFi, and Ethernet. All of these are discussed elsewhere in this book as they apply to networking (see Chapter 5 for further discussion of these topics).

Pointing and Input Devices

Pointing devices with laptops include such options as touchpads, point sticks, and track points. Some laptops come with only one of these, whereas others include a combination; and users can always opt for something else (such as a wireless mouse). Which you use is more a matter of preference and comfort than anything else.

Input devices can include a stylus, or *digitizer*. With this tool, a "pen" allows you to write directly on the screen, and the text written is digitized into data. When data is entered in this way, the laptop is often referred to as a *tablet PC*, maintaining the analogy of a tablet and pen.

You should also know that the Function (Fn) key on a laptop is typically combined with the function keys and a few other special keys to enable the laptop to perform tasks not present on a desktop. For example, pressing Fn and F8 on a Dell laptop toggles the display in three modes: in the first, the display goes only to the monitor; in the second, it goes to the monitor and an output device such as a projector; and in the third, it goes only to the output device.

It's typical to have Fn keys assigned for Standby and Hibernate modes as well as checking the battery status and toggling volume controls.

Power Management

Power management is essential with laptops. You don't want the system going dead when the battery gets low without properly warning you and doing everything possible to save the data. Although laptops include batteries and peripherals, the true strength in power management lies in the operating system.

With Windows XP, for example, you access the power options by choosing Start ➢ Control Panel ➢ Power Options to open a dialog box similar to that shown in Figure 2.1.

FIGURE 2.1   Power options in Windows XP

At least 10 power schemes are possible, including Home/Office Desk (which doesn't use power management), Portable/Laptop (the default on a laptop PC), Always On, Max Battery, and so on. From the Advanced tab, you can choose what happens when you close the lid, when you press the power button, and when you press the sleep button.

 You can select to "Always show icon on the taskbar" and then you can change power schemes by clicking on the icon, without going in the power properties of the system.

By default, the alarms are set to notify you when only 10 percent of the battery life is left and to put the system in hibernation when only 3 percent of the battery life is left. You can change all these options to fit individual circumstances.

Exam Essentials

Know the different types of PCMCIA cards.   PCMCIA cards are the expansion cards for notebook PCs. Most notebook PCs have a PCMCIA bay that can accept one Type III device or two Type I or Type II devices.

Know the different monitor resolutions.   The exam expects you to know four different types: XGA, SXGA+, UXGA, and WUXGA. Know the resolution for each of them.

Know the purpose of the Fn key.   You should know that the Function (Fn) key on a laptop is typically combined with the function keys and a few other special keys to enable the laptop to perform tasks not present on a desktop.

Know the peripherals discussed.   You should be familiar with docking stations and understand the principle reasons for their use.

Know about auto-switching and fixed-input power supplies.   You should understand that auto-switching allows the power supply to be used in other countries.

Upgrade and Optimize Laptops and Portable Devices

This objective is a continuation of 2.1 in that power management, batteries, and such also fall beneath 2.1.6. The following sections provide information specific to portable computers.

Power Management

The Advanced Configuration Power Interface (ACPI) must be supported by the system BIOS in order to work properly. With ACPI, it is the BIOS that provides the operating system with the necessary methods for controlling the hardware. This is in contrast to APM (Advanced Power Management), which only gave a limited amount of power to the operating system and let the BIOS do all the real work. Because of this, it is not uncommon to find legacy systems that can support APM but not ACPI.

There are three main states of power management common in most operating systems:

- Hibernate—This state saves all the contents of memory to the hard drive and preserves all data/applications/etc. exactly where they are. When the system comes out of hibernation, it returns to its previous state.

- Standby—This state leaves memory active but saves everything else to disk.

- Suspend—In most operating systems, this term is used interchangeably with Hibernate. In Windows XP, Hibernate is used instead of Suspend.

Removing and Replacing the Battery

Depending on the notebook model, the battery may be anywhere, but it's usually under the keyboard. On some models, you can slide the battery out the side by removing a panel or cover; on other models, you must lift the keyboard.

Pull out the battery, and insert a fresh battery in the same slot, pressing it firmly into place. Then, replace the cover over the battery's bay.

While manufacturers recommend a shutdown, in reality batteries are *hot-pluggable/swappable*, so you don't have to shut down in order to remove one. However, unless you have a second battery or are connected to AC power, you'll lose power and the PC will shut off when you remove the battery.

For purposes of exam study, hot-swappable and hot-pluggable are interchangeable terms.

Adding and Removing PC Card Devices

PC Card devices are designed to be easily removed and installed. They're approximately the size and shape of a thick credit card, and they fit into PC Card (PCMCIA) slots in the side of the notebook PC. PC Card devices can include modems, network interface cards (NICs), SCSI adapters, USB adapters, FireWire adapters, and wireless Ethernet cards.

To eject a PC Card device, press the eject button next to its slot. To insert a PC Card device, press the device into the slot. You can do this while the computer is running. (That's called *hot-plugging* or *hot-swapping*.) However, in Windows, it's a good idea to stop the PC Card device before ejecting it, to ensure that all operations involving it complete normally. To do so, double-click the Safely Remove Hardware icon in the system tray, click the device, and then click Stop.

Disassembling a Notebook PC

There are many designs of notebook PC cases, and each one disassembles a little differently. The best way to determine the proper disassembly method is to consult the documentation from the manufacturer.

Some models of notebook PCs require a special T-8 Torx screwdriver. Most PC toolkits come with a T-8 bit for a screwdriver with interchangeable bits, but you may find that the T-8 screws are countersunk in deep holes so that you can't fit the screwdriver into them. In such cases, you need to buy a separate T-8 screwdriver, available at most hardware stores or auto-parts stores.

Prepare a clean, well-lit, flat work surface, assemble your tools and manuals, and ensure that you have the correct parts. Shut down the PC, unplug it, and detach any external devices such as an external keyboard, mouse, or monitor.

Many laptop manufacturers will consider a warranty void if an unauthorized person opens a laptop case and attempts to repair a laptop.

Removing and Replacing Disk Drives

Accessing the hard disk drive usually involves lifting the keyboard or removing it entirely. The hard disk typically has a ribbon cable made of thin plastic; be very careful when detaching it so you don't bend or break it. The hard disk also usually has a power supply connector that is smaller than that of a typical hard disk in a desktop PC. After you disconnect the hard disk, remove the screws holding it in place and lift it out.

The procedure for removing the floppy disk and/or CD drive varies widely depending on the model. Some notebook PCs are fully modular, such that the floppy disk and CD drives pop out easily without any tools. On other models, you may need to completely disassemble the PC to access them. Consult the documentation from the manufacturer.

After you remove the old drive, insert the new one in the same spot and secure it with screws. Then, attach the power-supply cable and ribbon cable, and reassemble the PC.

Adding Memory

Most notebook PCs have a certain amount of memory hard-wired into them that you can't remove. They also typically have a memory expansion slot into which you can insert a single circuit board containing additional RAM.

If such an additional memory module has been installed, you can remove it if desired (perhaps to replace it with one that has larger capacity). Most notebook PCs have a panel on the bottom held in place by screws. Remove this panel to expose the memory expansion slot. Then, gently pull out the existing RAM module, if necessary, and insert the new RAM module.

Docking and Undocking

Some notebook PCs have optional accessories called *docking stations* or *port replicators*. These let you quickly connect/disconnect with external peripherals and may also provide extra ports that the notebook PC doesn't normally have.

Each docking station works a little differently, but there is usually a button you can press to undock the notebook from the unit. There may also be a manual release lever in case you need to undock when the button is unresponsive.

Because different hardware is available in docked versus undocked configurations, you may want to set up hardware profiles in Windows to account for the differences.

Exam Essentials

Know what hot-swappable means.   PC Card devices are hot-swappable, meaning you can remove and insert them while the computer is running. So are USB and FireWire devices. However, if you need to remove a drive, add or remove RAM, or connect or disconnect a monitor or a parallel or serial device, you must shut down the laptop.

Know where to look for the battery and for RAM expansion slots.   Batteries are usually accessed either from the sides of a laptop or from under the keyboard. RAM is usually accessed on the bottom of the laptop. There will also be some unremoveable RAM built into the motherboard.

Identify Tools and Diagnostic Procedures

Most of the tools used in diagnostics and troubleshooting are the same in the laptop world as in the desktop world, with few exceptions. This section looks at tools (many are just approaches to what is already there) you can use to work with laptops.

Critical Information

To solve a problem with a laptop or portable device (these terms are mostly used interchangeably by CompTIA), you should fully understand the hardware you're working with. The following list describes the items that CompTIA wants you to be comfortable with for this objective. Some may seem like common sense, in which case you should have no difficulty choosing the correct answer for questions about them on the exam:

AC power In the absence of AC power, the laptop will attempt to run off of the battery. This solution is good for a time, but AC power must be available to keep the battery charged and the laptop running. Most laptops have an indicator light showing whether AC power is being received, and the AC cord typically has an indicator light on it as well to show that it's receiving power (see Figure 2.2). If no lights are lit on the cord or the laptop indicating that AC power is being received, try a different outlet or a different cord.

FIGURE 2.2   A light on the power cord indicates that AC is being received.

Light

The presence of AC can affect the action of the NIC. To conserve power, the NIC is often configured not to be active when running on DC power (see Figure 2.3). You can access this dialog through Start ➢ Control Panel ➢ Internal NIC Configuration.

Stylus Issues A stylus may no longer work on a tablet computer due to damage or excessive wear. When this occurs, you can purchase replacement styluses for most units very inexpensively.

FIGURE 2.3   The NIC can be disabled when running on DC to conserve battery life.

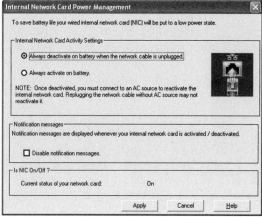

Antenna wires   Most laptops today include an internal wireless card. This is convenient, but it can be susceptible to interference (resulting in a low signal strength) between the laptop and the access point. Do what you can to reduce the number of items blocking the signal between the two devices, and you'll increase the strength of the signal.

Backlight functionality   The *backlight* is the light in the PC that powers the LCD screen. It can go bad over time and need to be replaced, and it can also be held captive by the inverter. The *inverter* takes the DC power the laptop is providing and boosts it up to AC to run the backlight. If the inverter goes bad, you can replace it on most models (it's cheaper than the backlight).

DC power   The biggest issue with DC power is the battery's inability to power the laptop as long as it should. This can be caused if the battery builds up a *memory* and thus doesn't offer a full charge. If a feature is available to fully drain the battery, you should use it to eliminate the memory (letting the laptop run on battery on a regular basis greatly helps). If you can't drain the battery and eliminate the memory, you should replace the battery.

External monitors   External monitors may be connected to the laptop directly or through a docking station. If you have an external monitor connected before you boot the laptop, many laptops automatically detect it and send the display there. If you connect after the laptop is booted, you should use the appropriate Fn key to send the display to the monitor.

Keyboards   Problems with keyboards can range from their collecting dust (in which case you need to blow them out) to their springs wearing out. If it's the latter, you can replace the keyboard (they cost about 10 times more than desktop keyboards) or choose to use an external one (provided the user isn't traveling and having to lug another hardware element with them).

Pointers   The pointer device used on the laptop, like the keyboard, can be affected by dirt/debris as well as by continual use. If the device fails to function properly after a good cleaning, you can replace it (expensive) or opt for an external pointer (such as a wireless mouse).

Unneeded peripherals   To keep the system running at peak efficiency, you should disconnect or disable unneeded peripherals. Every peripheral has the ability to drain power and resources from the PC, and you don't want that if it can be avoided.

Video   One of the biggest problems with video is incorrect settings. You can change the video settings easily on the laptop through the operating system. Make sure you have the correct—and most current—drivers.

 A few other miscellaneous topics—such as Fn toggling and wireless card issues—are listed by CompTIA beneath this objective, but they have been addressed elsewhere.

Exam Essentials

Know how to work with laptop components.   Understand the issues that can arise, and know what to look for to begin trying to fix them.

Know the power configuration settings.   Using power configuration, it's possible to disable the NIC and other devices to conserve power. You can also receive notification when the battery life reaches low levels.

Perform Preventative Maintenance for Laptops and Portable Devices

Taking care of your company's laptops can extend their life and save considerable money. Most of the actions necessary to maintain laptops fall under the category of what is reasonable, and you would undoubtedly think of them on your own.

Critical Information

Cleaning any computer—whether stationary or not—is the most important part of maintaining it. Dirt and debris of any type reduce the operating efficiency and life of computer systems. Much of the information on cleaning is the same for a laptop as for a desktop machine and is addressed many other times in this book: Chapter 1, for example, concluded by looking at preventative maintenance of desktop machines. To avoid repetition, what follows is an abstract of much of that information:

- Most computer cases and monitor cases can be cleaned using mild soap and water on a clean, lint-free cloth.

- Make sure the power is off before you put anything wet near a computer.

- Dampen (not soak) a cloth with a mild soap solution, and wipe the dirt and dust from the case.

- Wipe the moisture from the case with a dry, lint-free cloth.

- To clean a monitor screen, use glass cleaner designed specifically for monitors, and a soft cloth.

- To clean a keyboard, use canned air to blow debris out from under the keys, and use towelettes designed for use with computers to keep the key tops clean.

- To prevent a computer from becoming dirty in the first place, control its environment. Make sure there is adequate ventilation in the work area and that the dust level isn't excessive.

- Preventive maintenance for the software can include Disk Defragmenter, ScanDisk, Check Disk, and Disk Cleanup.

- Perform scheduled maintenance regularly to prolong the life of your equipment.

Exam Essentials

Know the importance of running scheduled maintenance.   Scheduled maintenance can prolong the life of your equipment and help ensure that your output continues to live up to the quality you expect.

Understand the importance of a suitable environment.   If you want your equipment to last as long as possible and deliver quality, you should pay attention to the environment in which you place it.

Review Questions

1. True or false: Because of the way the screen is refreshed, you typically cannot run LCD projectors, LCD panels, or other similar devices from passive matrix laptops.

2. What is the resolution for XGA?

3. What is the aspect ratio of WUGA?

4. What is cold docking?

5. What type of battery is lightweight and has a long life, and is not subject to problems with partial draining and recharging?

6. Which type of PCMCIA card is the thickest?

7. How many volts does Mini PCI operate at?

8. True or false: Batteries are hot-pluggable.

9. True or false: FireWire devices are hot-pluggable.

10. True or false: To clean a monitor screen, you should use glass cleaner designed specifically for monitors, and a soft cloth.

Answers to Review Questions

1. True. Because of the way the screen is refreshed, you typically cannot run LCD projectors, LCD panels, or other similar devices from passive matrix laptops.

2. XGA is a 1024×768 resolution.

3. WUGA has a 16:10 screen aspect ratio.

4. Cold docking means the laptop must be turned off and back on for a change to be recognized.

5. Lithium Ion batteries are lightweight and have a long life, plus they are not subject to problems with partial draining and recharging. They tend to be more expensive than NiCad or NiMH, however.

6. Type III cards are up to 10.5mm thick and are not commonly used.

7. Mini PCI operates at only 3.3 volts.

8. True. Batteries are hot-pluggable, so you do not have to shut down in order to remove one.

9. True. FireWire and USB devices are hot-pluggable.

10. True. To clean a monitor screen, use glass cleaner designed specifically for monitors, and a soft cloth.

Chapter

3

Operating Systems

COMPTIA A+ ESSENTIALS EXAM OBJECTIVES COVERED IN THIS CHAPTER:

✓ **3.1 Identify the fundamentals of using operating systems**

- Identify differences between operating systems (e.g., Mac, Windows, Linux) and describe operating system revision levels, including GIU, system requirements, application and hardware compatibility

- Identify names, purposes, and characteristics of the primary operating system components, including registry, virtual memory, and file system

- Describe features of operating system interfaces, for example:
    - Windows Explorer
    - My Computer
    - Control Panel
    - Command Prompt
    - My Network Places
    - Task bar / systray
    - Start Menu

- Identify the names, locations, purposes, and characteristics of operating system files, for example:
    - BOOT.INI
    - NTLDR
    - NTDETECT.COM
    - NTBOOTDD.SYS
    - Registry data files

- Identify concepts and procedures for creating, viewing, managing disks, directories, and files in operating systems, for example:
    - Disks (e.g., active, primary, extended and logical partitions)
    - File systems (e.g., FAT 32, NTFS)
    - Directory structures (e.g., create folders, navigate directory structures)
    - Files (e.g., creation, extensions, attributes, permissions)

✓ **3.2 Install, configure, optimize, and upgrade operating systems**

- Identify procedures for installing operating systems, including:
  - Verification of hardware compatibility and minimum requirements
  - Installation methods (e.g., boot media, such as CD, floppy, or USB, network installation, drive imaging)
  - Operating system installation options (e.g., attended / unattended, file system type, network configuration)
  - Disk preparation order (e.g., start installation, partition, and format drive)
  - Device driver configuration (e.g., install and upload device drivers)
  - Verification of installation
- Identify procedures for upgrading operating systems, including:
  - Upgrade considerations (e.g., hardware, application, and / or network compatibility)
  - Implementation (e.g., backup data, install additional Windows components)
- Install / add a device, including loading, adding device drivers, and required software, including:
  - Determine whether permissions are adequate for performing the task
  - Device driver installation (e.g., automated and / or manual search and installation of device drivers)
  - Using unsigned drivers (e.g., driver signing)
  - Verify installation of the driver (e.g., device manager and functionality)
- Identify procedures and utilities used to optimize operating systems, for example, virtual memory, hard drives, temporary files, service, startup, and applications

✓ **3.3 Identify tools, diagnostic procedures, and troubleshooting techniques for operating systems**

- Identify basic boot sequences, methods, and utilities for recovering operating systems
- Boot methods (e.g., safe mode, recovery console, boot to restore point)

- Automated System Recovery (ASR) (e.g., Emergency Repair Disk (ERD))
- Identify and apply diagnostic procedures and troubleshooting techniques, for example:
  - Identify the problem by questioning the user and identifying user changes to the computer
  - Analyze problem, including potential causes and initial determination of software and / or hardware problem
  - Test related components, including connections, hardware / software configurations, device manager, and consulting vendor documentation
  - Evaluate results and take additional steps if needed, such as consultation, alternate resources, and manuals
  - Document activities and outcomes
  - Recognize and resolve common operational issues, such as bluescreen, system lock-up, input / output device, application install, start or load, and Windows-specific printing problems (e.g., print spool stalled, incorrect / incompatible driver for print)
- Explain common error messages and codes, for example:
  - Boot (e.g., invalid boot disk, inaccessible boot drive, missing NTLDR)
  - Startup (e.g., device / service failed to start, device / program in registry not found)
  - Event Viewer
  - Registry
  - Windows reporting
- Identify the names, locations, purposes, and characteristics of operating system utilities, for example:
  - Disk management tools (e.g., DEFRAG, NTBACKUP, CHKDSK, Format)
  - System management tools (e.g., device and task manager, MSCONFIG.EXE)
  - File management tools (e.g,. Windows Explorer, ATTRIB.EXE)

✓ **3.4 Perform preventative maintenance on operating systems**

- Describe common utilities for performing preventative maintenance on operating systems, for example, software and Windows updates (e.g., service packs), scheduled backups / restore, restore points

In the last iteration of the A+ certification, operating systems existed only on the second exam and not in the core one. Not only does the domain now appear on the Essentials exam, but it's tied for the most heavily weighted (at 21 percent) of the eight domains. In addition, the domain also appears on the IT Technician (220-602) exam, where it has the highest weight of any at 20 percent; and on the Remote Support Technician (220-603) exam, where it again has the highest weight—29 percent. The topic is absent from the Depot Technician (220-604) exam.

Identify Operating System Fundamentals

This objective deals with two basic questions:

- What desktop components and interfaces form the Windows GUI?
- What are the differences among the various Windows versions?

It's essential to know the answers to both of these questions, both for the A+ exam and for real-world work in the PC field. You need to be able to navigate confidently in any operating system (OS) version and tailor your processes to the specific OS version present.

Critical Information

Some of this information about Windows functionality may be a review for you, but read through it anyway, to make sure nothing slips between the cracks in your education. Pay special attention to the material on differentiating the OS versions from one another, because you're sure to see some test questions on that topic.

Operating System Differences

Microsoft Windows isn't the only OS available, but is the one that this exam tests on primarily. CompTIA expects you to know that others exist but won't ask a great many questions on them.

Linux is an open source OS that runs on the same hardware platform as Windows. Instead of being from a single vendor, such as Microsoft, you can find Linux offerings from a number of distributors, including Red Hat, SuSE/Novell, and Ubuntu. Although the robustness of Linux increases greatly with each new build of the kernel, one of its biggest weaknesses for desktop use, when compared to Windows, is the reduced number of available applications.

CompTIA offers a certification and exam solely on Linux called Linux+. It's aimed at entry-level administrators.

Macintosh systems have recently gained the ability to run Windows on their hardware. Prior to these very modern developments, they ran only the Mac OS. Although it's hailed as an excellent operating system, the Mac OS has always had a smaller market share and reduced number of applications available, when compared to Windows.

In the Windows world, there have been multiple iterations of Windows. The term can be used to describe everything from Windows 3.1 to Windows 95, Windows Me, NT 4.0, and so on. This version of the A+ exam focuses on the Windows 2000 and Windows XP versions.

If you're unsure which version of Windows you have, there are multiple ways to find out. Two of the easiest are to choose System from the Control Panel or to type **ver** from a command prompt.

Major Operating System Functions

The A+ exam focuses only on Windows-based OSs available from Microsoft, and we'll give those systems the most time in this chapter. Although Macintosh has a strong following in certain niche markets, Intel/Windows machines dominate the corporate market almost completely.

The *operating system* provides a consistent environment for other software to execute commands. The OS gives users an interface with the computer so they can send commands to it (input) and receive feedback or results back (output). To do this, the OS must communicate with the computer hardware to perform the following tasks:

- Disk and file management
- Device access
- Memory management
- Input/output

Disk and File Management

The OS must be able to store and retrieve files on disks; this is one of its most primary functions. The system components involved in disk and file management include the following:

The filesystem   The organizational scheme that governs how files are stored on and retrieved from a disk. There are four major filesystems: the original 16-bit FAT system (a carryover from MS-DOS); the 32-bit version of it called FAT32; the NT File System (NTFS 4.0) supported by Windows NT 4.0; and the improved version of NTFS called NTFS 5.0, supported by Windows 2000/XP. Table 3.1 lists some of the filesystems and the Microsoft OSs that support them.

TABLE 3.1 Major Filesystems

Operating System	FAT16	FAT32	NTFS 4.0	NTFS 5.0
Windows NT 4.0	Yes	No	Yes	No
Windows 98	Yes	Yes	No	No
Windows 2000	Yes	Yes	No (must convert)	Yes
Windows XP	Yes	Yes	No (must convert)	Yes

Windows Explorer The primary file-management interface in Windows. It displays the list of files in the current location at the right and a folder tree of other locations at the left. (See Figure 3.1.) It starts with the My Documents folder as its default location when opened. Windows Explorer is available in all Windows versions and works approximately the same way in each.

My Computer Basically the same interface as Windows Explorer, except it doesn't show the folder tree by default, and it starts with a list of local drives. Originally, the two were separate; but in modern versions of Windows, you can click the Folders button on the toolbar to turn that folder tree on/off, making the two interfaces practically identical.

FIGURE 3.1 The Windows Explorer interface

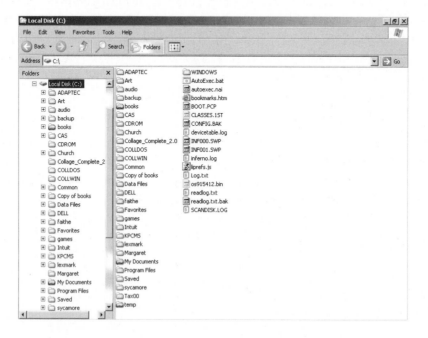

Control Panel   A folder that contains applets you can use to configure your system. Common applets beneath the Control Panel include Add Hardware, Add or Remove Programs, Display, System, and a surplus of others. Some of the entries here—such as Fonts—aren't applets themselves, but rather folders that hold additional entities.

Network Neighborhood/My Network Places   Again, basically the same interface as the others, but designed for browsing network computers and drives rather than local ones. In early versions of Windows, this was called Network Neighborhood; starting with Windows 2000, the name was changed to My Network Places.

Device Access

Another responsibility of the OS is to manage the way that software on the system interacts with the computer's hardware. More-advanced OSs have the ability to avoid conflicts between devices and to prevent applications from interfering with each other.

Windows handles device management by itself in most cases. In instances where users need to get involved, they can use the Device Manager interface. In Windows 2000/XP, you must display the System Properties box, click the Hardware tab, and then click Device Manager.

Memory Management

Computers are designed so that in order for information to be used by the processor, it must be in the machine's memory (RAM). How the OS manages the transfer of information from storage on the hard drive to a place in RAM is referred to as *memory management*.

Back in the days of MS-DOS, applications could run only in conventional memory—the first 640KB of RAM in the system. This severely limited the size of the applications that could be written, so various schemes for getting around that limitation were devised. Windows *9x* and higher get around it in the following ways:

Extended memory   PCs today have many megabytes and even gigabytes of RAM, and everything except the first megabyte is considered *extended memory*. Windows can address extended memory and apportion it out to applications as needed.

Virtual machines   Windows can *multitask* (that is, run more than one application at the same time) by creating a separate memory space for each application. It's almost like each of the applications is running on a separate PC, with the OS interface tying them all together. The separate space in which an application runs is called a *virtual machine*.

Virtual memory   Windows is such a large OS and requires so much overhead that sometimes a PC doesn't have enough RAM to accommodate its needs. Rather than giving an *out of memory* error message to the user, Windows has a workaround technique whereby it uses an unused part of the hard disk to simulate additional RAM, swapping data into and out of it from the real RAM. This is called *virtual memory*. The file on the hard disk used for the simulation is called a *paging file* or *swap file*.

Applications always use the memory out of the physical RAM, but the virtual memory is there to allow for a fast swap.

Input/Output

Generally called *I/O*, input/output is the process by which the machine accepts instructions (from the mouse, keyboard, and so on) and provides output (to a monitor, file, or printer). These operations happen behind the scenes with no user intervention in most cases. The user clicks the mouse or types on the keyboard, and input happens. Keyboard and mouse settings can be fine-tuned through Control Panel.

Major Operating System Components

All Windows versions have a similar look and feel in their user interface. Figure 3.2 shows Windows 2000, for example.

The main differences between Windows XP and all other Windows versions are the redesigned Start menu and the rounded look of the dialog boxes. Figure 3.3 shows a typical Windows XP screen.

Much of this information will be review for those of you who have experience using Windows OSs, but you may want to refresh your mind as to the specific names and attributes of these components.

FIGURE 3.2 The Windows 2000 interface

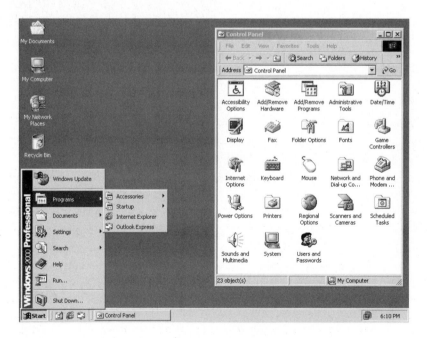

FIGURE 3.3   The Windows XP interface

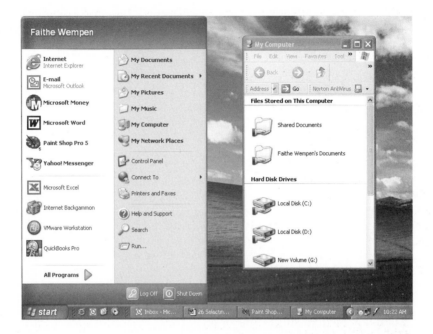

The Desktop

The Desktop is the virtual desk on which all of your other programs and utilities run. By default, it contains the Start menu, the Taskbar, and a number of icons. The Desktop can also contain additional elements, such as web page content, through the use of the Active Desktop option. Because it's the base on which everything else sits, how the Desktop is configured can have a major effect on how the GUI looks and how convenient it is for users.

You can change the Desktop's background patterns, screensaver, color scheme, and size by right-clicking any area of the Desktop that doesn't contain an icon. The menu that appears allows you to do several things, such as create new Desktop items, change how your icons are arranged, and select a special command called Properties. Right-click the Desktop and choose Properties to work with display properties.

Windows is designed to let each user access information in the way they're most comfortable with, and as such there are generally at least two ways to do everything. When you're getting ready for the test, try to make sure you know *all* the ways to perform a task, not just the way you're used to.

The Taskbar/System Tray

The *Taskbar* runs along the bottom of the Windows display. At the left is the Start button, which opens the menu system. At the right is the clock and the *System Tray (systray)*, also known as the *Notification Area*. The System Tray holds icons for programs that are running in the background, such as virus checkers, and also sometimes icons for frequently needed controls such as the sound volume.

In its center, the Taskbar displays buttons for each of the open windows. To bring a window or program to the front (or to maximize it if it's minimized), click its button on the Taskbar. As the middle area of the Taskbar fills up with buttons, the buttons become smaller so there is room to display them all.

There are different methods of managing situations where you have too many Taskbar buttons. One method is to drag the top border of the Taskbar upward, creating an extra row for the buttons. Another, which works only in later Windows versions like XP, is to allow Taskbar buttons to be grouped. For example, if you have four file-management windows open, they appear as a single button on the Taskbar. You can click that button to see the windows in menu form and make your selection. To set this up, right-click the Taskbar and choose Properties, and then mark the Group Similar Taskbar Icons check box. If there's no such check box, your version of Windows doesn't support this feature.

You can move the Taskbar to the top or sides of the screen by clicking the Taskbar and dragging it to the new location. This is important to know, because sometimes users accidentally do this and need help dragging the Taskbar back to the bottom.

The Start Menu

The Start button opens the Start menu, an entry point into a well-organized system of shortcuts to various utilities and applications you can run. Its top level has a few shortcut icons for some critical features, but most of the shortcuts are contained in a hierarchical system of submenus. To display a submenu, point at any item that has a right-pointing arrow to its right.

PROGRAMS SUBMENU

The Programs submenu holds the program groups and program icons that you can use. In Windows XP, it's called All Programs rather than Programs, but it's basically the same thing.

Shortcuts to programs are placed in the Programs menu when they're installed using a Windows-based setup utility, or when you manually place them there. There are a number of ways to create a new item on the Start menu or to reorganize items that are already there:

- Right-click the Taskbar, and choose Properties. Depending on the Windows version, different options may be available through this Properties box for customizing the Start menu.

- Right-click the Start button, and choose Open. The Start menu's content appears in a file-management window, and you can add and remove shortcuts.

- Drag and drop a shortcut from the Desktop. This works only in later Windows versions. Drag an icon to the Start menu, but don't release the mouse button. Just pause, and the Start menu will open. Then, pause over the Programs menu, and it will open. Keep going until you find the right spot, and then release the mouse button.

 Within the Programs submenu is an especially important submenu that is specifically mentioned in the exam objective: the Accessories/System Tools submenu. This menu is important because it contains shortcuts to some of the utilities needed for troubleshooting and preventive maintenance of a system.

DOCUMENTS SUBMENU

The Documents submenu has only one function: to keep track of the last 15 data files you opened (this number can be adjusted). Whenever you open a file, a shortcut to it is automatically added to this menu. Click the document in the Documents menu to reopen it in its associated application. In Windows XP, this submenu is called My Recent Documents.

SETTINGS SUBMENU

The Settings submenu provides easy access to the Windows configuration. It contains a shortcut to Control Panel, for example, and to the Printers folder. Additional menus are available depending on which version of Windows you're using. Windows XP has no Settings submenu; the shortcuts it would contain appear directly on the top level of the Start menu instead.

SEARCH SUBMENU

The Search submenu of Windows 2000/XP was known as Find in earlier operating systems, but it has the same functionality. In Windows XP, Search is a command that opens a Search window, rather than a submenu.

HELP COMMAND

Windows includes a *very* good Help system. Not only is it arranged by topic, but it's also fully indexed and searchable. Because of its usefulness and power, it was placed on the Start menu for easy access. When you select the Help command, it brings up Windows Help. From this screen, you can double-click a manual to show a list of subtopics and then click a subtopic to view the text of that topic. You can also view indexed help files or do a specific search through the help documents' text.

RUN COMMAND

The Run command can be used to start programs if they don't have a shortcut on the Desktop or in the Programs submenu. To execute a particular program, type its name and path in the Open field. If you don't know the exact path, you can browse to find the file by clicking the Browse button. Once you've typed in the executable name and path, click OK to run the program.

SHUT DOWN COMMAND

You probably already know that you should never shut down a Windows-based computer by pressing the power switch, because of the possibility of file corruption. Instead, you should shut it down through Windows' Shut Down command.

When you select Shut Down, you're provided a choice of several shutdown methods. They vary depending on the Windows version:

Shut Down This option writes any unsaved data to disk, closes any open applications, and either gets the computer ready to be powered off (on AT systems) or shuts off the computer's power (on ATX systems).

Restart This option works the same as the first option, but instead of shutting down completely, it automatically reboots the computer with a warm reboot.

Log Off If you have user profiles enabled, a Log Off option is available either from this menu or as a separate menu command. Profiles are automatic on NT/2000.

Stand By On laptops or other machines with power-management capability through their BIOS, the Stand By option may be available. It allows the machine to go into a sleep mode, where it shuts down most functions to save energy. Utilizing Stand By can significantly extend battery time on laptops.

Hibernate Hibernate copies the content of RAM to a reserved area on the hard disk and then shuts down the computer completely. When you turn it back on, it copies the data back into RAM, and startup is much faster than normal. This option has been available in most Windows versions and is available only on systems that support it through the BIOS.

Using a Command-Line Interface within Windows

Occasionally, you may need to run commands from an MS-DOS–style command prompt. To do so, there is a special command: either MS-DOS Prompt or Command Prompt, depending on the OS version. It may be on the first-level Programs menu, or it may be on the Accessories submenu, depending on the version.

This command opens a window containing a command prompt. From there, you can type commands and press Enter to execute them.

Contrasts between Windows Versions

Windows 2000 and XP are similar in their user interface. Windows XP is the dominant OS; it's based on Windows 2000 (which, in turn, was based on Windows NT 4.0). Although Windows XP comes in both Professional and Home versions, both are NT-based; the Home version is just the Pro version with some features stripped off.

The main user interface differences between 2000 and Windows XP are in its Start menu and differently styled windows. However, Windows XP can be set up to look just like Windows 2000. In the Display Properties, choose the Windows Classic appearance theme. Then, in the Taskbar Properties, select the Classic Start menu.

Although Windows 2000/XP make no claims about universal backward compatibility, in reality most MS-DOS and 16-bit Windows programs work fine under them. In addition, Windows XP comes with an Application Compatibility feature that helps the system emulate the earlier versions when needed.

Major System Files

By understanding the files used by various Windows versions for behind-the-scenes operations, you'll be better able to troubleshoot problems when they occur. That's the real purpose of memorizing all these filenames:

NTLDR   *Bootstraps* the system. In other words, starts the loading of an OS on the computer.

BOOT.INI   Holds information about which OSs are installed on the computer. This file is read by the BIOS at startup to determine the location of the Master Boot Record. This file is also used, when dual-booting, to display the boot menu.

NTDETECT.COM   Parses the system for hardware information each time Windows is loaded. This information is then used to create dynamic hardware information in the Windows Registry.

NTBOOTDD.SYS   Used to recognize and load the SCSI interface on a system with a SCSI boot device with the SCSI BIOS disabled. On enhanced IDE (EIDE) systems or SCSI systems with the BIOS enabled, this file isn't needed and isn't even installed.

System files   Besides the previously listed files, all of which are located in the root of the C: partition on the computer, Windows 2000 also needs a number of files from its system directories, including the hardware abstraction layer (HAL.DLL) and the Windows 2000 command file (WIN.COM).

Numerous other Dynamic Link Library (DLL) files are also required, but usually the lack or corruption of one of them produces a noncritical error, whereas the absence of WIN.COM or HAL.DLL causes the system to be nonfunctional.

The Windows2000/XP Registry

The Registry in Windows 2000/XP requires that each user have their own profile and maintains that profile automatically for them. The current user's settings are stored in the NTUSER.DAT file. The following files are then used to store the Registry settings:

SAM   Stores the machine's Security Accounts Management database, which is where the Registry stores information about user accounts and passwords.

SECURITY   Stores information about file and folder security on the machine.

SOFTWARE   Holds configuration data for programs and utilities installed on the machine. Also has numerous areas corresponding to the OS.

SYSTEM   Holds information that affects the OS's operation, especially during startup.

Exam Essentials

Know the major functions of Windows.   You should understand what an OS does, what systems it manages, and how it communicates with the human user.

Know which filesystems work with which Windows versions.   Refer back to Table 3.1 if you need to review this.

Understand virtual memory.   You should know the purpose of virtual memory and how it operates in terms of hard disk and physical RAM.

Be able to identify Windows display components.   Make sure you can point out the Task-bar, Start button, System Tray, Desktop, and other key features of the OS interface.

Understand version differences.   Be able to group the Windows versions according to similarity and explain how one group differs from the other.

Know the names of the system files.   You should be able to list the files and their purposes.

Install and Configure Operating Systems

This objective expects you to know the minimum requirements for the operating systems and different ways to install them. You should know the information at the level it is presented here. You aren't expected to know much about them above the basic knowledge level.

Critical Information

The operating systems focused on in this objective are Windows 2000 and Windows XP.

   Before performing any installation or upgrade, you must back up your existing files to removable media. Doing so provides you with an insurance policy in the event of an unforeseen disaster and, therefore, is highly recommended.

Given the timing of these updates, and the pending release of Vista, you may question the need to know this information. Nevertheless, it's tested on by CompTIA, and you should know the information given here in order to pass this exam.

Minimum Requirements for Windows 2000

Before installing any OS, you always want to make certain the hardware will meet (or, even better, exceed) the minimum system requirements. Windows 2000 Professional has the following minimum requirements:

- Pentium 133MHz or higher (Professional can support up to two processors)
- 32MB of RAM (64MB is recommended; the maximum supported is 4GB)
- 650MB free disk space
- VGA
- Keyboard and mouse (though the mouse is just "recommended," it truly is difficult to work without)

The Support folder on the Windows 2000 Professional CD contains an HCL.TXT file, which is the hardware compatibility list (HCL) of supported hardware. An updated version of this file is kept on the Microsoft website (http://www.microsoft.com). The latest release notes can also be found in text files located on the CD under the SETUPTXT folder.

Dual-booting requires that each operating system be stored in its own folder. The default folder under which Windows 2000 is installed is WINNT, but this can be changed to any valid folder name.

Minimum Requirements for Windows XP

To install Windows XP on a system, it needs to meet the following minimum requirements:

- Pentium 233MHz or higher (300MHz is recommended; it can also work with Celeron, AMD K6/Athlon/Duron or compatible processors)
- 128MB of RAM (64MB is the minimum supported)
- 1.5GB free disk space
- Super VGA
- CD-ROM and/or DVD drive
- Keyboard and mouse (or similar pointing device)

The same minimum requirements exist for both Windows XP Professional and Windows XP Home.

Installing Operating Systems

Operating systems can be installed in two generic ways: attended or unattended. During an attended installation, you walk through the installation and answer the questions as prompted. Questions typically ask for the product key, the directory in which you want to install the OS, and relevant network settings.

As simple as attended installations may be, they're time-consuming and administrator-intensive in that they require someone to fill in a fair number of fields to move through the process. Unattended installations allow you to configure the OS with little or no human intervention. Windows 2000 Professional offers three main methods for performing unattended installations: Remote Installation Service (RIS), System Preparation Tool, and Setup Manager.

The RIS is a service that runs on a Windows 2000 Server. Client machines to be converted to Windows 2000 Professional access the server service and run the installation across the network.

The System Preparation Tool takes a completely different approach. Sysprep.exe is used to prepare an ideal Windows 2000 Professional workstation so that an image can be made of it (this requires a third-party utility). That image, which lacks user/computer-specific information and SIDs (Security IDs), can then be loaded on other computers.

Setup Manager is used to create answer files (known as uniqueness database files [UDFs]) for automatically providing computer or user information during setup. Setup Manager, like Sysprep, isn't installed on the system by default but is stored within the Deploy cabinet file on the CD beneath Support\Tools.

Windows XP offers similar installation options as well. For the exam, you should be familiar with the attended installation and know that the other methods exist.

Working with Device Drivers

Device drivers are the software stubs that allow devices to communicate with the operating system. Called *drivers* for short, they're used for interacting with printers, monitors, network cards, sound cards, and just about every type of hardware attached to the PC. One of the most common problems associated with drivers isn't having the current version—as problems are fixed, the drivers are updated, and you can often save a great deal of time by downloading the latest drivers from the vendor's site early in the troubleshooting process.

Adding the /sos option to the operating system option in the BOOT.INI file will show the drivers as they're loaded in Windows 2000/XP.

The easiest way to see/change drivers in Windows 2000/XP is to click the Driver tab in the Properties for the device. For example, to see the driver associated with the hard drive in Windows XP, double-click the hard drive in Device Manager (Start ➤ Control Panel ➤ System, and then click the Hardware tab and the Device Manager button), and choose the Driver tab. Among other things, this shows the driver provider, date, version, and signer. You can choose to view details about it, update it, roll it back to a previous driver, or uninstall it.

Common Installation Problems

For the most part, the days of having to suffer through installation issues are a thing of the past. The wizards available in the Microsoft OSs tend to make installation errors much less common than they were with earlier operating systems. Several categories of errors and fixes that still crop up from time to time are as follows:

Installation disk errors   Retry the installation once more. If the errors persist, change to a new installation CD.

Inadequate disk space   Take corrective action to proceed with the installation, such as deleting temporary files, archiving old data, and so on.

Disk configuration errors   Make sure you're using hardware compatible with the operating system by checking the HCL.

Can't connect to a domain controller   Verify that you're entering the correct username and password and that the Caps Lock key isn't on.

Domain name error   Reselect/retype the correct domain name.

Upgrading Operating Systems

If you add an OS to a machine that doesn't currently have one (recently formatted, built from scratch, and so on), that is *installing*. If you add an OS such that you can dual-boot (choose which one to run at start), that is *installing*. If you replace one OS with another and attempt to keep the same data/application files, that is *upgrading*.

Whereas installation can typically be done over any existing OS, upgrading can only be done from OSs that are generally compatible with the one you're adding. For example, with Windows 2000, upgrades can only be done from the following programs:

- Windows 95
- Windows 98
- Windows NT Workstation 3.51
- Windows NT Workstation 4.0

WINNT32.EXE is the utility to use to initiate the upgrade. The Setup Wizard automatically creates a report of devices that can't be upgraded. Keep in mind that you must uncompress any DoubleSpace or DriveSpace volumes before you start an upgrade.

With Windows XP, you can upgrade to the Home version only from Windows 98 or Windows Me. You can upgrade to the Professional version from Windows 98, Windows Me, Windows NT Workstation 4.0, Windows 2000 Professional, or even from Windows XP Home.

Step-by-step upgrade information for Windows XP can be found at http://www.microsoft.com/windowsxp/using/setup/getstarted/default.mspx.

Keeping the System Current

Upgrades to Windows (2000 and XP) come in the form of *service packs*. Each service pack contains patches and fixes to OS components, as well as additional features. A service pack is a self-running program that modifies your OS. It isn't uncommon within the lifetime of an OS to have two or three service packs.

Successive service packs include all files that have been in previous ones. Therefore, if you perform a new installation, and the latest service pack is Service Pack 4, you don't need to install Service Packs 1, 2, and 3. You need install only Service Pack 4 after the installation to bring the OS up to the current feature set.

As they're released, service packs are shipped monthly for all Microsoft OSs with TechNet. TechNet is a subscription CD service available through Microsoft.

Exam Essentials

Know the system requirements of Windows.   You should know the minimum system requirements for Windows 2000 Professional and Windows XP Home/Professional.

Know the difference between attended and unattended installations.   Be able to identify the time savings that are present with an unattended installation.

Understand upgrading.   You should know that an installation overwrites any existing files whereas an upgrade keeps the same data/application files.

Identify Tools for Diagnostics and Troubleshooting

This is a catchall category, as are many in this domain. Some of the objectives here carry over from previous ones. It tests your ability to understand the boot sequence, use diagnostic procedures, recognize some common operational issues, explain a few error messages, and identify the names, locations, purposes, and characteristics of some common utilities (including the ability to display a command prompt and enter common commands using the correct syntax).

Critical Information

Both for the test and for real life, you should know how to recognize common problems with operating systems and make certain they're booting correctly. The sections that follow look at a number of topics related to keeping your OSs booting and running properly.

Working with the Boot Sequence

The first objective discussed in this chapter introduced the files used to boot the system. Under a normal boot, these files are accessed as needed, and the system is brought to its ready state. If problems are occurring, however, you may need to alter the boot method used. Windows offers a number of choices of altered boot sequences:

All of these are discussed in detail in Chapter 11, where the objectives require more detailed information.

Safe Mode   To access Safe Mode, you must press F8 when the OS menu is displayed during the boot process. A menu of Safe Mode choices appears, and you can select the mode you want to boot into. This is the mode to boot into if you suspect driver problems and want to load with a minimal set while you diagnose the problem.

Recovery Console   This is a command-line utility used for troubleshooting. From it, you can format drives, stop and start services, and interact with files stored on FAT, FAT32, or NTFS. The Recovery Console isn't installed on a system by default, but you can add it as a menu choice at the bottom of the startup menu.

Restore points   System Restore is arguably the most powerful tool in Windows XP. It allows you to restore the system to a previous point in time. This feature is accessed from Start ➤ All Programs ➤ Accessories ➤ System Tools ➤ System Restore and can be used to roll back as well as to create a restore point.

Automated System Recovery (ASR)   It's possible to automate the process of creating a system recovery set by choosing the ASR Wizard on the Tools menu of the Backup utility (Start ➤ All Programs ➤ Accessories ➤ System Tools ➤ Backup). This wizard walks you through the process of creating a disk that can be used to restore parts of the system in the event of a major system failure.

Emergency repair disk (ERD)   The Windows Backup and Recovery Tool/Wizard also allows you to create an ERD. As the name implies, this is a disk you can use to repair a portion of the system in the event of a failure.

Diagnostic Procedures

When it comes to diagnostic procedures with OSs, you need to memorize the steps that Comp-TIA wants you to take as you approach the problem. Much of this approach carries over to other domains (and objectives) as well. Your approach to the problem should be as follows:

1. Identify the problem by questioning the user and identifying user changes to the computer. Before you do anything else, ask the user what the problem is, when the last time was that the problem didn't exist, and what has changed since then.

2. Analyze the problem, including potential causes, and make an initial determination of whether it's a software and/or hardware problem. As you narrow down the problem, you need to determine whether it's hardware- or software-related so you can act accordingly.

3. Test related components, including connections and hardware/software configurations; use Device Manager; and consult vendor documentation. Whatever the problem may be, the odds are good that someone else has experienced it before. Use the tools at your disposal—including manuals and websites—to try to focus in on the problem as expeditiously as possible.

4. Evaluate the results, and take additional steps if needed, such as consultation, examining alternate resources, and looking in manuals. It's possible that more than one thing is causing the problem. If that is the case, you may need to solve one problem and then turn your attention to the next.

5. Document your activities and outcomes. Experience is a wonderful teacher, but only if you can remember what you've done. Documenting your actions and outcomes will help you (or a fellow admin) troubleshoot a similar problem when it crops up in the future.

Common Operational Issues

There are a number of operational issues that you should be familiar with. Although CompTIA calls them "common," they're nowhere near as common as they were in the past. Each successive release of the Windows OS and service packs has reduced the frequency of these operational conditions from occurring, to the point where many of them are on the verge of extinction.

Blue Screens

Once a regular occurrence when working with Windows, blue screens (also known as the Blue Screen of Death and bluescreens) have become mostly a thing of the past. Occasionally, systems will lock up, and you can usually examine the log files to discover what was happening when this occurred and take steps to correct it.

System Lockup

The difference between a blue screen and a system lockup is whether the dump message that accompanies a blue screen is present. With a regular lockup, things just stop working. As with blue screens, these are mostly a thing of the past (the only exception may occur with laptops, which go to hibernate mode). If they occur, you can examine the log files to discover what was happening and take steps to correct it.

Input/Output Device

Errors can occur with devices such as keyboards, printers, and mice. Often, those problems are caused by the hardware—or connections—and can be readily identified. Issues with the software are generally related to the drivers and have been mentioned before in this chapter.

Application Failures

If applications fail to install, start, or load, you should examine the log files associated with them to try to isolate the problem. Many applications write logs that can be viewed with Event Viewer (choose Application Logs); others (mostly legacy) write to text files that you can find in their own directories.

Common steps to try include closing all other applications and beginning this one, reinstalling fresh, and checking to see if the application works properly on another machine.

Printing Problems

Although the topic of Windows-specific printing problems is tossed in to this objective, it's discussed in detail in the Chapter 4.

Common Error Messages

Unfortunately, there are times when systems do fail. Fortunately, when they do, they now try to explain why. Depending on the OS and settings, it's possible that the user will be asked if they want a report sent to Microsoft, dump logs will be created, log files will be written to, and so on. All of this makes your job as a troubleshooting administrator much easier than it was in the days when the solution to every problem was Ctrl+Alt+Del.

Boot problems can occur with corruption of the boot files or missing components (such as the NTLDR file being "accidentally" deleted by an overzealous user). Luckily, during the installation of the OS, log files are created in the %SystemRoot% or %SystemRoot%\Debug folder (C:\WINNT and C:\WINNT\DEBUG, by default). If you have a puzzling problem, look at these logs and see if you can find error entries there.

During startup, problems with devices that fail to be recognized properly, services that fail to start, and so on, are written to the System log and can be viewed with Event Viewer. This utility provides information about what's been going on system-wise, to help you troubleshoot problems. Event Viewer shows warnings, error messages, and records of things happening successfully. It's found in NT versions of Windows only. You can access it through Computer Management, or you can access it directly from the Administrative Tools in Control Panel.

Configuration information for Windows is stored in a special configuration database known as the Registry. This centralized database contains environmental settings for various

Windows programs. It also contains what is known as *registration* information, which details the types of file extensions associated with applications. So, when you double-click a file in Windows Explorer, the associated application runs and opens the file you double-clicked.

The Registry Editor enables you to make changes to the large hierarchical database that contains all of Windows' settings. These changes can potentially disable the entire system, so they should not be made lightly.

WARNING   Changes made in the Registry Editor are implemented immediately; you don't have the opportunity to save or reject your changes.

As with `MSCONFIG`, there is no menu command for the Registry Editor. You must run it with the Run command. `REGEDIT` is the name of the program.

Windows 2000 includes a second Registry Editor program called `REGEDT32`. This alternative program accesses the same Registry, but it does so in a slightly different way; it shows each of the major key areas in a separate window. One nice thing is that `REGEDT32` provides a Read Only mode that allows you to read the Registry without any fear of making unintended changes.

NOTE   In Windows XP, the command `REGEDT32` is still present, but running it launches `REGEDIT`; they have been rolled into a single utility.

You can configure problems with system failure to write *dump files* (debugging information) for later analysis when they occur by going to the System applet in Control Panel, choosing the Advanced tab, and clicking Settings under Startup and Recovery. Here, in addition to choosing the default OS, you can configure whether events should be written to the system log, whether an alert should be sent to the administrator, and the type of memory dump to be written.

Operating System Utilities

There are a number of files to know for this exam (and for helping solve problems in the real world, as well). Some of these run within the graphical interface, whereas others run only from the command line. To display a command prompt from Windows NT/2000/XP, you can do either of the following:

- Choose Start ➤ Run, type **CMD**, and click OK.
- Choose Start ➤ Programs ➤ Accessories ➤ Command Prompt.

Most commands can be executed through the command prompt that appears with either of these methods. To return to Windows, type **EXIT** and press Enter. If that doesn't work, restart the computer.

NOTE   When you start a command prompt from within Windows, it's sometimes called *shelling out to DOS*, which means you're creating a *shell*, or user environment, that resembles MS-DOS from within Windows. EXIT returns you to Windows from a shell in most cases.

The three categories of tools you're asked to know about are

- Disk-management tools
- System-management tools
- File-management tools

All three are discussed in the sections that follow.

Disk-Management Tools

You should be familiar with four disk-management tools:

- Disk Defragmenter
- NTBACKUP
- CHKDSK
- FORMAT

DISK DEFRAGMENTER

Disk Defragmenter reorganizes the file storage on a disk to reduce the number of files that are stored noncontiguously. This makes file retrieval faster, because the read/write heads on the disk have to move less.

There are two versions of Disk Defragmenter: a Windows version that runs from within Windows and a DOS version (DEFRAG.EXE). The Windows version is located on the System Tools submenu on the Start menu (Start ➤ All Programs ➤ Accessories ➤ System Tools ➤ Disk Defragmenter).

The available switches for the command-line version (DEFRAG.EXE) are as follows:

-a   Analyze only

-f   Force defragmentation even if disk space is low

-v   Verbose output

NTBACKUP

With Windows 2000 and XP, you can access this utility from the System Tools menu or from the Tools tab in a hard disk's Properties box. Its purpose is to back up files in a compressed format, so the backups take up less space than the original files would if they were copied. To restore the backup, you must use the same utility again, but in Restore mode. The best insurance policy you have against devastating loss when a failure occurs is a backup of the data that you can turn to when the system is rebuilt.

When you start the program, by default it begins the Backup or Restore Wizard (you can disable this default action by deselecting the Always Start in Wizard Mode check box in the first dialog). The wizard will walk you through any backup/restore operation you want to do, or you can click Advanced Mode. As mentioned in this chapter, this tool is also used to create ASR and ERD recovery backups.

CHKDSK (CHECK DISK)

The fact that CHKDSK is specified as it is in the CompTIA list is an oddity, because it's an old MS-DOS utility that is used to correct logical errors in the FAT. The most common switch for CHKDSK is /F, which fixes the errors that it finds. Without /F, CHKDSK is an "information only" utility.

Check Disk, on the other hand (not to be confused with CHKDSK), is a Windows 2000/XP graphical utility for finding and fixing logical errors in the FAT, and optionally also for checking each sector of the disk physically and relocating any readable data from damaged spots.

Check Disk isn't a menu command on the Start menu. To run it, display the Properties box for a hard disk, and then select Check Disk for Errors from the Tools tab.

FORMAT

FORMAT is a command-line utility that allows you to prepare a disk to hold data. That FORMAT command can be used to format a disk. This utility is located in the C:\Windows\System32 folder but can be accessed from any prompt. Its switches are as follows:

/V[:*label*]	Specifies a volume label
/Q	Performs a quick format
/F:*size*	Specifies the formatted size; omit for default
/B	Allocates space on the formatted disk for system files to be added later
/S	Copies system files to the formatted disk
/T:*tracks*	Specifies the number of tracks per disk side
/N:*sectors*	Specifies the number of sectors per track
/1	Formats a single side of a floppy disk
/4	Formats a 5¼" 360KB floppy disk
/8	Formats eight sectors per track
/C	Tests clusters that are currently marked as bad

You can also access a Windows-based Format utility by right-clicking a drive icon in Windows and selecting Format.

However, there is more to the story that you should know about disks. Windows NT and 2000/XP use different tools to manage partitions. Windows NT has an icon for Disk Administrator in its Administrative Tools folder, whereas Windows 2000 has a Disk Management tool in its Computer Management utility.

Where's Disk Management? In Windows 2000/XP, go to Control Panel, choose Administrative Tools, and choose Computer Management. One of the items on the folder tree in the window that appears is Disk Management.

The two utilities are very similar; both allow you to modify partition information in a graphical manner. Figure 3.4 shows the Windows XP version of Disk Management.

Disk Administrator and Computer Management can also be used to format partitions. During a format, the surface of the hard-drive platter is briefly scanned to find any possible bad spots, and the areas surrounding a bad spot are marked as bad sectors. After this, magnetic tracks are laid down in concentric circles. These tracks are where information is eventually encoded.

FIGURE 3.4   The Disk Management utility (Windows XP version)

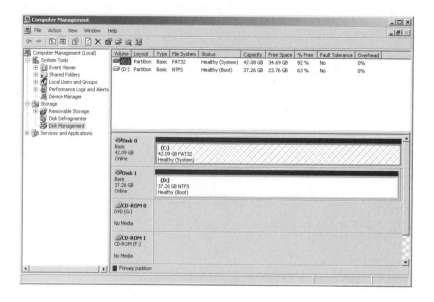

 Hard disks must be partitioned; removable disks such as CDs and floppy disks don't need this step.

 Windows 2000 and XP allow you to format as part of the install, so no advance preparation with FDISK or FORMAT is necessary when installing those OSs.

Beyond this, there are a number of options regarding how the system will store information. Each of these methods of storing information is known as a *filesystem*, and you should know about several of these:

FAT   Short for *File Allocation Table*. The FAT keeps track of where information is stored and how to retrieve it.

FAT16   Used with DOS and Windows 3.x, as well as early versions of Windows 95. FAT16 (generally just called FAT) has a number of advantages. First, it's extremely fast on small (under 500MB) drives. Second, it's a filesystem that nearly all OSs can agree on, making it excellent for dual-boot system. However, FAT also has limitations that began causing problems as Windows got bigger and faster. First, FAT has a limit of 4GB per partition. When you have hard drives that are 10GB to 30GB, this becomes a serious issue. Also, sectors on hard drives are arranged in what is called a *cluster* or *allocation unit*. In general, as a FAT16-formatted drive or drive partition increases in size, the number of sectors per cluster increases. A drive between 16MB and 128MB has 4 sectors per cluster, whereas a drive of up to 256MB has 8 sectors per cluster, and drives of up to 512MB have 16 sectors per cluster.

> Another aspect of FAT is so wonderfully obscure that test preparers rarely can resist it. The root of any FAT drive (C:\, D:\) has a hard-coded limit of 512 entries. This includes directories, files, and so on. Also, long filenames may take up more than one entry. If users reach this limit, they will be unable to save any other files in the root. This limit doesn't apply to subdirectories or to FAT32 or NTFS drives.

FAT32   Introduced with Windows 95 Release 2. FAT32 is similar to FAT but has a number of advantages. It supports larger drives and smaller allocation units. As a comparison of how the new system saves you space, a 2GB drive with FAT16 has clusters of 32KB; with FAT32, the clusters sizes are 4KB. If you save a 15KB file, FAT needs to allocate an entire 32KB cluster; FAT32 uses four 4KB clusters, for a total of 16KB. FAT32 wastes an unused 1KB, but FAT wastes 15 times as much!

The disadvantage of FAT32 is that it isn't compatible with older DOS, Windows 3.x, and Windows 95 OSs. This means that when you boot a Windows 95 Rev B. or Windows 98 FAT32-formatted partition with a DOS boot floppy, you can't read the partition.

Windows 98 includes the FAT32 Drive Converter tool (CVT1.EXE), which allows you to upgrade FAT disks to FAT32 without having to reformat them. This preserves all the information on the drive but allows you to take advantage of FAT32's enhancements.

NTFS4   Windows NT's filesystem. NTFS4 includes enhanced attributes for compressing files or for setting file security. Updating a FAT drive to NTFS is relatively easy and can be done through a command called CONVERT. This conversion doesn't destroy any information but updates the filesystem. NTFS4 is used only with Windows NT 4.0.

NTFS5   The NTFS system updated with Windows 2000. It includes enhancements such as file encryption. NTFS5 also includes support for larger drive sizes and a new feature called Dynamic Disks that does away with the concept of partitioning to improve drive performance. NTFS5 is used only with Windows 2000/XP.

System-Management Tools

There are three tools to know well for this section:

- Device Manager
- Task Manager
- MSCONFIG

We'll look at these in the following sections.

DEVICE MANAGER

Device Manager shows a list of all installed hardware and lets you add items, remove items, update drivers, and more. This is a Windows-only utility. In Windows 2000/XP, when you display the System Properties, click the Hardware tab, and then click the Device Manager button to display it.

TASK MANAGER

Task Manager shows running programs and the system resources they're consuming. It can be used for informational purposes, but it's most often used to shut down a nonresponsive application.

There are three ways to display the Task Manager. The first is to press Ctrl+Alt+Delete and click the Task Manager button. The second is to right-click in an empty location on the Taskbar and choose Task Manager from the pop-up menu. The third method is hold down Ctrl+Shift and press Esc.

A list of running tasks appears under the Applications tab; you can click one of them and then click End Task to shut it down. Because this shutdown method fails to close files gracefully, you should use it only as a last resort, not as a normal method of shutting down an application. You can also choose the Processes tab to see all processes—not just applications—running, or choose the Performance tab to see CPU, paging, memory, and other parameters. The Networking tab shows usage for all found connections, and the Users tab shows the current users and allows you to disconnect them, log them off, or send them a message.

SYSTEM CONFIGURATION EDITOR (*MSCONFIG*)

This utility, known as the System Configuration Editor, helps troubleshoot startup problems by allowing you to selectively disable individual items that normally are executed at startup. There is no menu command for this utility; you must run it with the Run command (on the Start menu). Choose Start ➢ Run, and type **MSCONFIG**. It works in most versions of Windows, although the interface window is slightly different among versions.

File-Management Tools

There are two tools to know well for this section:

- Windows Explorer
- `Attrib`

We'll look at each in the following sections.

WINDOWS EXPLORER

Discussed earlier in this chapter, Windows Explorer is a utility that allows you to accomplish a number of important file-related tasks from a single graphical interface.

Using Windows Explorer is simple; you need only a few basic instructions to start working with it. The Explorer interface has a number of parts, each of which serves a specific purpose. The top area of Explorer is dominated by a set of menus and toolbars that provide easy access to common commands. The main section of the window is divided into two panes: the left pane displays the drives and folders available to the user, and the right pane displays the contents of the currently selected folder. Along the bottom of the window, the status bar displays information about the used and free space on the current directory.

WARNING   Watch out for all the "Explorers" when you're reading test questions. Windows includes three different Explorers: Internet Explorer, Windows Explorer, and EXPLORER.EXE (the Windows shell program). Make sure you know which one the question is asking you about.

Some common actions in Explorer include the following:

Expanding a folder   You can double-click a folder to expand it (show its subfolders in the left panel) and display its contents in the right pane. Clicking the plus sign (+) to the left of a folder expands the folder without changing it.

Collapsing a folder   Clicking the minus sign (–) next to a folder collapses it.

Selecting a file   If you click a file in the right pane, Windows highlights the file by marking it with a darker color.

Selecting multiple files   The Ctrl and Shift keys allow you to select multiple files at once. Holding down Ctrl while clicking individual files selects each new file while leaving the currently selected file or files selected as well. Holding down Shift while selecting two files selects both of them and all files in between.

Opening a file   Double-clicking a file in the right pane opens the program if it's an application; if it's a file, Explorer opens it using the file extension that is configured for it.

Changing the view type   There are four primary view types: Large Icons, Small Icons, List, and Details. You can move between these views by clicking the View menu and selecting the view you prefer.

Creating new objects   To create a new file, folder, or other object, navigate to the location where you want to create the object, and then right-click in the right pane. In the menu that appears, select New, and then choose the object you want to create.

Deleting objects   To delete an object, select it, and press the Delete key on the keyboard; or right-click the object, and select Delete from the menu that appears. Doing so sends the file or folder to the Recycle Bin. To permanently delete the object, you must then empty the Recycle Bin. Alternatively, you can hold down Shift while deleting an object, and it will be permanently deleted immediately.

In addition to simplifying most file-management commands as shown here, Explorer also allows you to easily complete a number of disk-management tasks. You can format and label floppy disks, and copy the Windows system files to a floppy so that a disk may be used to boot a machine. Before you take the test, you should be extremely familiar with the Windows file-system and how these tasks are accomplished.

NOTE   *Labeling* is an optional process of giving a name to a disk. You can label both hard drives and floppies.

ATTRIB

`ATTRIB.EXE` displays or changes the attributes for one or more files. Used by itself, it displays a list of all files in the current location with attributes set. The attributes are Read Only (R), Hidden (H), System (S), and Archive (A). They can be turned off with a minus sign or turned on with a plus sign. Here are some examples:

`ATTRIB -R TEE.DOC`   Removes the read-only attribute from `TEE.DOC`.

`ATTRIB +H *.*`   Adds the Hidden attribute to all files in the current location.

Additional attributes become available in the operating system if NTFS (on NTFS-formatted disks only) is used. These additional attributes (beyond R-A-S-H) are as follows:

`Compress`   Specifies that the file is to be compressed when not in use. This saves space on the drive but slows access to the file (NTFS disks only).

`Index`   Allows the Index Service to add the file to its indexes. This increases the speed of any searches you do on the system (NTFS5 disks only).

`Encrypt`   Secures a file through an encryption algorithm. This makes it extremely difficult for anyone other than the user to access the file by encoding it using a public/private key technology (NTFS5 disks only).

Other Common Tools

You should be familiar with a handful of other utilities. Although they may not specifically be on the A+ exam, they're useful in troubleshooting problems:

`DIR`   Displays the contents of the current folder. Can be used by itself or with a file specification to narrow down the listing. Here are some examples:

   `DIR`   Displays all files in the current folder.

   `DIR ????.*`   Displays all files that are exactly four letters in name length, with any extension.

   `DIR /w`   Displays the listing in wide (multicolumn) format, with names only (fewer details).

   `DIR /p`   Displays the listing one screenful at a time. Press Enter to see the next screenful.

`VER`   Displays the current OS name and version.

`EDIT`   Opens the MS-DOS Editor utility, a text editor similar to Notepad. You can add a filename to open that file (if it exists) or create a new file (if it doesn't exist). Here is an example:

   `EDIT CONFIG.SYS`   Opens `CONFIG.SYS` if it's present in the current folder; otherwise creates it and opens it.

`COPY`   Copies files from one location to another. If the location for either the source or the destination isn't included in the command, it's assumed to be the current folder. Here are some examples:

   `COPY *.* A:\`   Copies all files from the current folder to the A: drive.

   `COPY C:\Windows\Myfile.txt`   Copies `Myfile.txt` from `C:\Windows` to the current folder.

XCOPY   Like COPY but also duplicates any subfolders. Here is an example:

XCOPY C:\BOOKS A: Copies everything from C:\BOOKS to the A: drive, and also copies any subfolders and their contents.

MD/CD/RD   Directory (folder) management commands. MD is Make Directory, CD is Change Directory, and RD is Remove Directory. When they're used without specifying a location, the current location is assumed. Here are some examples:

MD BACKUP   Makes a new directory called Backup in the current directory.

CD C:\SYSTEM   Changes to the System directory.

RD C:\SYSTEM   Deletes the System directory (assuming it's empty).

DEL   Deletes specified files. Doesn't work on folders (directories). Examples:

DEL C:\SYSTEM\BACKUP.DOC   Deletes the specified file in the specified location.

DEL *.*   Deletes all files in the current location.

    DEL doesn't act on hidden or read-only files. They will be ignored.

TYPE   Shows the text contained in the specified file on-screen. Useful for browsing through a group of text files without having to open them in an editing program. Here is an example:

TYPE CONFIG.SYS   Displays the complete contents of the file CONFIG.SYS on-screen.

Exam Essentials

Know how to boot into Safe Mode.   To access Safe Mode, you must press F8 when the operating system menu is displayed during the boot process.

Be able to identify the diagnostic procedures.   CompTIA wants you to take a systematic approach to the problem that helps you isolate the problem and quickly identify it. You should be able to list the steps given in order.

Know the filesystems.   Make sure you can explain the differences between FAT16, FAT32, NTFS4, and NTFS5 and tell which OSs they're compatible with.

Understand file attributes.   You should be able to explain the major file attributes and how to set them.

Use Windows Explorer.   This is somewhat of a no-brainer because it's a basic end-user skill, but you should be thoroughly familiar with using Windows Explorer to manage files and folders.

Preventative Operating System Maintenance

This objective requires you to know how to work with a number of utilities and covers a host of utility programs included in Windows that help technicians and experienced end users manage their systems.

Critical Information

It's important to keep your systems running at peak efficiency. One of the best ways to do this is to keep them current. Upgrades to Windows come in the form of service packs. Each service pack contains patches and fixes to OS components, as well as additional features. A service pack is a self-running program that modifies your OS. It isn't uncommon within the lifetime of an OS to have two or three service packs.

Successive service packs include all files that have been in previous ones. Therefore, if you perform a new installation, and the latest service pack is Service Pack 4, you don't need to install Service Packs 1, 2, and 3. You need install only Service Pack 4 after the installation to bring the OS up to the current feature set.

As they're released, service packs are shipped monthly for all Microsoft OSs with TechNet. (TechNet is a subscription CD service available through Microsoft.) You can also click Start ➢ Help and Support, and choose Keep Your Computer Up-to-Date with Windows Update to have the Microsoft website start an automatic check of your system and see whether your system is current. You can configure this to occur automatically by choosing the Automatic Updates applet in Control Panel. By default, this checks for updates every day at 3:00 A.M., but you can change it to any time you wish. You can also choose (although doing so isn't recommended) to not check for or install updates.

Other tools to be familiar with are discussed in the following sections.

Disk Cleanup

Disk Cleanup is a Windows-based utility that helps the user recover disk space by deleting unneeded files. It can be run from the System Tools submenu. In some versions of Windows, it automatically runs (or offers to run) when free disk space gets low.

Registry Backup

In Windows 2000, the Registry files aren't backed up automatically. You can back up the Registry using the Backup program or by creating an ERD. Note that when creating an ERD, you have to add the /s switch to back up the security information from the Registry. When the ERD is updated, the /REPAIR directory on the hard drive can also be updated with the same current configuration information that is written to the floppy disk.

Another option in all versions of Windows (2000 or XP) is to use REGEDIT or REGEDT32 to save the Registry out to a file, which can then be re-added later. This file can include all Registry information or only particular parts of the Registry's hierarchy.

 Be sure to use the Backup utility to create restore points in Windows XP.

Exam Essentials

Select the right utility for a scenario.   The test is likely to provide you with a troubleshooting or management scenario and ask you to identify which utility you would use. Familiarize yourself with all the utilities discussed.

Review Questions

1. True or false: Windows XP does not support FAT32.

2. With what Windows feature is a paging file associated?

3. What is another name for the System Tray?

4. To display a command-line interface in Windows XP, what would you execute from the Run command?

5. What files does Windows 2000/XP use to hold the Registry settings?

6. To select all files that have exactly four letters in their name and an extension that begins with D, what file specification would you use?

7. Which type of disk must be partitioned prior to formatting?

8. Which version(s) of Windows supports NTFS encryption on NTFS5 drives?

9. What utility is a Windows 2000/XP graphical utility for finding and fixing logical errors in the FAT?

10. Which Windows application most resembles the MS-DOS application EDIT?

Answers to Review Questions

1. False: Windows XP supports FAT32 as well as NTFS.
2. Virtual memory creates a paging file, or swap file, and then moves data into and out of RAM to it.
3. Microsoft uses the terms *System Tray* and *Notification Area* roughly synonymously to refer to the area where the clock and the icons for running background programs appear.
4. In Windows 2000 or XP, you use CMD.
5. Windows 2000 and XP use SAM, SECURITY, SOFTWARE, SYSTEM, and DEFAULT.
6. You would use ????.D*. The four letters in the name are represented by ????. The extension D* refers to any extension as long as it begins with *D*.
7. Hard disks must be partitioned; removable disks such as CDs and floppies do not need this step.
8. NTFS5 is used only with Windows 2000/XP.
9. Check Disk is a Windows 2000/XP graphical utility for finding and fixing logical errors in the FAT.
10. EDIT is a plain-text editor, so the answer is Notepad.

Chapter
4

Printers and Scanners

COMPTIA A+ ESSENTIALS EXAM OBJECTIVES COVERED IN THIS CHAPTER:

✓ **4.1 Identify the fundamental principles of using printers and scanners**

- Identify differences between types of printer and scanner technologies (e.g., laser, inkjet, thermal, solid ink, impact)
- Identify names, purposes, and characteristics of printer and scanner components (e.g., memory, driver, firmware) and consumables (e.g., toner, ink cartridge, paper)
- Identify the names, purposes, and characteristics of interfaces used by printers and scanners, including port and cable types; examples include the following:
  - Parallel
  - Network (e.g., NIC, print servers)
  - USB
  - Serial
  - IEEE 1394/FireWire
  - Wireless (e.g., Bluetooth, 802.11, infrared)
  - SCSI

✓ **4.2 Identify basic concepts of installing, configuring, optimizing, and upgrading printers and scanners**

- Install and configure printers/scanners
- Power and connect the device using a local or network port
- Install and update a device driver and calibrate the device
- Configure options and default settings
- Print a test page
- Optimize printer performance; for example, printer settings such as tray switching, print spool settings, device calibration, media types, and paper orientation

✓ **4.3 Identify tools, basic diagnostic procedures, and troubleshooting techniques for printers and scanners**

- Gather information about printer/scanner problems
- Identify symptoms
- Review device error codes, computer error messages, and history (e.g., event log, user reports)
- Print or scan a test page
- Use appropriate generic or vendor-specific diagnostic tools, including web-based utilities
- Review and analyze collected data
- Establish probable causes
- Review service documentation
- Review knowledge base and define and isolate the problem (e.g., software vs. hardware, driver, connectivity, printer)
- Identify solutions to identified printer/scanner problems
- Define specific cause and apply fix
- Replace consumables as needed
- Verify functionality and get user acceptance of problem fix

This domain covers a great deal of ground and accounts for 9 percent of the total exam. It appears on the IT Technician elective (where its weight is 14 percent) and on the Technical Support Technician elective (where it's 10 percent of the exam weight). The topic jumps in importance on the Depot Technician elective, where it's 20 percent of the exam.

Identify Principles of Printers and Scanners

This objective tests your knowledge of how printers work and how they connect to computers. Although the A+ exam has traditionally focused heavily on laser printers, you may also see questions about other printer types. Scanners have also been added to this iteration of the exam, and you should know their basic characteristics as well.

Critical Information

The three major areas of study for this objective are printer technologies, printer interfaces, and scanners. The printer technologies include laser, ink-jet (sometimes called ink dispersion), dot matrix, solid ink, thermal, and dye sublimation. The printer interfaces include parallel, network, and Universal Serial Bus (USB), among others.

 With regard to scanners, you're expected to know the different types of connections, which are—for the most part—identical to those for printers. Therefore, most of the focus here will be on printers.

The following sections provide details about various technologies of printers. These printers may be differentiated from one another in several ways, including the following:

Impact vs. nonimpact Impact printers physically strike an inked ribbon and therefore can print multipart forms; nonimpact printers deliver ink onto the page without striking it. Dot matrix is impact; everything else is nonimpact.

Continuous feed vs. sheet fed Continuous-feed paper feeds through the printer using a system of sprockets and tractors. Sheet-fed printers accept plain paper in a paper tray. Dot matrix is continuous feed; everything else is sheet fed.

Line vs. page Line printers print one line at a time; page printers compose the entire page in memory and then place it all on the paper at once. Dot matrix and ink-jet are line printers; laser is a page printer.

Dot-Matrix Printers

A dot-matrix printer is an impact printer; it prints by physically striking an inked ribbon, much like a typewriter. It's an impact, continuous-feed line printer.

The print head on a dot-matrix printer consists of a block of metal pins that extend and retract. These pins are triggered to extend in patterns that form letters and numbers as the print head moves across the paper. Early models, known as near letter quality (NLQ), printed using only nine pins. Later models used 21 pins and produced much better letter-quality (LQ) output.

The main advantage of dot matrix is its impact. Because it strikes the paper, you can use it to print on multipart forms. Nonimpact printers can't do that. Dot-matrix printers aren't commonly found in most offices these days because of their disadvantages, including noise, slow speed, and poor print quality.

Dot-matrix printers are still found in many warehouses, and other businesses, where multi-part forms are used.

Ink-Jet Printers

Ink-jet printers are one of the most popular types in use today. This type of printer sprays ink on the page to print text or graphics. It's a nonimpact, sheet-fed line printer.

Figure 4.1 shows an ink cartridge. Some cartridges, like this one, contain the print head for that color of ink; you get a new print head each time you replace the cartridge. On other printer models, the ink cartridge is just an ink reservoir, and the heads don't need replacing.

FIGURE 4.1   A typical ink cartridge (size: approximately 3 inches by 1 1/2 inches)

There are two kinds of ink-jet printers: *thermal* and *piezoelectric*. These terms refer to the way the ink is sprayed onto the paper. A thermal ink-jet printer heats the ink to about 400° F, creating vapor bubbles that force the ink out of the cartridge. Thermal ink-jets are also sometimes called *bubble-jets*. A piezoelectric printer does the same thing but with electricity instead of heat.

Ink-jet printers are popular because they can print in color and are inexpensive. However, their print quality isn't quite as good as that of a laser printer, and the per-page cost of ink is much higher than for a laser printer. Therefore most businesses prefer laser printers for their main printing needs, perhaps keeping one or two ink-jet printers around for situations requiring color printing.

Laser Printers

Laser printers are referred to as *page printers* because they receive their print job instructions one page at a time. They're sheet-fed, nonimpact printers. Another name for a laser printer is an *electrophotographic (EP)* printer.

LED printers are much like laser printers except they use light-emitting diodes (LEDs) instead of lasers. Their process is similar to that of laser printers. They're covered in more detail later in this chapter.

Parts of a Laser Printer

An electrophotographic laser printer consists of the following major components:

Printer controller A large circuit board that acts as the motherboard for the printer. It contains the processor and RAM to convert data coming in from the computer into a picture of a page to be printed.

Toner cartridge and drum A powdery mixture of plastic resin and iron oxide. The plastic allows it to be melted and fused to the paper, and the iron oxide allows it to be moved around via positive or negative charge. Toner comes in a cartridge, like the one shown in Figure 4.2.

The drum is light sensitive; it can be written to with the laser scanning assembly. The toner cartridge in Figure 4.2 contains the print drum, so every time you change the toner cartridge, you get a new drum. In some laser printers, the drum is a separate part that lasts longer, so you don't have to change it every time you change the toner.

FIGURE 4.2 An EP toner cartridge

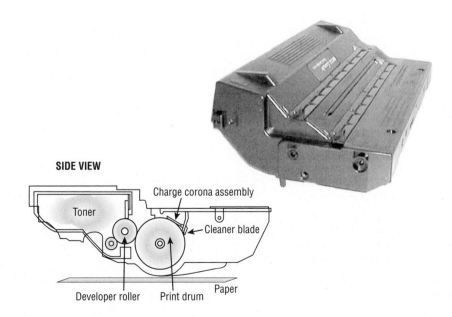

Primary corona (charge corona)   Applies a uniform negative charge (around –600V) to the drum at the beginning of the printing cycle.

Laser scanning assembly   Uses a laser beam to neutralize the strong negative charge on the drum in certain areas, so toner will stick to the drum in those areas. The laser scanning assembly uses a set of rotating and fixed mirrors to direct the beam, as shown in Figure 4.3.

Paper transport assembly   Moves the paper through the printer. The paper transport assembly consists of a motor and several rubberized rollers. These rollers are operated by an electronic stepper motor. See Figure 4.4 for an example.

FIGURE 4.3   The EP laser scanning assembly (side view and simplified top view)

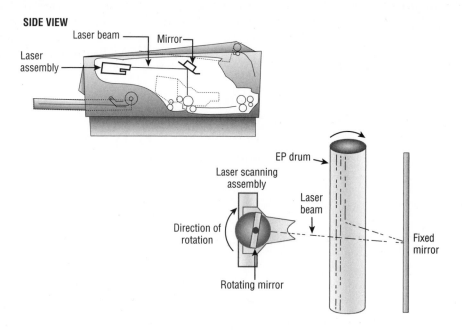

FIGURE 4.4   Paper transport rollers

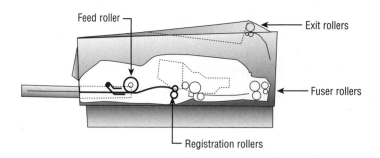

Transfer corona   Applies a uniform positive charge (about +600V) to the paper. When the paper rotates past the drum, the toner jumps off the drum and onto the paper. Then the paper passes through a static eliminator that removes the positive charge from it. (See Figure 4.5.) Some printers use a transfer corona wire; others use a transfer corona roller.

High-voltage power supply (HVPS)   Delivers the high voltages needed to make the printing process happen. It converts ordinary 120V household AC current into high-DC voltages used to energize the primary and transfer corona wires (discussed later).

DC power supply   Delivers lower voltages to components in the printer that need much lower voltages than the corona wires do (such as circuit boards, memory, and motors).

Fusing assembly   Melts the plastic resin in the toner so that it adheres to the paper. The fusing assembly contains a halogen heating lamp, a fusing roller made of Teflon-coated aluminum, and a rubberized pressure roller. The lamp heats the fusing roller, and as the paper passes between the two rollers, the pressure roller pushes the paper against the hot fusing roller, melting the toner into the paper. (See Figure 4.6.)

FIGURE 4.5   The transfer corona assembly

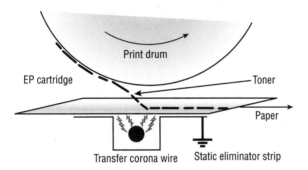

FIGURE 4.6   The fusing assembly

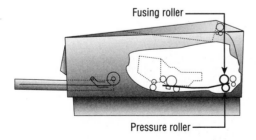

The Laser Printing Process

The laser (EP) print process consists of six steps. Here are the steps in the order you'll see them on the exam:

1. Cleaning
2. Conditioning (or charging)
3. Writing
4. Developing
5. Transferring
6. Fusing

STEP 1: CLEANING

In the first part of the laser print process, a rubber blade inside the EP cartridge scrapes any toner left on the drum into a used-toner receptacle inside the EP cartridge, and a fluorescent lamp discharges any remaining charge on the photosensitive drum (remember that the drum, being photosensitive, loses its charge when exposed to light). See Figure 4.7.

FIGURE 4.7   The cleaning step of the EP process

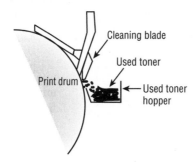

The EP cartridge is constantly cleaning the drum. It may take more than one rotation of the photosensitive drum to make an image on the paper. The cleaning step keeps the drum fresh for each use. If you didn't clean the drum, you would see ghosts of previous pages printed along with your image.

 The actual amount of toner removed in the cleaning process is quite small. The cartridge will run out of toner before the used toner receptacle fills up.

STEP 2: CONDITIONING

In the *conditioning step* (Figure 4.8), a special wire (called a *primary corona* or *charge corona*) within the EP toner cartridge (above the photosensitive drum) gets a high voltage from the HVPS. It uses this high voltage to apply a strong, uniform negative charge (around –600VDC) to the surface of the photosensitive drum.

FIGURE 4.8 The conditioning step of the EP process

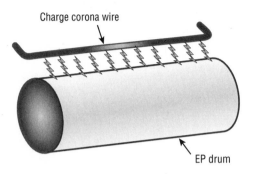

Charge corona wire

EP drum

STEP 3: WRITING

In the *writing step* of the EP process, the laser is turned on and scans the drum from side to side, flashing on and off according to the bits of information the printer controller sends it as it communicates the individual bits of the image. In each area where the laser touches the photosensitive drum, the drum's charge is severely reduced from –600VDC to a slight negative charge (around –100VDC). As the drum rotates, a pattern of exposed areas is formed, representing the images to be printed. Figure 4.9 shows this process.

At this point, the controller sends a signal to the pickup roller to feed a piece of paper into the printer, where it stops at the registration rollers.

FIGURE 4.9 The writing step of the EP process

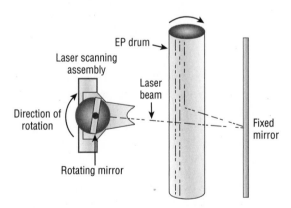

EP drum

Laser scanning assembly

Laser beam

Direction of rotation

Fixed mirror

Rotating mirror

STEP 4: DEVELOPING

Now that the surface of the drum holds an electrical representation of the image being printed, its discrete electrical charges need to be converted into something that can be transferred to a piece of paper. The EP process's *developing step* accomplishes this (Figure 4.10). In this step, toner is transferred to the areas that were exposed in the writing step.

FIGURE 4.10 The developing step of the EP process

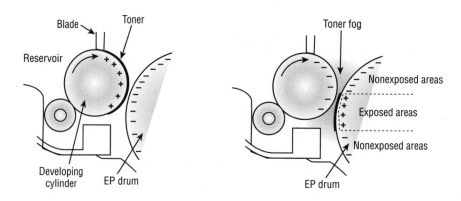

A metallic *developing roller* or *cylinder* inside an EP cartridge acquires a –600VDC charge (called a *bias voltage*) from the HVPS. The toner sticks to this roller because there is a magnet located inside the roller and because of the electrostatic charges between the toner and the developing roller. While the developing roller rotates toward the photosensitive drum, the toner acquires the charge of the roller (–600VDC). When the toner comes between the developing roller and the photosensitive drum, the toner is attracted to the areas that have been exposed by the laser (because these areas have a lesser charge, of –100VDC). The toner also is repelled from the unexposed areas (because they're at the same –600VDC charge, and like charges repel). This toner transfer creates a fog of toner between the EP drum and the developing roller.

The photosensitive drum now has toner stuck to it where the laser has written. The photosensitive drum continues to rotate until the developed image is ready to be transferred to paper in the next step.

STEP 5: TRANSFERRING

At this point in the EP process, the developed image is rotating into position. The controller notifies the registration rollers that the paper should be fed through. The registration rollers move the paper underneath the photosensitive drum, and the process of transferring the image can begin, with the *transferring step*.

The controller sends a signal to the corona wire or corona roller (depending on which one the printer has) and tells it to turn on. The corona wire/roller then acquires a strong *positive* charge (+600VDC) and applies that charge to the paper. The paper, thus charged, pulls the toner from the photosensitive drum at the line of contact between the roller and the paper, because the paper and toner have opposite charges. Once the registration rollers move the paper past the corona wire, the static-eliminator strip removes all charge from that line of the paper. Figure 4.11 details this step. If the strip didn't bleed this charge away, the paper would attract itself to the toner cartridge and cause a paper jam.

The toner is now held in place by weak electrostatic charges and gravity. It won't stay there, however, unless it's made permanent, which is the reason for the fusing step.

FIGURE 4.11   The transferring step of the EP process

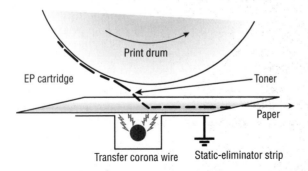

STEP 6: FUSING

In the final step, the *fusing step*, the toner image is made permanent. The registration rollers push the paper toward the fuser rollers. Once the fuser grabs the paper, the registration rollers push for only a short time more. The fuser is now in control of moving the paper.

As the paper passes through the fuser, the fuser roller melts the polyester resin of the toner, and the rubberized pressure roller presses it permanently into the paper (Figure 4.12). The paper continues on through the fuser and eventually exits the printer.

Once the paper completely exits the fuser, it trips a sensor that tells the printer to finish the EP process with the cleaning step. At this point, the printer can print another page, and the EP process can begin again.

FIGURE 4.12   The fusing step of the EP process

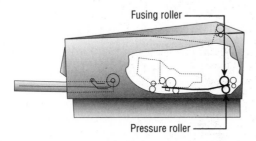

SUMMARY OF THE EP PRINT PROCESS

Figure 4.13 summarizes all the EP process printing steps. First, the printer uses a rubber scraper to clean the photosensitive drum. Then the printer places a uniform, negative, –600VDC charge on the photosensitive drum by means of a charge corona. The laser paints an image onto the photosensitive drum, discharging the image areas to a much lower voltage (–100VDC). The developing roller in the toner cartridge has charged (–600VDC) toner stuck to it. As it rolls the toner toward the photosensitive drum, the toner is attracted to (and sticks to) the areas of the photosensitive drum that the laser has discharged. The image is then transferred from the drum to the paper at its line of contact by means of the corona wire (or corona roller) with a +600VDC charge. The static-eliminator strip removes the high, positive charge from the paper, and the paper, now holding the image, moves on. The paper then enters the fuser, where the fuser roller and the pressure roller make the image permanent. The paper exits the printer, and the printer starts printing the next page or returns to its ready state.

FIGURE 4.13   The EP print process

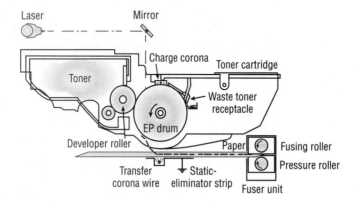

LED Printers

An LED printer uses a light-emitting diode instead of a laser. The LED isn't built into the toner cartridge; it's separate, so that when you replace the toner cartridge, all you get is new toner.

The LED printing process uses a row of small LEDs very close to the drum to expose it. Each LED is about the same size as the diameter of the laser beam used in a laser printer. Except for the writing stage, the operation is the same as the laser printing process.

LED printers are cheaper and smaller than lasers. However, they're considered lower-end printers, and they have a lower maximum dots per inch (dpi)—under 800dpi versus 1200 or more for a laser printer.

Other Printer Technologies

Besides the aforementioned technologies, you may see a question or two about several less popular ones on the A+ exam. They're all high-end color graphics printers designed for specialty professional usage:

Color laser   Works much like a regular laser printer except that it makes multiple passes over the page, one for each ink color. Consequently, the printing speed is rather low.

Thermal wax transfer   A color nonimpact line printer that uses a solid, wax-like ink. A heater melts the wax and then sprays it onto the page, somewhat like an ink-jet. The quality is very high, but so is the price ($2,500 or so). However, the wax is cheaper per page than ink-jet ink. The quality is as good as a color laser, but the speed is much faster because it needs only one pass.

Dye sublimation   Another color nonimpact line printer. This one converts a solid ink into a gas that is then applied to the paper. Color is applied in a continuous tone, rather than individual dots, and the colors are applied one at a time. The ink comes on film rolls. The paper is very expensive, as is the ink. Print speeds are very low. The quality is extremely high.

Printer Components

In addition to the physical body of the printer, components and consumables are associated with it as well. Components include the following:

Memory   As a general rule, the more memory the printer has, the better. The memory is used to hold the print jobs in the printer queue; the more users, and the larger the print jobs, the more memory you'll want.

Drivers   These are the software components of the printer (or scanner)—allowing the device to communicate with the operating system. It's important to always have the correct and most current drivers, for the greatest efficiency.

Firmware   Although drivers can be updated, firmware rarely is. Firmware is installed on the printer/scanner and can be thought of as the operating system for that device.

Consumables for printers are those items you must change as you use the printer—the variable items that get consumed and must be replenished. These include toner (or ink, depending on the type of printer you're using) and paper. Be sure to always order and use the consumables that are recommended for your machine.

Scanner Fundamentals

CompTIA has linked printers and scanners together in this objective, although they share little in common. Printers use consumables, but little is consumed by a scanner. Scanners do include firmware and drivers, and more attention is paid to that detail in the coverage of the topic for the elective exam.

Simply put: Printers are output devices, whereas scanners are input devices. You can purchase cheap scanners that work but do a poor job, and you can purchase expensive printers that can input documents all day long using a feeder. If you do a great deal of scanning, you'll want software that can convert the text on the pages scanned in to text that can be used by a word processor of your choice, and many such packages are available.

Printers and scanners use a common interface, which is discussed in the next section.

Printer and Scanner Interfaces

Besides understanding the printer's operation and the basics of a scanner, for the exam you need to understand how these devices talk to a computer. An *interface* is the collection of hardware and software that allows the device to communicate with a computer. Each printer, for example, has at least one interface, but some printers have several, in order to make them more flexible in a multiplatform environment. If a printer has several interfaces, it can usually switch between them on the fly so that several computers can print at the same time.

Communication Types

When we say *communication types*, we're talking about the hardware technologies involved in getting the information to and from the computer. There are eight major types:

Legacy serial   This is the traditional RS-232 serial port found on most PCs. The original printer interface on the earliest computers, it has fallen out of favor and is seldom used anymore for printing because it's so slow.

Legacy parallel   Until recently, the parallel port on a PC was the overwhelming favorite interface for connecting printers, to the point where the parallel port has become synonymous with *printer port*. It sends data 8 bits at a time (in parallel) and uses a cable with a male DB-25 connector at the computer and a 36-bin Centronics male connector at the printer. Its main drawback is its cable length, which must be less than 10 feet.

Universal Serial Bus (USB)   The most popular type of printer interface as this book is being written is the USB. It's the most popular interface for just about every peripheral. The benefit for printers is that it has a higher transfer rate than either serial or parallel and it automatically recognizes new devices. USB is also fully plug-and-play, and it allows several printers to be connected at once without adding ports or using up additional system resources.

Network   Most large-environment printers (primarily laser and LED printers) have a special interface that allows them to be hooked directly to a network. These printers have a network interface card (NIC) and ROM-based software that let them communicate with networks, servers, and workstations.

The type of network interface used on the printer depends on the type of network the printer is being attached to. For example, if you're using a Token Ring network, the printer should have a Token Ring interface.

SCSI   Although it isn't a common interface for printers, external SCSI can be used for a printer. See Chapter 1 for more information about SCSI.

IEEE 1394/FireWire   This is a high-speed serial alternative to USB. It's less commonly used for printers than USB is, but FireWire printer interfaces do exist.

Radio Wave   Bluetooth is an infrared technology that can connect a printer to a computer at a range of about 35 feet, provided there is an unblocked line of sight.

Wireless   A network-enabled printer that has a wireless adapter can participate in a wireless Ethernet (IEEE 802.11b, a, or g) network, just as it would as a wired network client.

Exam Essentials

Know the common types of printers.   Know and understand the types of printers, such as impact printers, ink-jet printers, and laser printers (page printers), as well as their interfaces and print media.

Know the fundamentals of scanners.   Whereas printers are output devices, scanners can be thought of as input devices.

Understand the process of printing for each type of printer.   Each type of printer puts images or text on paper. Understand the process that each type of printer uses to accomplish this task.

Know the specific components of each type of printer.   Each type of printer uses similar components to print. Know the different components that make up each type of printer, and their jobs.

Know and understand the print process of a laser printer.   You'll almost certainly be asked questions about certain processes of a laser printer. Know and understand the different steps that make up the print process of a laser printer.

Know the possible interfaces that can be used for printing.   The eight types are legacy parallel, legacy serial, USB, FireWire, network, wireless, infrared, and SCSI.

Work with Printers and Scanners

Knowing about printers and scanners isn't nearly enough. You must also know how to configure these to be able to use them and allow users to access them. Because much of this depends on the software involved, there is overlap between the material here and in Chapter 12.

Critical Information

It's important to install printers and scanners per the instructions included with the devices. Both of these can be connected locally or through a network, and you want to make sure they're functioning properly. Key components to making sure they're functioning properly—and continue to do so—include keeping the drivers and firmware updated and configuring them for optimal use in your setting.

Firmware Updates

Printers and scanners resemble a computer in many ways. Like a computer, they can have their own motherboard, memory, and CPU. They also have firmware—that is, software permanently stored on a chip. If you're using an old computer with a new operating system, an update may be available for the printer's or scanner's firmware. You can find out that information at the printer/scanner manufacturer's website and download the update from there along with a utility program for performing the update.

Printer Configuration

To add a printer, whether it's local or networked, you start the Add Printer Wizard found in Windows XP by accessing Start ➢ Printers and Faxes and then choosing Add a Printer. Once the printer is installed, you can right-click its icon at any time beneath this dialog and choose Properties from the pop-up menu. From here, you can print a test page and configure such items as sharing, ports, device settings (including tray selection) and so on. Figure 4.14 shows the spooling options and the settings to allow you to configure the printer to be available only at certain times, and Figure 4.15 shows the tray settings.

FIGURE 4.14   Configure the advanced options.

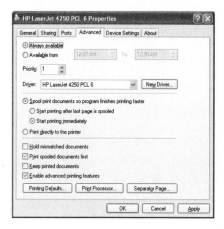

FIGURE 4.15   Configure the tray and other settings.

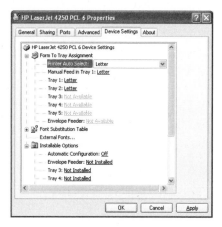

More information on printer installation/configuration, as it relates to the elective exams, can be found in Chapter 12.

Scanner Configuration

To add a scanner in Windows XP, you start the Scanner and Camera Installation Wizard found in Windows XP by accessing Start ➢ Control Panel ➢ Scanners and Cameras and then choosing Add an Imaging Device. Once the scanner is installed, you can right-click its icon at any time beneath this dialog and choose Properties from the pop-up menu. From here, you can test the scanner (as shown in Figure 4.16) and configure such items color management.

FIGURE 4.16   A command button allows you to test the scanner.

If the diagnostic test is successful, a dialog box telling you that it succeeded will appear.

Exam Essentials

Know how to install printers and scanners.   The manufacturer is the best source of information about installing printers and scanners. You should, however, know of the wizards available in Windows, as well.

Know to keep firmware up-to-date.   Firmware updates can be found at the manufacturer's website and installed according to the instructions accompanying them.

Recognize and Resolve Common Problems

Not only is troubleshooting on the test, but you may have to accomplish these tasks on a daily basis, depending on your environment. Your ability to get a down printer or scanner working will make you more valuable to your employer.

Critical Information

In the real world, you'll find that a large portion of all service calls relate to printing problems. This section will give you some general guidelines and common printing solutions to resolve printing problems.

Printer Driver Issues

Many problems with a printer that won't work with the operating system or that prints the wrong characters can be traced to problems with its software. Computers and printers can't talk to each other by themselves. They need interface software to translate software commands into commands the printer can understand.

For a printer to work with a particular operating system, a driver must be installed for it. This driver specifies the *page description language (PDL)* the printer understands, as well as information about the printer's characteristics (paper trays, maximum resolution, and so on). For laser printers, there are two popular PDLs: Adobe PostScript and Hewlett-Packard Printer Control Language (PCL). Almost all laser printers use one or both of these.

If the wrong printer driver is selected, the computer will send commands in the wrong language. If that occurs, the printer will print several pages of garbage (even if only one page of information was sent). This "garbage" isn't garbage at all, but the printer PDL commands printed literally as text instead of being interpreted as control commands.

 Although HP doesn't recommend using any printer driver other than the one designed for the specific printer, in some cases, you can increase the printing performance (speed) of HP LaserJet and DeskJet printers by using older drivers that don't support the newer high-definition printing. I have also had cases where software packages would not function with newer HP drivers. To increase speed or correct printing problems with HP LaserJet printers, follow this rule of thumb: If you're using a 5-series printer (5Si), try a 4-series driver; if that doesn't work, reduce the driver by one series. If a LaserJet III doesn't work, try the LaserJet driver, which should be last on your list of the default drivers built into Windows. In 90 percent of cases, this driver will fix printing problems with some applications.

Memory Errors

A printer can have several types of memory errors. The most common is insufficient memory to print the page. Sometimes you can circumvent this problem by doing any of the following:

- Turn off the printer to flush out its RAM, and then turn it back on and try again.

- Print at a lower resolution. (Adjust this setting in the printer's properties in Windows.)

- Change the page being printed so it's less complex.

- Try a different printer driver if your printer supports more than one PDL. (For example, try switching from PostScript to PCL or vice versa.) Doing so involves installing another printer driver.

Printer Hardware Troubleshooting

This section covers the most common types of hardware printer problems you'll run into. We'll break the information into three areas, for the three main types of printers in use today.

Dot-Matrix Printer Problems

Dot-matrix printers are relatively simple devices. Therefore, only a few problems usually arise. We'll cover the most common problems and their solutions here.

LOW PRINT QUALITY

Problems with print quality are easy to identify. When the printed page comes out of the printer, the characters may be too light or have dots missing from them. Table 4.1 details some of the most common print-quality problems, their causes, and their solutions.

TABLE 4.1   Common Dot-Matrix Print-Quality Problems

Characteristics	Cause	Solution
Consistently faded or light characters	Worn-out print ribbon	Replace ribbon with a new, vendor-recommended ribbon.
Print lines that go from dark to light as the print head moves across the page	Print ribbon advance gear slipping	Replace ribbon advance gear or mechanism.
A small, blank line running through a line of print (consistently)	Print-head pin stuck inside the print head	Replace the print head.
A small, blank line running through a line of print (intermittently)	A broken, loose, or shorting print-head cable, or a sticking print head	Secure or replace the print-head cable. Replace the print head, or clean it.
A small, dark line running through a line of print	Print-head pin stuck in the out position	Replace the print head. (Pushing in the pin may damage the print head.)
Printer makes a printing noise, but no print appears on the page	Worn, missing, or improperly installed ribbon cartridge, or the print head gap set too large	Replace the ribbon cartridge correctly, or adjust the print-head gap.
Printer prints garbage	Cable partially unhooked, wrong driver selected, or a bad printer control board (PCB)	Hook up the cable correctly, select the correct driver, or replace the PCB (respectively).

PRINTOUT JAMS INSIDE THE PRINTER

A paper jam happens when something prevents the paper from advancing through the printer evenly. Print jobs jam for two major reasons: an obstructed paper path or stripped drive gears.

An obstructed paper path is often difficult to find. Usually it means disassembling the printer to find the bit of paper or other foreign substance that's blocking the paper path. A common obstruction is a piece of the *perf*—the perforated sides of tractor-feed paper—that has torn off and gotten crumpled up and then lodged into the paper path. It may be necessary to remove the platen roller and feed mechanism to get at the obstruction.

STEPPER MOTOR PROBLEMS

A *stepper motor* is a motor that can move in very small increments. Printers use stepper motors to move the print head back and forth as well as to advance the paper (these are called the *carriage motor* and *main motor*, respectively). These motors get damaged when they're forced in any direction while the power is on. This includes moving the print head over to install a printer ribbon, as well as moving the paper-feed roller to align paper. These motors are very sensitive to stray voltages. And, if you're rotating one of these motors by hand, you're essentially turning it into a small generator, thereby damaging it!

A damaged stepper motor is easy to detect. Damage to the stepper motor will cause it to lose precision and move farther with each step. Lines of print will be unevenly spaced if the main motor is damaged (which is more likely). Characters will be scrunched together if the print-head motor goes bad. If the motor is bad enough, it won't move at all in any direction; it may even make high-pitched squealing noises. If any of these symptoms show themselves, it's time to replace one of these motors. Stepper motors are usually expensive to replace—about half the cost of a new printer. However, because dot-matrix printers are old technology and difficult to find, you may have no choice but to replace the motor if the printer is essential and is no longer available new.

Ink-Jet Printers

Ink-jet printers are the most commonly sold printers for home use. For this reason, you need to understand the most common problems with ink-jet printers so your company can service them effectively.

PRINT QUALITY

The majority of ink-jet printer problems are quality problems. Ninety-nine percent of these can be traced to a faulty ink cartridge. With most ink-jet printers, the ink cartridge contains the print head and the ink. The major problem with this assembly can be described by, "If you don't use it, you lose it." The ink will dry out in the small nozzles and block them if they aren't used at least once a week.

An example of a quality problem is when thin blank lines or colored stripes appear on the page. This is caused by a plugged hole in at least one of the small, pinhole ink nozzles in the print cartridge. Replacing the ink cartridge solves this problem easily. You may also be able to clear the clogged ink jet by running the printer's cleaning routine, either by pressing buttons on the printer or by issuing a command through the printer's driver in Windows.

If an ink cartridge becomes damaged or develops a hole, it can put too much ink on the page, and the letters will smear. Again, the solution is to replace the ink cartridge. (However, a very small amount of smearing is normal if the pages are laid on top of each other immediately after printing.)

One final print-quality problem that doesn't directly involve the ink cartridge is characterized by the print quickly going from dark to light and then to nothing. As we already mentioned, ink cartridges dry out if not used. That's why the manufacturers include a small suction pump inside the printer that primes the ink cartridge before each print cycle. If this priming pump is broken or malfunctioning, this problem will manifest itself, and the pump will need to be replaced.

If the problem of the ink quickly going from dark to light and then disappearing ever happens to you, and you really need to print a couple of pages, try this trick: Take the ink cartridge out of the printer. Squirt some window cleaner on a paper towel, and gently tap the print head against the wet paper towel. The force of the tap plus the solvents in the window cleaner should dislodge any dried ink, and the ink will flow freely again.

PAPER JAMS

Ink-jet printers usually have simple paper paths. Therefore, paper jams due to obstructions are less likely. They're still possible, however, so an obstruction shouldn't be overlooked as a possible cause of jamming.

Paper jams in ink-jet printers are usually due to one of two things:

- A worn pickup roller
- The wrong type of paper

The pickup roller usually has one or two D-shaped rollers mounted on a rotating shaft. When the shaft rotates, one edge of the D rubs against the paper, pushing it into the printer. When the roller gets worn, it becomes smooth and doesn't exert enough friction against the paper to push it into the printer.

If the paper used in the printer is too smooth, it causes the same problem. Pickup rollers use friction, and smooth paper doesn't offer much friction. If the paper is too rough, on the other hand, it acts like sandpaper on the rollers, wearing them smooth. Here's a rule of thumb for paper smoothness: paper slightly smoother than a new dollar bill will work fine.

Laser and Page Printers

Most of the problems with laser printers can be diagnosed with knowledge of the inner workings of the printer and a little common sense.

PAPER JAMS

Laser printers today run at copier speeds. As a result, their most common problem is paper jams. Paper can get jammed in a printer for several reasons. First, feed jams happen when the paper feed rollers get worn (similar to feed jams in ink-jet printers). The solution to this problem is easy: Replace the worn rollers.

If your paper-feed jams are caused by worn pickup rollers, there is something you can do to get your printer working while you're waiting for the replacement pickup rollers. Scuff the feed roller(s) with a Scotch-Brite pot-scrubber pad (or something similar) to roughen up the feed rollers. This trick works only once. After that, the rollers aren't thick enough to touch the paper.

Another cause of feed jams is related to the drive of the pickup roller. The drive gear (or clutch) may be broken or have teeth missing. Again, the solution is to replace it. To determine if the problem is a broken gear or worn rollers, print a test page, but leave the paper tray out. Look into the paper feed opening with a flashlight, and see if the paper pickup roller(s) are turning evenly and don't skip. If they turn evenly, the problem is more than likely worn rollers.

Worn exit rollers can also cause paper jams. These rollers guide the paper out of the printer into the paper-receiving tray. If they're worn or damaged, the paper may catch on its way out of the printer. These types of jams are characterized by a paper jam that occurs just as the paper is getting to the exit rollers. If the paper jams, open the rear door and see where the paper is. If the paper is very close to the exit roller, the exit rollers are probably the problem.

The solution is to replace all the exit rollers. You must replace all of them at the same time, because even one worn exit roller can cause the paper to jam. Besides, they're inexpensive. Don't be cheap and skimp on these parts if you need to have them replaced.

Paper jams can be the fault of the paper. If your printer consistently tries to feed multiple pages into the printer, the paper isn't dry enough. If you live in an area with high humidity, this could be a problem. I've heard some solutions that are pretty far out but that work (like keeping the paper in a Tupperware-type of airtight container or microwaving it to remove moisture). The best all-around solution, however, is humidity control and to keep the paper wrapped until it's needed. Keep the humidity around 50 percent or lower (but above 25 percent if you can, in order to avoid problems with electrostatic discharge).

Finally, a metal, grounded strip called the *static eliminator strip* inside the printer drains the corona charge away from the paper after it has been used to transfer toner from the EP cartridge. If that strip is missing, broken, or damaged, the charge will remain on the paper and may cause it to stick to the EP cartridge, causing a jam. If the paper jams after reaching the corona assembly, this may be the cause.

BLANK PAGES

Blank pages are a somewhat common occurrence in laser and page printers. Somehow, the toner isn't being put on the paper. The toner cartridge is the source for most quality problems, because it contains most of the image-formation pieces for laser and page printers. Let's start with the obvious. A blank page will come out of the printer if there is no toner in the toner cartridge. It's easy to check: Just open the printer, remove the toner cartridge, and gently shake it. You'll be able to hear if there's toner inside the cartridge. If it's empty, replace it with a known, good, manufacturer-recommended toner cartridge.

Another issue that crops up rather often is the problem of using refilled or reconditioned toner cartridges. During their recycling process, these cartridges may be filled with the wrong kind of toner (for example, one with an incorrect charge). This may cause toner to be repelled from the EP drum instead of attracted to it. Thus, there's no toner on the page because there was no toner on the EP drum to begin with. The solution is to replace the toner cartridge with the type recommended by the manufacturer.

A third problem related to toner cartridges happens when someone installs a new toner cartridge and forgets to remove the sealing tape that is present to keep the toner in the cartridge during shipping. The solution to this problem is as easy as it is obvious: remove the toner cartridge from the printer, remove the sealing tape, and reinstall the cartridge.

Another cause of blank pages is a damaged or missing corona wire. If a wire is lost or damaged, the developed image won't transfer from the EP drum to the paper. Thus, no image appears on the printout. To determine if this is causing your problem, do the first half of the self-test. If there is an image on the drum but not on the paper, you'll know that the corona assembly isn't doing its job.

To check whether the corona assembly is causing the problem, open the cover and examine the wire (or roller, if your printer uses one). The corona wire is hard to see, so you may need a flashlight. You'll know if it's broken or missing just by looking (it will either be in pieces or just not there). If it's not broken or missing, the problem may be related to the HVPS. The corona wire (or roller) is a relatively inexpensive part and can be easily replaced with some patience and the removal of two screws.

The HVPS supplies high-voltage, low-current power to both the charging and transfer corona assemblies in laser and page printers. If it's broken, neither will work properly. If the self-test shows an image on the drum but none on the paper, and the corona assembly is present and not damaged, then the HVPS is at fault.

ALL-BLACK PAGES

This happens when the charging unit (the charge corona wire or charge corona roller) in the toner cartridge malfunctions and fails to place a charge on the EP drum. Because the drum is grounded, it has no charge. Anything with a charge (like toner) will stick to it. As the drum rotates, all the toner will be transferred to the page, and a black page will form.

This problem wastes quite a bit of toner, but it can be fixed easily. The solution (again) is to replace the toner cartridge with a known, good, manufacturer-recommended one. If that doesn't solve the problem, then the HVPS is at fault (it's not providing the high voltage the charge corona needs to function).

REPETITIVE SMALL MARKS OR DEFECTS

Repetitive marks occur frequently in heavily used (as well as older) laser printers. The problem may be caused by toner spilled inside the printer. It can also be caused by a crack or chip in the EP drum (this mainly happens with recycled cartridges). These cracks can accumulate toner. In both cases, some of the toner will get stuck onto one of the rollers. Once this happens, every time the roller rotates and touches a piece of paper, it will leave toner smudges spaced a roller circumference apart.

The solution is simple: Clean or replace the offending roller. To help you figure out which roller is causing the problem, the service manuals contain a chart like the one in Figure 4.17. To use the chart, place the printed page next to the chart. Align the first occurrence of the smudge with the top arrow. The next smudge will line up with one of the other arrows. The arrow it lines up with tells you which roller is causing the problem. (This chart in the figure is only an example; your printer will have different-size rollers and will need a different chart. Also, this chart isn't to scale.)

FIGURE 4.17   Laser printer roller-circumference chart

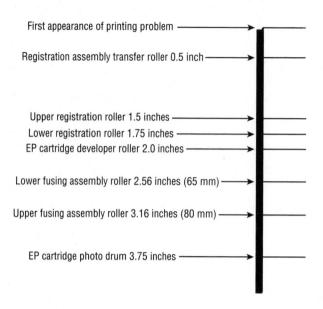

VERTICAL BLACK LINES ON THE PAGE

A groove or scratch in the EP drum can cause the problem of vertical black lines running down all or part of the page. Because a scratch is lower than the surface, it doesn't receive as much (if any) of a charge as the other areas. The result is that toner sticks to it as though it were discharged. Because the groove may go around the circumference of the drum, the line may go all the way down the page.

Another possible cause of vertical black lines is a dirty charge corona wire. A dirty charge corona wire prevents a sufficient charge from being placed on the EP drum. Because the EP drum has almost zero charge, toner sticks to the areas that correspond to the dirty areas on the charge corona wire.

The solution to the first problem is, as always, to replace the toner cartridge (or EP drum, if your printer uses a separate EP drum and toner). You can also solve the second problem with a new toner cartridge, but in this case that would be an extreme solution. It's easier to clean the charge corona with the brush supplied with the cartridge.

VERTICAL WHITE LINES ON THE PAGE

Vertical white lines running down all or part of the page are relatively common problems on older printers, especially ones that see little maintenance. They're caused by foreign matter (more than likely toner) caught on the transfer corona wire. The dirty spots keep the toner from being transmitted to the paper (at those locations, that is), with the result that streaks form as the paper progresses past the transfer corona wire.

The solution is to clean the corona wires. Some printers come with a small corona-wire brush to help in this procedure. To use it, remove the toner cartridge and run the brush in the charge corona groove on top of the toner cartridge. Replace the cartridge and use the brush to brush away any foreign deposits on the transfer corona. Be sure to put it back in its holder when you're finished.

IMAGE SMUDGING

If you can pick up a sheet from a laser printer, run your thumb across it, and have the image come off on your thumb, then you have a fuser problem. The fuser isn't heating the toner and fusing it into the paper. This could be caused by a number of things—but all of them can be taken care of with a fuser replacement. For example, if the halogen light inside the heating roller has burned out, that will cause the problem. The solution is to replace the fuser. The fuser can be replaced with a rebuilt unit, if you prefer. Rebuilt fusers are almost as good as new fusers, and some even come with guarantees. Plus, they cost less.

 The whole fuser may not need to be replaced. You can order fuser components from parts suppliers and then rebuild them. For example, if the fuser has a bad lamp, you can order a lamp and replace it in the fuser.

Another, similar problem happens when small areas of smudging repeat themselves down the page. Dents or cold spots in the fuser heat roller cause this problem. The only solution is to replace either the fuser assembly or the heat roller.

GHOSTING

Ghosting means you can see light images of previously printed pages on the current page. This is caused by one of two things: bad erasure lamps or a broken cleaning blade. If the erasure lamps are bad, the previous electrostatic discharges aren't completely wiped away. When the EP drum rotates toward the developing roller, some toner sticks to the slightly discharged areas. A broken cleaning blade, on the other hand, causes old toner to build up on the EP drum and consequently present itself in the next printed image.

Replacing the toner cartridge solves the second problem. Solving the first problem involves replacing the erasure lamps in the printer. Because the toner cartridge is the least expensive cure, you should try that first. Usually, replacing the toner cartridge will solve the problem. If it doesn't, you'll then have to replace the erasure lamps.

PRINTER PRINTS PAGES OF GARBAGE

This has happened to everyone at least once. You print a 1-page letter, and 10 pages of what looks like garbage come out of the printer. This problem comes from either the print driver software or the formatter board:

Printer driver   The correct printer driver needs to be installed for the printer you have. For example, if you have an HP LaserJet III, then that is the driver you need to install. Once the driver has been installed, it must be configured for the correct page description language: PCL or PostScript. Most HP LaserJet printers use PCL (but can be configured for PostScript). Determine what page description your printer has been configured for, and set the print driver to the same setting. If this isn't done, you'll get garbage out of the printer.

Most printers with LCD displays indicate that they're in PostScript mode with *PS* or *PostScript* somewhere in the display.

If the problem is the wrong driver setting, the garbage the printer prints looks like English. That is, the words are readable, but they don't make any sense.

Formatter board   The other cause of several pages of garbage being printed is a bad formatter board. This circuit board takes the information the printer receives from the computer and turns it into commands for the various components in the printer. Problems with the formatter board generally produce wavy lines of print or random patterns of dots on the page.

It's relatively easy to replace the formatter board in a laser printer. Usually this board is installed underneath the printer and can be removed by loosening two screws and pulling the board out. Typically, replacing the formatter board also replaces the printer interface, which is another possible source of garbage printouts.

Problems with Consumables

Just as it's important to use the correct printer interface and printer software, you must use the correct printer supplies. These supplies include the print media (what you print on) and the consumables (what you print with). The quality of the final print job has a great deal to do with the print supplies.

Paper

Most people don't give much thought to the kind of paper they use in their printers. It's a factor that can have a tremendous effect on the quality of the hard-copy printout, however, and the topic is more complex than people think. For example, if the wrong paper is used (too thick for your printer, etc.), it can cause the paper to jam frequently and possibly even damage components.

The way that you install the paper on a laser printer can determine whether you end up with a curl in it or not. Sometimes the arrow on the package really does matter.

Transparencies

Transparencies are still used for presentations made with overhead projectors, even with the explosion of programs like Microsoft PowerPoint and peripherals like LCD computer displays, both of which let you show a whole roomful of people exactly what's on your computer screen. PowerPoint has an option to print slides, and you can use any program to print anything you want on a transparent sheet of plastic or vinyl for use with an overhead projector. The problem is, these "papers" are *exceedingly* difficult for printers to work with. That's why special transparencies were developed for use with laser and ink-jet printers.

Each type of transparency was designed for a particular brand and model of printer. Again, check the printer's documentation to find out which type of transparency works in that printer. Don't use any other type of transparency.

Never run transparencies through a laser printer without first checking to see if they're the type recommended by the printer manufacturer. The heat from the fuser will melt most other transparencies, and they will wrap themselves around it. It's impossible to clean a fuser after this has happened. The fuser will have to be replaced. *Use only the transparencies that are recommended by the printer manufacturer.*

Ink, Toner, or Ribbon

Besides print media, other things in the printer run out and need to be replenished. These items are the print consumables. Most consumables are used to form the images on the print media. Printers today use two main types of consumables: ink and toner.

To avoid problems relating to the ink, toner, or ribbon, use only brand-new supplies from reputable manufacturers. Don't use remanufactured or refilled cartridges.

Cleaning Pads

Some toner cartridges come with a cleaning pad. It's a long, thin strip of felt mounted on a piece of plastic. If a toner cartridge includes one, then somewhere inside the printer is a dirty felt pad that needs to be swapped out with the new one. Failing to do this when you change toner cartridges can cause problems.

Environmental Issues for Printers

Just like computers, printers can suffer from operating in an inhospitable environment such as one that is extreme in temperature or very dusty or smoky. Printers work best in a cool, clean environment where the humidity is between 50 and 80 percent.

Scanner Issues

Color profiles are associated with scanners and accessible through the Color Management tab on the properties for the device. Settings within these profiles can affect the colors of your images; you can add/remove profiles as needed.

Many scanner issues can also be resolved by double-checking the connection—both cabling to the computer and power. You should always make sure you're using the latest drivers as well (check the manufacturer's website).

Exam Essentials

Know the common printing problems listed.   Understand the most common problems that occur in an environment.

Know the possible fixes for the common problem types.   Each type of printer has its own common issues. Be familiar with the most likely repair options for each common problem.

Know how to select good-quality, appropriate consumables.   Using appropriate paper and new (not remanufactured) toner, ink, or ribbon can prevent many problems.

Review Questions

1.   Give two examples of line printers.

2.   What advantage does dot matrix have over other printer technologies?

3.   What is the purpose of the primary corona in the laser printing process?

4.   List the six steps in the laser printing process in the correct order.

5.   If there is loose toner on the paper after a laser print, which part is defective?

6.   What are some advantages of USB as a printer interface, as opposed to legacy parallel?

7.   What do you need to do if there are stripes on an ink-jet printout?

8.   True or false: A laser printer that prints a completely black page may be suffering from a nonfunctioning fuser.

9.   Why should you not use transparency film designed for an ink-jet printer in a laser printer?

10. What is the most common cause of small marks or defects in the same spot on every page of a laser printer's printout?

Answers to Review Questions

1. Ink-jet, dot matrix

2. The ability to print on multipart forms

3. It applies a uniform negative charge to the drum.

4. Cleaning, conditioning, writing, developing, transferring, fusing

5. Fuser

6. USB is fully plug-and-play, it allows several printers to be connected at once without adding additional ports or using up additional system resources, and it is faster.

7. Clean the ink jets; one or more is clogged.

8. False. A completely black page results from the primary (charging) corona malfunctioning.

9. Because the laser printer's fuser will melt it.

10. A scratch on the drum

Chapter

5

Networks

COMPTIA A+ ESSENTIAL EXAM OBJECTIVES COVERED IN THIS CHAPTER:

✓ **5.1 Identify the fundamental principles of networks**

- Describe basic networking concepts

- Identify names, purposes, and characteristics of the common network cables

- Identify names, purposes, and characteristics of network cables (e.g., RJ45 and RJ11, ST/SC/LC, USB, IEEE 1394 / FireWire)

- Identify names, purposes, and characteristics (e.g., definition, speed, and connections) of technologies for establishing connectivity

✓ **5.2 Install, configure, optimize, and upgrade networks**

- Install and configure network cards (physical address)

- Install, identify, and obtain wired and wireless connections

✓ **5.3 Identify tools, diagnostic procedures, and troubleshooting techniques for networks**

- Explain status indicators (e.g., speed, connection and activity lights, and wireless signal strength)

CompTIA offers a number of other exams and certification on networking (Network+, i-Net+, and so on), but to become A+ certified, you must have good knowledge of basic networking skills. Not only do you need to know how networks operate, but you also need to know how to troubleshoot and identify common problems with them. Three subobjectives in this category focus more on general knowledge than specific. These topics are tested again—in more specific implementations—in the elective exam (see Chapter 13).

Identify the Fundamental Principles of Networks

You're expected to know the basic concepts of networking as well as the different types of cabling that can be used. For the latter, you should be able to identify connectors and cables from figures even if those figures are crude line art (think shadows) appearing in pop-up exhibit boxes.

Critical Information

It's important to know how network addressing works and the various protocols that are in use in networks today. Although TCP/IP has the lion's share of the networking market, it isn't the only protocol that may be used, and CompTIA expects you to have a broad range of knowledge in this category.

Basic Concepts

Duplexing is the means by which communication takes place. With *full duplexing*, everyone can send and receive at the same time. With *half duplexing*, communications travel in both directions but in only one direction at any given time. Think of a road where construction is being done on one lane—traffic can go in both directions but in only one direction at a time at that location.

Networks consist of servers and clients. A *server* is a dedicated machine offering services such as file and print sharing. A *client* is any individual workstation accessing the network. *Thin clients* are network clients that typically can't boot (and sometimes can't function) without the network. Normally, they lack a hard drive and must boot from the network in order to be operable.

A *local area network* (LAN) is a network that is geographically confined within a small space—a room, a building, and so on. Because it's confined, and does not have to span a great distance, it can normally offer higher speeds. A *wide area network* (WAN) is a collection of two or more LANs, typically connected by routers. The geographic limitation is removed, but WAN speeds are traditionally less than LAN speeds.

Segments are divisions of a LAN made possible if you're using certain topologies—think of them as subnets or logical groupings of computers. The division of the network into segments can be accomplished through the use of switching hubs, multiplexers, bridges, routers, or brouters.

A *server* is a computer that serves something to others with files, print capabilities, and so on. A *workstation* is a client machine that accesses services elsewhere (normally from a server). A *host* is any machine or interface that participates in a TCP/IP network – whether as a client or a server. Every interface on a TCP/IP network that must be issued an IP address is considered a host.

A peer-to-peer network—also known as a *workgroup*—consists of a number of workstations (two or more) that share resources among themselves (see Figure 5.1). The resources shared are traditionally file and print access, and every computer has the capacity to act as a workstation (by accessing resources from another machine) and as a server (by offering resources to other machines). The only security that can be placed on such an environment is *share-level*: It's on the resource that is being shared. If the user knows the password for that share (or there isn't one), then they're able to access it.

In a server-based network (known as a *client/server network*), users log on to the server by supplying a username and password (see Figure 5.2). They're then authenticated for the duration of their session. Rather than requiring users to give a password for every resource they want to access (share-level), security is based on how they authenticated themselves at the beginning of their session. This is known as *user-level* security, and it's much more powerful than share-level security.

The advantage of a peer-to-peer network is that the cost is lower—you need only add cards and cables to the computers you already have if you're running an operating system that allows such modifications. With a server-based network, you must buy a server—a dedicated machine—and thus the costs are higher. It's never recommended that a peer-to-peer network be used for more than 10 workstations, because the administration and management become so significant that a server-based network makes far greater sense.

FIGURE 5.1   The peer-to-peer model

FIGURE 5.2   The server-based model

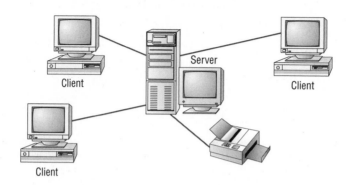

The *cable* is the physical pathway for communications, and the *network interface card* (NIC) is the physical entity that goes into the computer and is attached to the cable. A *router* is used to connect LANs together; you can even use a router to connect dissimilar topologies that use the same protocol, because it's operating high enough up the Open Systems Interconnection (OSI) model that physical specifications don't apply.

With *baseband*, the entire medium's capacity is used for one signal. The speed possibilities are thus increased because the entire channel is utilized. With *broadband*, the medium is used to carry multiple signals, but all unidirectionally. Some common implementations of broadband include DSL, cable, and satellite.

A *gateway* can have two meanings. In TCP/IP, a gateway is the address of the machine to send data to that isn't intended for a host on this network (in other words, a default gateway). A gateway is also a physical device operating between the Transport and Application layers of the OSI model that can send data between dissimilar systems. The best example of the latter is a mail gateway—it doesn't matter which two networks are communicating; the gateway allows them to exchange email.

The International Standards Organization (ISO) created the OSI model to outline networking. They defined the functions that must take place between machines in order to have a network and broke them into seven distinct parts, or layers. At the bottom of the layers, the network deals only with bits and signals; there is no intelligence. At the top layer, the model interacts with users and applications and has a great deal of intelligence built into it. Starting from the bottom, the OSI layers are as follows:

The Physical layer   This layer is made up of components you can see, feel, and touch: cards, cables, terminators, and so on. There is no intelligence; and devices that can operate here include repeaters and multiplexers. A repeater takes in a signal, amplifies it, and sends it on. If the signal coming in is garbage, then amplified garbage comes out—this layer performs no other function aside from boosting the signal.

The Data Link layer   This layer takes data from the upper layers and prepares it to be sent across the Physical layer. It's the only layer divided into subcomponents—the Logical Link

Control (LLC) and Media Access Control (MAC). In addition to communicating with NICs, it also performs error checking and manages link control. Bridges and Layer 2 switches can and do operate at this layer.

The Network layer   This layer directs the flow of data from a source to a destination, regardless of whether there is a dedicated connection. It's responsible for translating names into addresses, monitoring traffic, and finding the best route. Routers operate at this level.

All switching operates at Layer 2 using MAC addresses. Layer 3 switches are so named because they can perform a routing function as well as a switching function. Most switches operate only at the Data Link layer.

The Transport layer   This layer handles packets and network transmissions. Its primary responsibility is to make certain packets transmitted by the Network layer get to where they are going. A gateway is the physical device capable of working at this and all upper layers.

The Session layer   This layer determines the synchronization rules the two computers will use and establishes the rules for dialogue (communications). It also contains protocols that are primarily responsible for establishing connections between computers and terminating the connections when the transmission is complete.

The Presentation layer   This layer translates data between the Application layer above it and all other layers. It can perform compression and encryption, and it's the redirector from the application to the network.

The Application layer   This layer is the interface to network services. All data originates here before going across the network and concludes here on the other side. Possible services include print, file, messaging, database, and so on.

Data originates in the Application layer of the source computer and travels down through subsequent layers. Each layer adds a header to the data and passes it to the next lower layer until it reaches the Physical layer. At the Physical layer, the data travels across the wire to the target computer, where it enters at the Physical layer and begins moving up the layers. On the target computer, each layer strips the header intended for it and passes the data up until it reaches the Application layer once more.

Large numbers of protocols and services operate at various layers of the OSI model. In many cases, a protocol or service can function at multiple layers. A summation of protocols, services, and hardware is shown in Table 5.1.

Integrated Services Digital Network (ISDN) is a WAN technology that performs link management and signaling by virtue of packet switching. The original idea behind it was to let existing phone lines carry digital communications by using multiplexing to support multiple channels. ISDN works with the bottom four layers of the OSI model: Transport, Network, Data Link, and Physical.

TABLE 5.1 Networking Layer Breakout

Layer	Hardware	Protocols and Services	Data Type
Application	Gateway	SMB, NCP, NFS, SNMP, Telnet	Message, user data
Presentation	Gateway	NCP, NFS, SNMP	Packet
Session	Gateway	NFS, SNMP, RPC	Packet
Transport	Gateway	TCP, UDP, SPX, NetBEUI	Segment, datagram, packet
Network	Router, brouter, switch	IP, IPX, NetBEUI, ICMP, ARP, RARP, RIP, OSPF, DLC, DecNET	Datagram, packet
Data Link	Bridge, brouter, switch	LLC, MAC	Frame
Physical	Repeater, multiplexer	None	Bit, signal

Network Protocols

Hosts on a network communicate using a common language called a protocol. A *protocol* is nothing more than a set of rules that governs the communications between the hosts. Just as humans can speak more than one language, so too can networked hosts—but it's critically important that the hosts speak a common language, or they won't be able to communicate, and no networking will take place.

NetBEUI/NetBIOS

NetBIOS Enhanced User Interface (NetBEUI) is a protocol that Microsoft came up with as an outgrowth of *Network Basic Input Output System (NetBIOS)*. It's very small, has virtually no overhead, and was used in all of Microsoft's early networking products: Windows for Workgroups, LAN Manager, and so on.

Although NetBEUI is ideal for a small network or workgroup, its giant downfall is that it can't be routed. This limits your network to a single location, unless you use a bridge (a device of days gone by).

IPX/SPX

Internetwork Packet Exchange/Sequenced Packet Exchange (IPX/SPX) is the proprietary protocol that Novell developed for networking NetWare. Far more robust than NetBEUI and some of the others that were around at the time, it's routable, but it requires configuration and consumes overhead. This protocol is still available for use, but Novell has included TCP/IP as the default with NetWare since version 5.0.

Microsoft created NetWare Link (NWLINK), a reverse-engineered version of IPX/SPX that is included with (or available for) most Windows operating systems. This protocol allows you to add Windows clients to an existing IPX/SPX network.

TCP/IP

Every computer, interface, or device on a *Transmission Control Protocol/Internet Proto-col* (TCP/IP) network is issued a unique identifier known as an *IP address* that resembles 209.110.12.123. TCP/IP is the most commonly used networking protocol today. You can easily see that it's difficult for most users to memorize these numbers, so host names are used in their place. *Host names* are alphanumeric values assigned to a host; any host may have more than one host name.

For example, the host 209.110.12.123 may be known to all users as Gemini, or it may be known to the sales department as Gemini and to the marketing department as Apollo9. All that is needed is a means by which the alphanumeric name can be translated into its IP address. There are four methods of so doing:

- On a small network, you can use HOSTS files. These are ASCII text files located in the /etc directory of every machine that performs the translation. When a new host is added to the network, every host must have its HOSTS file updated to include the new entry. HOSTS files work with every platform and every operating system, but they require con-stant manual updating and editing to keep them current—impractical on large networks.

- On a large network, you can add a server to be referenced by all hosts for the name resolution. The server runs Domain Name Services (DNS) and resolves Fully Qualified Domain Names (FQDNs) from www.ds-technical.com into their IP address. Multiple DNS servers can serve an area and provide fault tolerance for one another. In all cases, the DNS servers divide their area into zones; every zone has a primary server and any number of secondary servers. DNS, like HOSTS, works with any operating system and any version.

- If the network within which you work is all Microsoft (Windows 2000, Windows XP, and so on), then you're accustomed to using NetBIOS names as computer names. On a small network, you can use LMHOSTS files to translate computer names to IP addresses—much like HOSTS does. The big difference is that NetBIOS (computer) names exist only on the Microsoft platform, and LMHOSTS files can't be used with Unix or other operating systems.

- If you have a large Microsoft-only network, you can stop editing the LMHOSTS files manually and use a server running Windows Internet Naming Service (WINS). The WINS server dynamically maps NetBIOS names to IP addresses and keeps your network mappings cur-rent. Again, this is a replacement for LMHOSTS and works only in the Microsoft world.

You can use a WINS proxy to let Unix and other clients resolve names using the WINS database.

Whether the files/services are case-sensitive or not depends on the operating system. If you're using HOSTS files in Unix and have a host named GEMINI, you must have the following entry in the file:

```
209.110.12.123 GEMINI
```

In Windows, however, neither the operating system nor the HOSTS file is case sensitive, and

```
209.110.12.123 Gemini
```

delivers the same result when trying to resolve *GEMINI*, as do references to *gemini*, *gemInI*, and so on.

HOSTS files are limited to 256 characters per line, and the pound sign (#) is used as the comment character. Wherever the pound sign is found, the rest of the line is ignored. For example:

```
#This is the first line
209.110.123.4 MARS #This is the second line
```

Line one is completely ignored, and line two is processed up to the space following the *S*. LMHOSTS files also use the pound sign as the comment character.

The FQDNs mentioned earlier identify the host and information about it. The first part, www, identifies the type of service to use. The second part, ds-technical, identifies the entity, and com identifies the type of entity. Known as a *domain*, the entity type can be any of the values shown in Table 5.2.

TABLE 5.2   Common Domains

Domain	Meaning
biz	Business
com	Commercial
edu	Educational
info	Information
mil	Military
gov	Government
net	Network—ISP
org	Original—organization
xx	Two-character country identifier, such as ca for Canada

Dynamic Host Configuration Protocol (DHCP) falls into a different category. Whereas the other services described concentrate on resolving names to IP addresses, DHCP issues IP configuration data.

Rather than an administrator having to configure a unique IP address for every host added on a network (and *default gateway* and *subnet mask*), they can use a DHCP server to issue these values. That server is given a number of addresses in a range that it can supply to clients.

For example, the server may be given the IP range (or *scope*) 209.110.12.1 to 209.11.12.200. When a client boots, it sends out a request for the server to issue it an address (and any other configuration data) from that scope. The server takes one of the numbers it has available and leases it to the client for a length of time. If the client is still using the configuration data when 50 percent of the lease has expired, it requests a renewal of the lease from the server; under normal operating conditions, the request is granted. When the client is no longer using the address, the address goes back in the scope and can be issued to another client.

DHCP is built on the older Bootstrap Protocol (BOOTP) that was used to allow diskless workstations to boot and connect to a server that provided them an operating system and applications. The client uses broadcasts to request the data and thus—normally—can't communicate with DHCP servers beyond their own subnet (broadcasts don't route). A DHCP Relay Agent, however, can be employed to allow DHCP broadcasts to go from one network to another.

IP addresses are 32-bit binary numbers. Because numbers of such magnitude are difficult to work with, they're divided into four octets (eight bits) and converted to digital. Thus, 01010101 becomes 85. This is important because the limits on the size of the digital number are due to the reality that they're representations of binary numbers. The range must be from 0 (00000000) to 255 (11111111) per octet, making the lowest possible IP address 0.0.0.0 and the highest 255.255.255.255. Many IP addresses aren't available because they're reserved for diagnostic purposes, private addressing, or some other function.

Three classes of IP addresses are available; they're identified by the first octet. Table 5.3 shows the class and the range the first octet must fall into to be within that class.

If you're given a Class A address, then you're assigned a number such as 125. With a few exceptions, this means you can use any number between 0 and 255 in the second field, any number between 0 and 255 in the third field, and any number between 0 and 255 in the fourth field. This gives you a total number of hosts that you can have on your network in excess of 16 million.

TABLE 5.3   IP Address Classes

Class	Range
A	1–126
B	128–191
C	192–223

If you're given a Class B address, then you're assigned a number such as 152.119. With a few exceptions, this means you can use any number between 0 and 255 in the third field and any number between 0 and 255 in the fourth field. This gives you a total number of hosts that you can have on your network in excess of 65,000.

If you're given a Class C address, then you're assigned a number such as 205.19.15. You can use any number between 1 and 254 in the fourth field, for a total of 254 possible hosts (0 and 255 are reserved).

The class, therefore, makes a tremendous difference in the number of hosts your network can have. In most cases, the odds of having all hosts at one location are small. Assuming you have a Class B address, will there be 65,000 hosts in one room, or will they be in several locations? Most often, it's the latter.

Subnetting your network is the process of taking the total number of hosts available to you and dividing it into smaller networks. When you configure TCP/IP on a host, you must only give three values: a unique IP address, a default gateway (router) address, and a subnet mask. The default subnet mask for each class of network is shown in Table 5.4.

TABLE 5.4   Default Subnet Values

Class	Default Subnet Mask
A	255.0.0.0
B	255.255.0.0
C	255.255.255.0

When you use the default subnet mask, you're allowing for all hosts to be at one site and not subdividing your network. Any deviation from the default signifies that you're dividing the network into multiple subnetworks.

TCP/User Datagram Protocol (UDP) uses port numbers to listen for and respond to requests for communications. RFC 1060 defines common port numbers for a number of services, generally below 1024. You can, however, reconfigure your service to use another port number (preferably much higher) if you're concerned about security and you don't want your site to be available to anonymous traffic.

Common port assignments are listed in Table 5.5.

TABLE 5.5   Common Port Assignments

Service	Port
FTP	21
Telnet	23

TABLE 5.5   Common Port Assignments *(continued)*

Service	Port
SMTP	25
HTTP	80
NNTP	119
SSL	443

AppleTalk

AppleTalk is the default network operating system of Macintosh computers included with every Mac OS. Many other operating systems can also communicate via AppleTalk, but it isn't their default. The Apple File Protocol (AFP) is used to provide the sharing capabilities across the network. AppleTalk uses zones to define the network, as Windows uses domains, and so on. The Apple Printer Utility is used to configure printers and tell them which zone they belong to so they can be reached by the clients within that area.

Status Indicators

Link lights appear on a hub to show when a connection to a computer is present. If a network cable is plugged into the hub and the light isn't lit, there isn't a valid connection between the hub and the client, or the correct drivers and configuration aren't present. On most hubs, the link lights blink when traffic is traveling through that port. On 10/100 hubs, a different color can be used for the light to indicate whether the connection is made at 10Mbps or 100Mbps. Lit link lights on the NIC card also indicate that a connection is present.

Collision lights are used on hubs, bridges, and so on to indicate when a collision has occurred. Collisions can happen whenever more than one device attempts to send data at a time. Under normal conditions, both devices wait a short time (milliseconds) and then attempt to resend. Under this condition, the collision lights blink occasionally and go off. If they're on regularly, you don't have enough bandwidth to handle your traffic. Switched hubs can often be used to reduce the number of collisions on a network; you can also increase the bandwidth of the network (from 10Mbps to 100Mbps, for example).

Cabling

A number of choices are available when you're cabling a network. Twisted-pair wiring is one of the most common; it's made up of pairs of wires twisted around each other, as shown in Figure 5.3.

Unshielded twisted pair (UTP) offers no shielding (hence the name) and is the network cabling type most prone to outside interference. The interference can be from a fluorescent light ballast, electrical motor, or other such source (known as *electromagnetic interference [EMI]*) or from wires being too close together and signals jumping across them (known as *crosstalk*).

FIGURE 5.3   Twisted-pair cable

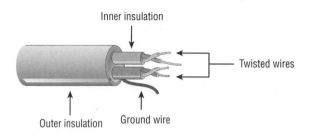

Shielded twisted pair (STP) adds a braided foil shield around the twisted wires to protect against EMI.

Twisted-pair cabling is most often used in 10BaseT/100BaseT networks. There are different grades, which are given as categories; and as you may guess, the higher the grade, the more expensive the cabling, and the higher the data rate it can support. The breakout is as follows:

Category 1   For voice-only transmissions. Used in most phone systems today. It contains two twisted pairs.

Category 2   Transmits data at speeds up to 4Mbps. It contains four twisted pairs of wires. It's also not used in networks and is suitable only for voice grade.

Category 3   Transmits data at speeds up to 10Mbps. It contains four twisted pairs of wires with three twists per foot. This is the lowest-level cabling you can safely use in a network.

Category 4   Transmits data at speeds up to 16Mbps. It contains four twisted pairs of wires.

Category 5   Transmits data at speeds up to 100Mbps. It contains four twisted pairs of copper wire to give the most protection.

Category 5e   Transmits data at speeds up to 1Gbps. It also contains four twisted pairs of copper wire, but they're physically separated and contain more twists per foot than Category 5 to provide maximum interference protection.

Category 6   Transmits data at speed up to 2Gbps. It contains four twisted pairs of copper wire.

10BaseT networks require a minimum of Cat 3 cabling, whereas 100BaseT requires an upgrade to Cat 5 cabling. You can often use the network type to compute the required length and speed of your cabling. For example, 10BaseT tells you three things:

1.   10—The speed of the network, 10Mbps.

2.   Base—the technology used (either baseband or broadband).

3.   T—Twisted-pair cabling. In the case of 10BaseT, it's generally UTP.

Most UTP cable uses RJ-45 connectors that look like telephone connectors (RJ-11) but have eight wires instead of four. STP cable, on the other hand, uses IBM data connector (IDC) or universal data connector (UDC) ends and connects to token ring networks. The common types of STP cable are as follows:

Type 1   The most common STP cable type. Contains two pairs.

Type 2   Like Type 1, but adds two pairs of voice wires.

Type 3   Contains four pairs.

Type 6   Patch cable, used for connecting token ring hubs.

Type 8   A flat type of STP cable used for running under carpets.

Type 9   A two-pair, high-grade type of STP.

Fiber-optic cabling is the most expensive type of those discussed for this exam. Although it's an excellent medium, it's often not used because of the cost of implementing it. It can be single-mode or multi-mode—if the cable supports only one mode, it is called single-mode; otherwise it is multi-mode.

It has a glass core within a rubber outer coating and uses beams of light rather than electrical signals to relay data (see Figure 5.4). Because light doesn't diminish over distance the way electrical signals do, this cabling can run for distances measured in kilometers with transmission speeds from 100Mbps up to 1Gbps or higher.

FIGURE 5.4   Fiber-optic cable

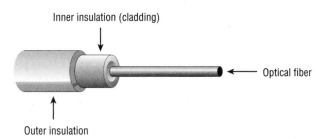

Often, fiber is used to connect runs to wiring closets where they break out into UTP or other cabling types, or as other types of backbones. Fiber-optic cable can use either ST or SC connectors: ST is a barrel-shaped connector, and SC is squared and easier to connect in small spaces.

Table 5.6 lists the cabling types discussed and various attributes of each.

 FC or LC connectors may also be used, but are not as common.

TABLE 5.6   Cable Types

Characteristic	Unshielded Twisted Pair	Shielded Twisted Pair	Fiber-Optic
Cost	Least expensive	Moderate	Expensive
Maximum Length	100m (328ft)	100m (328ft)	>10 miles
Transmission Rates	10Mbps to 2Gbps	10Mbps to 2Gbps for Ethernet, Fast Ethernet, and Gigabit Ethernet; 16Mbps for token ring	100Mbps or more
Flexibility	Most flexible	Fair	Fair
Ease of Installation	Very easy	Very easy	Difficult
Interference	Susceptible	Not as susceptible as UTP	Not susceptible
Preferred Uses	10/100/1000BaseT	10/100/1000BaseT or token ring	Network segments requiring high-speed transmission
Connector	RJ-45	RJ-45 for Ethernet; IDC/UDC for Token Ring	ST/SC

Miscellaneous

There are a few odd topics that CompTIA has placed beneath this objective. While they do not fit well here, they must be discussed and understood here in order to round out this objective. Those topics include the following:

- Cellular networks work like those for telephones. Radio cells are created through the use of transmitters and they provide coverage within their own specific area.

- Dial-up networking is the traditional method of remote access. It has been fading in popularity recently due to its poor connectivity speed. Virtual Private Networks (VPNs) have been replacing dial-up on a consistent basis.

- IEEE 1394/ FireWire is a serial bus interface that has been replacing SCSI for many implementations (such as camcorders and such) due to its flexibility and high speeds.

- Plenum/PVC cable is a specific type of cable that is rated for use in plenum spaces. Plenum spaces are those in a building used for heating and air conditioning systems. Most cable cannot be used in the plenum because of the danger of fire (or the fumes the cables give off as they burn). Plenum cable is fire-rated and meets the necessary standards which make it OK to use in these locations.

- RS-232 is the standard serial port. You can connect modems and other networking devices to it, but this has been losing popularity in favor of USB and other ports.

- Voice-over IP (VoIP) is a technology that allows you to route voice traffic across the IP network. A number of companies (including most cable providers) offer this as a service, and it offers the advantage of allowing you to save long-distance phone charges.

Wireless networking, infrared, and BlueTooth are also listed here but discussed in detail in the next objective.

Exam Essentials

Understand basic networking concepts.   A network is a collection of computers that can interact with each other and share files and resources. The network may be peer-to-peer or client/server-based.

Know the network cable types.   UTP is the cheapest type of cable to implement, but it's also the weakest. STP is more expensive, but it isn't subject to EMI. Fiber-optic cabling is the most expensive and most difficult to implement, but it offers the greatest combination of speed and distance.

Know the categories of networking connectivity.   LANs are confined to local, whereas WANs expand that limit. ISDN, broadband, and cellular are methods of establishing network connections.

Install, Configure, Optimize, and Upgrade Networks

This objective tests your knowledge of networking cards and wireless networking connectivity. It expects you to understand the terms and topics and be able to work with them in the real world.

Critical Information

A NIC is a physical card installed within a computer than allows it to communicate on the network. This NIC can allow the system to operate on a wired or wireless network and must be there for communication to be possible.

The Network Interface Card

The NIC provides the physical interface between computer and cabling. It prepares data, sends data, and controls the flow of data. It can also receive and translate data into bytes for the CPU to understand. It communicates at the Physical layer of the OSI model and comes in many shapes and sizes.

Installation

The physical installation of a NIC is the same as with any other internal circuit board. It fits into an ISA or PCI expansion slot in the motherboard or in a USB port as with a USB NIC.

When choosing a NIC, use one that fits the bus type of your PC. If you have more than one type of bus in your PC (for example, a combination ISA/PCI), use a NIC that fits into the fastest type (PCI, in this case). This is especially important in servers, because the NIC can quickly become a bottleneck if you don't follow this guideline.

Configuration

The NIC's configuration includes such things as a manufacturer's hardware address, IRQ address, base I/O port address, and base memory address. Some NICs may also use direct memory access (DMA) channels to offer better performance.

Each card has a unique MAC address, which is hard-wired into the card during its manufacture. It consists of six two-digit hexadecimal numbers; the first three represent the manufacturer, and the second three are the unique serial number of the card. The MAC address is separate from any logical address that might be assigned to the PC by the networking system, such as an IP address.

Configuring a NIC is similar to configuring any other type of expansion card. Token-ring cards often have two memory addresses that must be allocated in reserved memory for them to work properly.

Drivers

For the computer to use the NIC, it's very important to install the proper device drivers. These drivers communicate directly with the network redirector and adapter. They operate in the MAC sublayer of the Data Link layer of the OSI model.

Media Access Methods

You've put the network together in a topology. You've told the network how to communicate and send the data, and you've told it how to send the data to another computer. You also have the communications medium in place. The next problem you need to solve is how to put the data on the cable. What you need now are the *cable access methods*, which define a set of rules for how computers put data onto and retrieve it from a network cable. The four most common methods of data access are shown here:

- Carrier Sense Multiple Access with Collision Detection (CSMA/CD)
- Carrier Sense Multiple Access with Collision Avoidance (CSMA/CA)
- Token passing
- Polling

Carrier Sense Multiple Access with Collision Detection

NICs that use CSMA/CD listen to, or "sense," the cable to check for traffic. They compete for a chance to transmit. Usually, if access to the network is slow, it means that too many computers are trying to transmit, causing traffic jams.

Carrier Sense Multiple Access with Collision Avoidance

Instead of monitoring traffic and moving in when there is a break, CSMA/CA allows the computers to send a signal that they're ready to transmit data. If the ready signal transmits without a problem, the computer then transmits its data. If the ready signal isn't transmitted successfully, the computer waits and tries again. This method is slower and less popular than CSMA/CD on wired networks. CSMA/CA is the carrier access method used for most wireless networks today.

Token Passing

Token passing is a way of giving every NIC equal access to the cable. A special packet of data is passed from computer to computer. Any computer that wants to transmit has to wait until it has the token. It can then transmit its data.

This is an old method that was used on IBM token-ring networks of the past. It's also sometimes used on fiber rings today.

Polling

Polling is an old method of media access. Not many topologies support polling anymore, mainly because it has special hardware requirements. This method requires a central, intelligent device (meaning that the device contains either hardware or software intelligence to enable it to make decisions) that asks each workstation in turn if it has any data to transmit. If the workstation answers "yes," the controller allows the workstation to transmit its data.

The polling process doesn't scale well—that is, you can't take this method and apply it to any number of workstations. In addition, the high cost of the intelligent controllers and cards has made the polling method all but obsolete.

Wireless Networks

One of the most fascinating cabling technologies today—actually, it doesn't really *use* cable— is wireless. Wireless networks offer the ability to extend a LAN without the use of traditional cabling methods. Wireless transmissions are made through the air by infrared light, laser light, narrow-band radio, microwave, or spread-spectrum radio.

Wireless LANs are becoming increasingly popular as businesses are becoming more mobile and less centralized. You can see them most often in environments where standard cabling methods aren't possible or wanted.

Wireless networking requires much the same type of equipment as traditional networking; the main difference is that the special versions of each item rely on radio frequency (RF) signals or infrared instead of cables. For example, each node needs a NIC that has a transceiver in it instead of a cable jack; and there must be a central wireless access point (WAP), the equivalent of a hub, with which the wireless NICs communicate.

The first wireless networking standard to become commercially popular was *IEEE 802.11b*, which could send and receive at up to 11Mbps. At this writing, a newer standard, *IEEE 802.11a*, has extended that to 54Mbps and will reach over 100Mbps in the next two years.

BlueTooth is a wireless standard that uses radio waves in the 2.4 to 2.485 GHz range. It's limited to about 35 feet in range, so it hasn't become widely used except for communications between notebook PCs and PDAs.

Exam Essentials

Understand network cards and their purpose.   A network interface card (NIC) is the physical component that allows a host to connect to a network at the Physical layer.

Understand wired and wireless connectivity.   Networks work the same whether there is a physical wire between the hosts or that wire has been replaced by a wireless signal. The same order of operations and steps are carried out regardless of the medium employed.

Identify Tools, Diagnostic Procedures, and Troubleshooting Techniques for Networks

There is some overlap between this objective and the coverage of status indicators in objective 5.1. The information that is unique to this domain focuses on how to approach troubleshooting and the tools to use (with operating system–specific tools being a component of the elective exams as opposed to the core).

Critical Information

It's imperative that you understand proper troubleshooting procedures and know the tools available for your use before you begin trying to diagnose problems with the network. The sections that follow will focus on the key issues associated with this function.

A Systematic Approach

A systematic approach to troubleshooting a network problem always begins with trying to isolate the issue and determine how broad an area is affected. There is some overlap between what is expected in terms of knowledge here and on the Network+ exam, where you are to select the appropriate next step based on this approach:

1. Determine whether the problem exists across the network.
2. Determine whether the problem is with the workstation, workgroup, LAN, or WAN.
3. Determine whether the problem is consistent and replicable.
4. Use standard troubleshooting methods.

In a more scenario-focused view, this translates into selecting the appropriate next step based on this approach:

1. Identify the exact issue.

2. Re-create the problem.

3. Isolate the cause.

4. Formulate a correction.

5. Implement the correction.

6. Test.

7. Document the problem and the solution.

8. Give feedback.

Some standard ways you can do this are as follows:

1. Have a second operator perform the same task on an equivalent workstation.

2. Have a second operator perform the same task on the original operator's workstation.

3. See whether operators are following standard operating procedure.

Common Problems and Tools

DNS, WINS, HOSTS files, and LMHOSTS files are all used to resolve host names to IP addresses. You'll know whether any of them have a problem if you can ping a remote host by its IP address but not by its host name. Problems that can occur include the following:

- Case-sensitivity

- Misspelling

- Non-unique host names

A *crossover cable* reverses wiring pairs in UTP cabling (typically 10BaseT) and contains male connectors on both ends. This allows you to directly connect two computers without the need for a hub.

A *hardware loopback* can be any board or adapter that completes the circuit without having anything else there—emulating, if you will, what the system expects to find. Loopback adapters/boards are available for most components, including ISA slots, serial ports, and so on. Never forget that the IP address 127.0.0.1 is the loopback address for testing the TCP/IP implementation.

A *tone generator* is used for wire tracing—it's known as a *fox*. Its companion, a *tone locator*, is also known as a *hound*. The fox (generator) sends distinct tones down the wire for tracing. The hound utilizes a hi-gain (often hi-impedance) amplifier to find the tone and locate the cable. The hound works without the need to break the cable and can often be used through non-metal surfaces (wood, drywall, and so on).

Table 5.7 lists some other tools you can use for network troubleshooting.

TABLE 5.7   Network Troubleshooting Tools

Tool	Purpose
Digital voltmeter	Determines whether cables are faulty; tests power supply voltage
Time domain reflectometer (TDR)	Determines the distance to the break in the cable
Advanced cable tester	Analyzes network traffic, and finds excessive collisions
Protocol analyzer	Finds faulty NIC cards, bridges, and routers
Terminator	Finds breaks in the cable

Wireless Issues

One of the biggest problems with wireless networks is being able to find and maintain a strong, usable signal. While the distance between the client and the access point is a crucial factor, so is the environment that exists between the two. Such elements as metal filing cabinets, cinder-block walls, and similar items can greatly reduce the strength of the signal to the point where the user cannot function.

Repeaters can help improve the strength of the signal and should be used as needed within the worksite.

To see the signal strength a Windows XP client is receiving, go to Network Connections (Start > My Network Places > View Network Connections), right-click on the wireless network icon, and choose Status. This will show the speed being attained.

Exam Essentials

Know the steps of troubleshooting.   Always begin troubleshooting by trying to isolate the problem and understanding how widespread it is. Before you begin drastic operations, make certain the issue isn't confined to just one user.

Know what troubleshooting tools exist.   Be familiar with the network troubleshooting tools that exist and what each one can do.

Review Questions

1. What is the difference between full and half duplexing?

2. What is another name for a server-based network?

3. What is the difference between baseband and broadband?

4. Which layer of the OSI model takes data from the upper layers and prepares it for sending across the Physical layer?

5. At which layers of the OSI model does a gateway operate?

6. What is the term for the rules that govern the communications between network hosts called?

7. Which Microsoft protocol is compatible with IPX/SPX?

8. Which type of server translates host names to IP addresses?

9. What is the default subnet value for a host with a Class B address?

10. What is BlueTooth?

Answers to Review Questions

1. Duplexing is the means by which communication takes place. With full duplexing, everyone can send and receive at the same time. With half duplexing, communications travel in both directions but in only one direction at any given time.

2. A server-based network is also known as a client/server network.

3. With baseband, the entire medium's capacity is used for one signal. The speed possibilities are thus increased because the entire channel is utilized. With broadband, the medium is used to carry multiple signals, but all unidirectionally.

4. The Data Link layer takes data from the upper layers and prepares it for sending across the Physical layer.

5. A gateway operates at the top four layers: Application, Presentation, Session, and Transport.

6. A protocol is a set of rules that governs the communications between the hosts.

7. The NWLINK protocol, from Microsoft, is compatible with IPX/SPX—a proprietary protocol from Novell.

8. A Domain Name Service (DNS) server translates host names to IP addresses.

9. The default subnet value for a host with a Class B address is 255.255.0.0.

10. BlueTooth is an infrared wireless standard that uses light rather than radio waves.

Chapter

6

Security

COMPTIA A+ ESSENTIALS EXAM OBJECTIVES COVERED IN THIS CHAPTER:

✓ **6.1 Identify the fundamental principles of security**

   ▪ Identify names, purposes, and characteristics of hardware and software security

   ▪ Identify names, purposes, and characteristics of wireless security

   ▪ Identify names, purposes, and characteristics of data and physical security

   ▪ Describe importance and process of incidence reporting

   ▪ Recognize and respond appropriately to social engineering situations

✓ **6.2 Install, configure, upgrade, and optimize security**

   ▪ Install, configure, upgrade, and optimize hardware, software, and data security

✓ **6.3 Identify tools, diagnostic procedures, and troubleshooting techniques for security**

   ▪ Diagnose and troubleshoot hardware, software, and data security issues

✓ **6.4 Perform preventative maintenance for computer security**

   ▪ Implement software security preventative maintenance techniques, such as installing service packs and patches and training users about malicious software prevention technologies

Reflecting the increased visibility of the need for security knowledge in the real world, CompTIA added emphasis in its current A+ exams. Security has always been an important topic (as witnessed by the popularity of the Security+ exam), but it's now something about which every administrator—not just the security professional—must have a basic knowledge and understanding. The four subobjectives in this category do a good job of providing a thorough overview of the topic, and it's visited again in the Technicians exams (see Chapter 14).

Identify the Fundamental Principles of Security

Security is unlike any other topic in computing. The word *security* is so encompassing that it's impossible to know exactly what you mean when you say it. When you talk about security, do you mean physical security of servers and workstations from those who might try to steal them, or damage that may occur if the side of the building collapses? Or, do you mean the security of data from viruses and worms and the means by which you keep those threats from entering the network? Or, do you mean security of data from hackers and miscreants who have targeted you and have no other purpose in life than to keep you up at night? Or is security the comfort that comes from knowing you can restore files if a user accidentally deletes them?

The first problem with security is that it's next to impossible to have everyone agree on what it means, because it can include all these items. The next problem is that we don't *really* want things to be completely secured. For example, if you wanted your customer-list file to be truly secure, you wouldn't put it on the server and make it available. It's on the server because you need to access it, and so do 30 other people. In this sense, security means that only 30 select people can get to the data.

The next problem is that although everyone wants security, no one wants to be inconvenienced by it. To use an analogy, few travelers don't feel safer by watching airport personnel pat down everyone who heads to the terminal—they just don't want it to happen to them. This is true in computing, as well; we all want to make sure data is accessed only by those who truly should be working with it, but we don't want to have to enter 12-digit passwords and submit to retinal scans.

As a computer professional, you have to understand all these concerns. You have to know that a great deal is expected of you, but few people want to be hassled or inconvenienced by the measures you must put in place. You have a primary responsibility to protect and safeguard the information your organization uses. Many times, that means educating your users and making certain they understand the "why" behind what is being implemented.

Critical Information

When discussing computer security, you must be able to identify the names, purposes, and characteristics of three key areas: hardware/software security, wireless security, and physical/data security. These three topics are discussed in the sections that follow.

Hardware and Software Security

When it comes to hardware, CompTIA expects you to understand that although the user interacts with software, the hardware actually stores the data. The hardware in question can be a hard disk, a backup tape, or some other storage device. This overly simplistic concept is important when it comes to choosing how to dispose of hardware.

If it's possible to verify beyond a reasonable doubt that a piece of hardware that's no longer being used doesn't contain any data of a sensitive or proprietary nature, then that hardware can be recycled (sold to employees, sold to a third party, donated to a school, and so on). That level of assurance can come from wiping a hard drive, reformatting it, or using specialized utilities. When computer systems are retired, the disk drives should be zeroed out, and all magnetic media should be degaussed. Degaussing involves applying a strong magnetic field to initialize the media (this is also referred to as *disk wiping*). Erasing files on a computer system doesn't guarantee that the information isn't still on the disk; a low-level format can be performed on the system, or a utility can be used to completely wipe the disk clean. This process helps ensure that information doesn't fall into the wrong hands.

If you can't be assured that the hardware in question doesn't contain important data, then the hardware should be destroyed. You cannot, and should not, take a risk that the data your company depends on could fall into the wrong hands.

Other topics beneath this objective focus on specific subjects and are discussed in the following sections.

Smart Cards

A *smart card* is a type of badge or card that gives you access to resources including buildings, parking lots, and computers. It contains information about your identity and access privileges. Each area or computer has a card scanner or a reader in which you insert your card.

The reader is connected to the workstation and validates against the security system. This increases the security of the authentication process, because you must be in physical possession of the smart card to use the resources. Of course, if the card is lost or stolen, the person who finds the card can access the resources it allows.

    Most smart cards also require the use of a PIN, just in case the card is lost or stolen.

Biometrics

Biometric devices use physical characteristics to identify the user. Such devices are becoming more common in the business environment. Biometric systems include hand scanners, retinal scanners, and soon, possibly, DNA scanners. To gain access to resources, you must pass a physical screening process. In the case of a hand scanner, this may include identifying fingerprints, scars, and markings on your hand. Retinal scanners compare your eye's retinal pattern to a stored retinal pattern to verify your identity. DNA scanners will examine a unique portion of your DNA structure in order to verify that you are who you say you are.

Key Fobs

Key fobs are named after the chains that used to hold pocket watches to clothes. They are security devices that you carry with you that display a randomly generated code that you can then use for authentication. This code usually changes very quickly (every 60 seconds is probably the average) and you combine this code with your PIN for authentication.

Authentication Issues to Consider

You can set up many different parameters and standards to force the people in your organization to conform. In establishing these parameters, it's important that you consider the capabilities of the people who will be working with these policies. If you're working in an environment where people aren't computer savvy, you may spend a lot of time helping them remember and recover passwords. Many organizations have had to reevaluate their security guidelines after they've invested great time and expense to implement high-security systems.

Setting authentication security, especially in supporting users, can become a high-maintenance activity for network administrators. On one hand, you want people to be able to authenticate themselves easily; on the other hand, you want to establish security that protects your company's resources.

Be wary of popular names or current trends that make certain passwords predictable. For example, during the first release of *Star Wars*, two of the most popular passwords used on college campuses were C3PO and R2D2. This created a security problem for campus computer centers.

Understanding Software Exploitation

The term *software exploitation* refers to attacks launched against applications and higher-level services. They include gaining access to data using weaknesses in the data-access objects of a database or a flaw in a service. This section briefly outlines some common exploitations that have been successful in the past. The following exploitations can be introduced using viruses, as in the case of the Klez32 virus, or by using access attacks described later in this chapter:

Database exploitation   Many database products allow sophisticated access queries to be made in the client/server environment. If a client session can be hijacked or spoofed, the attacker can formulate queries against the database that disclose unauthorized information. For this attack to be successful, the attacker must first gain access to the environment through one of the attacks outlined later.

Application exploitation   The macro virus is another example of software exploitation. A macro virus is a set of programming instructions in a language such as VBScript that commands an application to perform illicit instructions. Users want more powerful tools, and manufacturers want to sell users what they want. The macro virus takes advantage of the power offered by word processors, spreadsheets, or other applications. This exploitation is inherent in the product, and all users are susceptible to it unless they disable all macros.

E-mail exploitation   Hardly a day goes by without another e-mail virus being reported. This is a result of a weakness in many common e-mail clients. Modern e-mail clients offer many shortcuts, lists, and other capabilities to meet user demands. A popular exploitation of e-mail clients involves accessing the client address book and propagating viruses. There is virtually nothing a client user can do about these exploitations, although antivirus software that integrates with your e-mail client does offer some protection. To be truly successful, the software manufacturer must fix the weaknesses—an example is Outlook's option to protect against access to the address book. This type of weakness isn't a bug, in many cases, but a feature that users wanted.

One of the most important measures you can take to proactively combat software attacks is to know common file extensions and the applications they're associated with. For example, .scr files are screensavers, and viruses are often distributed through the use of these files. No legitimate user should be sending screensavers via e-mail to your users, and all .scr attachments should be banned from entering the network.

Table 6.1, although not comprehensive, contains the most common file extensions that should or should not, as a general rule, be allowed into the network as e-mail attachments.

TABLE 6.1   Common File Extensions for E-mail Attachments

Should Be Allowed	Should *Not* Be Allowed
DOC	BAT
PDF	COM
TXT	EXE
XLS	HLP
ZIP	PIF
	SCR

Spyware   *Spyware* differs from other malware in that it works—often actively—on behalf of a third party. Rather than self-replicating, like viruses and worms, spyware is spread to machines by users who inadvertently ask for it. The users often don't know they have asked for it, but have done so by downloading other programs, visiting infected sites, and so on.

The spyware program monitors the user's activity and responds by offering unsolicited pop-up advertisements (sometimes known as *adware*), gathers information about the user to pass on to marketers, or intercepts personal data such as credit-card numbers. One thing separating spyware from most other malware is that it almost always exists to provide commercial gain. The operating systems from Microsoft are the ones most affected by spyware, and Microsoft has released Microsoft AntiSpyware to combat the problem.

Rootkits   Recently, *rootkits* have become the software exploitation program du jour. Rootkits are software programs that have the ability to hide certain things from the operating system. With a rootkit, there may be a number of processes running on a system that don't show up in Task Manager, or connections may be established/available that don't appear in a netstat display—the rootkit masks the presence of these items. The rootkit does this by manipulating function calls to the operating system and filtering out information that would normally appear.

Unfortunately, many rootkits are written to get around antivirus and antispyware programs that aren't kept up-to-date. The best defense you have is to monitor what your system is doing and catch the rootkit in the process of installation.

Viruses   A *virus* is a piece of software designed to infect a computer system. The virus may do nothing more than reside on the computer. A virus may also damage the data on your hard disk, destroy your operating system, and possibly spread to other systems. Viruses get into your computer in one of three ways: on a contaminated floppy or CD-ROM, through e-mail, or as part of another program.

Viruses can be classified as several types: polymorphic, stealth, retroviruses, multipartite, armored, companion, phage, and macro viruses. Each type of virus has a different attack strategy and different consequences.

Trojan Horses   *Trojan horses* are programs that enter a system or network under the guise of another program. A Trojan horse may be included as an attachment or as part of an installation program. The Trojan horse can create a back door or replace a valid program during installation. It then accomplishes its mission under the guise of another program. Trojan horses can be used to compromise the security of your system, and they can exist on a system for years before they're detected.

The best preventive measure for Trojan horses is to not allow them entry into your system. Immediately before and after you install a new software program or operating system, back it up! If you suspect a Trojan horse, you can reinstall the original programs, which should delete the Trojan horse. A port scan may also reveal a Trojan horse on your system. If an application opens a TCP or IP port that isn't supported in your network, you can track it down and determine which port is being used.

Worms   A *worm* is different from a virus in that it can reproduce itself, it's self-contained, and it doesn't need a host application to be transported. Many of the so-called viruses that have made the papers and media were actually worms. However, it's possible for a worm to contain or deliver a virus to a target system.

By their nature and origin, worms are supposed to propagate, and they use whatever services they're capable of to do that. Early worms filled up memory and bred inside the RAM of the target computer. Worms can use TCP/IP, e-mail, Internet services, or any number of possibilities to reach their target.

Spam   *Spam* is defined as any unwanted, unsolicited e-mail. Not only can the sheer volume of it be irritating, but it can often open the door to larger problems. Some of the sites advertised in spam may be infected with viruses, worms, and other unwanted programs. If users begin to respond to spam by visiting those sites, then your problems will only multiply.

Just as you can, and must, install good antivirus software programs, you should also consider similar measures for spam. Filtering messages and preventing them from ever entering the network is the most effective method of dealing with the problem.

Grayware   *Grayware* is a term used to describe any application that is annoying or is negatively affecting the performance of your computer. If an application doesn't fall into the virus or Trojan category, it can get lumped under grayware. Spyware and adware are often considered types of grayware, as are programs that log user keystrokes, and certain hacking programs.

Firewalls

Firewalls are one of the first lines of defense in a network. There are different types of firewalls, and they can be either stand-alone systems or included in other devices such as routers or servers. You can find firewall solutions that are marketed as hardware-only and others that are software-only. Many firewalls, however, consist of add-in software that is available for servers or workstations.

 Although solutions are sold as hardware-only, the hardware still runs some sort of software. It may be hardened and in ROM to prevent tampering, and it may be customized—but software is present, nonetheless.

The basic purpose of a firewall is to isolate one network from another. Firewalls are becoming available as appliances, meaning they're installed into the network between two networks. *Appliances* are freestanding devices that operate in a largely self-contained manner, requiring less maintenance and support than a server-based product.

Firewalls function as one or more of the following:

- Packet filter
- Proxy firewall
- Stateful inspection

A firewall operating as a *packet filter* passes or blocks traffic to specific addresses based on the type of application. The packet filter doesn't analyze the contents of a packet; it decides whether to pass it based on the packet's addressing information. For instance, a packet filter may allow web traffic on port 80 and block Telnet traffic on port 23. This type of filtering is included in many routers. If a received packet request asks for a port that isn't authorized, the filter may reject the request or ignore it. Many packet filters can also specify which IP addresses can request which ports and allow or deny them based on the security settings of the firewall.

You can think of a *proxy firewall* as an intermediary between your network and any other network. Proxy firewalls are used to process requests from an outside network; the proxy firewall examines the data and makes rules-based decisions about whether the request should be forwarded or refused. The proxy intercepts all the packages and reprocesses them for use internally. This process includes hiding IP addresses.

Stateful inspection is also referred to as *stateful packet filtering*. Most of the devices used in networks don't keep track of how information is routed or used. Once a packet is passed, the packet and path are forgotten. In stateful inspection (or stateful packet filtering), records are kept using a state table that tracks every communications channel. Stateful inspections occur at all levels of the network and provide additional security, especially in connectionless protocols.

Filesystem Security

Microsoft's earliest filesystem was referred to as File Allocation Table (FAT). FAT was designed for relatively small disk drives. It was upgraded first to FAT-16 and finally to FAT-32. FAT-32 (also written as FAT32) allows large disk systems to be used on Windows systems.

FAT allows only two types of protection: share-level and user-level access privileges. If a user has write or change access to a drive or directory, they have access to any file in that directory. This is very unsecure in an Internet environment.

The New Technology File System (NTFS) was introduced with Windows NT to address security problems. Before Windows NT was released, it had become apparent to Microsoft that a new file system was needed to handle growing disk sizes, security concerns, and the need for more stability. NTFS was created to address those issues.

With NTFS, files, directories, and volumes can each have their own security. NTFS's security is flexible and built in. Not only does NTFS track security in Access Control Lists (ACLs), which can hold permissions for local users and groups, but each entry in the ACL can also specify what type of access is given—such as Read-Only, Change, or Full Control. This allows a great deal of flexibility in setting up a network. In addition, special file-encryption programs were developed to encrypt data while it was stored on the hard disk.

Microsoft strongly recommends that all network shares be established using NTFS.

Wireless Security

Wireless systems are those that don't use wires to send information, but rather transmit data through the air. The growth of wireless systems creates several opportunities for attackers. These systems are relatively new, they use well-established communications mechanisms, and they're easily intercepted. Wireless controllers use special ID numbers called *service-set identifiers* (SSIDs) that must be configured in the network cards to allow communications. However, using SSID number configurations doesn't necessarily prevent wireless networks from being monitored.

This section discusses the various types of wireless systems that you'll encounter, and it mentions some of the security issues associated with this technology. Specifically, this section deals with Wireless Transport Layer Security (WTLS), the IEEE 802 wireless standards, Wired Equivalent Privacy (WEP) / Wireless Applications Protocol (WAP) applications, and the vulnerabilities that each presents.

Wireless Transport Layer Security

Wireless Transport Layer Security (WTLS) is the security layer of WAP, discussed in the section "WEP/WAP." WTLS provides authentication, encryption, and data integrity for wireless devices. It's designed to utilize the relatively narrow bandwidth of these types of devices, and it's moderately secure. WTLS provides reasonable security for mobile devices, and it's being widely implemented.

WTLS is part of the WAP environment: WAP provides the functional equivalent of TCP/IP for wireless devices. Many devices, including newer cell phones and PDAs, include support for WTLS as part of their networking protocol capabilities.

IEEE 802.11x Wireless Protocols

The IEEE 802.11x family of protocols provides for wireless communications using radio frequency transmissions. The frequencies in use for 802.11 standards are the 2.4GHz and the 5GHz frequency spectrums. Several standards and bandwidths have been defined for use in wireless environments, and they aren't extremely compatible with each other:

802.11 The *802.11* standard defines wireless LANs transmitting at 1Mbps or 2Mbps bandwidths using the 2.4GHz frequency spectrum and using either frequency-hopping spread spectrum (FHSS) or direct-sequence spread spectrum (DSSS) for data encoding.

802.11a The *802.11a* standard provides wireless LAN bandwidth of up to 54Mbps in the 5GHz frequency spectrum. The 802.11a standard also uses orthogonal frequency division multiplexing (OFDM) for encoding rather than FHSS or DSSS.

802.11b The *802.11b* standard provides for bandwidths of up to 11Mbps (with fallback rates of 5.5, 2, and 1Mbps) in the 2.4GHz frequency spectrum. This standard is also called *WiFi* or *802.11 high rate*. The 802.11b standard uses only DSSS for data encoding.

802.11g The *802.11g* standard provides for bandwidths of 20Mbps+ in the 2.4GHz frequency spectrum.

Three technologies are used to communicate in the 802.11 standard:

Direct-sequence spread spectrum (DSSS) DSSS accomplishes communication by adding the data that is to be transmitted to a higher-speed transmission. The higher-speed transmission contains redundant information to ensure data accuracy. Each packet can then be reconstructed in the event of a disruption.

Frequency-hopping spread spectrum (FHSS) FHSS accomplishes communication by hopping the transmission over a range of predefined frequencies. The changing or hopping is synchronized between both ends and appears to be a single transmission channel to both ends.

Orthogonal frequency division multiplexing (OFDM) OFDM accomplishes communication by breaking the data into subsignals and transmitting them simultaneously. These transmissions occur on different frequencies or subbands.

The mathematics and theories of these transmission technologies are beyond the scope of this book and far beyond the scope of this exam.

WEP/WAP

Wireless systems frequently use WAP for network communications. WEP is intended to provide the equivalent security of a wired network protocol. This section briefly discusses these two terms and provides you with an understanding of their relative capabilities.

WAP

The *Wireless Access Protocol (WAP)* is the technology designed for use with wireless devices. WAP has become a standard adopted by many manufacturers, including Motorola, Nokia, and others. WAP functions are equivalent to TCP/IP functions in that they're trying to serve the same purpose for wireless devices. WAP uses a smaller version of HTML called *Wireless Markup Language (WML)*, which is used for Internet displays. WAP-enabled devices can also respond to scripts using an environment called *WMLScript*. This scripting language is similar to Java, which is a programming language.

The ability to accept web pages and scripts produces the opportunity for malicious code and viruses to be transported to WAP-enabled devices. No doubt this will create a new set of problems, and antivirus software will be needed to deal with them.

WAP systems communicate using a WAP gateway system. The gateway converts information back and forth between HTTP and WAP, and it also encodes and decodes the security protocols. This structure provides a reasonable assurance that WAP-enabled devices can be secured. If the interconnection between the WAP server and the Internet isn't encrypted, packets between the devices may be intercepted, creating a potential vulnerability. This vulnerability is called a *gap in the WAP*.

WEP

Wired Equivalent Privacy (WEP) is a relatively new security standard for wireless devices. WEP encrypts data to provide data security. The protocol has always been under scrutiny for not being as secure as initially intended.

WEP is vulnerable due to weaknesses in the encryption algorithms. These weaknesses allow the algorithm to potentially be cracked in less than five hours using available PC software. This makes WEP one of the more vulnerable protocols available for security. WEP is a relatively new technology and will no doubt improve as it moves into the mainstream.

MAC Filtering can be used on a wireless network to prevent certain clients from accessing the Internet. You can choose to deny service to a set list of MAC addresses (and allow all others) or only allow service to a set list of MAC addresses (and deny all others).

Wireless Vulnerabilities to Know

Wireless systems are vulnerable to all the different attacks that wired networks are vulnerable to. However, because these protocols use radio frequency signals, they have an additional weakness: All radio frequency signals can be easily intercepted. To intercept 802.11x traffic, all you need is a PC with an appropriate 802.11x card installed. Simple software on the PC can capture the link traffic in the WAP and then process this data in order to decrypt account and password information.

An additional aspect of wireless systems is the *site survey*. Site surveys involve listening in on an existing wireless network using commercially available technologies. Doing so allows intelligence, and possibly data capture, to be performed on systems in your wireless network.

The term *site survey* initially meant determining whether a proposed location was free from interference. When used by an attacker, a site survey can determine what types of systems are in use, the protocols used, and other critical information about your network. It's the primary method used to gather data about wireless networks. Virtually all wireless networks are vulnerable to site surveys.

Data and Physical Security

Physical security, as the name implies, involves protecting your assets and information from physical access by unauthorized personnel. In other words, you're trying to protect those items that can be seen, touched, and stolen. These threats often present themselves as service technicians, janitors, customers, vendors, or even employees. They can steal your equipment, damage it, or take documents from offices, garbage cans, or filing cabinets. Their motivation may be retribution for some perceived misgiving, a desire to steal your trade secrets to sell to a competitor as an act of vengeance, or just greed. They might steal $1,000 worth of hardware that they can sell to a friend for a fraction of that and have no concept of the value of the data stored on the hardware.

Physical security is relatively easy to accomplish. You can secure facilities by controlling access to the office, shredding unneeded documents, installing security systems, and limiting access to sensitive areas of the business. Most office buildings provide perimeter and corridor security during unoccupied hours, and it isn't difficult to implement common-sense measures during occupied hours as well. Sometimes just having a person present—even a guard who spends much of the time sleeping—can be all the deterrent needed to prevent petty thefts.

Many office complexes also offer roving security patrols, multiple-lock access control methods, and electronic or password access. Typically, the facility managers handle these arrangements. They won't generally deal with internal security as it relates to your records, computer systems, and papers; that is your responsibility in most situations.

The first component of physical security involves making a physical location less tempting as a target. If the office or building you're in is open all the time, gaining entry into a business in the building is easy. You must prevent people from seeing your organization as a tempting target. Locking doors and installing surveillance or alarm systems can make a physical location a less desirable target. You can also add controls to elevators requiring keys or badges in order to reach upper floors. Plenty of wide-open targets are available, involving less risk on the part of the people involved. Try to make your office not worth the trouble.

The second component of physical security involves detecting a *penetration* or theft. You want to know what was broken into, what is missing, and how the loss occurred. Passive videotape systems are one good way to obtain this information. Most retail environments routinely tape key areas of the business to identify how thefts occur and who was involved. These tapes are admissible as evidence in most courts. Law enforcement should be involved as soon as a penetration or theft occurs. More important from a deterrent standpoint, you should make it well known that you'll prosecute anyone caught in the act of theft to the fullest extent of the law. Making the video cameras as conspicuous as possible will deter many would-be criminals.

The third component of physical security involves recovering from a theft or loss of critical information or systems. How will the organization recover from the loss and get on with normal business? If a vandal destroyed your server room with a fire or flood, how long would it take your organization to get back into operation and return to full productivity?

Recovery involves a great deal of planning, thought, and testing. What would happen if the files containing all your bank accounts, purchase orders, and customer information became a pile of ashes in the middle of the smoldering ruins that used to be your office? Ideally, critical copies of records and inventories should be stored off site in a secure facility.

Encryption Technologies

Cryptographic algorithms are used to encode a message from its unencrypted or clear text state into an encrypted message. The three primary methods are hashing, symmetric, and asymmetric.

Hashing is the process of converting a message, or data, into a numeric value. The numeric value that a hashing process creates is referred to as a *hash total* or *value*. Hashing functions are considered either one-way or two-way. A one-way hash doesn't allow a message to be decoded back to the original value. A two-way hash allows a message to be reconstructed from the hash. Most hashing functions are one-way hashing. Two primary standards exist that use the hashing process for encryption:

Secure Hash Algorithm (SHA)   The *Secure Hash Algorithm (SHA)* was designed to ensure the integrity of a message. The SHA is a one-way hash that provides a hash value that can be used with an encryption protocol. This algorithm produces a 160-bit hash value. SHA has been updated; the new standard is SHA-1.

Message Digest Algorithm (MDA)   The *Message Digest Algorithm (MDA)* also creates a hash value and uses a one-way hash. The hash value is used to help maintain integrity. There are several versions of MD; the most common are MD5, MD4, and MD2.

Symmetric algorithms require both ends of an encrypted message to have the same key and processing algorithms. Symmetric algorithms generate a secret key that must be protected. A secret key—sometimes referred to as a *private key*—is a key that isn't disclosed to people who aren't authorized to use the encryption system. The disclosure of a private key breaches the security of the encryption system. If a key is lost or stolen, the entire process is breached. These types of systems are common.

Asymmetric algorithms use two keys to encrypt and decrypt data. These keys are referred to as the *public key* and the *private key*. The public key can be used by the sender to encrypt a message, and the private key can be used by the receiver to decrypt the message. Symmetrical systems require the key to be private between the two parties, but with asymmetric systems, each circuit has one key.

The public key may be truly public or it may be a secret between the two parties. The private key is kept private and is known only by the owner (receiver). If someone wants to send you an encrypted message, they can use your public key to encrypt the message and then send you the message. You can use your private key to decrypt the message. One of the keys is always kept private. If both keys become available to a third party, the encryption system won't protect the privacy of the message.

Perhaps the best way to think about this system is that it's similar to a safe-deposit box. Two keys are needed: The box owner keeps the public key, and the bank retains the second or private key. In order to open the box, both keys must be used simultaneously.

Backups

Backups are duplicate copies of key information, ideally stored in a location other than the one where the information is currently stored. Backups include both paper and computer records. Computer records are usually backed up using a backup program, backup systems, and backup procedures.

The primary starting point for disaster recovery involves keeping current backup copies of key data files, databases, applications, and paper records available for use. Your organization must develop a solid set of procedures to manage this process and ensure that all key information is protected. A security professional can do several things in conjunction with systems administrators and business managers to protect this information. It's important to think of this problem as an issue that is larger than a single department.

The information you back up must be immediately available for use when needed. If a user loses a critical file, they won't want to wait several days while data files are sent from a remote storage facility. Several different types of storage mechanisms are available for data storage:

Working copies   *Working copy* backups—sometimes referred to as *shadow copies*—are partial or full backups that are kept at the computer center for immediate recovery purposes. Working copies are frequently the most recent backups that have been made.

Typically, working copies are intended for immediate use. These copies are typically updated on a frequent basis.

Many file systems used on servers include *journaling*. Journaled file systems (JFS) include a log file of all changes and transactions that have occurred within a set period of time (last few hours, and so on). If a crash occurs, the operating system can look at the log files to see what transactions have been committed and which ones haven't. This technology works well and allows unsaved data to be written after the recovery and the system, usually, to be successfully restored to its pre-crash condition.

Onsite storage   *Onsite storage* usually refers to a location on the site of the computer center that is used to store information locally. Onsite storage containers are available that allow computer cartridges, tapes, and other backup media to be stored in a reasonably protected environment in the building.

Onsite storage containers are designed and rated for fire, moisture, and pressure resistance. These containers aren't *fireproof* in most situations, but they're *fire-rated*: A fireproof container should be guaranteed to withstand damage regardless of the type of fire or temperatures, whereas fire ratings specify that a container can protect the contents for a specific amount of time in a given situation.

If you choose to depend entirely on onsite storage, make sure the containers you acquire can withstand the worst-case environmental catastrophes that could happen at your location. Make sure, as well, that those containers are in locations where you can easily find them after the disaster and access them (near exterior walls, and so on).

Offsite storage   *Offsite storage* refers to a location away from the computer center where paper copies and backup media are kept. Offsite storage can involve something as simple as keeping a copy of backup media at a remote office, or it can be as complicated as a nuclear-hardened high-security storage facility. The storage facility should be bonded, insured, and inspected on a regular basis to ensure that all storage procedures are being followed.

Determining which storage mechanism to use should be based on the needs of the organization, the availability of storage facilities, and the budget available. Most offsite storage facilities charge based on the amount of space you require and the frequency of access you need to the stored information.

Three methods exist to back up information on most systems:

Full backup   A *full backup* is a complete, comprehensive backup of all files on a disk or server. The full backup is current only at the time it's performed. Once a full backup is made, you have a complete archive of the system at that point in time. A system shouldn't be in use while it undergoes a full backup because some files may not get backed up. Once the system goes back into operation, the backup is no longer current. A full backup can be a time-consuming process on a large system.

Incremental backup   An *incremental backup* is a partial backup that stores only the information that has been changed since the last full or the last incremental backup. If a full backup were performed on a Sunday night, an incremental backup done on Monday night would contain only the information that changed since Sunday night. Such a backup is typically considerably smaller than a full backup. This backup system requires that each incremental backup be retained until a full backup can be performed. Incremental backups are usually the fastest backups to perform on most systems, and each incremental tape is relatively small.

Differential backup   A differential backup is similar in function to an incremental backup, but it backs up any files that have been altered since the last full backup; it makes duplicate copies of files that haven't changed since the last differential backup. If a full backup were performed on Sunday night, a differential backup performed on Monday night would capture the information that was changed on Monday. A differential backup completed on Tuesday night would record the changes in any files from Monday and any changes in files on Tuesday. As you can see, during the week each differential backup would become larger; by Friday or Saturday night, it might be nearly as large as a full backup. This means the backups in the earliest part of the weekly cycle will be very fast, and each successive one will be slower.

When these backup methods are used in conjunction with each other, the risk of loss can be greatly reduced. You should never combine an incremental backup with a differential backup. One of the major factors in determining which combination of these three methods to use is time—ideally, a full backup would be performed every day. Several commercial backup programs support these three backup methods. You must evaluate your organizational needs when choosing which tools to use to accomplish backups.

Almost every stable operating system contains a utility for creating a copy of configuration settings necessary to reach the present state after a disaster. In Windows Server 2003, for example, this is accomplished with an Automated System Recovery (ASR) disk. Make certain you know how to do an equivalent operation for the operating system you're running.

As an administrator, you must know how to do backups and be familiar with all the options available to you.

Incident Reporting

Incident Response policies define how an organization will respond to an incident. These policies may involve third parties, and they need to be comprehensive. The term *incident* is somewhat nebulous in scope; for our purposes, an incident is any attempt to violate a security policy, a successful penetration, a compromise of a system, or any unauthorized access to information. This term includes systems failures and disruption of services in the organization.

It's important that an Incident Response policy establish the following, at minimum:

- Outside agencies that should be contacted or notified in case of an incident
- Resources used to deal with an incident
- Procedures to gather and secure evidence
- List of information that should be collected about the incident
- Outside experts who can be used to address issues if needed
- Policies and guidelines regarding how to handle the incident

According to CERT, a Computer Security Incident Response Team (CSIRT) can be a formalized team, or ad hoc. You can toss a team together to respond to an incident after it arises; but investing time in the development process can make an incident more manageable, because many decisions about dealing with an incident will have been considered earlier. Incidents are high-stress situations; therefore, it's better to simplify the process by considering important aspects in advance. If civil or criminal actions are part of the process, evidence must be gathered and safeguarded properly.

Assume you've discovered a situation where a fraud has been perpetrated internally using a corporate computer. You're part of the investigating team. Your Incident Response policy lists the specialists you need to contact for an investigation. Ideally, you've already met the investigator or investigating firm, you've developed an understanding of how to protect the scene, and you know how to properly deal with the media (if they become involved).

Social Engineering

Social engineering is a process in which an attacker attempts to acquire information about your network and system by social means, such as talking to people in the organization. A social engineering attack may occur over the phone, by e-mail, or by a visit. The intent is to acquire access information, such as user IDs and passwords.

These types of attacks are relatively low-tech and are more akin to con jobs. Take the following example. Your Help Desk gets a call at 4:00 a.m. from someone purporting to be the vice president of your company. She tells the Help Desk personnel that she is out of town to attend a meeting, her computer just failed, and she is sitting in a Kinko's trying to get a file from her desktop computer back at the office. She can't seem to remember her password and user ID. She tells the Help Desk representative that she needs access to the information right away or the company could lose millions of dollars. Your Help Desk rep knows how important this meeting is and gives the vice president her user ID and password over the phone.

Another common approach is initiated by a phone call or e-mail from your software vendor, telling you that they have a critical fix that must be installed on your computer system. If this patch isn't installed right away, your system will crash and you'll lose all your data. For some reason, you've changed your maintenance account password and they can't log on. Your systems operator gives the password to the person. You've been hit again.

Exam Essentials

Know the names, purpose, and characteristics of hardware and software security.   Many types of hardware and software are used to provide security to an organization. These can range from firewalls (which can be software- or hardware-based) to smart cards. It's important to also know the different types of authentication technologies available and the various types of malicious software that exist.

Know the names, purpose, and characteristics of wireless security.   Wireless networks can be encrypted through WEP and WAP technologies. Wireless controllers use special ID numbers (SSIDs) and must be configured in the network cards to allow communications. However, using ID number configurations doesn't necessarily prevent wireless networks from being monitored, and there are vulnerabilities specific to wireless devices.

Know the names, purpose, and characteristics of data and physical security.   Know the different types of backups that can be done, as well as the basics of encryption. You should also be aware of social-engineering concerns and the need for a useful Incident Response policy.

Install, Configure, Upgrade, and Optimize Security

The topics beneath this objective and the following one closely mirror each other. In addition to this, there is a fair amount of overlap from the previous objective.

Critical Information

For this objective, you're expected to know the basics of the following items:

- BIOS
- Smart cards
- Authentication technologies
- Malicious-software protection
- Data access
- Backup procedures and access to backups

- Data migration

- Data/remnant removal

Each of these items is discussed in the sections that follow, as well as in the section called "Identify Tools, Diagnostic Procedures, and Troubleshooting Techniques for Security."

BIOS Security

The system Basic Input/Output System (BIOS) is used to power up the system and can also allow you to assign a password. Once enabled/activated, that password is stored in CMOS and must be given before the system will fully boot.

This provides a simple—and somewhat efficient—security solution for a workstation/laptop. For the casual hacker, the only way around giving the password is to remove the battery (thus erasing the CMOS). You should be aware, however, that many BIOS manufacturers include a backdoor password that can be given to bypass the one set by the user. Many of these values can be found on the Internet and are known by more-professional hackers.

Smart-Card Security

Smart cards are generally used for access control and security purposes. The card itself usually contains a small amount of memory that can be used to store permissions and access information.

Smart cards are difficult to counterfeit, but they're easy to steal. Once a thief has a smart card, they have all the access the card allows. To prevent this, many organizations don't put any identifying marks on their smart cards, making it harder for someone to utilize them. Many modern smart cards require a password or PIN to activate the card, and employ encryption to protect the card's contents.

Many European countries are beginning to use smart cards instead of magnetic-strip credit cards because they offer additional security and can contain more information.

Authentication Technologies

Authentication proves that a user or system is actually who they say they are. This is one of the most critical parts of a security system. It's part of a process that is also referred to as *Identification and Authentication (I&A)*. The identification process starts when a user ID or logon name is typed into a sign-on screen. Authentication is accomplished by challenging the claim about who is accessing the resource. Without authentication, anybody can claim to be anybody.

Authentication systems or methods are based on one or more of these three factors:

- Something you know, such as a password or PIN

- Something you have, such as a smart card or an identification device

- Something physically unique to you, such as your fingerprints or retinal pattern

Systems authenticate each other using similar methods. Frequently, systems pass private information between each other to establish identity. Once authentication has occurred, the two systems can communicate in the manner specified in the design.

Several common methods are used for authentication. Each has advantages and disadvantages that must be considered when you're evaluating authentication schemes.

Username/Password

A username and password are unique identifiers for a logon process. When users sit down in front of a computer system, the first thing a security system requires is that they establish who they are. Identification is typically confirmed through a logon process. Most operating systems use a user ID and password to accomplish this. These values can be sent across the connection as plain text or can be encrypted.

The logon process identifies to the operating system, and possibly the network, that you are who you say you are. Figure 6.1 illustrates this logon and password process. Notice that the operating system compares this information to the stored information from the security processor and either accepts or denies the logon attempt. The operating system may establish privileges or permissions based on stored data about that particular ID.

FIGURE 6.1 A logon process occurring on a workstation

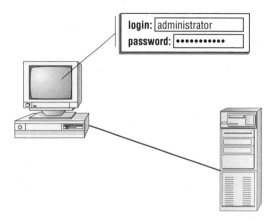

Logon or security server

Password Authentication Protocol (PAP)

Password Authentication Protocol (PAP) offers no true security, but it's one of the simplest forms of authentication. The username and password values are both sent to the server as clear text and checked for a match. If they match, the user is granted access; if they don't match, the user is denied access. In most modern implementations, PAP is shunned in favor of other, more secure, authentication methods.

Challenge Handshake Authentication Protocol (CHAP)

Challenge Handshake Authentication Protocol (CHAP) challenges a system to verify identity. CHAP doesn't use a user ID/password mechanism. Instead, the initiator sends a logon request from the client to the server. The server sends a challenge back to the client. The challenge is encrypted and then sent back to the server. The server compares the value from the client and, if the information matches, grants authorization. If the response fails, the session fails, and the request phase starts over. Figure 6.2 illustrates the CHAP procedure. This handshake method involves a number of steps and is usually automatic between systems after it's configured.

FIGURE 6.2   CHAP authentication

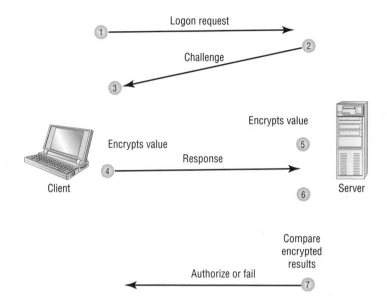

Certificates

Certificates are another common form of authentication. A server or *certificate authority (CA)* can issue a certificate that will be accepted by the challenging system. Certificates can be either physical access devices, such as smart cards, or electronic certificates that are used as part of the logon process. A *Certificate Practice Statement (CPS)* outlines the rules used for issuing and managing certificates. A *Certificate Revocation List (CRL)* lists the revocations that must be addressed (often due to expiration) in order to stay current.

A simple way to think of certificates is like hall passes at school. Figure 6.3 illustrates a certificate being handed from the server to the client once authentication has been established. If you have a hall pass, you can wander the halls of your school. If your pass is invalid, the hallway monitor can send you to the principal's office. Similarly, if you have a certificate, then you can prove to the system that you are who you say you are and are authenticated to work with the resources.

Security Tokens

Security tokens are similar to certificates. They contain the rights and access privileges of the token bearer as part of the token. Think of a token as a small piece of data that holds a sliver of information about the user.

Many operating systems generate a token that is applied to every action taken on the computer system. If your token doesn't grant you access to certain information, then either that information won't be displayed or your access will be denied. The authentication system creates a token every time a user connects or a session begins. At the completion of a session, the token is destroyed. Figure 6.4 shows the security token process.

FIGURE 6.3   A certificate being issued once identification has been verified

FIGURE 6.4   Security token authentication

Kerberos

Kerberos is an authentication protocol named after the mythical three-headed dog that stood at the gates of Hades. Originally designed by MIT, Kerberos is becoming very popular as an authentication method. It allows for a single sign-on to a distributed network.

Kerberos authentication uses a *Key Distribution Center* (*KDC*) to orchestrate the process. The KDC authenticates the *principal* (which can be a user, a program, or a system) and provides it with a ticket. Once this ticket is issued, it can be used to authenticate against other principals. This occurs automatically when a request or service is performed by another principal.

Kerberos is quickly becoming a common standard in network environments. Its only significant weakness is that the KDC can be a single point of failure. If the KDC goes down, the authentication process will stop. Figure 6.5 shows the Kerberos authentication process and the ticket being presented to systems that are authorized by the KDC.

FIGURE 6.5   Kerberos authentication process

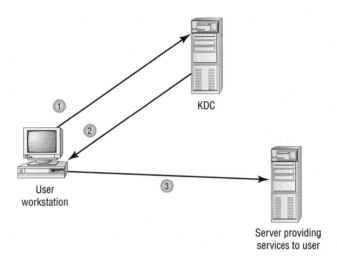

KDC

User
workstation

Server providing
services to user

1 User requests access to service running on a different server
2 KDC authenticates user and sends a ticket to be used between the user and the service on the server
3 User's workstation sends a ticket to the service

Multifactor Authentication

When two or more access methods are included as part of the authentication process, you're implementing a *multifactor* system. A system that uses smart cards and passwords is referred to as a *two-factor authentication* system. Two-factor authentication is shown in Figure 6.6. This example requires both a smart card and a logon password.

Malicious-Software Protection

Computer *viruses*—applications that carry out malicious actions—are one of the most annoying trends happening today. It seems that almost every day, someone invents a new virus. Some of these viruses do nothing more than give you a big "gotcha"; others destroy systems, contaminate networks, and wreak havoc on computer systems. A virus may act on your data or your operating system, but it's intent on doing harm, and doing so without your consent. Viruses often include replication as a primary objective and try to infect as many machines as they can, as quickly as possible.

The business of providing software to computer users to protect them from viruses has become a huge industry. Several very good and well-established suppliers of antivirus software exist, and new virus-protection methods come on the scene almost as fast as new viruses. Antivirus software scans the computer's memory, disk files, and incoming and outgoing e-mail. The software typically uses a virus-definition file that is updated regularly by the manufacturer. If these files are kept up-to-date, the computer system will be relatively secure. Unfortunately, most people don't keep their virus definitions up-to-date. Users will exclaim that a new virus has come out, because they just got it. Upon examination, you'll often discover that their virus-definition file is months out of date. As you can see, the software part of the system will break down if the definition files aren't updated on a regular basis.

Data Access

Access control defines the methods used to ensure that users of your network can access only what they're authorized to access. The process of access control should be spelled out in the organization's security policies and standards. Several models exist to accomplish this. This section will briefly explain the following models:

- Bell La-Padula
- Biba
- Clark-Wilson
- Information Flow model
- Noninterference model

Bell La-Padula Model

The *Bell La-Padula model* was designed for the military to address the storage and protection of classified information. The model is specifically designed to prevent unauthorized access to classified information. It prevents the user from accessing information that has a higher security rating than they're authorized to access. The model also prevents information from being written to a lower level of security.

FIGURE 6.6   Two-factor authentication

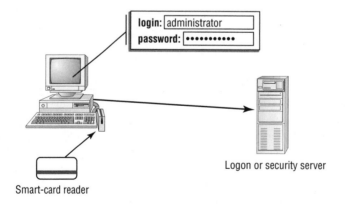

Logon or security server

Smart-card reader

Both factors must be valid:
• User ID and password
• Smart card

For example, if you're authorized to access Secret information, you aren't allowed to access Top Secret information, nor are you allowed to write to the system at a level lower than the Secret level. This creates upper and lower bounds for information storage. This process is illustrated in Figure 6.7. Notice in the illustration that you can't *read up* or *write down*. This means that a user can't read information at a higher level than they're authorized to access. A person writing a file can't write down to a lower level than the security level they're authorized to access.

FIGURE 6.7   The Bell La-Padula model

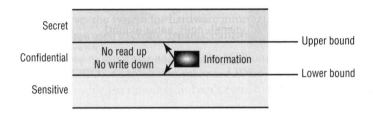

The process of preventing a write down keeps a user from accidentally breaching security by writing Secret information to the next lower level, Confidential. In our example, you can read Confidential information, but because you're approved at the Secret level, you can't write to the Confidential level. This model doesn't deal with integrity, only confidentiality. A user of Secret information can potentially modify other documents at the same level they possess.

To see how this model works, think about corporate financial information. The chief financial officer (CFO) may have financial information about the company that they need to protect. The Bell La-Padula model keeps them from inadvertently posting information at an access level lower than their access level (writing down), thus preventing unauthorized or accidental disclosure of sensitive information. Lower-level employees can't access this information because they can't read up to the level of the CFO.

The Biba Model

The *Biba model* was designed after the Bell La-Padula model. It's similar in concept to the Bell La-Padula model, but it's more concerned with information integrity, an area that the Bell La-Padula model doesn't address. In this model, there is no write up or read down. In short, if you're assigned access to Top Secret information, you can't read Secret information or write to any level higher than the level to which you're authorized. This keeps higher-level information pure by preventing less-reliable information from being intermixed with it. Figure 6.8 illustrates this concept in more detail. The Biba model was developed primarily for industrial uses, where confidentiality is usually less important than integrity.

Think about the data that is generated by a researcher for a scientific project. The researcher is responsible for managing the results of research from a lower-level project and incorporating it into their research data. If bad data were to get into their research, the whole research project would be ruined. With the Biba model, this accident can't happen. The researcher doesn't have access to the information from lower levels: That information must be promoted to the level of the researcher. This system keeps the researcher's data intact and prevents accidental contamination.

FIGURE 6.8   The Biba model

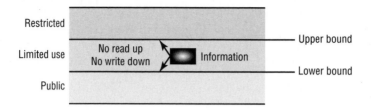

The Clark-Wilson Model

The *Clark-Wilson model* was developed after the Biba model. The approach is a little different from either the Biba or the Bell La-Padula method. In this model, data can't be accessed directly; it must be accessed through applications that have predefined capabilities. This process prevents unauthorized modification, errors, and fraud from occurring. If a user needs access to information at a certain level of security, a specific program is used. This program may allow only read access to the information. If a user needs to modify data, another application must be used. This allows a separation of duties in that individuals are granted access to only the tools they need. All transactions have associated audit files and mechanisms to report modifications. Figure 6.9 illustrates this process. Access to information is gained by using a program that specializes in access management; this can be either a single program that controls all access or a set of programs that controls access. Many software-management programs work using this method of security.

FIGURE 6.9   The Clark-Wilson model

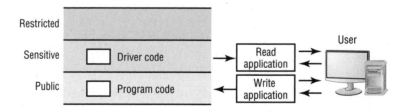

Let's say you're working on a software product as part of a team. You may need to access certain code to include in your programs. You aren't authorized to modify this code; you're merely authorized to use it. You use a checkout program to get the code from the source library. Any attempt to put modified code back is prevented. The developers of the code in the source library are authorized to make changes. This process ensures that only people authorized to change the code can accomplish the task.

Information Flow Model

The *Information Flow model* is concerned with the properties of information flow, not only the direction of the flow. Both the Bell La-Padula and Biba models are concerned with information flow in predefined manners; they're considered information-flow models. However, this particular Information Flow model is concerned with all information flow, not just up or down. This model requires that each piece of information have unique properties, including operation capabilities. If an attempt is made to write lower-level information to a higher level, the model evaluates the properties of the information and determines whether the operation is legal. If the operation is illegal, the model prevents it from occurring. Figure 6.10 illustrates this concept.

FIGURE 6.10   The Information Flow model

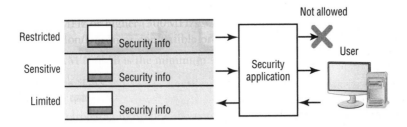

Let's use the previous software project as an example. A developer may be working with a version of the software to improve functionality. When the programmer makes improvements to the code, they want to put that code back into the library. If the attempt to write the code is successful, the code replaces the existing code. If a subsequent bug is found in the new code, the old code has been changed. The solution is to create a new version of the code that incorporates both the new code and the old code. Each subsequent change to the code requires a new version to be created. This process may consume more disk space, but it prevents things from getting lost, and it provides a mechanism to use or evaluate an older version of the code.

Noninterference Model

The *Noninterference model* is intended to ensure that higher-level security functions don't interfere with lower-level functions. In essence, if a higher-level user changes information, the lower-level user doesn't know about and isn't affected by the changes. This approach prevents the lower-level user from being able to deduce what changes are being made to the system. Figure 6.11 illustrates this concept. Notice that the lower-level user isn't aware that any changes have occurred above them.

FIGURE 6.11   The Noninterference model

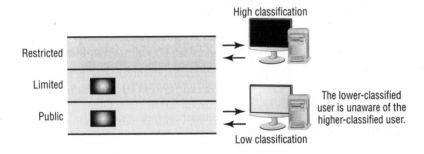

Let's take one last look at the software project with which we've been working. If a systems developer is making changes to the library that's being used by a lower-level programmer, changes may be made to the library without the lower-level programmer being aware of them. This lets the higher-level developer work on prototypes without affecting the development effort of the lower-level programmer. When the developer finishes the code, they publish it to lower-level programmers. At this point, all users have access to the changes, and they can use them in their programs.

Backup Procedures

An organization's *backup policy* dictates what information should be backed up and how it should be backed up. Ideally, a backup plan is written in conjunction with the Business Continuity Plan.

Backup policies also need to set guidelines for information archiving. Many managers and users don't understand the difference between a backup and an archive. A *backup* is a restorable copy of any set of data that is needed on the system; an *archive* is any collection of data that is removed from the system because it's no longer needed on a regular basis.

Data Migration

When migrating data, it's imperative that you focus on availability and reparability. Depending on the migration being undertaken, it's possible that the system you're migrating to doesn't use the same ACLs, granularity, or defaults that exist on the system you're coming from. To identify and plan for this scenario, it's important to always do a test of the migration in a controlled environment (lab, pilot, and so on) before instigating it on production systems.

It's also crucial that you do a full backup of all data before the migration. That backup can't be considered complete until you verify that you can restore it. The last thing you want is to need to restore data, only to find out that the media was improperly formatted and you're unable to do so.

Data Remnant Removal

When data ages, it must often be archived and removed from live systems. Policies should be in place to dictate who has access to the archives, how and where the archives are stored, and how they're cataloged. The latter is of key importance because you want to be able to find data as expeditiously as possible, even when it has been removed from the system.

Exam Essentials

Install, configure, upgrade, and optimize hardware, software, and data security. For this objective, you're expected to know the basics of the following items: BIOS, smart cards, authentication technologies, malicious-software protection, data access, backup procedures and access to backups, data migration, and data remnant removal.

Identify Tools, Diagnostic Procedures, and Troubleshooting Techniques for Security

This objective closely mirrors the previous objective. It also gets revisited in Chapter 14, which focuses on the methods used on each operating system.

Critical Information

The topics beneath this objective have been addressed before; the key difference here is that the focus is on identifying problems with each of the items/technologies. Table 6.2 summarizes the areas where problems may occur and ways to identify that a problem exists.

TABLE 6.2   Identifying Problem Issues

Area	Identifying Symptoms
BIOS	Problems/compromises involving the BIOS typically prevent the system from starting properly. You may be required to enter a password you don't know, or control of the system is never handed to the OS after POST.
Smart cards	Problems with smart cards become apparent when users are unable to access data, or logs show that they accessed data they never truly did.
Biometrics	If there is a problem with biometrics, the user is unable to authenticate and unable to access resources.
Malicious software	Malicious software should be first detected by an antivirus program or other routine operation. If not, it will begin to show itself in the actions taking place on the system (deletion of executables, mass mailing, and so on).
File system	File-system problems can fall into the category of users not being able to access data as they need to, or everyone being granted access to data that they should not see.
Data access	Data-access problems, like file-system issues, are usually those where users legitimately needing access to data can't access it, or too much permission is granted to users who don't need such access. Chapter 14 deals with specific OS approaches to data access.

TABLE 6.2 Identifying Problem Issues *(continued)*

Area	Identifying Symptoms *(continued)*
Backup	Issues with backups are their inability to successfully complete and include all files, or media failure when a restore needs to be done. Always verify that the backup completed successfully, and routinely verify that you can restore.
Data migration	Data-migration problems, as they pertain to security, usually result from the source and target not having the same one-to-one permission sets. Work closely with test data ahead of time to work out any issues that may arise before doing a migration of production data.

Exam Essentials

Diagnose and troubleshoot procedures and troubleshooting techniques for security. It's important to know the symptoms that may arise in the problem areas and to be able to quickly identify them. This allows you to then hone in on the source of the problem and begin troubleshooting in earnest.

Perform Preventative Maintenance for Computer Security

This objective tests your knowledge of preventative measures you should take on a regular basis to keep your system secure.

Critical Information

The landscape of security is changing at a very fast pace. You, as a security professional, are primarily responsible for keeping current on the threats and changes that are occurring. You're also responsible for ensuring that systems are kept up-to-date. The following list briefly summarizes the areas you must be concerned about:

Operating system updates Make sure all scheduled maintenance, updates, and service packs are installed on all the systems in your environment. Many manufacturers are releasing security updates on their products to deal with newly discovered vulnerabilities. For example, Novell, Microsoft, and Linux manufacturers offer updates on their websites. In some cases, you can have the OS automatically notify you when an update becomes available; this notification helps busy administrators remember to keep their systems current.

As a security administrator, you understand the importance of applying all patches and updates to keep systems current and to close found weaknesses.

Application updates   Make sure all applications are kept to the most current levels. Older software may contain vulnerabilities that weren't detected until after the software was released. New software may have recently discovered vulnerabilities as well as yet-to-be-discovered ones. Apply updates to your application software when they're released to help minimize the impact of attacks on your systems.

One of the biggest exploitations that occurs today involves application programs such as e-mail clients and word-processing software. The manufacturers of these products regularly release updates to attempt to make them more secure. Like operating system updates, these should be checked regularly and applied.

Network device updates   Most newer network devices can provide high levels of security, or they can be configured to block certain types of traffic and IP addresses. Make sure logs are reviewed and, where necessary, ACLs are updated to prevent attackers from disrupting your systems. These network devices are also frequently updated to counter new vulnerabilities and threats. Network devices should have their BIOS updated when the updates become available; doing so allows for an ever-increasing level of security in your environment.

Cisco, 3Com, and other network manufacturers regularly offer network updates. These can frequently be applied online or by web-enabled systems. These devices are your front line of defense: you want to make sure they're kept up-to-date.

Policies and procedures   A policy that is out-of-date may be worse than no policy. Be aware of any changes in your organization and in the industry that make existing policies out-of-date. Many organizations set a review date as part of their policy-creation procedures. Periodically review your documentation to verify that your policies are effective and current.

In addition to focusing on these areas, you must also stay current on security trends, threats, and tools available to help you provide security. The volume of threats is increasing, as are the measures, methods, and procedures being used to counter them.

You must keep abreast of what is happening in the field, as well as the current best practices of the systems and applications you support. You're basically going to be functioning as a clearinghouse and data repository for your company's security. Make it a point to become a walking encyclopedia on security issues: Doing so will improve your credibility and demonstrate your expertise. Both of these aspects enhance your career opportunities and equip you to be a leader in the field.

You should also make it a priority to train and educate users about malicious software. The more they know about the threats that are present—and the harm those threats can inflict—the more likely they are to act accordingly when they encounter a possible threat.

Exam Essentials

Implement software security preventative maintenance techniques.   Know the importance of keeping the systems current, applying patches as they're released/needed, and keeping your knowledge/skills up-to-date.

Review Questions

1. What is physical security?

2. What does Kerberos use to authenticate a principal?

3. Which authentication method sends a challenge to the client that is encrypted and then sent back to the server?

4. Which type of authentication method uses more than one authentication process for a logon?

5. What type of technology relies on a physical characteristic of the user to verify identity?

6. In which type of attack does someone try to con your organization into revealing account and password information?

7. What type of malicious code attempts to replicate using whatever means are available?

8. Which type of malware enters the system along with a legitimate program?

9. What could be one cause of unusual activity on the system disk when no user is accessing the system?

10. What do packet filters prevent?

Answers to Review Questions

1. Physical security is primarily concerned with the loss or theft of physical assets. This would include theft, fire, and other acts that physically deny a service or information to the organization.

2. Kerberos uses a Key Distribution Center to authenticate a principle. The KDC provides a credential that can be used by all Kerberos-enabled servers and applications.

3. Challenge Handshake Authentication Protocol (CHAP) sends a challenge to the originating client. This challenge is sent back to the server, and the encryption results are compared. If the challenge is successful, the client is logged on.

4. A multifactor authentication process uses two or more processes for logon. A two-factor method might use smart cards and biometrics for logon.

5. Biometric technologies rely on a physical characteristic of the user to verify identity. Biometric devices typically use either a hand pattern or a retinal scan to accomplish this.

6. Someone trying to con your organization into revealing account and password information is launching a social-engineering attack.

7. A worm is a type of malicious code that attempts to replicate using whatever means are available.

8. A Trojan horse enters with a legitimate program to accomplish its evil deeds.

9. A symptom of many viruses is unusual activity on the system disk. This is caused by the virus spreading to other files on your system.

10. Packet filters prevent unauthorized packets from entering or leaving a network. Packet filters are a type of firewall that block specified port traffic.

Chapter 7

Safety and Environmental Issues

COMPTIA A+ ESSENTIALS EXAM OBJECTIVES COVERED IN THIS CHAPTER:

✓ **7.1 Describe the aspects and importance of safety and environmental issues**

- ▪ Identify potential safety hazards and take preventative action
- ▪ Use Material Safety Data Sheets (MSDS) or equivalent documentation and appropriate equipment documentation
- ▪ Use appropriate repair tools
- ▪ Describe methods to handle environmental and human (e.g., electrical, chemical, physical) accidents, including incident reporting

✓ **7.2 Identify potential hazards and implement proper safety procedures, including ESD precautions and procedures, safe work environment, and equipment handling**

✓ **7.3 Identify proper disposal procedures for batteries, display devices, and chemical solvents and cans**

At one point in time, the objectives this chapter covers stood within their own domain and were combined with routine cleaning (then called Safety and Preventive Maintenance). In the previous version of the A+ exam, however, they were lumped beneath the Preventive Maintenance domain and safety was taken out. With this rendition of the certification/exam, CompTIA has brought them back into a domain of their own, removed the preventive maintenance (actually, it is now in objective 1.4), and made the topics worth 10 percent of the weighting.

Describe Safety and Environmental Issues

This objective requires you to know the potential safety hazards that exist when working with computer elements, and how to address them. There is a fair amount of overlap between this objective and the other two in this chapter, but is imperative that you understand such issues as *Material Safety Data Sheets* (*MSDS*) and know how to reference them when needed.

Critical Information

Any type of chemical, equipment, or supply that has the potential to harm the environment or people has to have an MSDS associated with it. These are traditionally created by the manufacturer and you can obtain them from the manufacturer, or from the Environmental Protection Agency at www.epa.gov.

Preventing Harm to Humans

Computers, display monitors, and printers can be dangerous if not handled properly. Computers not only use electricity, but they store electrical charge after they're turned off, in components called *capacitors*. The monitor and the power supply have large capacitors, capable of delivering significant shock, so they should not be disassembled except by a trained electrical repairperson.

In addition, various parts of the printer run at extremely high temperatures, and you can get burned if you try to handle them immediately after they've been in operation. Two examples are the CPU chip and the fusing unit inside a laser printer.

Extinguishing Electrical Fires

Repairing a computer is not often the cause of an electrical fire. However, you should know how to extinguish such a fire properly. Three major classes of fire extinguishers are available, one for each type of flammable substance: A for wood and paper fires, B for flammable liquids, and C for electrical fires. The most popular type of fire extinguisher today is the multipurpose, or ABC-rated, extinguisher. It contains a dry chemical powder that smothers the fire and cools it at the same time. For electrical fires (which may be related to a shorted-out wire in a power supply), make sure the fire extinguisher will work for class-C fires. If you don't have an extinguisher that is specifically rated for electrical fires (type C), you can use an ABC-rated extinguisher.

Power Supply Safety

Although it is possible to work on a power supply, doing so is *not* recommended. Power supplies contain several capacitors that can hold *lethal* charges *long after they have been unplugged*! It is extremely dangerous to open the case of a power supply. Besides, power supplies are inexpensive, so it would probably cost less to replace one than to try to fix it, and it would be much safer.

The number of volts in a power source represents its potential to do work, but volts don't do anything by themselves. Current (amperage, or amps) is the actual force behind the work being done by electricity. Here's an analogy to help explain this concept. Say you have two boulders; one weighs 10 pounds, the other 100 pounds, and each is 100 feet off the ground. If you drop them, which one will do more work? The obvious answer is the 100-pound boulder. They both have the same potential to do work (100 feet of travel), but the 100-pound boulder has more mass, and thus more force. Voltage is analogous to the distance the boulder is from the ground, and amperage is analogous to the mass of the boulder.

This is why we can produce static electricity on the order of 50,000 volts and not electrocute ourselves. Even though this electricity has a great *potential* for work, it does very little work because the amperage is so low. This also explains why we can weld metal with only 110 volts. Welders use only 110 (sometimes 220) volts, but they also use anywhere from 50 to 200 amps!

Printer Safety

Printer repair has hazards and pitfalls. Some of them are discussed here:

- When handling a toner cartridge from a laser printer or page printer, do not vigorously shake the cartridge or turn it upside down. You will find yourself spending more time cleaning the printer and the surrounding area than you would have spent to fix the printer.

- Do not put any objects into the feeding system (in an attempt to clear the path) while the printer is running.

- Laser printers generate a laser that is hazardous to your eyes. Do not look directly into the source of the laser.

- If it's an ink-jet printer, do not try to blow into the ink cartridge to clear a clogged opening— that is, unless you like the taste of ink. Most printers come with software that provides a cleaning method for the cartridge.

- Some parts of a laser printer (such as the EP cartridge) will be damaged if touched. Your skin produces oils and has a small surface layer of dead skin cells. These substances can collect on the delicate surface of the EP cartridge and cause malfunctions. Bottom line: Keep your fingers out of where they don't belong!

Monitor Safety

Other than the power supply, one of the most dangerous components to try to repair is the monitor, or cathode ray tube (CRT). We recommend that you *not* try to repair monitors. To avoid the extremely hazardous environment contained inside the monitor—it can retain a high-voltage charge for hours after it's been turned off—take it to a certified monitor technician or television repair shop. The repair shop or certified technician will know and understand the proper procedures to discharge the monitor, which involves attaching a resistor to the flyback transformer's charging capacitor to release the high-voltage electrical charge that builds up during use. They will also be able to determine whether the monitor can be repaired or needs to be replaced. Remember, the monitor works in its own extremely protective environment (the monitor case) and may not respond well to your desire to try to open it. The CRT is vacuum-sealed. Be extremely careful when handling it—if you break the glass, the CRT will implode, which can send glass in any direction.

Even though we recommend not repairing monitors, the A+ exam does test your knowledge of the safety practices to use when you need to do so. If you have to open a monitor, you must first discharge the high-voltage charge on it using a high-voltage probe. This probe has a very large needle, a gauge that indicates volts, and a wire with an alligator clip. Attach the alligator clip to a ground (usually the round pin on the power cord). Slip the probe needle under the high-voltage cup on the monitor. You will see the gauge spike to around 15,000 volts and slowly reduce to zero. When it reaches zero, you may remove the high-voltage probe and service the high-voltage components of the monitor.

Reporting Incidents

As careful as you try to be, there is always the possibility for accidents to occur. Accidents can be environment-related (for example, a flash flood no one could predict suddenly overtakes the server room and shorts out the wiring), or caused by humans (someone mixes the wrong cleaning chemicals together to try and make their own concoction). Regardless of the cause or circumstances, one thing is written in stone: you must fully and truthfully document the problem.

While that documentation must be seen by internal parties (managers, human resources, etc.), it may also need to be seen by external parties. The latter depends on the type of industry that you are in and the type of incident that occurred. For example, if a large amount of battery acid is spilled in the ground, you should contact the Environmental Protection Agency (see reporting procedures at www.epa.gov). If employees are injured, you may need to be contact the Occupational Safety and Health Administration (OSHA). On their website (www.osha.gov), you can find links to information on issues of compliance, laws and regulation, and enforcement.

It is your responsibility, as an administrator and a professional, to know—or learn—the reporting procedures for incidents that you are faced with and to act accordingly.

Exam Essentials

Know what an MSDS is.   An MSDS is a Material Safety Data Sheet containing instructions for handling an item. It can be acquired from the manufacturer or from the EPA.

Know the fire extinguisher types.   Class C is the type of fire extinguisher needed for electrical fires.

Know that a monitor stores high voltage.   Monitors and power supplies carry the greatest potential for human harm. This is due to their capacitors, which store high-voltage electrical charges. A monitor in particular can store thousands of volts of charge for weeks after it has been unplugged.

Know that you may need to report incidents.   When incidents happen, you must always document them and every attempt should be made to do so both fully and truthfully. Depending upon the type of incident, you may also need to report it to other authorities, such as the EPA or OSHA.

Identify Potential Hazards

This objective deals with potential hazards, both to you and to the computer system. It focuses on protecting humans from harm due to electricity, heat, and other hazards, and on protecting computer components from harm due to electrostatic discharge (ESD).

Critical Information

ESD is one of the most dangerous risks associated with working with computers. Not only does ESD have the potential to damage and harm components of the computer, but it can also injure you. Not understanding the proper way to avoid it could get you killed.

The ESD that we are speaking about here does not have the capability to kill you since it doesn't have the amperage. What does represent a threat, though, is using a wrist strap of your own design that does not have the resistor protection built into it and then accidentally touching something with high voltage while wearing the wrist strap. Without the resistor in place, the high voltage would be grounded through you!

Minimizing Electrostatic Discharge (ESD)

Electrostatic discharge (ESD) is the technical term for what happens whenever two objects of dissimilar charge come in contact—think of rubbing your feet on a carpet and then touching a light switch. The two objects exchange electrons in order to standardize the electrostatic charge between them, with the object of higher charge passing voltage to the object of lower charge. If it happens to be an electronic component that receives the charge, there is a good chance that it can be damaged.

The likelihood that a component will be damaged increases with the increasing use of Complementary Metallic Oxide Semiconductor (CMOS) chips, because these chips contain a thin metal oxide layer that is hypersensitive to ESD. The previous generation's Transistor-Transistor Logic (TTL) chips are more robust than the newer CMOS chips because they don't contain this metal oxide layer. Most of today's ICs are CMOS chips, so ESD is more of a concern lately.

The lowest-static voltage transfer that you can feel is around 3,000 volts (it doesn't electrocute you because there is extremely little current). A static transfer that you can *see* is at least 10,000 volts! Just by sitting in a chair, you can generate around 100 volts of static electricity. Walking around wearing synthetic materials can generate around 1,000 volts. You can easily generate around 20,000 volts simply by dragging your smooth-soled shoes across a shag carpet in the winter. (Actually, it doesn't have to be winter to run this danger; it can occur in any room with very low humidity. It's just that heated rooms in wintertime generally have very low humidity.)

It would make sense that these thousands of volts would damage computer components. However, a component can be damaged with as little as 80 volts. That means if your body has a small charge built up in it, you could damage a component without even realizing it.

Antistatic Wrist Strap

There are measures you can implement to help contain the effects of ESD. The easiest one to implement is the *antistatic wrist strap*, also referred to as an ESD strap. You attach one end of the ESD strap to an earth ground (typically the ground pin on an extension cord) and wrap the other end around your wrist. This strap grounds your body and keeps it at a zero charge. Figure 7.1 shows the proper way to attach an antistatic strap.

FIGURE 7.1   Proper ESD strap connection

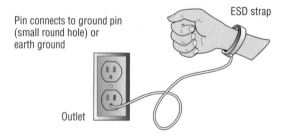

Pin connects to ground pin (small round hole) or earth ground

ESD strap

Outlet

If you do not have a grounded outlet available, you can achieve partial benefit simply by attaching the strap to the metal frame of the PC case. Doing so keeps the charge equalized between your body and the case, so that there is no electrostatic discharge when you touch components inside the case.

WARNING   An ESD strap is a specially designed device to bleed electrical charges away *safely*. It uses a 1-megaohm resistor to bleed the charge away slowly. A simple wire wrapped around your wrist will not work correctly and could electrocute you!

WARNING   Do not wear the antistatic wrist strap when there is the potential to encounter a high-voltage capacitor, such as when working on the inside of a monitor or power supply. The strap could channel that voltage through your body.

Antistatic Bags for Parts

Antistatic bags protect sensitive electronic devices from stray static charges. The bags are designed so that static charges collect on the outside of the bags rather than on the electronic components. You can obtain these bags from several sources. The most direct way to acquire antistatic bags is to go to an electronics supply store and purchase them in bulk. Most supply stores have several sizes available. Perhaps the easiest way to obtain them, however, is to hold onto the ones that come your way. That is, when you purchase any new component, it usually comes in an antistatic bag. Once you have installed the component, keep the bag. It may take you a while to gather a sizable collection of bags if you take this approach, but eventually you will have a fairly large assortment.

ESD Static Mats

It is possible to damage a device simply by laying it on a bench top. For this reason, you should have an ESD mat in addition to an ESD strap. This mat drains excess charge away from any item coming in contact with it (see Figure 7.2). ESD mats are also sold as mouse/keyboard pads to prevent ESD charges from interfering with the operation of the computer.

FIGURE 7.2   Proper use of an ESD mat

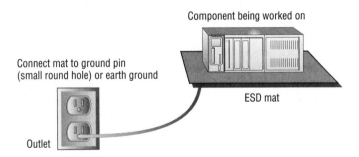

Vendors have methods of protecting components in transit from manufacture to installation. They press the pins of ICs into antistatic foam to keep all the pins at the same potential, and circuit boards are shipped in antistatic bags, discussed earlier. However, keep in mind that unlike antistatic mats, antistatic bags do not drain the charges away—they should never be used in place of antistatic mats.

Modifying the Relative Humidity

Another preventive measure you can take is to maintain the relative humidity at around 50 percent. Be careful not to increase the humidity too far—to the point where moisture starts to condense on the equipment! Also, use antistatic spray, which is available commercially, to reduce static buildup on clothing and carpets. In a pinch, a solution of diluted fabric softener sprayed on these items will do the same thing.

At the very least, you can be mindful of the dangers of ESD and take steps to reduce its effects. Beyond that, you should educate yourself about those effects so you know when ESD is becoming a major problem.

Exam Essentials

Understand ESD. Electrostatic discharge occurs when two objects of unequal electrical potential meet. The object of higher potential transfers some charge to the other one, just as water flows into an area that has a lower water level.

Understand the antistatic wrist strap. The antistatic wrist strap is also referred to as an ESD strap. To use the ESD strap, you attach one end to an earth ground (typically the ground pin on an extension cord) and wrap the other end around your wrist. This strap grounds your body and keeps it at a zero charge, preventing discharges from damaging the components of a PC.

Identify Proper Disposal Procedures

This objective expects you to know the various components involved in computing that must be disposed of in ways other than just dumping them in the trash. Some of these components could harm the environment, while others may be hazardous to humans if disposed of improperly.

Critical Information

It is estimated that more than 25 percent of all the lead in landfills today comes from consumer electronics components. Because consumer electronics contain hazardous substances, many states require that they be disposed of as hazardous waste. Computers are no exception. Monitors contain several carcinogens and phosphors, as well as mercury and lead. The computer itself may contain several lubricants and chemicals as well as lead. Printers contain plastics and chemicals such as toners and inks that are also hazardous. All of these items should be disposed of properly.

Recycling Computers

We recycle cans, plastic, and newspaper, so why not recycle computer equipment? The problem is that most computers contain small amounts of hazardous substances. Some countries are exploring the option of recycling electrical machines, but most have not enacted appropriate measures to enforce their proper disposal. However, we can do a few things as consumers and environmentalists to promote the proper disposal of computer equipment:

- Check with the manufacturer. Some manufacturers will take back outdated equipment for parts.
- Disassemble the machine and reuse the parts that are good.
- Check out businesses that can melt down the components for the lead or gold plating.

- Contact the Environmental Protection Agency (EPA) for a list of local or regional waste disposal sites that will accept used computer equipment.
- Check with local nonprofit or education organizations interested in using the equipment.
- Check out the Internet for possible waste disposal sites. Table 7.1 gives a few websites that deal with disposal of used computer equipment.

TABLE 7.1   Computer Recycling Websites

Site Name	Web Address
Computer Recycle Center	www.recycles.com/
PC Disposal	www.pcdisposal.com
Re-PC	www.repc.com/

Disposing of Batteries

In particular, you should make a special effort to recycle batteries. Batteries contain several chemicals that are harmful to our environment, such as nickel and lead, and won't degrade safely. Batteries should not be thrown away; they should be recycled according to your local laws. Check with your local authorities to find out how batteries should be recycled.

Disposing of CRTs

A CRT contains phosphors on the inside of the screen that can harm the environment if placed in a landfill. The large boxy shell of the CRT also takes up a lot of space in a landfill. Dispose of a monitor at your local hazardous-waste recycling center.

Disposing of Circuit Boards

Circuit boards contain lead in their soldering, so they should not be put in the regular trash. Take them to the local hazardous-waste disposal site, or contract with a company that handles them.

Disposing of Ink and Toner Cartridges

Ink and toner cartridges should be taken to recycling centers for proper disposal. It may also be possible to sell them to companies that refill and reuse them, but some people feel that this is not a good idea. Those re-manufactured cartridges sometimes do not work very well, and can damage the printers they are installed in, and by selling such companies your "empties" you are encouraging that industry.

Disposing of Cleaning Chemicals

The most common cleaning chemicals used for computers are alcohol and water, neither of which are particularly hazardous to the environment. However, if you use other chemical products, consult an MSDS for the product or consult the manufacturer to find out whether any special disposal is required.

Exam Essentials

Know what components are not suitable for a landfill.   Batteries, CRTs, and circuit boards are all examples of items that should not be thrown away normally because of the elements used in them. Batteries contain metals such as lead and nickel, circuit boards contain lead solder, and CRTs contain phosphors.

Review Questions

1. From which government agency can you find Material Safety Data Sheets?

2. What is the environmentally unfriendly part of laser printers?

3. True or false: An ESD strap should connect to the ground of an electrical outlet.

4. What is the danger to humans when disassembling and working on a monitor?

5. What type of fire extinguisher is appropriate for electrical fires?

6. True or false: ESD occurs when two objects of unequal electrical charge touch, with the object of higher charge passing some of its voltage to the object of lower charge.

7. Given that static electricity can exceed 10,000 volts, why does it not electrocute you?

8. As room humidity goes up, what happens to the potential for ESD damage?

9. True or false: A CRT should not be thrown in a landfill because it contains lead and nickel.

10. What is the name of the document that contains information about handling and disposal of a potentially hazardous item?

Answers to Review Questions

1. The EPA (Environmental Protection Agency) keeps a copy of Material Safety Data Sheets.

2. Toner. You must be careful not to spill it and to send used cartridges to recycling centers.

3. True. An ESD strap should connect to the ground of an electrical outlet.

4. A high-voltage capacitor inside the monitor retains a charge even long after the monitor has been unplugged.

5. Class C.

6. True.

7. Low current (amps).

8. It decreases.

9. False. A CRT is not landfill-safe, but not because of nickel or lead. Instead, it's due to the phosphors on the glass and the CRT's large size and hollow center.

10. Material Safety Data Sheet (MSDS).

Chapter

8

Professionalism and Communication

COMPTIA A+ ESSENTIALS EXAM OBJECTIVES COVERED IN THIS CHAPTER:

✓ **8.1 Use good communication skills, including listening and tact / discretion, when communicating with customers and colleagues**

- Use clear, concise, and direct statements
- Allow the customer to complete statements—avoid interrupting
- Clarify customer statements—ask pertinent questions
- Avoid using jargon, abbreviations, and acronyms
- Listen to customers

✓ **8.2 Use job-related professional behavior, including notation of privacy, confidentiality, and respect for the customer and customers' property**

- Behavior
  - Maintain a positive attitude and tone of voice
  - Avoid arguing with customers and / or becoming defensive
  - Do not minimize customers' problems
  - Avoid being judgmental and / or insulting or calling the customer names
  - Avoid distractions and / or interruptions when talking with customers
- Property
  - Telephone, laptop, desktop computer, printer, monitor, etc.

When the A+ certification was first released by CompTIA, it included a domain on Customer Satisfaction that tested "soft skills." In recent years, those questions were removed from the exams and weren't tested on (or taught in corresponding classes). Reflecting the value that CompTIA ascribes to these fundamentals, however, CompTIA has added these types of questions back into the exams—now under the moniker of Professionalism and Communication.

On the Essentials exam, this domain has the lowest weighting—only 5 percent—but you should study the topic well. Not only does it have great value in the real world, but it's also weighted heavier on some of the electives.

Use Good Communication Skills

It's possible that you chose computers as your vocation instead of public speaking because you want to interact with people on a one-to-one basis. As unlikely as that possibility may be, it still exists.

Whether or not you enjoy one-to-one communication, you should know the basics. Fortunately, the multiple-choice questions you'll be asked require more common sense than anything else, and you shouldn't find this domain to be a stumbling block. If the following discussion seems like second nature, you should feel confident that this objective won't be one with which you'll have trouble.

Critical Information

Good communication includes listening to what the user/manager/developer is telling you and making certain that you understand completely what they are trying to say. Just because a user or customer doesn't understand the terminology/syntax/concepts that you do doesn't mean they don't have a real problem that needs addressing. You must, therefore, be skilled not only at listening, but also at translating. Professional conduct encompasses politeness, guidance, punctuality, and accountability. Always treat the customer with the same respect and empathy you would expect if the situation were reversed. Likewise, guide the customer through the problem and the explanation. Tell them what has caused the problem they're currently experiencing and the best solution to prevent it from reoccurring.

Customer satisfaction goes a long way toward generating repeat business. If you can *meet* the customer's expectations, you'll almost assuredly hear from them again when another problem arises. If you can *exceed* the customer's expectations, you can almost guarantee that they will call you the next time a problem arises.

Customer satisfaction is important in all communication media—whether you're on site, providing phone support, or communicating through email or other correspondence. If you're on site act in accordance with the following points:

- When you arrive, immediately look for the person (user, manager, administrator, and so on) who is affected by the problem. Announce that you're there, and assure them that you'll do all you can to remedy the problem.

- Listen intently to what your customer is saying. Make it obvious to them that you're listening and respecting what they're telling you. If you have a problem understanding them, go to whatever lengths you need to in order to remedy the situation. Look for verbal and nonverbal cues that can help you isolate the problem.

- Share the customer's sense of urgency. What may seem like a small problem to you can appear to the customer as if the whole world is collapsing around them.

- Be honest and fair with the customer, and try to establish a personal rapport. Tell them what the problem is, what you believe is the cause, and what can be done in the future to prevent it from reoccurring.

- Handle complaints as professionally as possible. Accept responsibility for errors that may have occurred on your part, and never try to pass the blame. Avoid arguing with a customer, because doing so serves no purpose; resolve their anger with as little conflict as possible. Remember: the goal is to keep them as a customer, not to win an argument.

- When you finish a job, notify the user that you're done. Make every attempt to find the user and inform them of the resolution. If it's impossible to find them, leave a note for them to find when they return, explaining the resolution. You should also leave a means by which they can contact you, should they have a question about the resolution or a related problem. In most cases, the number you leave should be that of your business during working hours and your pager, where applicable, after hours.

If you're providing phone support, do the following:

- Always answer the telephone in a professional manner, announcing the name of the company and yourself.

- Make a concentrated effort to ascertain the customer's technical level, and communicate at that level, not above or below it.

- The most important skill you can have is the ability to listen. You have to rely on the customer to tell you the problem and describe it accurately. They can't do that if you're second-guessing them or jumping to conclusions before the whole story is told. Ask questions that are broad at first and then narrow down to help isolate the problem. It's your job to help guide the user's description of the problem. Here are some examples:
  - Is the printer plugged in?
  - Is it online?
  - Are any lights flashing on it?

- Complaints should be handled in the same manner as if you were on site. Make your best effort to resolve the problem and not argue its points. Again: you want to keep the customer more than you want to accomplish any other goal.

- Close the incident only when the customer is satisfied that the solution you have given them is the correct one and the problem has gone away.

- End the telephone call in a courteous manner. Thanking the customer for the opportunity to serve them is often the best way.

Talking to the user is an important first step in the troubleshooting process. Your first contact with a computer that has a problem is usually through the customer, either directly or by way of a work order that contains the user's complaint. Often, the complaint is something straightforward, such as "There's a disk stuck in the floppy drive." At other times, the problem is complex, and the customer doesn't mention everything that has been going wrong.

Eliciting Problem Symptoms from Customers

The act of diagnosis starts with the art of customer relations. Go to the customer with an attitude of trust: believe what the customer is saying. At the same time, go to the customer with an attitude of hidden skepticism, meaning *don't* believe that the customer has told you everything. This attitude of hidden skepticism isn't the same as distrust; just remember that what you hear isn't always the whole story, and customers may inadvertently forget to give a crucial detail.

For example, a customer may complain that their CD-ROM drive doesn't work. What they fail to mention is that it has never worked and that they installed it. When you examine the machine, you realize that the customer mounted the drive with screws that are too long and that prevent the tray from ejecting properly.

Having Customers Reproduce Errors as Part of the Diagnostic Process

The most important part of this step is to have the customer show you what the problem is. An excellent method is to say, "Show me what 'not working' looks like." That way, you see the conditions and methods under which the problem occurs. The problem may be a simple matter of an improper method. The user may be doing an operation incorrectly or doing the process in the wrong order. During this step, you have the opportunity to observe how the problem occurs, so pay attention.

Identifying Recent Changes to the Computer Environment

The user can give you vital information. The most important question is, "What changed?" Problems don't usually come out of nowhere. Was a new piece of hardware or software added? Did the user drop some equipment? Was there a power outage or a storm? These are the types of questions you can ask a user in trying to find out what is different.

If nothing changed, at least outwardly, then what was going on at the time of failure? Can the problem be reproduced? Can the problem be worked around? The point here is to ask as many questions as you need to in order to pinpoint the trouble.

Using the Information

Once the problem or problems have been clearly identified, your next step is to isolate possible causes. If the problem can't be clearly identified, then further tests are necessary. A common technique for hardware and software problems alike is to strip the system down to bare-bones basics. In a hardware situation, this may mean removing all interface cards except those absolutely required for the system to operate. In a software situation, this may mean disabling elements within Device Manager.

Then, you can gradually rebuild the system toward the point where the trouble started. When you reintroduce a component and the problem reappears, you know that component is the one causing the problem.

Putting It in Perspective

Whether you're dealing with customers in person or on the phone, CompTIA expects you to adhere to five rules. These were implied in the discussion previously, but you must understand them and hold fast to their precepts for the exam:

- Use clear, concise, and direct statements—customers want to know what is going on. They want to know that you understand the problem and can deal with it. Being honest and direct is almost always appreciated.

- Allow the customer to complete statements, and avoid interrupting them. Everyone has been in a situation where they haven't been able to fully tell what they wanted to without being interrupted or ignored. It isn't enjoyable in a social setting, and it's intolerable in a business setting.

- Clarify customer statements, and ask pertinent questions. The questions you ask should help guide you toward isolating the problem and identifying possible solutions.

- Avoid using jargon, abbreviations, and acronyms. Every field has its own language that can make those from outside the field feel lost. Put yourself in the position of someone not in the field, and explain what is going on using words they can relate to.

- Listen to customers. This is the most important rule of all—people like to feel they're being listened to. As simple an act as it is, it can make all the difference in making customers at ease with your work.

Exam Essentials

Use good communication skills.   Listen to the customer. Let them tell you what they understand the problem to be, and then interpret the problem and see if you can get them to agree to what you're hearing them say. Treat the customer, whether an end user or a colleague, with respect, and take their issues and problems seriously.

Use Appropriate Job-Related Behavior

Whether you're representing a company or yourself, you should always act in a professional manner. Your appearance and demeanor have a great deal to do with the lasting impression that stays with the customer. Always go to great lengths to instill confidence and a sense of security in their minds.

This objective tests your knowledge of what is—and isn't—appropriate behavior for this line of work, and your ability to respect the customer's property.

Critical Information

Critical to appropriate behavior is treating the customer, or user, the way you want to be treated. Much has been made of the Golden Rule—treating others the way you would have them treat you. Six key elements, from a business perspective, are punctuality, accountability, flexibility, confidentiality, respect, and privacy. The following sections discuss each of these.

Punctuality

Punctuality is important and should be a part of your planning process before you ever arrive at the site: If you tell the customer you'll be there at 10:30, you need to make every attempt to be there at that time. If you arrive late, you have given them false hope that the problem would be solved by a set time. That false hope can lead to anger when you arrive late and appear to not be taking their problem as seriously as they are. Punctuality continues to be important throughout the service call and doesn't end with your arrival. If you need to leave to get parts, tell the customer when you'll be back, and then be there at that time. If for some reason you can't return at the expected time, alert the customer and inform them of your new return time.

In conjunction with time and punctuality, if a user asks how much longer the server will be down, and you respond that it will up in five minutes, only to have it remain down for five more hours, you're creating resentment and possibly anger. When estimating downtime, always allow for more time than you think you'll need, just in case other problems occur. If you greatly underestimate the time, always inform the affected parties and give them a new time estimate. Here's an analogy that will put it in perspective: If you take your car to get the oil changed, and the counter clerk tells you it will be "about 15 minutes," the last thing you want is to be sitting there four hours later.

Accountability

Accountability is a trait that's well respected in every technician. When problems occur, you need to be accountable for them and not attempt to pass the buck. You can no doubt think of people who have a sense of accountability, and you can also think of some who don't. It's equally easy for a customer to identify this trait in a technician. For example, suppose you're called to a site to put a larger hard drive into a server. While performing this operation, you inadvertently scrape your feet across the carpeted floor, build up energy, and zap the memory in the server. Some technicians would pretend the electrostatic discharge (ESD) never happened, put in the new hard drive, and then act baffled by the fact that problems unrelated to the hard drive are occurring. An accountable technician will explain exactly what happened to the customer and suggest ways of proceeding from that point—addressing and solving the problem as quickly and efficiently as possible.

Flexibility

Flexibility is another important trait for a service technician. Although it's important that you respond to service calls promptly and close them (solve them) as quickly as you can, you must also be flexible. If a customer can't have you on site until the afternoon, make your best attempt to work them into your schedule around the time most convenient for them. Likewise, if you're called to a site to solve a problem, and they're having another problem that they bring to your attention while you're there, make every attempt to address that problem as well. Under no circumstances should you ever give a customer the cold shoulder or not respond to their problems because they weren't on an initial incident report.

You should take all this advice in the context of general information and follow the express guidelines of the company you work for.

Confidentiality

The goal of *confidentiality* is to prevent or minimize unauthorized access to files and folders and disclosure of data and information. In many instances, laws and regulations require specific information confidentiality. For example, Social Security records, payroll and employee records, medical records, and corporate information are high-value assets. This information could create liability issues or embarrassment if it fell into the wrong hands. Over the last few years, there have been several cases in which bank-account and credit-card numbers were published on the Internet. The costs of these types of breaches of confidentiality far exceed the actual losses from the misuse of this information.

Confidentiality entails ensuring that data expected to remain private is seen only by those who should see it. Confidentiality is implemented through authentication and access controls.

Just as confidentiality issues are addressed early in the design phase of a project, you—as a computer professional—are expected to uphold a high level of confidentiality. Should a user approach you with a sensitive issue—telling you their password, asking for assistance obtaining access to medical forms, and so on—it's your obligation as a part of your job to make certain that information passes no further.

Respect

Much of the discussion in this chapter is focused on respecting the customer as an individual. In addition to respecting them as a person, you must also respect the tangibles that are important to them. Although you may look at a monitor they're using and recognize it as an outdated piece of equipment that should be scrapped, the customer may see it as a gift from their children when they first started their business.

Treat the customer's property as if it has value, and you'll win their respect. Their property includes the system you're working on (laptop/desktop computer, monitor, peripherals, and so on) as well as other items associated with their business. Don't use their telephone to make personal calls or unnecessarily call other customers while you're at this site. Don't use their printers or other equipment unless it's in a role associated with the problem you've been summoned to fix.

Privacy

Although there is some overlap between confidentiality and privacy, *privacy* is an area of computing that is becoming considerably more regulated. As a computing professional, you must stay current with applicable laws, because you're often one of the primary agents expected to ensure compliance.

 In addition to the federal laws, most states have laws on computer crime as well. Check http://nsi.org/Library/Compsec/computerlaw/statelaws.html for information on your state.

Computer Fraud and Abuse Act

The Computer Fraud and Abuse Act was introduced into law in 1986. The original law was passed to address issues of fraud and abuse that weren't well covered under existing statutes. The law was updated in 1994, in 1996, and again in 2001.

This act gives federal authorities, primarily the FBI, the ability to prosecute hackers, spammers, and others as terrorists. The law is primarily intended to protect government and financial computer systems from intrusion. Technically, if a governmental system, such as an Internet server, were used in the commission of the crime, virtually any computer user of that system could be prosecuted.

The law is comprehensive and allows for stiff penalties, fines, and imprisonment of up to 10 years for convictions under this statute.

 For more information on this act, visit http://cio.doe.gov/Documents/ CFA.HTM.

Computer Security Act of 1987

The Computer Security Act requires federal agencies to identify and protect computer systems that contain sensitive information. This law requires agencies that keep sensitive information to conduct regular training and audits and to implement procedures to protect privacy. All federal agencies must comply with this act.

 For more information on this act, visit www.epic.org/crypto/csa/.

Cyberspace Electronic Security Act

The Cyberspace Electronic Security Act (CESA) gives law enforcement the right to gain access to encryption keys and cryptography methods. The initial version of this act allowed federal law enforcement agencies to secretly use monitoring, electronic capturing equipment, and other technologies to access and obtain information. These provisions were later stricken from the act, although federal law-enforcement agencies were given a large amount of latitude to conduct investigations relating to electronic information. This act is generating a lot of discussion about what capabilities should be given to law enforcement in the detection of criminal activity.

 For more information on this act, visit www.cdt.org/crypto/CESA/.

Cyber Security Enhancement Act of 2002

The Cyber Security Enhancement Act allows federal agencies relatively easy access to ISPs and other data-transmission facilities to monitor communications of individuals suspected of committing computer crimes using the Internet. The act is also known as Section 225 of the Homeland Security Act of 2002.

 For more information on this act, visit www.usdoj.gov/criminal/cybercrime/homeland_CSEA.htm.

Patriot Act

The Uniting and Strengthening America by Providing Appropriate Tools Required to Intercept and Obstruct Terrorism (USA PATRIOT) Act of 2001 was passed partially because of the World Trade Center attack. This law gives the United States government extreme latitude in pursuing criminals who commit terrorist acts. The definition of a terrorist act is broad.

The law provides for relief to victims of terrorism, as well as the ability to conduct virtually any type of surveillance of a suspected terrorist. This act is currently under revision, and it will probably be expanded.

 For more information on this act, visit www.cbo.gov/showdoc.cfm?index=3180&sequence=0&from=6.

Putting It in Perspective

When it comes to behavior, CompTIA expects you to adhere to five rules. These were implied in the discussion of privacy, confidentiality, and respect, but specifically they're as follows:

- Maintain a positive attitude and tone of voice.

- Avoid arguing with customers and/or becoming defensive.

- Don't make light of the customer's problem. Although it may be a situation you see every day, it's a crisis to them.

- Avoid being judgmental and/or insulting or calling the customer names.

- Avoid distractions and/or interruptions when talking with customers.

Exam Essentials

Use job-related professional behavior.   The Golden Rule should govern your professional behavior. Six key elements to this, from a business perspective, are punctuality, accountability, flexibility, confidentiality, respect, and privacy.

Review Questions

1. A customer is trying to explain a problem to you when you arrive on site, but you cannot understand their dialect. What should you do?

2. A customer becomes physically abusive by pushing you. What should you do?

3. A customer tells you that they are really glad to see you and not Tony—the tech they had last time, whom they describe as a real jerk. How should you respond?

4. A user in the next department has been on the phone with you for 30 minutes describing their desktop problem. No matter how many times you explain it to them, they do not understand what you are saying. What should you do?

5. A customer complains that the printer on system A no longer prints after you were there working on system B. What should you do?

6. While troubleshooting a customer's LAN, you determine the server must be rebooted. This will affect over a dozen current users. What should you do?

7. A customer complains that he cannot print to the workgroup laser printer. What should be the first question you ask?

8. A customer states that they may need to reach you quickly for troubleshooting a mission-critical application, and asks for your pager number. What should you do?

9. Which act gives law enforcement the right to gain access to encryption keys and cryptography methods?

10. Which act gives the United States government extreme latitude in pursuing criminals who commit terrorist acts?

Answers to Review Questions

1. You should see if another person can be found on site who is capable of helping with the translation. They will likely be familiar with the user and know about the issues they are discussing.

2. You should try to calm the individual and explain that their anger isn't helping the situation. If you cannot calm them down and create a secure environment, you should leave the premises.

3. You should thank the person for their confidence and support and then ask to see the system in question. Do not join in the discussion of the other co-worker or give them reason to later quote you in any discussion of this individual or their abilities.

4. Given the close proximity of the user in question, you should visit their machine and solve the problem from there. Not only is it easier to solve the issue when you are sitting at the machine, but it will save time as well.

5. Ask questions about the connections/network between A and B. Ask about the similarities and differences between the two. It will serve no purpose for you to become defensive. Once you have collected information, you can approach troubleshooting the problem as you would any other.

6. A message should be sent to all users notifying them that the system will be going down and giving an estimate of how long the users will be affected. The estimate should include time to address any other issues that you fear may crop up.

7. One of the first questions you should ask the user is if they have ever printed to that printer. This can then be followed up with questions as to how recently they did so and what has changed since then.

8. You should adhere to policies of the company you work for on this matter. Some companies do not mind customers having the pager number for a technician, whereas others want all calls to come to a central location so the calls can be processed more efficiently. Whichever situation applies, you should carefully explain it to your customer and let them know the rules of response time, escalation, and other issues.

9. The Cyberspace Electronic Security Act (CESA) gives law enforcement the right to gain access to encryption keys and cryptography methods.

10. The Uniting and Strengthening America by Providing Appropriate Tools Required to Intercept and Obstruct Terrorism (USA PATRIOT) Act of 2001 gives the United States government extreme latitude in pursuing criminals who commit terrorist acts. The definition of a terrorist act is broad.

Chapter

9

Personal Computer Components

COMPTIA A+ 220-602 EXAM OBJECTIVES COVERED IN THIS CHAPTER:

✓ **1.1 Install, configure, optimize, and upgrade personal computer components**

- Add, remove, and configure personal computer components, including selection and installation of appropriate components, for example:
  - Storage devices
  - Motherboards
  - Power supplies
  - Processors / CPUs
  - Memory
  - Display devices
  - Input devices (e.g., basic, specialty, and multimedia)
  - Adapter cards
  - Cooling systems

✓ **1.2 Identify tools, diagnostic procedures, and troubleshooting techniques for personal computer components**

- Identify and apply basic diagnostic procedures and troubleshooting techniques
- Isolate and identify the problem using visual and audible inspection of components and minimum configuration
- Recognize and isolate issues with peripherals, multimedia, specialty input devices, internal and external storage, and CPUs
- Identify the steps used to troubleshoot components (e.g., check proper seating, installation, appropriate components, settings, and current driver), for example:
  - Power supply
  - Processor / CPUs and motherboards

- Memory
- Adapter cards
- Display and input devices
- Recognize names, purposes, characteristics, and appropriate application of tools, for example:
  - Multi-meter
  - Anti-static pad and wrist strap
  - Specialty hardware / tools
  - Loop back plugs
  - Cleaning products (e.g., vacuum, cleaning pads)

✓ **1.3 Perform preventative maintenance on personal computer components**

- Identify and apply common preventative maintenance techniques for personal computer components, for example:
  - Display devices (e.g., cleaning, ventilation)
  - Power devices (e.g., appropriate source such as power strip, surge protector, ventilation, and cooling)
  - Input devices (e.g., covers)
  - Storage devices (e.g., software tools, such as DEFRAG and cleaning of optics and tape heads)
  - Thermally sensitive devices, such as motherboards, CPU, adapter cards memory (e.g., cleaning, air flow)

COMPTIA A+ 220-603 EXAM OBJECTIVES COVERED IN THIS CHAPTER:

✓ **1.1 Install, configure, optimize, and upgrade personal computer components**

- Add, remove, and configure display devices, input devices, and adapter cards, including basic input and multimedia devices

✓ **1.2 Identify tools, diagnostic procedures, and troubleshooting techniques for personal computer components**

- Identify and apply basic diagnostic procedures and troubleshooting techniques, for example:
  - Identify and analyze the problem/potential problem
  - Test related components and evaluate results

- Identify additional steps to be taken if/when necessary
- Document activities and outcomes
- Recognize and isolate issues with display, peripheral, multimedia, specialty input device, and storage
- Apply steps in troubleshooting techniques to identify problems (e.g., physical environment, functionality, and software/driver settings) with components, including display, input devices, and adapter cards

✓ **1.3 Perform preventative maintenance on personal computer components**

- Identify and apply common preventative maintenance techniques for storage devices, for example:
  - Software tools (e.g., Defrag, CHKDSK)
  - Cleaning (e.g., optics, tape heads)

COMPTIA A+ 220-604 EXAM OBJECTIVES COVERED IN THIS CHAPTER:

✓ **1.1 Install, configure, optimize, and upgrade personal computer components**

- Add, remove, and configure internal storage devices, motherboards, power supplies, processor/CPU's, memory, and adapter cards, including:
  - Drive preparation
  - Jumper configuration
  - Storage device power and cabling
  - Selection and installation of appropriate motherboard
  - BIOS set-up and configuration
  - Selection and installation of appropriate CPU
  - Selection and installation of appropriate memory
  - Installation of adapter cards, including hardware and software/drivers
  - Configuration and optimization of adapter cards, including adjusting hardware settings and obtaining network card connection
- Add, remove, and configure systems

✓ **1.2 Identify tools, diagnostic procedures, and troubleshooting techniques for personal computer components**

- Identify and apply basic diagnostic procedures and troubleshooting techniques, for example:
  - Identify and isolate the problem using visual and audible inspection of components and minimum configuration
- Identify the steps used to troubleshoot components (e.g., check proper seating, installation, appropriate component, settings, current driver), for example:
  - Power supply
  - Processor/CPU's and motherboards
  - Memory
  - Adapter cards
- Recognize names, purposes, characteristics, and appropriate application of tools, for example:
  - Multi-meter
  - Anti-static pad and wrist strap
  - Specialty hardware/tools
  - Loop back plugs
  - Cleaning products (e.g., vacuum, cleaning pads)

✓ **1.3 Perform preventative maintenance on personal computer components**

- Identify and apply common preventative maintenance techniques, for example:
  - Thermally sensitive devices (e.g., motherboards, CPU's, adapter cards, memory)
  - Cleaning
  - Air flow (e.g., slot covers, cable routing)
  - Adapter cards (e.g., driver/firmware updates)

You can't become A+ certified without knowing personal computers inside and out. This domain was heavily weighted on the A+ Essentials exam, and it's heavily weighted on the in the technician exams as well. For the IT Technician (220-602) exam, it's an incredible 45 percent of the exam. For the Remote Support Technician (220-603) exam, it's weighted at 18 percent of the exam; and for the Depot Technician (220-604) exam, it's 15 percent.

Along with Printers and Scanners, and Security, it's one of a very small group of domains that appears in the Essentials exam as well as in every elective.

Install, Configure, Optimize, and Upgrade Personal Computer Components

Depending on which technician exam you're studying for, the scope of this objective can include only a few things or quite a number of them. Regardless of the elective exam, you'll want to reread Chapter 1, which you'll need to know for the Essentials exam; make certain you know each component's purpose and some of its basics.

Critical Information

This objective demands that you be able to add, remove, and configure a number of different devices. At some point, every computer will need to be upgraded. Upgrading usually means one of two things: replacing old technology with new technology or adding functionality to an existing system. An example of upgrading old technology is replacing a slower, older modem with a faster, newer one. An example of adding functionality to an existing system is adding more RAM to increase performance. In either case, upgrading usually involves adding a new component. This process consists of several basic steps, each of which must be carefully followed. In this section, we'll cover the following steps:

- Disassembly

- Inspection

- Part replacement and reassembly

As you work inside a PC, be aware of safety hazards both to yourself and to the equipment.

When you choose an area in which to work on a computer, pick a workspace that is sturdy enough to support the weight of a computer and any peripherals you're adding to your system. The area must also be well lit, clean, and large enough to hold all the pieces and necessary tools.

Disassembling the Computer

You don't need to disassemble the computer completely to perform most upgrade and repair jobs; part of being a successful technician is being able to identify what parts must be removed for each job. For example, replacing a motherboard requires almost complete disassembly, but replacing a disk drive doesn't require any disassembly at all in most cases (except for removing the drive itself).

Preparing Your Work Area

For any work you do on a computer, you must have an adequate workspace. First, the work area must be flat. Second, the area must be sturdy. Make sure the work surface you're using can support the weight of the components. Third, the area must be well lit, clean, and large enough to hold all pieces (assembled and disassembled) and all necessary tools.

Before you begin, make sure all necessary tools are available and in working order. Also make sure the documentation for the system you're working on is available (including owner's manuals, service manuals, and Internet resources).

The final guideline to preparing your work area is to set aside plenty of time to complete the task. Estimate the time required to complete the entire task (disassembly, installation, reassembly, and testing).

Once you've prepared your work area and gathered your tools, you're ready to begin the actual disassembly of the computer. The steps are basically the same for all brands and types of computers.

Disassembly Prerequisites

You need to do several things before you even move the computer to your work area:

1. Shut down any running programs, and turn off the computer.

2. Remove all cables that are attached to the computer.

3. Remove any floppy disks from their drives.

4. Check to see that all the prerequisites have been met, and move the computer to the work surface.

Disconnect the Display Devices

You should disconnect the monitor and any other display devices (projector, and so on) that may be connected to the system. Although some cases can be opened without disconnecting the monitor cable, you run the risk of damaging the display or card if you don't.

Removing Input Devices

External devices such as the keyboard and mouse should be unplugged before you open the case. Although this step isn't necessary for every upgrade, it makes it easier to remove the case cover because the cords and connectors aren't in the way.

From CompTIA's perspective, input devices can include basic items such as keyboards and mice as well as specialty items such as tablets, joysticks, and microphones. Multimedia devices such as web cameras can fall beneath this category as well. In all cases, know that you should disconnect them before working on the PC and add them per the vendor's documentation.

Removing the Case Cover

Now you can unfasten the computer's cover by removing any retaining screws at the back of the computer. Some cases don't have screws; instead, they have a sliding bar or latches that release the cover. Many of today's PCs can be completely disassembled without a single tool.

Then, remove the cover by sliding or lifting it. The exact procedure varies greatly depending on the case; Figure 9.1 shows an example for a desktop-style case.

FIGURE 9.1   Removing the case cover on a desktop case

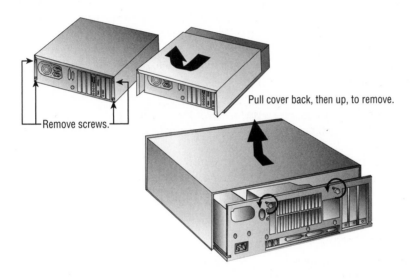

Pull cover back, then up, to remove.

Remove screws.

Don't remove *all* the screws at the back of the computer! Some of these screws hold vital components (such as the power supply) to the case, and removing them will cause those components to drop into the computer.

Removing the Expansion/Adapter Cards

The next step in disassembly is to put on an antistatic wrist strap, plugging one end into the ground plug of an outlet. Then, you can start to remove any *expansion cards*. There are four major steps in removing the expansion cards, as shown in Figure 9.2:

1. Remove any internal or external cables or connectors.

2. Remove any mounting screws that are holding the boards in place, and put the screws somewhere where they won't be lost.

3. Grasp the board by the top edge with both hands and gently rock it front to back (not side to side).

4. Once the board is out, place it in an antistatic bag to help prevent electrostatic discharge (ESD) damage while the board is out of the computer.

Duplicate this procedure for each card.

FIGURE 9.2   Removing an expansion board

1. Remove any connectors (diagramming them first).
2. Remove the board's mounting screws.
3. Grasp the board along its top edge and rock it *gently* up and out.
4. Once the board is out of its slot, avoid touching the edge connector.

Rock gently front to back (not side to side).

Motherboard

Be sure to note the slot from which you remove each card, because some bus types (including Peripheral Component Interconnect [PCI]) keep track of the slots in which the expansion boards are installed. Reinstalling an expansion card in a different slot later probably won't cause a problem, because the Plug and Play BIOS should redetect it, but better safe than sorry.

Removing the Power Supply

Before you remove the power supply from the computer, you must do two things: disconnect the power-supply connectors from the internal devices, and remove the mounting hardware for the power supply, as shown in Figure 9.3.

FIGURE 9.3   Removing power-supply connectors

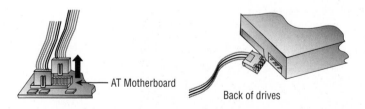

AT Motherboard

Back of drives

Grasp the connector (*not* the wires), and gently wiggle it out of its receptacle. Then, proceed to the next connector. The system board and disk drives both use power connectors. Make sure all of them are removed. AT cases have power leads connected to a switch at the front of the case that also need to be removed.

An AT PC power supply has two connectors to the motherboard; these plug into receptacles that are side by side. If you get confused about how these connectors attach, the general rule is black-to-black. An ATX power supply has a single 20-wire connector to the motherboard.

Once all the power-supply connectors are disconnected from their devices, you can remove the mounting hardware. You can usually detach the power supply from the case by removing four screws. Some power supplies don't need to have screws removed; instead, they're installed on tracks or into slots in the case and need only to be slid out or lifted out.

Removing the Storage Devices

To remove a disk drive, first disconnect it from the power supply (if you haven't done so already), and then disconnect the ribbon cable that runs from the drive to the motherboard (or drive controller board). Then, physically remove the drive from its bay. On some cases, drives are secured in the bays with screws in the sides, as in Figure 9.4; on other cases they slide in and out on rails with clips that release and retain them.

Most servers have *hot-pluggable* drives, which means they can be added or removed while the computer is running. You remove them by depressing a retaining clip or button. Consult the documentation provided with the machine or drives for the exact details.

Removing the Motherboard

The motherboard is held away from the metal case using brass or plastic spacers called *stand-offs* and is secured and grounded using mounting screws. To remove the motherboard, you must remove the screws holding the motherboard to the case floor. On an ATX motherboard, you then lift the motherboard out of the case. On an AT motherboard, as in Figure 9.5, you must slide the motherboard about 1 inch to one side to release its plastic stand-offs from the mounting holes in the case floor.

FIGURE 9.4   Removing the hard drive

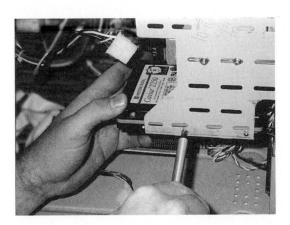

FIGURE 9.5 Removing the motherboard

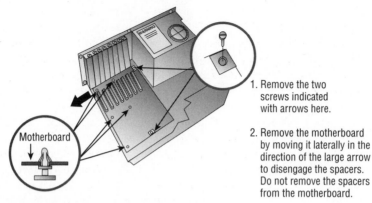

1. Remove the two screws indicated with arrows here.

2. Remove the motherboard by moving it laterally in the direction of the large arrow to disengage the spacers. Do not remove the spacers from the motherboard.

There are five spacers holding the motherboard off the case. A spacer is shown above, viewed from its side.

Removing the Memory

Memory is held in place by retaining clips at both ends of the module. For a single inline memory module (SIMM), the retaining clips are metal. Pull them back, tilt the SIMM back to a 45-degree angle with the motherboard, and then lift it out of the slot. For a dual inline memory module (DIMM), the retaining clips are plastic. Push them down (away from the DIMM), and the DIMM will pop free from its slot automatically; you can just lift it out. Place the removed memory in an antistatic bag to prevent damage.

Inspecting the Computer

Inspecting the computer is an important step in the disassembly and reassembly of the system. You should check the components for any damage and gather any documentation. Damage is sometimes visible on motherboards. Discolored areas on the board are often caused by power surges.

After a component is removed, it's a good idea to create a parts list on a notepad and make sure you have all the supporting documentation and device drivers. If you don't have them, then it's good practice to download them from the manufacturer's website or from a multivendor information site.

Part Replacement and Reassembly

The reassembly of the machine is almost an exact reversal of its disassembly. Once you have all the necessary documentation and device drivers, the process is simple: you reassemble the computer by replacing the hard-to-reach items first and then attaching the supporting devices.

Installing the System Board

The motherboard attaches to the case by the spacers (stand-offs) that hold it away from the metal case. There are two kinds. AT systems use plastic stand-offs that fit into holes in the motherboard and then slide into channels in the case floor. Both AT and ATX systems use brass stand-offs that attach to the floor of the case and have screw holes in their tops for attaching the motherboard screws.

Before you reattach the motherboard, it's best to make sure that the memory and the processor are properly secured and seated in the slots. Doing so will help prevent damage to the chips and protect your hand from cuts, because installing them after the board is secured will leave you with limited space. After you've snapped the board onto its spacers, one or two retaining screws normally need to be attached. When attaching these screws, be sure not to over-tighten them and damage the board.

Installing the Power Supply

The power supply should be installed next. Attach it with the screws you removed during its disassembly. After it's secure, reattach the power leads to their respective connectors on the motherboard. If it's an AT system, make sure the black wires on the motherboard power connectors (usually labeled P8 and P9) are oriented together on the connector.

Installing Drives/Storage Devices

The drives are the next components you attach. First, attach the floppy drive. The ribbon cable and the power connector connect to the back of the drive as they were removed. Be sure to check the ribbon cable's attachment, because it's the most commonly reversed item on the PC. The red stripe on the cable indicates 1, which should be oriented closest to the power connector on the drive.

Next, attach the Integrated Drive Electronics (IDE) drives, such as hard drives and CD drives. They connect to the motherboard's IDE interface via ribbon cable, and they connect to the power supply via a Molex power connector.

Installing PCI, ISA, and AGP Devices

After the drives are attached, add any PCI, Industry Standard Architecture (ISA), and Accelerated Graphics Port (AGP) devices the system uses, such as a video card, sound card, or modem. If the motherboard has any of these components built in, their ports may be built into the side of the motherboard (typical of an ATX motherboard) or may require you to attach a port to the back of the case and then run a small ribbon cable to connect that port to the motherboard.

Closing the Case

After you install all the components, slide the cover over the metal frame of the case. This may be a challenging part of the repair. Cases are generally designed to be the most inexpensive part of the PC. They're disassembled much more easily than they're reassembled. Tighten the screws on the outside of the case, or make sure the case has snapped into the proper position.

Attaching Input Devices

Input devices such as the keyboard and mouse should be attached in the same ports from which they were removed. Be sure the keyboard and mouse are plugged into the correct ports if they both use a PS/2 connector. A good rule of thumb is that the keyboard attaches to the port closest to the outside of the machine.

Other input devices can be connected through USB or FireWire connections and should be configured per the vendor's documentation.

Attaching Display Devices

Connect the display devices to the system using the connectors discussed in Chapter 1. Display devices can include a simple monitor, a projector, or any of several other choices. In all cases, you should follow the vendor's documentation when adding a new display device to the system.

Optimizing the Personal Computer

The most common need for an upgrade is to increase system performance. Over time, a computer's performance will decrease as newer software is added. In most cases, newer versions of software require additional resources that aren't available. The PC was originally configured to run at certain performance levels that considered the applications and peripherals available when it was produced. Upgrades increase the system's performance to accommodate newer software and peripheral devices.

Toward the end of the system's life expectancy, it may become necessary to upgrade the system for required programs or for new hardware to function. If the system is too antiquated, it may be more cost efficient to replace the entire computer. However, in many cases, the system's performance can be enhanced to acceptable levels by adding resources.

Memory

As we mentioned earlier in this chapter, RAM is used to store data temporarily while the PC is operating. The operating system and applications utilize RAM, so if the amount of available RAM is insufficient, the operating system will utilize hard-disk space to store some of the data. Because the speed at which the data stored on a hard drive is considerably lower than the speed at which data can be accessed in RAM, the performance of the system will degrade as more and more information is stored on the hard drive.

Both Windows 2000 Professional and Windows XP require a minimum of 64MB RAM. This should truly be at least 128MB for daily use on a workstation; and generally, the more you can add to the system, the better the performance you can expect.

Disk Subsystem

The disk subsystem consists of the hard drives, the controllers, and the cables used to connect them.

HARD DRIVES

Hard drives are most commonly replaced because the system runs out of space to store data and program files. A small hard drive is replaced with one of larger capacity, or an additional hard disk is added.

Another reason to upgrade a hard drive is to increase the speed at which data can be written to or read from the drive. For example, replacing an old hard disk that conforms to ATA-3 standards with a newer one that conforms to ATA-6 (UltraATA/100) results in a disk that has a much faster access time and data-transfer rate (provided the IDE controller and the cable are of the correct type to support it).

There are two common ways to replace a disk drive in a computer: adding a drive or completely replacing the disk. Each approach has benefits and drawbacks.

Complete replacement   If you need additional hard-disk capacity and don't have the physical room for a second drive inside the computer's case, or you don't want to manage two drives, complete replacement is necessary. Complete replacement requires reinstalling or restoring the operating system, program files, and data on the new drive. Because this is a considerable undertaking, drive-image tools have been developed to aid in this process. A *drive-image tool* takes a snapshot of the drive and allows you to create an image that can be expanded on the larger drive, avoiding reinstallation.

These images are normally compressed and require less space than the actual contents of the drive, allowing the images to be placed on a CD-ROM or other storage media. Some examples of this type of data transfer programs are Norton Ghost and Seagate Power Quest Drive Image. Larger corporations use these tools to create a basic image of the operating system and commonly used programs to decrease downtime and lower upgrade and repair costs.

Adding drives   The simplest way to increase hard-drive capacity is to add another drive. Most desktop PCs have IDE controllers built into the motherboard. These controllers allow for two devices to be connected to both the primary and secondary controller. With this type of architecture, four IDE devices can be installed in a PC, if space permits.

After adding the drive, you can place data and programs on it. This type of installation doesn't require the reinstallation or restoration of the operating system and program files on the new drive.

CONTROLLER CARD

If the motherboard is more than a few years old, its IDE interface may not support the latest, fastest UltraATA standards. To get the highest performance out of a new hard drive, you may want to install an IDE controller card that supports the same standard as the new drive (for example, UltraATA/100 or ATA-6).

CABLE

UltraATA/66 and UltraATA/100 work only with a special 80-wire ribbon cable; when installing such drives on an existing IDE interface you'll probably also want to replace the 40-wire cable with an 80-wire one. Most new hard disks come with the 80-wire cable.

CPU Upgrade

The frequency at which the processor operates (MHz) determines the speed at which data passes through the processor. Upgrading the processor to a higher frequency will provide a dramatic improvement in the system's overall performance.

It's important to remember that replacing a processor requires some research. Most motherboards support a certain class of processor; they don't have the capacity to upgrade to a different class of chip. For example, it isn't possible to upgrade a Pentium-class chip to a Pentium II–class chip. This relates not only to the processor slots, but also to the power requirements of the chip. You must consider the additional cooling requirements of the new chip, as well. In most cases, processor upgrades are accomplished by replacing the motherboard and processor using a special overdrive chip. Overdrive chips are also discussed in Chapter 1.

Some motherboards support the use of multiple CPUs, and in such motherboards, additional CPUs can improve overall system performance. Although the system doesn't run at a faster speed (in terms of MHz), an additional CPU makes the system able to process more operations per second.

Upgrading the BIOS

When the BIOS no longer supports all the devices that need to be connected to the PC, an upgrade is needed. There are two ways to upgrade the BIOS chip: by manually replacing the chip or by using special flash software.

MANUAL CHIP REPLACEMENT

Manual chip replacement requires you to remove the old chip and replace it with a new chip provided by the motherboard manufacturer. Manual replacement isn't an option in today's PCs.

FLASH BIOS REPLACEMENT

Flash BIOS is the modern way of upgrading a computer's BIOS. By placing the BIOS update disk in the floppy drive and booting the machine, a technician can reprogram the system's BIOS to handle new hardware devices that the manufacturer has included.

This works because the BIOS in modern systems is written in an electrically erasable programmable ROM (EEPROM) chip. This chip is normally read-only, but when it receives a stronger-than-normal voltage of electricity, it can temporarily become rewriteable. The utility for updating the BIOS includes instructions to the motherboard to deliver this extra-strong electricity prior to the new BIOS update being sent to the chip.

Manufacturers periodically post the flash upgrades on their websites for you to download. Be aware that you must take care in this process, because the BIOS could be disabled and require the motherboard to be shipped back to the manufacturer. In most cases, the flash program will give you the opportunity to save the current software and settings to a restore disk that can reverse the changes if necessary.

Upgrading the Cooling System

The cooling system consists of the fan in the power supply, the fan or heat sink on the CPU, and any additional heat sinks or fans in the case. If a system is inadequately cooled, lockups and spontaneous reboots may occur.

Liquid-cooled cases are now available that use circulating water rather than fans to keep components cool. These cases are typically more expensive than standard ones and may be more difficult to work on for an untrained technician, but they result in an almost completely silent system.

Air cooling is the most common cooling method used in PCs. CPUs typically have *active* heat sinks, which are heat sinks that include an electric fan that constantly channels heat away. A CPU that is running too hot may benefit from a better cooling fan. The heat sink portion is a block of spikes that channel heat away from the CPU.

Most *passive heat sinks* (that is, heat sinks that don't include a fan) are attached to the CPU using a glue-like thermal compound. This makes the connection between the heat sink and the

CPU more seamless and direct. Thermal compound can be used on active heat sinks, too, but generally it isn't because of the possibility that the fan may stop working and need to be replaced.

In addition to the main fan in the power supply, you can also install additional cooling fans in a case that help circulate air through the case.

Upgrading to a Faster NIC

The typical speed for an Ethernet network today is 100BaseT, or 100MBps. This speed requires a 100BaseT network card. 10BaseT network cards can coexist on a 100BaseT network but will send and receive data at only 10MBps. Upgrading to a higher-speed network card can improve network performance in such a case.

In addition, new Ethernet technologies such as Gigabit Ethernet are becoming popular; they push the speed beyond 100MBps. Upgrading to a network interface card (NIC) that supports these even faster speeds may be advantageous if the PC is on a network that supports them.

Specialized Video Cards

A standard 2D video card is adequate for business use, but for the serious graphic artist or gamer, a 3D video card with acceleration features can provide much better performance. These video cards include extra RAM buffers for holding video data, better on-board processing assistance for motion video, and support for the application programming interfaces (APIs) that the popular applications and games are written for, such as DirectX.

Drivers for Legacy Devices

A *legacy device* is one that is based on old technology. Examples include an ISA expansion card or a device that connects to a COM or LPT port rather than using the newer USB port. The term *legacy* can also refer to a piece of used hardware that is based on older technology internally.

Windows supports a wide variety of legacy devices with its own native drivers, but you may sometimes need to seek out a driver for a legacy device to run under a particular operating system version. The best source is the website of the device manufacturer. Other sources are also available, such as driver repositories on the Web.

Bus Types and Characteristics

When you're selecting upgrade devices, you may have a choice of bus types to which to connect the new device. It's important to understand the benefits of the various buses so you can choose wisely.

For example, you may have a choice of an ISA or PCI internal modem, or a COM port or USB external modem. Or you may need to choose between an AGP and a PCI video card.

For external ports, USB is better and faster than both COM (legacy serial) and LPT (legacy parallel). It's further advantageous because of its seamless Plug and Play integration and its hot-plugging ability.

For internal buses, AGP is the fastest and best, but it's only for video cards. PCI is the next most desirable. ISA is old technology and nearly obsolete, and you should avoid it whenever possible. One possible exception is an internal modem. Because an internal modem operates at a maximum of only 56Kbps, it will be least affected by being relegated to the ISA bus. In contrast, a video card will suffer greatly on ISA.

Table 9.1 describes the speeds and characteristics of internal expansion buses.

TABLE 9.1   Comparison of ISA, PCI, and AGP Buses

Bus	Width	Speed	Uses
ISA	8-bit or 16-bit	8MHz	Avoid if possible, or use for slow devices like modems
PCI	32-bit	33MHz	All nonvideo internal expansion boards
AGP	64-bit	66MHz to 133MHz	The primary video card in the system

Memory Capacity and Characteristics

When you're selecting RAM for a memory upgrade, it's important to buy the right kind. On a modern system, you must match the RAM to the motherboard's needs in the following areas:

Physical size   168-pin or 184-DIMMs, or 184-pin RIMMs.

Type   SDRAM, double data rate (DDR) SDRAM, or Rambus RAM.

Speed   PC100, PC133, and up. Faster RAM than is required will work, but not slower.

Capacity   64MB, 128MB, and up. Older systems may use SIMMs, which have somewhat more complex shopping issues:

> **Physical size**   30-pin (8-bit) or 72-pin (32-bit).
>
> **Parity**   Some SIMMs have an extra chip for parity checking. Some motherboards require parity RAM; others make it optional or forbid it.
>
> **Refresh technology**   Some SIMMs are extended data out (EDO), allowing for better performance through less frequent refreshing. Some motherboards require it; others make it optional or forbid it.

Capacity   Varies greatly, from 256KB up to 64MB or more.

When you're shopping for RAM for a system that uses SIMMs, it's important to consult the motherboard manual to find out any special rules for installation. Some motherboards have complex charts showing the combinations and positions of the SIMMs they will allow.

Motherboards may combine one or more RAM slots into a single logical bank, and all the RAM installed in that set of slots must be identical in every way. Check the motherboard documentation. On systems that use 30-pin SIMMs, four slots typically combine to create a single bank. On 486 systems that use 72-pin SIMMs, each SIMM slot is a separate bank. On Pentium systems that use 72-pin SIMMs, two SIMM slots together form a bank.

System/Firmware Limitations

One of the most common problems in upgrading to a larger hard disk is the BIOS's inability to support the larger disk size. In the original IDE specification, the size limit was 540MB. This limitation was upped to 8GB with the introduction of *Logical Block Addressing (LBA)* in 1996, which the BIOS must support. A BIOS update may be available for the motherboard to enable LBA if needed.

The 8GB limitation can be broken if the BIOS supports Enhanced BIOS Services for Disk Drives, a 1998 update. Again, a BIOS update for the motherboard may enable this support if it's lacking.

If no BIOS update is available, the choices are to replace the motherboard, to use the drive at the maximum size the BIOS can recognize, or to install a utility program (usually provided with the hard disk) that extends the BIOS to recognize the new drive. Such utilities are useful but can introduce some quirks in the system that can't be easily undone, so their usage isn't recommended except where no other alternative exists.

Power-Supply Output Capacity

A power supply has a rated output capacity in watts, and when you fill a system with power-hungry devices, you must make sure that maximum capacity isn't exceeded. Table 1.4 in Chapter 1 offered estimates of power consumption.

Selecting a CPU for a Motherboard

The CPU must be compatible with the motherboard in the following ways:

Physical connectivity   The CPU must be in the right kind of package to fit into the motherboard.

Speed   The motherboard's chipset dictates its external data-bus speed; the CPU must be capable of operating at that external speed.

Instruction set   The motherboard's chipset contains an instruction set for communicating with the CPU; the CPU must understand the commands in that set. For example, a motherboard designed for an AMD Athlon CPU can't accept an Intel Pentium CPU, because the instruction set is different.

Voltage   The CPU requires a certain voltage of power to be supplied to it via the motherboard's interface. This can be anywhere from +5V for a very old CPU down to around +2.1V for a modern one. The wrong voltage can ruin the CPU.

Miscellaneous Elements and the 220-604 Exam

A few miscellaneous components can fall beneath this objective, depending on the elective exam you're studying for. For example, the 22-604 exam's objectives list jumper configuration, and drive preparation. Those not covered here are addressed in detail in Chapter 1, or further down in this chapter.

You'll find that the multiple-choice questions on the CompTIA exams require a great deal of common sense to be mixed with knowledge. Read each question for what it's worth—don't read more into it than what is there—choose the best answer (sometimes you can argue that there isn't a right answer), and move on.

Exam Essentials

Know when to attach an antistatic wrist strap.   One thing from this chapter that will be on the test is attaching an antistatic wrist strap. You should attach one of these to a ground mat every time you open a computer. More components are damaged from static discharge than from anything else.

Know the "black wires together" rule.   When you're attaching an AT power supply to a motherboard, the connector will be in two pieces, P8 and P9. These must be oriented so the black wires on each connector are near the black wires on the other connector. Otherwise, damage to the motherboard can result.

Know what performance enhancements are achieved by upgrading memory.   Upgrading the amount of RAM a computer has will increase the speed of the machine by preventing the use of the hard drive to store data that is being accessed.

Know what performance enhancements are achieved by upgrading the hard drive, the IDE controller, and the IDE ribbon cable.   Replacing the hard drive can allow you to add to the overall storage capacity of the machine. In some cases, read/write performance can be improved by upgrading. Understand the UltraATA/66 and UltraATA/100 requirements.

Know what performance enhancements are achieved by updating the BIOS.   Replacing the BIOS can increase the number of supported devices.

Understand the benefits of improving system cooling.   Make sure you know what symptoms are produced by inadequate cooling and what options are available for upgrading the cooling system.

Using Tools and Diagnostic Procedures for Personal Computer Components

The various tools that you can use to discover the available resources on a PC can make installing new hardware a lot easier. Unfortunately, the tools are of little use unless you understand the information they present. In this section, we discuss the various resources that may be used by PC components and how those resources are used.

Interrupt request lines, direct memory access channels, and input/output addresses are configurable aspects of the communication between the devices inside a PC. *Interrupt request (IRQ) lines* are used to signal that an event has taken place that requires the attention of the CPU. *Input/output (I/O) addresses* refer to the hardware communication lines that carry data between the CPU and the bus slots of the PC. *Direct memory access (DMA) channels* allow a storage device or adapter card to send information directly into memory without passing through the CPU, which results in a faster data-transfer rate.

Critical Information

At some point, every computer will require the installation of a new component, whether it's a new sound card, a memory upgrade, or the replacement of a failed device. As a technician, you'll be required to perform this task time and time again. You should be well versed in determining the installation configuration and resources.

Whenever a new component is installed into a PC, its resources must be correctly configured, or the device won't function correctly (those resources may be IRQs, I/O addresses, and/or DMA channels). This is the most common problem when installing new circuit boards.

Understanding Computer Resources

In general, there are four main types of PC resources you may need to be aware of when installing a new component: IRQ lines, memory addresses, DMA channels, and I/O addresses.

Interrupt Request Lines

IRQs are appropriately named. Interrupts are used by peripherals to *interrupt*, or stop, the CPU and demand attention. When the CPU receives an interrupt alert, it stops whatever it's doing and handles the request.

Each device is given its own interrupt to use when alerting the CPU. (There are exceptions; some PCI devices can share with one another, for example, and USB devices all use a single interrupt.) AT-based PCs have 16 interrupts available. Given the limited number of available interrupts, it's critical that you assign them wisely! Table 9.2 lists the standard use and other uses associated with each interrupt.

TABLE 9.2   AT Interrupts

Interrupt	Most Common Use	Other Common Uses
0	System timer	None
1	Keyboard	None
2	None; this interrupt is used to cascade to the upper eight interrupts (see note following this table)	None
3	COM2	COM4
4	COM1	COM3
5	Sound card	LPT2
6	Floppy-disk controller	Tape controllers

TABLE 9.2   AT Interrupts *(continued)*

Interrupt	Most Common Use	Other Common Uses
7	LPT1	Any device
8	Real-time clock	None
9	None	Any device
10	None	Any device
11	None	Any device
12	PS/2-style mouse	Any device
13	Floating-point coprocessor	None
14	Primary IDE channel	SCSI controllers
15	Secondary IDE channel	SCSI controllers and network adapters

Interrupt 2 is a special case. Earlier (XT-based) PCs had only eight interrupts because those computers used an 8-bit bus. With the development of the AT, eight more interrupts were created (to match the 16-bit bus), but no mechanism was available to use them. Rather than redesign the entire interrupt process, AT designers decided to use interrupt 2 as a gateway, or *cascade*, to interrupts 9–15. In reality, interrupt 2 is the same as interrupt 9. You should never configure your system so that both interrupt 2 and 9 are used.

Most experienced field technicians have the standards (listed in the table) memorized. In studying for the exam, make sure you know all the default assignments, as well as the assignments for COM1–COM4 and LPT1–LPT2.

Memory Addresses

Many components use blocks of memory as part of their normal functioning. NICs often buffer incoming data in a block of memory until it can be processed. Doing so prevents the card from being overloaded if a burst of data is received from the network.

When the device driver loads, it lets the CPU know which block of memory should be set aside for the exclusive use of the component. This prevents other devices from overwriting the information stored there. Certain system components also need a memory address. Memory addresses are usually expressed in a hexadecimal range with eight digits, such as 000F0000–000FFFFF.

Direct Memory Access

DMA allows a device to bypass the CPU and place data directly into RAM. To accomplish this, the device must have a DMA channel devoted to its use.

All DMA transfers use a special area of memory known as a *buffer*, which is set aside to receive data from the expansion card (or CPU, if the transfer is going the other direction). The basic architecture of the PC DMA buffers is limited in size and memory location.

No DMA channel can be used by more than one device. If you accidentally choose a DMA channel that another card is using, the usual symptom is that no DMA transfers occur, and the device is unavailable.

Certain DMA channels are assigned to standard AT devices. DMA is no longer as popular as it once was, because of advances in hardware technology, but it's still used by floppy drives and some keyboards and sound cards. The floppy-disk controller typically uses DMA channel 2. A modern system isn't likely to run short on DMA channels because so few devices use them anymore.

I/O Addresses

I/O addresses, also known as *port addresses*, are specific areas of memory that components use to communicate with the system. Although they sound like memory addresses, the major difference is that memory addresses are used to store information that will be used by the device itself. I/O addresses are used to store information that will be used by the system. An I/O address is typically expressed using only the last four digits of the full address, such as 03E8. I/O addresses are usually expressed as a range, such as 03E8–03EF. The exam asks about a few I/O addresses; Table 9.3 provides a list of some hexadecimal addresses you should know.

TABLE 9.3 I/O Addresses

Port	I/O Address
COM1	03F8–03FF
COM2	02F8–02FF
COM3	03E8–03EF
COM4	02E8–02EF
LPT1	0378–037F
LPT2	0278–027F
Primary IDE	01F0–01F7
Secondary IDE	0170–0177

Determining Available Resources

The best way to determine the PC's available resources is by using hardware-configuration-discovery utilities. These software programs talk to the PC's BIOS as well as the pieces of hardware in the computer and display which IRQ, DMA, and memory addresses are being used. Most operating systems include some way of determining this information, including Device Manager in Windows 2000/XP. To display it in Windows 2000 and XP, right-click My Computer and choose Properties, click the Hardware tab, and then click Device Manager.

To display a device's resources, open the category by clicking the plus sign next to it and double-clicking the device name. Then, look in the Resources tab for that device. (See Figure 9.6.)

You can also get this same information through the System Information utility. To run it, choose Start ➢ (All) Programs ➢ Accessories ➢ System Tools ➢ System Information. Then, click one of the categories in the left pane to see the information in the right pane. (See Figure 9.7.)

FIGURE 9.6 Device Manager under Windows XP

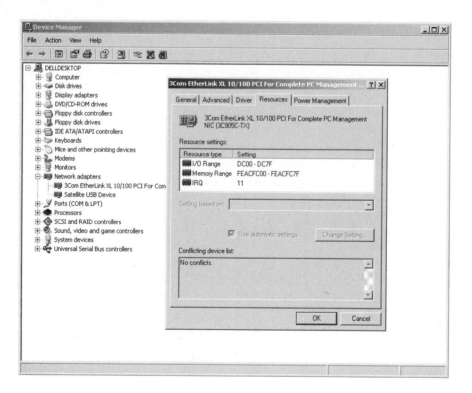

FIGURE 9.7   System Information under Windows XP

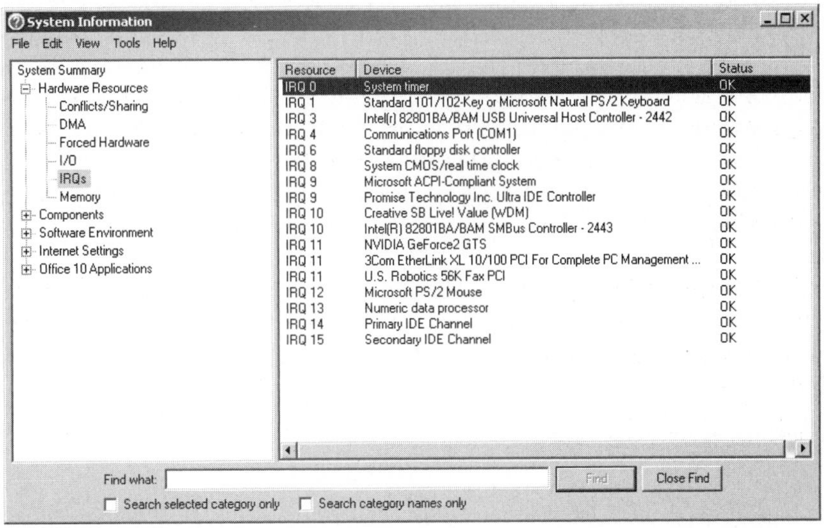

Manually Specifying a Resource Assignment

In Windows' Device Manager, you can manually specify the resources for a device to solve a problem with a *resource conflict*—that is, a situation in which two or more devices lay claim to the same resource. A resource conflict usually appears as a yellow exclamation point next to a device's name in Device Manager. Double-clicking the device opens its Properties box; on the Resources tab, you'll find an explanation of the problem in the Conflicting Device List.

To change a device's resource assignments, clear the Use Automatic Settings check box, and select a different configuration from the Setting Based On list. (See Figure 9.8.) If none of the alternate configurations resolves the conflict, you can double-click a specific resource on the Resource Type list and enter a manual setting for it.

Most modern computers use a power management and configuration method called Advanced Configuration Power Interface (ACPI), which helps prevent resource conflicts but which also limits the amount of tinkering you can do with manual resource assignments. If you get a message that a particular resource can't be changed, or if the Use Automatic Settings check box is unavailable, it's probably because of ACPI.

If the device isn't Plug and Play–compatible, it may have jumpers for hard-setting the resources assigned to it. If that's the case, Windows won't be able to change these assignments; it will use the assignments the device requires.

FIGURE 9.8 Manually changing a resource assignment

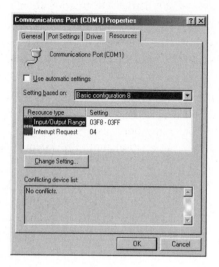

Diagnostic Resources

When you're stumped by a computer problem, where do you turn? The exam objectives specify that you should know about the following resources:

User/installation manuals Consult the manuals that came with the hardware and software.

Internet/Web resources Consult the websites of the companies that make the hardware and software. Updates and patches are often available for download, or the websites may be knowledge bases of troubleshooting information.

Training materials If you've taken a class pertaining to the hardware or software, consult the materials you received for that class.

Diagnostic Tools and Utilities

A big part of being a successful technician is knowing what tools are appropriate to correct which problems. The following diagnostic tools and utilities are ones you should be comfortable with:

Task Manager Lets you shut down nonresponsive applications selectively in all Windows versions. In Windows 2000/XP, it does much more, allowing you to see which processes and applications are using the most system resources. To display Task Manager, press Ctrl+Alt+Delete. It appears immediately in some operating systems, while in others you must click the Task Manager button to display it after pressing Ctrl+Alt+Delete. Use Task Manager whenever the system seems bogged down by an unresponsive application.

Dr. Watson This tool enables detailed logging of errors. Use it whenever you think an error is likely to occur (for example, when you're trying to reproduce an error).

Event Viewer   This tool enables you to see what's been going on behind the scenes in Windows NT/2000/XP. Use Event Viewer when you want to gather information about a system or hardware problem.

Device Manager   As already mentioned, Device Manager shows you what hardware is installed and lets you check its status. Use this when a device isn't functioning and you're trying to figure out why.

WinMSD   Another name for System Information, the same utility you can select from the System Tools menu. (Running it at the Run command with WINMSD is an alternative.) WinMSD provides comprehensive information about the system's resource usage, hardware, and software environments. Use it when you need to gather information about the system.

Recovery CD   Some computers that come with Windows preinstalled don't come with a full version of Microsoft Windows; instead they come with a recovery CD that can be used to return the PC to its original factory configuration. The important thing to know about these recovery CDs is that they wipe out all user data and applications. Use one only when you can't restore system functionality in any less-drastic way.

Hardware Tools

In addition to the software tools included with the operating system, you should be familiar with a number of hardware tools. The exam objectives specifically mention familiarity with these tools:

Multi-meter   A multi-meter (also written *multimeter*) combines a number of tools into one. There can be slight deviations, but a multi-meter always includes a voltmeter, an ohmmeter, and an ammeter (and is sometimes called VOM as an acronym).

Antistatic pad and wrist strap   The need for an antistatic strap was discussed in the first objective of this chapter. A properly grounded strap can save you from suffering a nasty jolt. An antistatic pad works similarly and can not only protect you, but also protect sensitive equipment from static damage.

    Another option is antistatic spray. Usually applied as a mist to carpets, chairs, and so on, this spray reduces the amount of static electricity present and can save computers and components.

Specialty hardware/tools   Specialty tools can include anything needed for a specific purpose, but there are a few things you should always have: a parts grabber for picking up pieces that have fallen or are hard to hold on to, a chip extractor, and wire cutters/strippers/crimpers. These tools can be used to solve a number of problems.

Loopback plugs   Also called wrap plugs, loopback plugs take the signal going out and essentially echo it back. This allows you to test parallel and serial ports to make certain they're working correctly.

Cleaning products   A good hand vacuum is a necessity. You need to be able to vacuum up dust, debris, and even toner on occasions. So, you want a vacuum that is capable of collecting small particles and won't pass them through the bag and back into the air. Spend the money on a good vacuum, and you'll be glad you did.

An assortment of other cleaning supplies should also be available. These include cleaning pads for monitors, contact cleaner, compressed air, and CD-cleaning supplies.

Exam Essentials

Know the default IRQs for COM ports and common devices.   Know the default IRQs for COM ports and common devices such as modems, sound cards, disk drives, and so on.

Be familiar with Device Manager.   Device Manager can display information about the computer's memory, I/O ports, IRQs being used, and many other PC resources.

Understand how manual resource assignments are set.   Manual resource assignments for Plug and Play devices are set on the Resources tab of the device's Properties box. For a non-PnP device, resource assignments are controlled by jumpers on the device itself.

Know the hardware tools mentioned.   Be able to name the hardware tools and their purposes.

Performing Preventative Maintenance for Personal Computer Components

Chapter 1 included a great deal of information on preventive maintenance products and procedures. Be sure you understand that information; the content here builds on it.

Critical Information

CompTIA expects you to know the preventative maintenance information covered in Chapter 1 for this objective as well. In addition, CompTIA expects you to know information on the following topics:

Display devices   Keep them clean to prevent overheating, and make sure there is adequate ventilation. Depending on the type and size of monitor, it may be able to generate a considerable amount of heat. This heat needs to be vented away to keep the device working properly, and you should take care that the heat from the monitor doesn't go into other devices that are also heat sensitive.

Power devices   In the days of old, it was common procedure to turn off a computer's power and solve your problems with a reboot. Today, there are so many open files on a system at any given time that doing so can cause irreparable harm to data. Just as you would no longer pull the plug, you should make sure this isn't done outside of your control by adding surge protectors, power strips, uninterruptible power supplies (UPSs), and other devices to the PCs. Most UPSs now include software that can trigger the PC to safely shut down if the power stays off for a long enough period of time that the battery in the UPS begins to get low.

Input devices   If you're working in an environment with a high degree of contaminants (a factory floor, for example), you should consider covering the input devices. Many supply houses carry disposable covers that can be placed over keyboards and other devices to keep dirt, liquid, grime, and other impurities out in these environments.

Storage devices   Keep the hard drives defragmented as much as possible (use DEFRAG) to keep them working optimally. Monitor them for adequate storage space, and replace/add to them as needed.

Thermally sensitive devices   Motherboards, CPUs, adapter cards, and almost everything else in the PC will react negatively to high temperatures. Make sure there is adequate ventilation for your PCs and that you keep them clean to keep the heat down.

As with so many other topics on the exam, common sense should be your guide when answering questions about preventative maintenance and computer components.

Exam Essentials

Know the need to keep systems well ventilated.   Heat can be a negative force to almost any PC component, and ventilation can help ensure there isn't excessive heat buildup.

Review Questions

1. When working on a computer, what do you need for an adequate workspace?

2. When removing the case cover, why should you not remove all screws from the back of the PC?

3. What should an antistatic strip be connected to?

4. Before you remove a power supply, what two things must you do?

5. What are hot-pluggable drives?

6. What are stand-offs?

7. Name the default IRQs for COM1 and COM2.

8. In what Windows utility would you manually change a hardware resource assignment?

9. What is one of the most common problems in upgrading to a larger hard disk?

10. What is the default I/O address for LPT1?

Answers to Review Questions

1. First, the work area must be flat. Second, the area must be sturdy. Third, the area must be well lit, clean, and large enough to hold all pieces and necessary tools.

2. Some of these screws hold vital components (such as the power supply) to the case, and removing them will cause those components to drop into the computer.

3. You should plug one end of the antistatic wrist strap into the ground plug of an outlet.

4. Before you remove the power supply from the computer, you must disconnect the power supply connectors from the internal devices, and remove the mounting hardware for the power supply.

5. Hot-pluggable drives are those that can be added or removed while the computer is running.

6. The motherboard is held away from the metal case using brass or plastic spacers called stand-offs.

7. COM1 is usually IRQ4, and COM2 is usually IRQ3.

8. Device Manager

9. One of the most common problems in upgrading to a larger hard disk is the BIOS's inability to support the larger disk size.

10. 0378-037F

Chapter

10

Laptops and Portable Devices

COMPTIA A+ 220-602 EXAM OBJECTIVES COVERED IN THIS CHAPTER:

✓ **2.1 Identify fundamental principles of using laptops and portable devices**

- Identify appropriate applications for laptop-specific communication connections, such as Bluetooth, infrared, cellular WAN, and Ethernet

- Identify appropriate laptop-specific power and electrical input devices and determine how amperage and voltage can affect performance

- Identify the major components of the LCD, including inverter, screen, and video card

✓ **2.2 Install, configure, optimize, and upgrade laptops and portable devices**

- Removal of laptop-specific hardware, such as peripherals, hot-swappable and non-hot-swappable devices

- Describe how video sharing affects memory upgrades

✓ **2.3 Use tools, diagnostic procedures, and troubleshooting techniques for laptops and portable devices**

- Use procedures and techniques to diagnose power conditions, video, keyboard, pointer, and wireless card issues, for example:

  - Verify AC power (e.g., LEDs, swap AC adapter)

  - Verify DC power

  - Remove unneeded peripherals

  - Plug in external monitor

  - Toggle Fn keys

  - Check LCD cutoff switch

  - Verify backlight functionality and pixilation

- Stylus issues (e.g., digitizer problems)
- Unique laptop keypad issues
- Antenna wires

COMPTIA A+ 220-604 EXAM OBJECTIVES COVERED IN THIS CHAPTER:

✓ **2.1 Identify the fundamental principles of using laptops and portable devices**

- Identify appropriate applications for laptop-specific communication connections, for example:
    - Bluetooth
    - Infrared devices
    - Cellular WAN
    - Ethernet
- Identify appropriate laptop-specific power and electrical input devices, for example:
    - Output performance requirements for amperage and voltage
- Identify the major components of the LCD (e.g., inverter, screen, video card)

✓ **2.2 Install, configure, optimize, and upgrade laptops and portable devices**

- Demonstrate the safe removal of laptop-specific hardware, including peripherals, hot-swappable and non hot-swappable devices
- Identify the affect of video sharing on memory upgrades

✓ **2.3 Identify tools, diagnostic procedures, and troubleshooting techniques for laptops and portable devices**

- Use procedures and techniques to diagnose power conditions, video issues, keyboard and pointer issues, and wireless card issues, for example:
    - Verify AC power (e.g., LED's, swap AC adapter)
    - Verify DC power
    - Remove unneeded peripherals
    - Plug in external monitor

- Toggle Fn keys
- Check LCD cutoff switch
- Verify backlight functionality and pixilation
- Stylus issues (e.g., digitizer problems)
- Unique laptop keypad issues
- Antenna wires

This domain is weighted at 9 percent of the IT Technician (220-602) exam and 20 percent of the Depot Technician (220-604) exam (it doesn't appear on the Remote Support [220-603] exam). Almost all of the material in the technician exams appears in the Essentials exam, with few exceptions. This chapter will recap the content that appeared in Chapter 2 and focus on the issues that are new to this exam.

Identify Principles of Laptops and Portable Devices

Contrary to the name, this objective doesn't expect you to know everything there is to know about laptops—you had to do much of that for the Essentials exam. Instead, this objective focuses on three key areas: communication connections, electrical issues, and LCDs.

Critical Information

This exam focuses on three key areas, regardless of the elective you've chosen to take. These three are discussed in the following sections. Some of this material is overlap from Chapter 2, and you should be able to breeze through it fairly quickly.

Communication Connections

Communication connections were discussed in Chapter 5 as they relate to networking, but this objective wants you to know about the following as they apply to laptops: Bluetooth, infrared, cellular WAN, and Ethernet.

Bluetooth

Bluetooth is a wireless standard that works best within a very close range—usually about 35 feet, so it hasn't become widespread in use except for communications between notebook PCs and PDAs.

Infrared

Infrared is a type of networking that requires line of sight and is useful for small areas, but it isn't used much beyond that. Many printers have infrared (IrDA) capabilities, as do mice and other wireless peripherals.

Cellular WAN

Cellular networks for computers work like those for voice communication. Radio cells are created through the use of transmitters and provide coverage within a specific area.

Ethernet

Ethernet is the traditional method most people think of when networking comes to mind. Most Ethernet networks use cabling, such as 10BaseT, to connect laptops to a hub and on to a network.

Electrical Issues

Electrical issues can be either AC- or DC-related. AC is the standard current coming from the outlet to the power cord. The power supply converts AC to DC, and the computer runs on DC power (which is why it can run on a battery for so long).

In the absence of AC power, the laptop will attempt to run off of the battery. Although this solution is good for a time, AC power must be available to keep the battery charged and the laptop running. Most laptops have an indicator light that shows whether AC power is being received; the AC cord typically has an indicator light as well, to show that it's receiving power. If no lights are lit on the cord or the laptop, indicating that AC power is being received, try a different outlet or a different cord.

One item the AC presence can affect is the action of the network card. In order to conserve power, the network card is often configured to not be active when running on DC power. You can access the relevant dialog through Start ➢ Control Panel ➢ Internal NIC Configuration.

The biggest issue with DC power problems is a battery's inability to power the laptop as long as it should. This can be caused by an older battery building up a memory and thus not offering a full charge (lithium ion batteries don't suffer this fate). If a feature is available to fully drain the battery, you should use it to eliminate the memory (letting the laptop run on battery on a regular basis greatly helps). If you can't drain the battery and eliminate the memory, you should replace the battery.

LCDs

The liquid crystal display (LCD) consists of three key elements: the screen, the inverter, and the video card. The screen is made of liquid crystals to reduce power consumption and the thickness of the monitor (it's a flat panel made from two polarized glass panes with liquid between them). The panels are made of columns and rows called a *matrix*.

Depending on the capability of the display, most panels fall into the category of *active* matrix or *passive* matrix. With a passive matrix, the display is essentially created at one time, and changes take place to an entire column; with an active matrix, a single liquid crystal (pixel) can be changed. Chapter 2 listed the different types of passive and active displays and gave some resolutions that you should know.

Exam Essentials

Know the different types of communication options available.   The exam expects you to know four different types: Bluetooth, infrared, cellular WAN, and Ethernet.

Know the various electrical issues discussed.   Power supplies convert AC to DC power and problems can occur within either current.

Upgrade and Optimize Laptops and Portable Devices

This objective is a mirror of Objective 2.2 in the Essentials exam, but it adds video sharing. Rather than repeating all the information on removing and replacing components, we assume you can skim Chapter 2 for that information. The focus here is solely on video sharing.

Critical Information

Video sharing is extremely popular, whether it's done through streaming media from a popular website (such as YouTube), by sending digital videos from your home camera to grandma and grandpa, or using any of a hundred other possibilities. One affect of the increased use of video is a greater need for memory. The more memory—and the faster the memory—that is installed in a system, the more potential it has to be able to queue/cache the video and deliver it seamlessly.

Although memory is the key element beneath this objective, you should know that the increased use of video has the potential to bottleneck other areas as well. Some to be aware of are the speed of the network connection (never view an episode of your favorite television show across a dial-up connection) and the computer itself (processor).

Exam Essentials

Know the need for memory when working with video.   Video sharing is popular and requires a lot of resources to function properly. One such resource is memory, and—as a general rule—the more memory, and the faster the memory, the better the performance.

Identify Tools and Diagnostic Procedures

Most of the tools used in diagnostics and troubleshooting are the same in the laptop world as in the desktop world, with few exceptions. This section contains virtually the same information that appeared in Chapter 2, due to identical exam objectives between the Essentials exam and the two electives.

Critical Information

To solve a problem with a laptop or portable device (the terms are mostly used interchangeably by CompTIA), you should fully understand the hardware you're working with. The following list describes those things CompTIA wants you to be comfortable with for this objective. Some may seem like common sense, in which case you should have no difficulty choosing the correct answers on the exam:

AC power issues In the absence of AC power, the laptop will attempt to run off of the battery. Although this solution is good for a time, AC power must be available to keep the battery charged and the laptop running. Most laptops have an indicator light that shows whether AC power is being received; the AC cord typically has an indicator light on it, as well, to show that it's receiving power. If no lights are lit on the cord or the laptop indicating that AC power is being received, try a different outlet or different cord.

Antenna wires Most laptops today include an internal wireless card. This is convenient, but it can be susceptible to interference (resulting in a low signal strength) between the laptop and the access point. Do what you can to reduce the number of items blocking the signal between the two devices, and you'll increase the strength of the signal.

Backlight functionality The *backlight* is the light in the PC that powers the LCD screen. It can go bad over time and need to be replaced, and it can also be held captive by the inverter. The inverter takes the DC power the laptop is providing and boosts it up to AC to run the backlight. If the inverter goes bad, you can replace it on most models (it's cheaper than the backlight).

DC power problems The biggest issue with DC power problems is a battery's inability to power the laptop as long as it should. This can be caused by the battery building up a memory and thus not offering a full charge. If a feature is available to fully drain the battery, you should use it to eliminate the memory (letting the laptop run on battery on a regular basis greatly helps). If you can't drain the battery and eliminate the memory, you should replace the battery.

External monitors An external monitor may be connected to the laptop directly or through a docking station. With many laptops, if the external monitor is connected before you boot the laptop, the laptop will automatically detect the monitor and send the display there. If you connect after the laptop is booted, you should use the appropriate Fn key to send the display to the monitor.

Keyboard problems   Problems with keyboards can range from collecting dust (in which case you need to blow them out) to their springs wearing out. In the latter case, you can replace the keyboard (they cost about 10 times more than desktop keyboards) or choose to use an external one (providing the user isn't traveling and having to lug another hardware element with them).

LCD cutoff switch   A thermal cutoff switch is often included in laptops to turn off the system if the temperature rises too high. Although this switch may go bad and cause the laptop to unduly turn off, usually a shutdown is a symptom of another problem; you should try to isolate what is causing the heat (dirt, debris, and so on) and address that issue.

Pointer difficulties   The pointer device used on the laptop, like the keyboard, can be affected by dirt/debris as well as by continual use. If the device fails to function properly after a good cleaning, you can replace it (expensive) or opt for an external pointer (such as a wireless mouse).

Stylus issues   A stylus may no longer work on a tablet computer due to damage or excessive wear. When this occurs, you can purchase inexpensive replacement styluses for most units.

Unneeded peripherals   To keep the system running at peak efficiency, you should disconnect or disable unneeded peripherals. Every peripheral has the ability to drain power and resources from the PC, and you don't want that if it can be avoided.

Video issues   One of the biggest problems with video is incorrect settings. You can change the video settings easily on the laptop through the operating system. Make sure you have the correct—and most current—drivers.

A few other miscellaneous topics—such as Fn toggling and wireless card issues—are listed by CompTIA beneath this objective, but they have been addressed elsewhere and there is nothing additional to say about them.

Exam Essentials

Know how to work with laptop components.   Understand the issues that can arise, and know what to look for to begin trying to fix them.

Know the power configuration settings.   Using power configuration, it's possible to disable the NIC and other devices to conserve power. It's also possible to receive notification when the battery life reaches low levels.

Review Questions

1. What range is Bluetooth limited to?

2. What is the acronym used for *infrared*?

3. What is used to create cells within a cellular network?

4. True or false: Most laptop electrical cords include a light to show that AC current is being received.

5. What are the three elements of an LCD?

6. What is the difference between active and passive matrix displays?

7. True or false: Video sharing is very memory-intensive.

8. What is used to turn off a system if the heat rises too high?

9. True or false: When a stylus no longer works, you can purchase inexpensive replacement styluses for most units.

10. True or false: Every peripheral has the ability to drain power and resources from the PC.

Answers to Review Questions

1. It is usually limited to about 10 feet of effective range.

2. It is IrDA.

3. Radio cells are created through the use of transmitters. They provide coverage within a specific area.

4. True. Most laptop electrical cords include a light to show that AC current is being received.

5. The liquid crystal display (LCD) consists of three key elements: the screen, the inverter, and the video card.

6. With a passive matrix, the display is essentially created at one time, and changes take place to an entire column. With an active matrix, a single liquid crystal (pixel) can be changed.

7. True. Video sharing is very memory-intensive.

8. A thermal cutoff switch is often included in laptops to turn off the system if the temperature rises too high.

9. True. You can purchase inexpensive replacement styluses for most units.

10. True. Every peripheral has the ability to drain power and resources from the PC.

Chapter 11

Operating Systems

COMPTIA A+ 220-602 EXAM OBJECTIVES COVERED IN THIS CHAPTER:

✓ **3.1 Identify the fundamental principles of operating systems**

- Use command-line functions and utilities to manage operating systems, including proper syntax and switches, for example:
  - CMD
  - HELP
  - DIR
  - ATTRIB
  - EDIT
  - COPY
  - XCOPY
  - FORMAT
  - IPCONFIG
  - PING
  - MD / CD / RD
- Identify concepts and procedures for creating, viewing and managing disks, directories, and files on operating systems
- Disks (e.g., active, primary, extended and logical partitions, and file systems, including FAT32 and NTFS)
- Directory structures (e.g., create folders, navigate directory structures)
- Files (e.g., creation, attributes, permissions)
- Locate and use operating system utilities and available switches, for example:
  - Disk management tools (e.g., DEFRAG, NTBACKUP, CHKDSK, Format)
  - System management tools
  - Device and Task Manager

- MSCONFIG.EXE
- REGEDIT.EXE
- REGEDT32.EXE
- CMD
- Event Viewer
- System Restore
- Remote Desktop
- File management tools (e.g., Windows EXPLORER, ATTRIB.EXE)

✓ **3.2 Install, configure, optimize, and upgrade operating systems**

- Identify procedures and utilities used to optimize operating systems, for example:
    - Virtual memory
    - Hard drives (e.g., disk defragmentation)
    - Temporary files
    - Services
    - Startup
    - Application

✓ **3.3 Identify tools, diagnostic procedures, and troubleshooting techniques for operating systems**

- Demonstrate the ability to recover operating systems (e.g., boot methods, recovery console, ASR, ERD)
- Recognize and resolve common operational problems, for example:
    - Windows specific printing problems (e.g., print spool stalled, incorrect / incompatible driver form print)
    - Auto-restart errors
    - Bluescreen error
    - System lock-up
    - Device drivers failure (input / output devices)
    - Application install, start or load failure
- Recognize and resolve common error messages and codes, for example:
    - Boot (e.g., invalid boot disk, inaccessible boot drive, missing NTLDR)

- Startup (e.g., device / service failed to start, device / program in registry not found)
- Event Viewer
- Registry
- Windows reporting

- Use diagnostic utilities and tools to resolve operational problems, for example:
  - Bootable media
  - Startup modes (e.g., safe mode, safe mode with command prompt or networking, step-by-step / single step mode)
  - Documentation resources (e.g., user / installation manuals, internet / web based, training materials)
  - Task and Device Manager
  - Event Viewer
  - MSCONFIG
  - Recover CD / recovery partition
  - Remote Desktop Connection and Assistance
  - System File Checker (SFC)

✓ **3.4 Perform preventative maintenance for operating systems**

- Demonstrate the ability to perform preventative maintenance on operating systems, including software and Windows updates (e.g., service packs), scheduled backups / restore, restore points

---

COMPTIA A+ 220-603 EXAM OBJECTIVES COVERED IN THIS CHAPTER:

✓ **2.1 Identify the fundamental principles of using operating systems**

- Use command-line functions and utilities to manage Windows 2000, XP Professional, and XP Home, including proper syntax and switches, for example:
  - CMD
  - HELP

- DIR
- ATTRIB
- EDIT
- COPY
- XCOPY
- FORMAT
- IPCONFIG
- PING
- MD / CD / RD

- Identify concepts and procedures for creating, viewing, managing disks, directories, and files in Windows 2000, XP Professional, and XP Home, for example:
  - Disks (e.g., active, primary, extended and logical partitions)
  - File systems (e.g., FAT 32, NTFS)
  - Directory structures (e.g., create folders, navigate directory structures)
  - Files (e.g., creation, extensions, attributes, permissions)
- Locate and use Windows 2000, XP Professional, and XP Home utilities and available switches
- Disk Management Tools (e.g., DEFRAG, NTBACKUP, CHKDSK, Format)
- System Management Tools
- Device and Task Manager
- MSCONFIG.EXE
- REGEDIT.EXE
- REGEDT32.EXE
- CMD
- Event Viewer
- System Restore
- Remote Desktop
- File Management Tools (e.g., Windows Explorer, ATTRIB.EXE)

✓ **2.2 Install, configure, optimize, and upgrade operating systems**

- Identify procedures and utilities used to optimize the performance of Windows 2000, XP Professional, and XP Home, for example:
  - Virtual memory
  - Hard drives (i.e. disk defragmentation)
  - Temporary files
  - Services
  - Startup
  - Applications

✓ **2.3 Identify tools, diagnostic procedures, and troubleshooting techniques for operating systems**

- Recognize and resolve common operational problems, for example:
  - Windows-specific printing problems (e.g., print spool stalled, incorrect/incompatible driver form print)
  - Auto-restart errors
  - Bluescreen error
  - System lock-up
  - Device drivers failure (input/output devices)
  - Application install, start or load failure
- Recognize and resolve common error messages and codes, for example:
  - Boot (e.g., invalid boot disk, inaccessible boot device, missing NTLDR)
  - Startup (e.g., device/service has failed to start, device/program references in registry not found)
  - Event viewer
  - Registry
  - Windows
- Use diagnostic utilities and tools to resolve operational problems, for example:
  - Bootable media
  - Startup Modes (e.g., safe mode, safe mode with command prompt or networking, step-by-step/single step mode)

- Documentation resources (e.g., user/installation manuals, internet/web-based, training materials)
- Task and Device Manager
- Event Viewer
- MSCONFIG
- Recovery CD / Recovery partition
- Remote Desktop Connection and Assistance
- System File Checker (SFC)

✓ **2.4 Perform preventative maintenance for operating systems**

- Perform preventative maintenance on Windows 2000, XP Professional, and XP Home, including software and Windows updates (e.g., service packs)

There is one sizable difference between this domain as it exists on the Essentials exam and in the Technician exams. On the Essentials exam, it focuses mostly on Windows-based operating systems but isn't limited to those operating systems. In the elective exams, the only operating systems focused on are those that are Windows-based.

This domain is weighted more heavily than any other on both the 220-602 (IT Technician) exam (at 20 percent) and 220-603 (Remote Support Technician) exam (at 29 percent). It isn't present on the 220-604 elective exam.

Operating System Fundamentals

This objective requires you to know three major concepts, all of which are necessary for working with operating systems in the real world:

- Common command-line utilities
- How to work with disks and directory structures
- Administrative tools

A great deal of the material here overlaps with that discussed in Chapter 3, but you'll want to make certain you know each and every utility discussed.

Critical Information

Although most of the information presented about Windows utilities and administration should seem like second nature to you (on-the-job experience is expected for A+ certification), you should thoroughly read these sections to make certain you can answer any questions that may appear about them.

Common Command-Line Utilities

The A+ objective's topic list expects you to know how to use certain specific commands at a prompt. The following list summarizes them:

ATTRIB This command displays or changes the attributes for one or more files. Used by itself, it displays a list of all files in the current location with attributes set. The attributes are

Read Only (R), Hidden (H), System (S), and Archive (A). They can be turned off with a minus sign or turned on with a plus sign. Here are some examples:

ATTRIB -R TEE.DOC   This command removes the read-only attribute from TEE.DOC.

ATTRIB +H *.*   This command adds the Hidden attribute to all files in the current location.

CD   This command serves two purposes. When typed at the command line without any parameters, CD (Current Directory) shows you the directory that you're currently in. When given a directory to change to, the CD (Change Directory) utility changes your current directory to the one given.

You can specify the directory to change to as either an absolute or a relative path. An absolute path gives the full path regardless of the directory you're currently in (for example, C:\Documents and Settings\All Users). A relative path tells the utility to change you to a location relative to where you currently are. For example, if you're in the C:\Documents and Settings directory, you can move to C:\Documents and Settings\All Users by giving the command

    CD ALL USERS

With relative addressing, you can use two periods (..) to indicate the parent directory or one period (.) to indicate the present directory.

CMD   Within Windows 2000 and the XP varieties, this utility is used to display a command prompt. You can either choose Start ≻ Run, type **CMD**, and click OK, or choose Start ≻ Programs ≻ Accessories ≻ Command Prompt to open the command prompt and be able to execute command-line utilities. When you're finished and want to return to Windows, type **EXIT** and press Enter.

COPY   This command copies files from one location to another. If the location for either the source or the destination isn't included in the command, it's assumed to be the current folder. Here are some examples:

COPY *.* A: This command copies all files from the current folder to the A: drive.

COPY C:\Windows\Myfile.txt   This command copies Myfile.txt from C:\Windows to the current folder.

DIR   This command displays the contents of the current folder. You can use it by itself or with a file specification to narrow down the listing. Here are some examples:

DIR ????.*   This command displays all files that are exactly four letters in name length, with any extension.

DIR /w   This command displays the listing in wide (multicolumn) format, with names only (fewer details).

DIR /p   This command displays the listing one screenful at a time. Press Enter to see the next screenful.

EDIT   This command opens the MS-DOS Editor utility, a text editor similar to Notepad. You can add a filename to open that file (if it exists) or create a new file (if it doesn't exist). Here's an example:

EDIT CONFIG.SYS   This command opens CONFIG.SYS if it's present in the current folder or otherwise creates it and opens it.

The switches for EDIT are listed in Table 11.1.

TABLE 11.1   The EDIT Switches

Switch	Description
/B	Forces monochrome mode
/H	Displays the maximum number of lines possible for your hardware
/R	Loads the file(s) in read-only mode
/S	Forces the use of short filenames
/<nnn>	Loads binary file(s), wrapping lines to <nnn> characters wide
[file]	Specifies an initial file to load

FORMAT   This command prepares a floppy or hard disk for use by applying a certain filesystem to it. You can use the FORMAT command at a command prompt to format a disk. It's located in the C:\Windows\System32 folder, but it can be accessed from any prompt.

Its switches are listed in Table 11.2.

TABLE 11.2   The FORMAT Switches

Switch	Description
/V[:label]	Specifies a volume label
/Q	Performs a quick format
/F:size	Specifies the formatted size; omit for default
/B	Allocates space on the formatted disk for system files to be added later
/S	Copies system files to the formatted disk

TABLE 11.2   The FORMAT Switches *(continued)*

Switch	Description
/T:*tracks*	Specifies the number of tracks per disk side
/N:*sectors*	Specifies the number of sectors per track
/1	Formats a single side of a floppy disk
/4	Formats a 5¹/₄″ 360KB floppy disk
/8	Formats eight sectors per track
/C	Tests clusters that are currently marked as bad

You can also access a Windows-based Format utility by right-clicking a drive icon in Windows and selecting Format.

HELP   This command can be used to give you the syntax and a short description of any command-line utility you want information on. You can obtain essentially the same information by following the command with /?. Because of this, the following two commands are identical:

    HELP CD

and

    CD /?

IPCONFIG   You can use IPCONFIG to view the current IP configuration for the client. It can also be used with a number of switches to change the IP address settings. Here are some examples:

    IPCONFIG /release   This command releases the IP address leased from a DHCP server.

    IPCONFIG /renew   This command renews an IP address leased from a DHCP server.

MD   MD (Make Directory) is used as the name implies. For example, MD BACKUP makes a new directory called Backup in the current directory.

PING   This command allows you to check a particular IP address or domain name on a network for reachability. For example, PING microsoft.com tells you whether Microsoft's website is up.

RD   RD (Remove Directory) is used to delete a directory from the system from the command line. For example, RD C:\EDULANEY deletes the EDULANEY directory (assuming it's empty). You cannot delete a directory that has files in it without using the /S parameter.

XCOPY   This command is like COPY, but it also duplicates any subfolders. For example, XCOPY C:\BOOKS A:\ copies everything from C:\BOOKS to the A: drive and also copies any subfolders and their contents.

Working with Disks and Directories

The basic building block of storage is the disk. Disks are partitioned (primary, logical, extended) and then formatted for use. With the Windows operating systems this exam focuses on, you can choose to use either FAT32 or NTFS, the advantage of the latter being that it offers security and many other features that FAT32 can't handle.

> If you're using FAT32 and want to change to NTFS, the convert utility will allow you to do so. For example, to change the E: drive to NTFS, the command is convert e: /FS:NTFS.

Once the disk is formatted, the next building block is the directory structure, in which you divide the partition into logical locations for storing data. Whether these storage units are called directories or folders is a matter of semantics—they tend to be called *folders* when viewed in the graphical user interface (GUI) and *directories* when viewed from the command line.

You can create directories from the command line using the MD command and from within the GUI by right-clicking in a Windows Explorer window and choosing New ➢ Folder. Once the folder exists, you can view/change its properties, as shown in Figure 11.1, by right-clicking the icon of its folder and choosing Properties.

In the Attributes section, you can choose to make the directory read-only or hidden. By clicking the Advanced button, you can configure indexing, archiving, encryption, and compression settings.

FIGURE 11.1 Change the attributes associated with a directory

Even though encryption and compression settings appear in the same frame on the dialog box, the two features are mutually exclusive.

The building blocks of directories are files. You can create a file either from within an application or by right-clicking, choosing New, and then selecting the type of item you want to create, as shown in Figure 11.2.

FIGURE 11.2   You can create files of various types with a right-click.

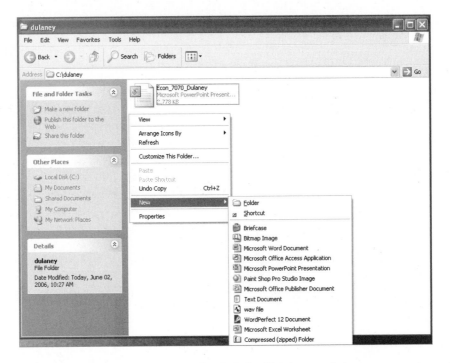

Once the file has been created, you can right-click the file's icon and change properties and permissions associated with the file by choosing Properties from the pop-up menu.

Administrative Tools

The administrative tools that fall beneath this section are the primary tools used on a regular basis. Most of them relate to data and drives, but that isn't true of all of them. The tools that CompTIA wants you to know are as follows:

CHKDSK   CHKDSK is an old MS-DOS utility that is used to correct logical errors in the FAT. The most common switch for CHKDSK is /F, which fixes the errors that it finds. Without /F, CHKDSK is an information-only utility.

DEFRAG   This tool runs the Disk Defragmenter utility. It works only under MS-DOS or from startup disks. Disk Defragmenter reorganizes the file storage on a disk to reduce the number of files that are stored noncontiguously. This makes file retrieval faster, because the read/write heads on the disk have to move less.

There are two versions of Disk Defragmenter: a DOS version, and a Windows version that runs from within Windows. The Windows version is located on the System Tools submenu on the Start menu (Start ➤ All Programs ➤ Accessories ➤ System Tools ➤ Disk Defragmenter).

The available switches for the DOS version (`defrag.exe`) include the following:

-a   Analyze only

-f   Force defragmentation even if disk space is low

-v   Verbose output

Device Manager   Device Manager shows a list of all installed hardware and lets you add items, remove items, update drivers, and more. This is a Windows-only utility. In Windows 2000/XP, you display the System Properties, click the Hardware tab, and then click the Device Manager button to display it. Figure 11.3 shows an example.

Event Viewer   This utility provides information about what's been going on system-wise, to help you troubleshoot problems. Event Viewer shows warnings, error messages, and records of things happening successfully. It's found in NT-based versions of Windows only (which includes Windows 2000, and Windows XP). You can access it through Computer Management, or you can access it directly from the Administrative Tools in Control Panel. Figure 11.4 shows an example.

FIGURE 11.3   The Device Manager in Windows XP

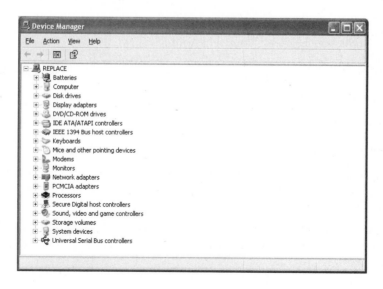

MSCONFIG (System Configuration Utility) This utility helps troubleshoot startup problems by allowing you to selectively disable individual items that normally are executed at startup. There is no menu command for this utility; you must run it with the Run command (on the Start menu). Choose Start ➢ Run, and type **MSCONFIG**. It works in most versions of Windows, although the interface window is slightly different among versions. Figure 11.5 shows an example in Windows XP.

FIGURE 11.4 The Event Viewer in Windows XP

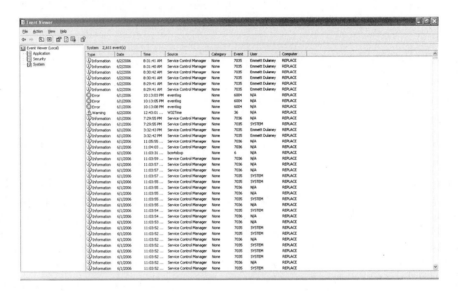

FIGURE 11.5 MSCONFIG in Windows XP

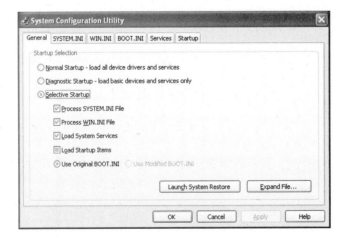

FIGURE 11.6   The Backup Utility in Windows XP

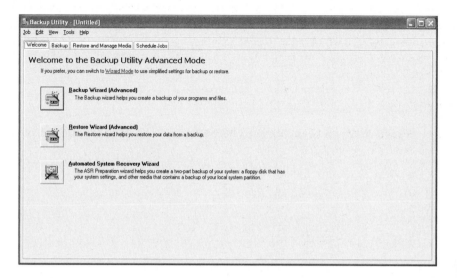

NTBACKUP   With Windows 2000 and XP, you can access this utility from the System Tools menu, or from the Tools tab in a hard disk's Properties box. Its purpose is to back up files in a compressed format, so the backups take up less space than the original files would if they were copied. To restore the backup, you must use the same utility again, but in Restore mode. The best insurance policy you have against devastating loss when a failure occurs is a backup of the data that you can turn to when the system is rebuilt.

When you start the program, by default it begins the Backup or Restore Wizard (you can disable this default action by deselecting Always Start in Wizard Mode on the first dialog). The wizard will walk you through any backup/restore operation you want to do, or you can click Advanced Mode to get to the interface shown in Figure 11.6.

Five backup type choices are available:

Normal   A full backup of all files, regardless of the state of the archive bit (the default). After the files are backed up, the archive bit is turned off.

Copy   A full backup of all files, regardless of the state of the archive bit. The archive bit is left in its current state.

Incremental   Backs up only files for which the archive bit is currently turned on. After the files are backed up, the archive bit is turned off.

Differential   Backs up only files for which the archive bit is currently turned on. The archive bit is left in its current state.

Daily   Backs up only those files with today's date, regardless of archive bit status.

You can also perform backups from the command line by using the `ntbackup.exe` executable. You can't restore files from the command line with this utility, however. Options include the following:

/A   Performs an append.

/F   Identifies the disk path and filename.

/HC:{on|off}   Toggles hardware compression on or off.

/J   Signifies the job name.

/M   Must be followed by a backup type name: `copy`, `daily`, `differential`, `incremental`, or `normal`.

/N   Signifies a new tape name; can't be used in conjunction with /A.

/P   Signifies the media pool name.

/T   Followed by the tape name.

/V:{yes|no}   Toggles whether to do verification after the completion of the backup.

REGEDIT and REGEDT32 (Registry Editor)   The Registry Editor is used to change values and variables stored in a configuration database known as the Registry. This centralized database contains environmental settings for various Windows programs along with registration information, which details the types of file extensions associated with applications. So, when you double-click a file in Windows Explorer, the associated application runs and opens the file you double-clicked.

The Registry Editor, shown in Figure 11.7, enables you to make changes to the large hierarchical database that contains all of Windows' settings. These changes can potentially disable the entire system, so they should not be made lightly.

FIGURE 11.7   The Registry Editor in Windows XP

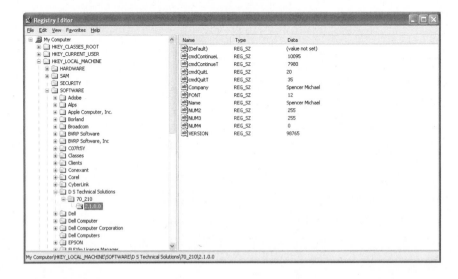

There is no menu command for the Registry Editor. You must run it with the Run command. REGEDIT is the name of the program. Windows 2000 includes a second Registry Editor program called REGEDT32. This alternative program accesses the same Registry but does so in a slightly different way; it shows each of the major key areas in a separate window. In Windows XP, the command REGEDT32 is present, but running it launches REGEDIT; they have been rolled into a single utility.

The Registry holds great power but can also cause great harm. Never edit the Registry without being completely sure what you're doing.

Remote Desktop   The Remote Desktop feature of Windows XP allows you to remotely connect to your workstation and use it for a variety of purposes—work from home, teach a user how to do a task, and so on. Two elements are involved:

Turning on the ability to access remotely

Accessing remotely

To do the first, access the System Properties, click the Remote tab, and select the Allow Users to Connect Remotely to This Computer Under Remote Desktop check box. Click Apply, and then click OK to exit.

To access the computer from another XP workstation, go to Start ➢ All Programs ➢ Accessories ➢ Communications, and choose Remote Desktop Connection. If you click the Options button, you'll see choices similar to those in Figure 11.8

FIGURE 11.8   The Remote Desktop Connection dialog in Windows XP

One of the simplest ways to connect is to enter the IP address of the host. Once you give a valid username and password, you're connected to the host and able to work remotely.

System Restore   System Restore is arguably the most powerful tool in Windows XP. It can allow you to restore the system to a previous point in time. You can access it from Start > All Programs ➢ Accessories ➢ System Tools ➢ System Restore and use it to roll back, as well as to create a restore point, as shown in Figure 11.9.

In addition to letting you manually create a restore point, Windows XP creates a restore point automatically every 24 hours, as well as when you install unsigned device drivers or install (or uninstall) a program with Windows Installer or InstallShield. By default, restore points are kept for 90 days and then deleted in order to conserve space.

FIGURE 11.9   Create a restore point or return to one with System Restore.

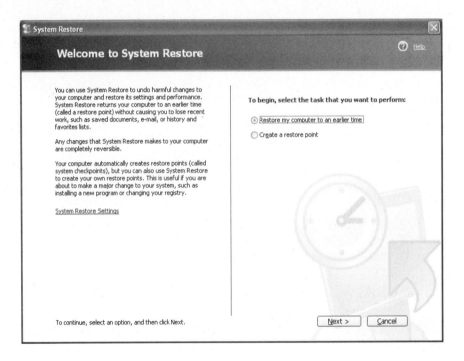

   You must be a member of Computer Administrators to run System Restore.

Task Manager   Task Manager shows running programs and the system resources they're consuming. It can be used for informational purposes, but it's most often used to shut down a nonresponsive application.

There are three ways to display the Task Manager. The first is to press Ctrl+Alt+Delete and click the Task Manager button (if required). The second is to right-click in an empty location on the Taskbar and choose Task Manager from the pop-up menu. The third method is to hold down Ctrl+Shift and press Esc.

A list of running tasks appears under the Applications tab; you can click one of them and then click End Task to shut it down. Because this shutdown method fails to close files gracefully, you should use it only as a last resort, not as a normal method of shutting down an application. You can also choose the Processes tab to see all processes—not just applications—running, or choose Performance to see CPU, paging, memory, and other parameters. The Networking tab shows usage for all found connections, and the Users tab shows the current users and lets you disconnect them, log them off, or send them a message.

Windows Explorer   Windows Explorer is the primary file-management interface in Windows. It displays the list of files in the current location at the right and a folder tree of other locations at the left. It starts with the My Documents folder as its default location when opened. Windows Explorer is available in all Windows versions and works approximately the same way in each.

Exam Essentials

Know the main command-line utilities.   Those discussed in this chapter include the ones CompTIA wants you to know for the exam.

Know the disk/directory structure.   You should be able to create folders from within Windows as well as from the command line. You should also be able to create files and copy them from one location to another.

Know the main administrative tools.   You should know the primary graphical tools for troubleshooting Windows and working with the operating system.

Optimizing Operating Systems

This objective expects you to know the minimum requirements for the operating systems and different ways to install them—all of which was discussed in Chapter 3. It also expects you to know how to optimize the operating systems, and that is the focus of this discussion.

Critical Information

The operating system can be optimized for different installations and scenarios in order to allow the user or administrator to get the most out of it. This section focuses on optimizing Windows.

Virtual Memory

Windows offers two types of memory: RAM and virtual memory. *RAM* is the physical (hardware) memory installed by means of chips. *Virtual memory* can include RAM and the hard drive (paging file); it allows Windows to run more applications than it has physical RAM for. In an ideal situation, Windows would have enough RAM for all the applications currently running, with a small amount of space to use for file caching. In other words, you can seldom go wrong by adding RAM, because it can improve disk performance by allowing you to hold more files in RAM, which allows for quicker access than from the hard drive. However, this will increase performance only when Windows has memory that isn't being used by applications.

You can use a couple of utilities to identify memory problems. The first is the Performance tool. The object to monitor is Memory, and the counters to watch include the following:

Committed Bytes   This counter shows how much memory (virtual and physical) is in use. If this number always exceeds the physical RAM by more than a few megabytes, you probably don't have sufficient RAM. As the counter's value increases, the system will have to page memory in and out more frequently to keep the running programs in memory.

Pages/Sec   This counter indicates how many pages per second are being moved to and from memory to satisfy requests. This number should be less than 100; a higher value can indicate that the system is RAM-starved. The counter won't drop to 0 even on a system that has plenty of RAM because some activity must always occur.

You can also gather memory statistics by using Task Manager. The Performance tab shows current utilization and a graph of recent history. A bar-graph icon appears in the System Tray when Task Manager is running. This is an active link to the CPU Usage graph on the Performance tab and can be used to visually gauge CPU activity even when Task Manager is minimized.

You can configure virtual memory parameters from the System applet in Control Panel. To access these settings, follow these steps:

1. Double-click the System applet in Control Panel.

2. Choose the Advanced tab.

3. In the Performance frame, click the Settings (for Windows XP) or Performance Options (for Windows 2000) button. With Windows XP, you must take the extra step of choosing the Advanced tab.

4. Click the Change button. The Virtual Memory dialog box shown in Figure 11.10 appears.

The initial paging file size is the amount of contiguous space claimed at each boot. The paging file is dynamic and can always grow. However, if it grows into noncontiguous space, performance can be greatly degraded. It is, therefore, preferable to have the initial size set to a number larger than you expect the file size to grow to.

Hard Drives

One of the biggest factors affecting hard-drive performance over time is fragmentation. The more files are read, added to, and rewritten, the more fragmentation is likely to occur. The Disk Defragmenter utility discussed earlier in this chapter is the best tool for correcting fragmentation.

You access the tool in Windows XP from Start ➤ All Programs ➤ Accessories ➤ System Tools ➤ Disk Defragmenter. Before doing any operation, you should run Analyze. This will check the volume and recommend an action, as shown in Figure 11.11.

If you chose View Report, you can see the files that are most fragmented in successive order.

FIGURE 11.10 The virtual memory settings in Windows XP

FIGURE 11.11 The Disk Defragmenter will recommend needed action in Windows XP.

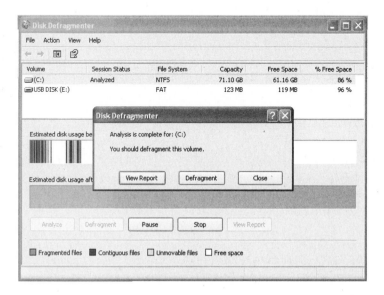

Temporary Files

Temporary files are written to a system on an almost nonstop basis. In addition to temporary files used for print queues, you also have cache from Internet sites and many other programs. You can manually pick and choose files to delete, but one of the simplest solutions is to choose Properties for a drive and then click the General tab. A command button for the Disk Cleanup utility will appear, which you can use to delete most common temporary files, including the following:

- Downloaded program files
- Temporary Internet files
- Offline web pages
- Office setup files
- Recycle Bin contents
- Setup log files
- Temporary files
- WebClient/Publisher temporary files
- Temporary offline files
- Offline files
- Catalog files for the Content Indexer

Services

The more operations your system is trying to perform, the more it must juggle between operations. For this reason—not to mention security—you should limit the services running on a system to only those that you want. Unfortunately, many services are often installed by default, and you have to remove or disable them.

To interact with services, access the Administrative Tools section of Control Panel and choose Services. This starts up the console shown in Figure 11.12. You can right-click any service and choose to Start, Stop, Pause, Resume, or Restart it. You can also double-click it to access its properties and configure such things as the startup type, dependencies, and other variables.

Startup

The programs to begin at startup can be configured through the MSCONFIG utility (discussed previously in this chapter) as well as by right-clicking the Start button, choosing Open, and then selecting Programs and Startup. Those that appear here are few, whereas a much greater number appear in MSCONFIG, because it can access other locations.

FIGURE 11.12   Working with services in Windows XP

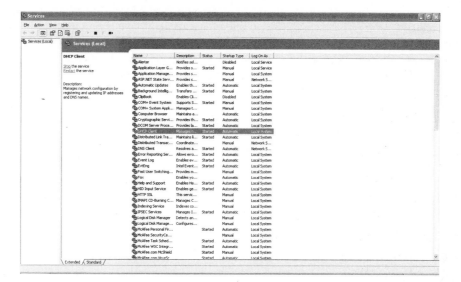

Exam Essentials

Know the primary ways to optimize Windows.   The utilities and tools discussed in this section are those you must know for the exam.

Diagnostics and Troubleshooting

The four primary topics beneath this objective involve recovering operating systems, resolving common operational problems, looking at error messages, and using diagnostic tools. Each of these topics are examined within this section.

Critical Information

As an administrator, you must be able to do all the functions this exam focuses on. But none will make you shine in the eyes of users as much as the ability to get systems back up and running after problems have occurred. The topics beneath this objective focus on that part of the job and your skill set.

Recovering Operating Systems

Windows includes a number of tools to simplify recovering an operating system after a serious problem has occurred. System Restore is one such tool, as discussed previously. Three others we'll look at here are the recovery console, Automated System Recovery (ASR), and emergency repair disks (ERDs).

Recovery Console

The Recovery Console is a command-line utility used for troubleshooting. From it, you can format drives, stop and start services, and interact with files. The latter is extremely important because many boot/command-line utilities bring you into a position where you can interact with files stored on FAT or FAT32, but not NTFS. The Recovery Console can work with files stored on all three filesystems.

The Recovery Console isn't installed on a system by default. To install it, use the following steps:

1. Place the Windows CD in the system.

2. From a command prompt, change to the i386 directory of the CD.

3. Type **winnt32 /cmdcons**.

4. A prompt appears, alerting you to the fact that 7MB of hard drive space is required and asking if you want to continue. Click Yes.

Upon successful completion of the installation, the Recovery Console (Microsoft Windows 2000 Recovery Console, for example) is added as a menu choice at the bottom of the startup menu. To access it, you must choose it from the list at startup. If more than one installation of Windows 2000 or Windows NT exists on the system, another boot menu will appear, asking which you want to boot into, and you must make a selection to continue.

To perform this task, you must give the administrator password. You'll then arrive at a command prompt. You can give a number of commands from this prompt, two of which are worth special attention: EXIT restarts the computer, and HELP lists the commands you can give. Table 11.3 lists the other commands available, most of which will be familiar to administrators who have worked with MS-DOS.

TABLE 11.3   Recovery Console Commands

Command	Purpose
ATTRIB	Shows the current attributes of a file or folder, and lets you change them.
BATCH	Runs the commands within an ASCII text file.
CD	Used without parameters, it shows the current directory. Used with parameters, it changes to the directory specified.
CHDIR	Works the same as CD.
CHKDSK	Checks the disk for errors.

TABLE 11.3   Recovery Console Commands *(continued)*

Command	Purpose
CLS	Clears the screen.
COPY	Allows you to copy a file (or files, if used with wildcards) from one location to another.
DEL	Deletes a file.
DELTREE	Recursively deletes files and directories.
DIR	Shows the contents of the current directory.
DISABLE	Allows you to stop a service/driver.
DISKPART	Shows the partitions on the drive, and lets you manage them.
EXPAND	Extracts compressed files.
ENABLE	Allows you to start a service/driver.
FIXBOOT	Writes a new boot sector.
FIXMBR	Checks and fixes (if possible) the master boot record.
FORMAT	Allows you to format a floppy or partition.
LISTSVC	Shows the services/drivers on the system.
LOGON	Lets you log on to Windows 2000.
MAP	Shows the maps currently created.
MD	Makes a new folder/directory.
MKDIR	Works the same as MD.
MORE	Shows only one screen of a text file at a time.
RD	Removes a directory or folder.
REN	Renames a file or folder.
RENAME	Works the same as REN.

T A B L E   1 1 . 3   Recovery Console Commands *(continued)*

Command	Purpose
RMDIR	Works the same as RD.
SYSTEMROOT	Works like CD but takes you to the system root of whichever OS installation you're logged on to.
TYPE	Displays the contents of an ASCII text file.

During the installation of the Recovery Console, a folder named Cmdcons is created in the root directory to hold the executable files and drivers it needs. A file named Cmldr, with attributes of System, Hidden, and Read-Only, is also placed in the root directory.

If you want to delete the Recovery Console (to prevent users from playing around, for example), you can do so by deleting the Cmldr file and the Cmdcons folder, and removing the entry from the Boot.ini file.

Automated System Recovery

It's possible to automate the process of creating a system recovery set by choosing the ASR Wizard on the Tools menu of the Backup utility (Start ➢ All Programs ➢ Accessories ➢ System Tools ➢ Backup). This wizard walks you through the process of creating a disk that can be used to restore parts of the system in the event of a major system failure.

The default name of this file is BACKUP.BKF; it requires a floppy disk. The backup set contains all the files necessary for starting the system, whereas the floppy becomes a bootable pointer to that backup set and can access/decompress it.

 A weakness of this tool is its reliance on a bootable floppy in a day when many new systems no longer include a 3.5″ drive.

Emergency Repair Disk

The Windows Backup and Recovery Tool/Wizard allows you to create an emergency repair disk (ERD). As the name implies, this is a disk you can use to repair a portion of the system in the event of a failure.

When you choose this option, the tab changes to the Backup tab, and a prompt tells you to install a blank, formatted floppy disk. A check box inquires whether you want to save the Registry as well. (The default is no.) If you don't choose to save the Registry, the following files are placed on the floppy disk:

- SETUP.LOG
- CONFIG.NT
- AUTOEXEC.NT

This doesn't leave you much to work with. The disk isn't bootable and contains only three minor configuration utilities.

If you check the box to include the Registry in the backup, the floppy disk contains the preceding files plus the following:

- `SECURITY._`
- `SOFTWARE._`
- `SYSTEM._`
- `DEFAULT._`
- `SAM._`
- `NTUSER.DAT`
- `USRCLASS.DAT`

The user profile (`NTUSER.DAT`) is for the default user; the files with the `._` extension are compressed files from the Registry. The compression utility used is `EXPAND.EXE`, which offers you the flexibility of restoring any or all files from any Microsoft operating system, including this utility (Windows 95/98, Windows NT, and so on). Because this floppy contains key Registry files, it's important that you label it appropriately and store it in a safe location, away from users who should not have access to it.

> During the process of creating the floppy, the Registry files are also backed up (in uncompressed state) to `%systemroot%\repair\RegBack`.

As before, the floppy isn't bootable, and you must bring the system up to a point (booted) where the floppy can be accessed before it's of any use.

Common Operational Problems

CompTIA wants you to be aware of six somewhat common operational problems that can occur with Windows. All six are discussed in this section.

Printing Problems

Most printing problems today are due to either improper configuration or actual physical problems with the printer. Physical printer problems are addressed in two other chapters in this book, and so configuration is the focus here.

The Windows architecture is such that when a client wants to print to a network printer, a check is first done to see if the client has the latest printer driver. If it doesn't—as judged by the print server—the new driver is sent from the server to the client, and then the print job is accepted. This is an enormous help to the administrator, for when a new driver comes out, all the administrator must do is install it on the server, and the distribution to the clients becomes automatic.

Errors occur when a client is configured with a printer different from the one in use. For example, suppose the network has an ABC 6200 printer, but you don't see that among the list of choices when you install the printer. Rather than taking the time to get the correct driver, you choose the ABC 6000, because you've been told that it's compatible. All will work well in this scenario until a new driver is released and loaded on the server. This client won't update (while all others configured with 6200 will), and thus there is the potential for printing problems to occur.

You can solve most other problems using the Printing Troubleshooter (go to Start ➤ Help and Support, and type in **Printing Troubleshooter**). It will walk you through solving individual printing problems.

Auto-Restart Errors

If the system is automatically restarting, there is the possibility that it has a virus or is unable to continue current operations (has become unstable). To solve issues with viruses/Trojans and the like, install virus-detection software on every client (as well as on the server), keep the definitions current, and run them often.

If the problem is with the system being unstable, examine the log files and try to isolate the problem. Reboot in Safe Mode, and correct any incompatibility issues. You can also deselect the Automatically Restart on Startup and Recovery option of the System applet (Advanced tab) in Control Panel to prevent the system from rebooting

Occasionally, systems reboot when they have been updated. This is a necessary process, and users are always given warning before the reboot is to occur. If no one is present to choose to reboot later (it's the middle of the night, for example) the reboot will take place.

Blue Screens

Once a regular occurrence when working with Windows, blue screens (also known as the Blue Screen of Death and bluescreens) have become mostly a thing of the past. Occasionally, systems will lock up; you can usually examine the log files to discover what was happening when this occurred and take steps to correct it.

System Lockup

The difference between a blue screen and a system lockup is whether the dump message that accompanies a blue screen is present. With a regular lockup, things just stop working. As with blue screens, these are mostly a thing of the past (the exception may be laptops, which go to hibernate mode). If they occur, you can examine the log files to discover what was happening and take steps to correct it.

Driver Failure

Drivers are associated with devices, and you can access them by looking at the Properties for the device. The following, for example, are the three tabs of an adapter's Properties dialog box:

General   This tab displays the device type, manufacturer, and location. It also includes text regarding whether the device is currently working properly and a Troubleshooter command button to walk you through diagnostics.

Driver   Access this tab to view information on the current driver and digital signer. Three command buttons allow you to see driver details and uninstall or update the driver.

Resources   This tab shows the system resources in use (I/O, IRQ, and so on) and whether there are conflicts.

In Device Manager, you can also expand the Monitors tree, right-click Shown Monitors, and choose Properties from the pop-up menu. Doing so shows the General and Driver tabs discussed in the preceding list, but not Resources.

Application Failures

If applications fail to install, start, or load, you should examine the log files associated with them to try to isolate the problem. Many applications write logs that can be viewed with Event Viewer (choose Application Logs), and others (mostly legacy) write to text files that you can find in their own directories.

Common steps to try include closing all other applications and beginning this one, reinstalling fresh, and checking to see whether the application works properly on another machine.

Common Error Messages

When things fail, they try to tell you why—this is a vast improvement in Windows over the old days when cryptic messages were the best you could hope for. Event Viewer is the primary tool for finding problems and uncovering what is going on. Other issues that can occur, however, include problems with booting, and system failure.

Booting problems can occur with corruption of the boot files or missing components. Luckily, during the installation of the operating system, log files are created in the %SystemRoot% and %SystemRoot%\Debug folders (C:\WINNT and C:\WINNT\DEBUG, by default). If you have a puzzling problem, look at these logs and see if you can find error entries there. With Windows 2000, for example, the following six files are created:

Comsetup.log   This log file holds information about the COM+ installation and any optional components installed. Of key importance are the last lines of the file, which should always show that the setup completed. If the last lines don't show this, they depict where the errors occurred.

MMDET.LOG   This file is used to hold information relevant to the detection of multimedia devices and ports. On most systems used for business, this file is very small and contains only a few lines.

NETSETUP.LOG   This file differs from all the others in that it's in the DEBUG folder and not just %SystemRoot%. Entries in it detail the workgroup and domain options given during installation.

SETUPACT.LOG   Known as the Action log, this file is a chronological list of what took place during the setup. There is a tremendous amount of information here; of key importance is whether errors occurred. The last lines of the file can show which operation was transpiring when the installation failed, or whether the installation ended with errors. Like all the log files created during setup, this file is in ASCII text format and can be viewed with any viewer (WordPad, Word, and so on).

SETUPAPI.LOG   This file shows every line run from an INF file and the results. Not only is this file created during installation, it continues to get appended to afterward. Of key importance is whether the commands are able to complete without error.

SETUPERR.LOG   The Error log, as this file is commonly called, is written to at the time errors are noted in other log files. For example, an entry in `Setupact.log` may show that an error occurred, and additional information on it will be found in `Setuperr.log`. Not only are the errors here, but also the severity of each is given.

You can configure problems with system failure to write dump files (debugging information) for later analysis when they occur by going to the System applet in Control Panel, choosing the Advanced tab, and clicking Settings under Startup and Recovery. Here, in addition to choosing the default operating system, you can configure whether events should be written to the system log, whether an alert should be sent to the administrator, and the type of memory dump to be written.

Diagnostic Tools

Most of the tools that fall beneath this section have already been covered elsewhere in this chapter. Those that have not already been addressed are the boot menu and System File Checker.

Safe Mode

If, when you boot, Windows won't come all the way up (it hangs or is otherwise corrupt), you can often solve the problem by booting into Safe Mode. Safe Mode is a concept borrowed from Windows 95 wherein you can bring up part of the operating system by bypassing the settings, drivers, or parameters that may be causing it trouble during a normal boot. The goal of Safe Mode is to provide an interface with which you're able to fix the problems that occur during a normal boot and then reboot in normal mode.

To access Safe Mode, you must press F8 when the operating system menu is displayed during the boot process. A menu of Safe Mode choices will then appear, as listed in Table 11.4. Select the mode you want to boot into.

TABLE 11.4   Safe Mode Startup Menu

Choice	Loaded
Safe Mode	Provides the VGA monitor, Microsoft mouse drivers, and basic drivers for the keyboard (storage system services, no networking)
Safe Mode with Networking	Same as Safe Mode, but with networking
Safe Mode with Command Prompt	Same as Safe Mode, but without the interface and drivers/services associated with it
Enable Boot Logging	Creates `ntbtlog.txt` in the root directory during any boot—normal attempted
Enable VGA Mode	Normal boot with only basic video drivers

TABLE 11.4   Safe Mode Startup Menu *(continued)*

Choice	Loaded
Last Known Good Configuration	Uses the last backup of the Registry to bypass corruption caused during the previous session
Debugging Mode	Sends information through the serial port for interpretation/troubleshooting at another computer
Boot Normally	Bypasses any of the options here
Return to OS Choices Menu	Gives you an out in case you pressed F8 by accident

You need to keep a few rules in mind when booting in different modes:

- If problems don't exist when you boot to Safe Mode but do exist when you boot to normal mode, the problem isn't with basic services/drivers.

- If the system hangs when you load drivers, the log file can show you the last driver it attempted to load, which is usually the cause of the problem.

- If you can't solve the problem with Safe Mode, restore the Registry from the ERD to a state known to be good. Bear in mind that doing so will lose all changes that have occurred since the last ERD was made.

System File Checker

The purpose of this utility is to keep the operating system alive and well. SFC.EXE automatically verifies system files after a reboot to see if they were changed to unprotected copies. If an unprotected file is found, it's overwritten by a stored copy of the system file from %systemroot%\system32\dllcache. (%systemroot% is the folder into which the operating system was installed.)

 Storing system files (some of which can be quite large) in two locations consumes a large amount of disk space. When you install Windows 2000 Professional, make sure you leave ample hard drive space on the %systemroot% drive for growth.

Only users with the Administrator group permissions can run SFC. It also requires the use of a parameter. The valid parameters are as follows:

Parameter	Function
/CACHSIZE=	Sets the size of the file cache
/CANCEL	Stops all checks

Parameter	Function
/ENABLE	Returns to normal mode
/PURGECACHE	Clears the cache
/QUIET	Replaces files without prompting
/SCANBOOT	Checks system files on every boot
/SCANNOW	Checks system files now
/SCANONCE	Checks system files at the next boot

Exam Essentials

Know the recovery options. Be familiar with the recovery console, ASR, and ERD.

Know the common operational problems. Blue screens and lockups are far less common that they used to be, but they do occasionally occur. Know how to deal with them and the other issues listed.

Know the common errors. Be able to identify how to get to error logs, and know the logs created during installation.

Know the boot menu options. Know how to access the boot menu and what options appear there.

Operating System Preventative Maintenance

Preventative maintenance is a broad category that includes many items already discussed in this chapter. For example, you should know how to configure restore points, how to do backups, and so on. One item not yet discussed is the importance of applying updates: in particular, service packs.

Upgrades to Windows come in the form of service packs. Each service pack contains patches and fixes to operating system components, as well as additional features. A service pack is a self-running program that modifies your operating system. It isn't uncommon within the lifetime of an operating system to have two or three service packs.

Successive service packs include all files that have been in previous ones. If you perform a new installation, and the latest service pack is Service Pack 4, you don't need to install Service Packs 1, 2, and 3. You need to install only Service Pack 4 after the installation to bring the operating system up to the current feature set.

As they're released, service packs are shipped monthly for all Microsoft Operating Systems with TechNet. TechNet is a subscription CD service available through Microsoft. You can also click Start ➢ Help and Support and choose Keep Your Computer Up-to-Date with Windows Update to start an automatic check with the Microsoft site to see if your system is current. You can configure this check to occur automatically by choosing the Automatic Updates applet in Control Panel. By default, it checks for updates every day at 3:00 A.M., but it can be changed to any time you wish. You can also choose to not check for or install updates (although doing so isn't recommended).

After any updates are downloaded/installed, you often must reboot the system. With Automatic Updates, this is done after a period of inactivity, as shown in Figure 11.13.

FIGURE 11.13   Automatic Updates reboots the system after making changes.

Exam Essentials

Know the importance of keeping the system current.   You want to keep your system current so it's operating at an optimal level. You should incorporate all operating-system fixes and enhancements that Microsoft has released.

Review Questions

1. Which command-line utility displays or changes the attributes for one or more files?

2. You have opened a command window with CMD and now want to close it. What command should you use to do this?

3. At the command line, what switch can be used with DIR to see the listing one screenful at a time?

4. You are in the directory C:\Documents and Settings\edulaney\photos. Where will the command cd .. take you?

5. What is the command—and syntax—that should be used to change the G: drive from FAT32 to NTFS without losing data?

6. Which command is used to start the System Configuration Editor?

7. Which type of backup copies only the files for which the archive bit is currently turned on, and turns off the archive bit after the files are backed up?

8. When does Windows XP automatically create restore points?

9. What are the three ways to start Task Manager?

10. What is the command used to install the Recovery Console from the CD?

Answers to Review Questions

1. ATTRIB displays or changes the attributes for one or more files.
2. EXIT closes the CMD window.
3. DIR /P displays the listing one screenful at a time. Press Enter to see the next screenful.
4. This will take you to the directory C:\Documents and Settings\edulaney.
5. The command is convert G: /FS:NTFS.
6. The command is MSCONFIG. You can start it by going to Start ➤ Run, and typing the command.
7. An incremental backup copies only the files for which the archive bit is currently turned on. After the files are backed up, the archive bit is turned off.
8. Windows XP creates restore points automatically every 24 hours, as well as when you install unsigned device drivers or install (or uninstall) a program with Windows Installer or InstallShield.
9. The first way to display the Task Manager is to press Ctrl+Alt+Delete and click the Task Manager button (if needed). The second is to right-click an empty location on the Taskbar and choose Task Manager from the pop-up menu. The third method is to hold down Ctrl+Shift and press Esc.
10. Type winnt32 /cmdcons.

Printers and Scanners

COMPTIA A+ IT TECHNICIAN EXAM OBJECTIVES COVERED IN THIS CHAPTER:

✓ **4.1 Identify the fundamental principles of using printers and scanners**

  ▪ Describe processes used by printers and scanners, including laser, ink dispersion, thermal, solid ink, and impact printers and scanners

✓ **4.2 Install, configure, optimize, and upgrade printers and scanners**

  ▪ Install and configure printers / scanners

  ▪ Power and connect the device using local or network port

  ▪ Install and update device driver and calibrate the device

  ▪ Configure options and default settings

  ▪ Install and configure print drivers (e.g., PCL, Postscript, GDI)

  ▪ Validate compatibility with operating system and applications

  ▪ Educate user about basic functionality

  ▪ Install and configure printer upgrades, including memory and firmware

  ▪ Optimize scanner performance, including resolution, file format, and default settings

✓ **4.3 Identify tools and diagnostic procedures to troubleshooting printers and scanners**

  ▪ Gather information about printer / scanner problems

  ▪ Review and analyze collected data

  ▪ Isolate and resolve identified printer / scanner problem, including defining the cause, applying the fix, and verifying functionality

  ▪ Identify appropriate tools used for troubleshooting and repairing printer / scanner problems

  ▪ Multi-meter

  ▪ Screwdrivers

- Cleaning solutions
- Extension magnet
- Test patterns

✓ **4.4 Perform preventative maintenance of printers and scanners**

- Perform scheduled maintenance according to vendor guidelines (e.g., install maintenance kits, reset page counts)
- Ensure a suitable environment
- Use recommended supplies

COMPTIA A+ REMOTE SUPPORT TECHNICIAN EXAM OBJECTIVES COVERED IN THIS CHAPTER:

✓ **3.1 Identify the fundamental principles of using printers and scanners**

- Describe processes used by printers and scanners, including laser, ink dispersion, impact, solid ink, and thermal printers.

✓ **3.2 Install, configure, optimize, and upgrade printers and scanners**

- Install and configure printers and scanners
- Power and connect the device using network or local port
- Install/update the device driver and calibrate the device
- Configure options and default settings
- Install and configure print drivers (e.g., PCL, Postscript and GDI)
- Validate compatibility with OS and applications
- Educate user about basic functionality
- Optimize scanner performance for example: resolution, file format and default settings

✓ **3.3 Identify tools, diagnostic procedures, and troubleshooting techniques for printers and scanners**

- Gather information required to troubleshoot printer/scanner problems
- Troubleshoot a print failure (e.g., lack of paper, clear queue, restart print spooler, recycle power on printer, inspect for jams, check for visual indicators)

COMPTIA A+ DEPOT TECHNICIAN EXAM OBJECTIVES COVERED IN THIS CHAPTER:

✓ **3.1 Identify the fundamental principles of using printers and scanners**

- Describe the processes used by printers and scanners, including laser, inkjet, thermal, solid ink, and impact printers

✓ **3.2 Install, configure, optimize, and upgrade printers and scanners**

- Identify the steps used in the installation and configuration processes for printers and scanners, for example:
  - Power and connect the device using network or local port
  - Install and update the device driver
  - Calibrate the device
  - Configure options and default settings
  - Print test page
  - Install and configure printer/scanner upgrades, including memory and firmware

✓ **3.3 Identify tools, diagnostic methods ,and troubleshooting procedures for printers and scanners**

- Gather data about printer/scanner problem
- Review and analyze data collected about printer/scanner problems
- Implement solutions to solve identified printer/scanner problems
- Identify appropriate tools used for troubleshooting and repairing printer/scanner problems
- Multi-meter
- Screw drivers
- Cleaning solutions
- Extension magnet
- Test patterns

✓ **3.4 Perform preventative maintenance of printer and scanner problems**

- Perform scheduled maintenance according to vendor guidelines (e.g., install maintenance kits, reset page counts)
- Ensure a suitable environment
- Use recommended supplies

This domain is one of the few that appears on all three technician exams. It's weighted at 14 percent of the IT Technician exam, 10 percent of the Remote Support Technician exam, and a stunning 20 percent of the Depot Technician exam. It would be great to be able to say that there are quite a few differences between the content here and in the Essentials exam (Chapter 4), but in reality most of the differences are only superficial. The operating systems focused on continue to be Windows 2000 and Windows XP.

> This chapter is heavy on printers, and light on scanners. While scanners are lumped with printers in this domain, the truth of the matter is that they generally don't require a lot of optimizing and upgrading.

Identify the Principles of Printers and Scanners

This objective tests your knowledge of some of the basic operations of printers and scanners, with a primary emphasis on printers. You should read Chapter 4 to understand the basic elements of these devices; the content here will expand on that as well as focus on the operations and interactions with the operating system.

Critical Information

There are several ways to interact with a device, check its status, configure it, and so on. We'll first look at printers and then scanners.

Checking Printer Status

The simplest is to choose Start ➤ Printers and Faxes, right-click the icon of an installed printer, and choose Properties. Depending on the printer and its capabilities, you'll see a number of tabs, such as those shown in Figure 12.1.

FIGURE 12.1   Typical property tabs available for a printer in Windows XP

Notice that from here you can choose the Color Management tab (for a color printer) and change the profile used. You can also choose the Maintenance tab and do such operations as

- Cleaning
- Deep cleaning
- Roller cleaning
- Nozzle check
- Print-head alignment
- Custom dettings (typically involves setting the printer to enhanced capabilities port [ECP] mode)

Most printers—particularly those intended for use on networks—include additional software for interacting with them. Figure 12.2 shows the Toolbox program included with several HP LaserJet printers.

In addition to being able to see the status of the toner and maintenance kit via Toolbox, you can also click Troubleshooting and access the following:

- Print-quality tools (general troubleshooting and print-quality troubleshooting)
- Maintenance
- Error messages (understand the messages as well as the accessory lights)
- Paper jams
- Supported media (always use parts for the specific printer model you have, to prevent a surfeit of problems)
- Printer pages (you can print out the configuration page, the supplies pages, the event log page, and the usage page)

FIGURE 12.2   Vendors generally offer utilities for advanced interaction with printers.

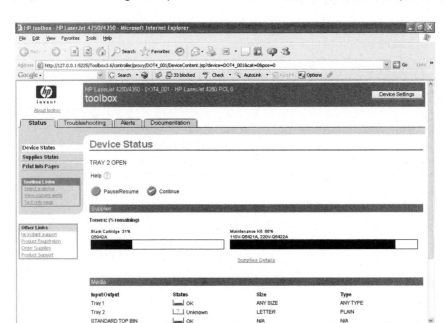

Checking Scanner Status

With most scanners, there is usually little beyond the Properties page (the General tab allows you to test the scanner [click Test Scanner], while the Color Management tab lets you work with profiles) and software from the vendor. Some high-end scanners include software similar to that found with printers, but most do little beyond what is found in Properties.

Exam Essentials

Know how to interact with printers and scanners.   Know that the Properties page for each, available from Windows, allows you to interact with them, but many printers also include advanced utilities that go beyond basic interaction.

Install and Optimize Printers and Scanners

Whereas Chapter 4 focused on the physical installation of the printer/scanner, this chapter looks more at the software side of things. The physical installation depends on your environment and the requirements of the manufacturer. The software interaction in Windows follows similar procedures regardless of the type of printer used.

Critical Information

It's important to install printers and scanners per the instructions included with the devices. Once the physical connection is established, you can use the wizards included with Windows to complete the installation.

Add a Printer

To add a printer in Windows, start the Add Printer Wizard by going to Start ➤ Printers and Faxes and clicking Add a Printer. To add a printer, you must have Administrator or Power User rights. The wizard begins the process and then either initiates the Add New Hardware Wizard (if a printer isn't already attached) or asks which port you want to use. You can't proceed until you've selected one of the available ports or added a new port.

Next, you must specify the manufacturer and model of the new printer, choosing from the list displayed. If your printer isn't listed, click the Have Disk button and install the driver from a disk.

Now, you must supply a printer name. The next choice you make here is whether you want the printer to become the default printer for Windows-based programs.

The printer name can contain up to 32 characters; it doesn't have to reflect the name of the driver in use. As you can with other resources and shares, you can place a dollar sign ($) at the end of the name to prevent it from being visible to all other users even though you may choose to share it.

The next choice, coincidentally, is whether you want to share the printer with other computers on the network. You must provide a share name if you're going to share it. (The default is the name you entered in the previous screen.)

If you're sharing the printer, you can add entries to the Location and Comment fields to be associated with the printer. While the Comment field is mostly free text, the Location value can be associated with a subnet and therefore allow an easy search for the printer in a Windows 2000 or Windows 2003 Active Directory. Finally, you're given the choice of printing a test page. (The default is Yes.) When you finish the installation, the wizard shows you all your choices and allows you one last chance to make changes (which you do by using the Back command button) before finishing.

Add a Network or Internet Printer

This is a much simpler operation than installing a printer locally. In the first screen of the Add Printer Wizard, click the Network Printer option. Doing so opens the Locate Your Printer dialog box, which asks for the name of the shared printer you want to connect to.

If the printer is networked and you don't know the path, you can leave the field blank and click Next to invoke the Browse feature. No such feature is available for the Internet printer option, however, so you *must* specify a URL in order to proceed to the next dialog box.

Prior to completion, the wizard asks if you want the printer to serve as a default printer. It then completes the installation by placing an icon for the printer in the Printers folder.

Internet printing is made possible by Internet Printing Protocol (IPP). It's a low-level protocol that is encapsulated within HTTP. When accessing a printer through a browser, the system first attempts to connect using RPC (Remote Procedure Calls).

Configure a Printer

All standard configuration settings for a Windows printer are available through three options of the Printers folder's File menu:

- Printing Preferences
- Server Properties
- Properties

Although the properties were discussed already, there is more to know; the options are discussed here, along with the other two entries.

Printing Preferences

To set the printing preferences, select the printer, choose File, and select Printing Preferences (or right-click the printer icon, and choose Printing Preferences from the pop-up menu). Both methods open a dialog box that differs significantly based on the type of printer in question. On a standard black-and-white laser printer, there are often only two tabs:

- Layout
- Paper/Quality

When you click the Advanced button on the Layout tab, you're given options for changing the graphics resolution, color adjustment, print quality, size, source, and orientation settings. On a bubble-jet printer, the choices change to the following:

- Main (select the print mode)
- Paper
- Control

In all cases, the purpose of Printing Preferences is to configure the printer you use most often for proper handling of the print jobs you most often submit.

Server Properties

The Print Server Properties dialog box contains information specific to the computer's print-server activities. The dialog box is independent of any particular type of printer. To get to it, select the printer, choose File, and click Server Properties.

The Print Server Properties dialog box contains the following four tabs:

Forms   Defines the print forms available on the computer.

Ports   Maintains a list of available ports. You can add, delete, or configure a port.

Drivers   Displays information about the installed print drivers (version, environment, and so on) and lets you update, add, or remove them.

Advanced   Provides the location of the spooler and an assortment of logging and notification options.

Properties

Most configuration settings for a printer are located in the printer's Properties dialog box. To open a particular printer's Properties dialog box, select a printer in the Printers folder, right-click it, and then choose Properties. The following sections discuss the tabs of the printer's Properties dialog box.

 The Ports tab in the Server Properties dialog box is the same as the one in the Add Printer Wizard, with one exception: You don't have to select a port here because you're viewing the available ports and aren't associating a port with a particular printer.

THE GENERAL TAB

The General tab, discussed previously, lets you install a new driver for the printer. There are two buttons on this tab:

- The Print Test Page button enables you to test a printer connection.

- The Printing Preferences button brings up the same printing preferences discussed earlier, in the section "Printing Preferences."

THE SHARING TAB

This tab lets you share the printer with other computers on the network. This option is useful if you didn't originally install the printer as a shared printer but later decide you want to share it.

THE PORTS TAB

The Ports tab lets you choose a port for the printer and add or delete a port. The Configure Port button also lets you specify the Transmission Retry time for all printers that use the same driver.

Of particular note are the two options at the bottom, with which you can enable printer pooling and bidirectional support. Printer pooling is discussed in detail in a later section of this chapter. Bidirectional support allows the printer to send unsolicited messages (such as out of paper, low on toner, and so on) to the workstation. In order to send such data, the printer in question must have bidirectional capabilities, and the cabling used must also support it.

THE ADVANCED TAB

This tab combines the features of the Scheduling tab and the command buttons from the General tab of previous versions of Windows. It lets you determine when the printer will be available and unavailable, and to set the printer priority.

Note the three command buttons along the bottom of the dialog box:

- Printing Defaults takes you back (yet again) to Printing Preferences.

- Print Processor allows you to select the processor. By default, this is WINPRINT.DLL, but it can be updated or replaced. WINPRINT.DLL supports the following eight data choices in Windows 2000:

  - RAW

  - RAW (FF appended)

  - RAW (FF auto)

  - NT EMF 1.003

  - NT EMF 1.006

- NT EMF 1.007

- NT EMF 1.008

- TEXT

- Separator Page lets you choose one of three predefined separator pages or create one of your own. By default, Windows doesn't separate print jobs or use a separator page. However, the following options are available with Windows 2000:

  - PCL.SEP switches Hewlett-Packard printers to Printer Control Language (PCL) mode.

  - PSCRIPT.SEP switches Hewlett-Packard printers to PostScript mode.

  - SYSPRINT.SEP is a separator page for PostScript printers.

  - SYSPRTJ.SEP is the Japanese version of SYSPRINT.SEP.

 The printer priority is in no way related to the print-job priority. Although the priority for a printer defaults to 1, it can be any number between 1 and 99. When more than one printer is printing to the same printing device, it's useful to change priorities (to allow the one with the highest priority to print first). Take the following scenario: If GroupA submits large jobs that hold up everyone else, you can 1) add a new printer and set a very high priority for it (97, for example), and then 2) deny print permissions to GroupA. This will allow all others to print to this printer first, going to the original printer only if it's free.

THE SECURITY TAB

This tab lets you configure permissions, auditing, and ownership for the printer (through the Advanced tab). Like all Windows objects, printers are protected by the Windows NT security model. The possible permission levels for printer access/denial are outlined here:

Print Allows a user or group to submit a print job and to control the settings and print status for that job.

Manage Printers Allows a user to submit a print job and to control the settings and print status for all documents, as well as for the printer itself. In addition, the user or group may share, stop sharing, change permissions for, and even delete the printer.

Manage Documents Allows a user or group to submit a print job and to control the settings and print status for all print jobs.

A key thing to remember is that these permissions affect both local and remote users. The following list summarizes the default permissions on newly created printers in Windows 2000:

Administrators	All - Allow
Creator/Owner	Manage Documents
Everyone	Print
Power Users	All - Allow

To change the permission level for a group, select the group from the Name list and either enter the new permission level in the Permissions combo boxes or open the Advanced dialog box. You can add a group or user to the permissions list by clicking the Add button and making your changes in the Add Users and Groups dialog box that appears.

The Security tab also enables you to set up auditing for the printer and to take ownership of the printer through the Advanced button.

THE PRINTER PROPERTIES DEVICE SETTINGS TAB

The Device Settings tab contains settings for the printing device, which differ depending on the printing device.

Set Up a Printer Pool

A printer pool offers an efficient means of streamlining the printing process in many environments. By the simplest definition, a *printer pool* is a single logical printer that prints to more than one printing device. It prints jobs sent to it to the first available printing device and provides the throughput of multiple printing devices with the simplicity of a single printer definition. Windows 2000 ensures that no single device is ever sent more than one document at a time if other devices are currently available. This ensures efficient utilization of all printing devices.

The following criteria must be met before a network can use a printer pool:

- A minimum of two printing devices must be capable of using the same printer driver. Because the pool is seen and treated as a single logical device, it must be managed by a single printer driver.

- Although not required, the printing devices should be located in close proximity to one another. This is because users have no means of specifying a device within the pool and are given no notification as to which printer actually printed the job. Users should not have to walk from floor to floor to find their documents; instead, they should be able to check all printing devices quickly.

You create a printer pool by configuring the printer to print to more than one port. Naturally, you must also attach a printing device to each of the ports.

Print from MS-DOS–Based Applications

DOS-based applications differ from Windows-based applications in that they provide their own printer drivers. They typically also render data to the RAW data type or to straight ASCII text. Because of this, an application that prints graphics and formatted text must have its own printer driver for the printing device, whereas the application can print ASCII text without a vendor-supplied printer driver.

Most DOS-based applications can't handle Universal Naming Convention (UNC) names. Therefore, when you print to a remote printer, you must often map a physical port to the remote printer. To do so, use the following command: NET USE LPTX: *PSERVER**PRINTER_NAME*

Add a Scanner

To add a scanner to a client, once the physical connection has been established, go to Start ➤ Control Panel ➤ Scanners and Cameras and click Add an Imaging Device or Allow This Computer to Use a Network Scanner. If you choose the latter, you must choose to configure Windows Firewall to allow the computer to use a scanner on the network (with Windows XP, it isn't allowed by default).

The Scanner and Camera Installation Wizard, shown in Figure 12.3, helps you install any scanner (or camera) that wasn't automatically detected. This is a crucial point to understand: most locally installed scanners should be automatically detected, and you should need to do nothing more for their installation.

FIGURE 12.3 The Scanner and Camera Installation Wizard in Windows XP

When using this wizard, you must first choose the manufacturer and model (or choose Have Disk). Typically, an installation of this type requires a restart of the system to be active.

Calibrating Printers and Scanners

Under most circumstances, there is little you need to do to get Windows to recognize your device once you have installed it using the appropriate wizard. The wizard adds the driver, and most printers and scanners will work fine at this point and you will not need to do anything further for them to function. An exception to this would be some inkjet printers and a few scanners: they require calibration (sometimes called alignment) in order for the end product to look as it should (color matching, no blank lines, uneven spaces, etc.).

Every manufacturer, and in fact many similar devices from the same manufacturer, has a slightly different process for performing this action. A typical printer calibration would follow these steps:

1. The installation wizard asks you during the installation if you want to calibrate and you say Yes (OK).

2. If it is a printer, a sheet with multiple sets of numbered lines will print out and each set of lines represents an alignment possiblity.

3. You are asked to choose which set looks best, you enter the corresponding number, and click OK (Continue).

4. You click Finish to end the alignment routine.

With a scanners, the calibration may need to be done so the colors on the monitor are reflective of the colors on the item scanned in. Typically, there is a test pattern included with the scanner (called an *IT8 scanner target)* that you scan in and then walk through the software to match up what you see with what was on the paper.

Upgrades

Upgrades can be applied to printers in the form of adding memory or changing firmware. New versions of the firmware can be downloaded from the manufacturer's website and installed per the directions given there.

You can add memory to printers to allow them to hold additional jobs and perform more efficiently. Printer memory must be congruent with that already installed and should be 100 percent compatible with that produced by the manufacturer. The HP LaserJet 4250, for example, uses PC-2100 memory and has two memory sockets. By default, it comes with 48MB of RAM but supports up to 512MB. For optimal performance, both memory sockets should hold the maximum amount of RAM. Figure 12.4 shows the Toolbox program (also shown in Figure 12.2), with the information depicting the memory presently installed.

FIGURE 12.4   The Toolbox program shows the current memory installed.

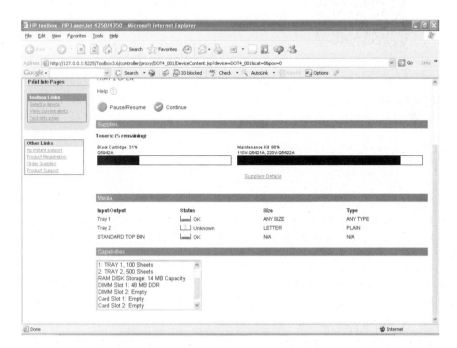

This same program also shows the firmware date, code, and related information.

Exam Essentials

Know how to install printers and scanners.   The manufacturer's information is the best source of information for installing printers and scanners. You should, however, know about the wizards available in Windows, as well.

Know to keep firmware up to date.   Firmware updates can be found at the manufacturer's website and installed according to the instructions accompanying them.

Identify Tools and Diagnostic Procedures for Troubleshooting

Not only is troubleshooting on the test, but you may have to accomplish these tasks on a daily basis, depending on your environment. Your ability to get a downed printer or scanner working will make you more valuable to your employer.

Critical Information

To solve a problem of any type, you must always approach it from a systematic position. Solving printer problems is no different than solving network problems, and a recommended approach is as follows.

Gather as much information as you can about the problem. For example, when a user calls to report that they can't print to a network printer, you should immediately ask when they were last able to do so and what has changed since then.

Review and analyze the data you've collected. Now that you've accumulated it, you need to look for the story it's telling you.

Isolate the problem. Is it confined to a single user, a group of users, a room, a floor, or a building, or is everyone affected? Knowing how narrowly you can isolate the issue can help you define the problem and come up with a fix.

Use the appropriate tools. Many times, the tools to use are available within the operating system (think of the Troubleshooters in Windows), and you can solve them easily. Other times, you have to turn to physical tools to help you solve a problem. The following is a list of tools you should be familiar with for printer and scanner problems:

Multi-meter   A multi-meter can be an invaluable resource in identifying electrical problems. The "multi" part comes from the fact that this device usually combines a voltmeter, an ohm-meter, and an ammeter into one (and is occasionally referred to as a VOM meter).

Screwdrivers   A good set of quality screwdrivers fitted to the job you're working on is essential. Never try to force a larger screwdriver into a small slot, or you may do far more damage than was there when you began.

Cleaning solutions   Most liquids don't mix with computer elements, including printers and scanners. A few exceptions are those solutions created specifically for the purpose. Scanner windows can be carefully cleaned using Windex, but you should be extremely careful to limit the amount used.

Extension magnet   This can be used when you're working in tight places, to make certain you don't drop small parts. Be very careful, however, in using any magnet around a device that stores data magnetically (such as a hard drive); use these sparingly.

Test patterns   One of the simplest tools of all is to print a test pattern and compare the results you get to those you desire. Almost every printer allows you to print a test, and this should be one of the first things you do when beginning to tackle a problem.

Other printing problems that can occur on an irregular basis include the following:

The computer won't work while the printer is printing   If your operating system supports background printing (spooling, and so on), make certain those features are turned on.

A print job is clobbered by another   If you share a network printer, check the printer time-out settings on your workstation. If the number of seconds is too low, a printer can think it has received all of a print job when it hasn't, and accept the next incoming job.

Printing stops before it's done   Check the power being delivered to the printer, particularly if it's a laser printer. Because of the high charges and other operations going on, a laser printer pulls a lot of power. If you're sharing a circuit with a number of other things, problems may occur. A typical workgroup laser printer consumes 330 watts when printing, requires a minimum of 8 amps circuit capacity, and has a line voltage requirement of 50-60Hz.

Some specific troubleshooting tips based on printer type follow.

Troubleshooting Dot-Matrix Printers

A dot-matrix print head reaches high temperatures, and care must be taken to avoid a user or technician touching it and getting burned. Most dot-matrix printers include a temperature sensor to tell if the print head is getting too hot. The sensor interrupts printing to let the print head cool down and then allows printing to start again. If this sensor becomes faulty, it can cause the printer to print a few lines, stop for a while, print more, stop, and so on.

The print head should never be lubricated, but you can clean off debris with a cotton swab and denatured alcohol. Print pins missing from the print head will cause incomplete images or characters or white lines running through the text. This can be remedied by replacing the print head.

If the print head isn't at fault, make certain it's close enough to the platen to make the right image. The print head can be moved closer and farther from the platen depending on the thickness of the paper and other considerations.

The most common other culprit is the ribbon. A tight ribbon, or one that isn't advancing properly, will cause smudges or overly light printout.

Preventive maintenance includes keeping the print head dry and clean, and vacuuming paper shreds from inside the machine.

Troubleshooting Ink-Jet Printers

Ink-jet printers encounter few problems. If the ink becomes goopy on the paper, make certain the nozzles are clean and the heating transistors are working properly. If the ink is drying out quickly, make certain the print head is reaching the park position after print jobs are completed.

Troubleshooting Laser Printers

Just as laser printers are the most complicated of the types (and offer the most capabilities), they also have the most that can go awry. A thermal fuse is included to keep the system from overheating, and if it becomes faulty, it can prevent the printer from printing. Many high-capacity laser printers also include an ozone filter to prevent the corona's ozone output from reaching too high a level. On these printers, the filter should be changed as a part of regular maintenance.

Other common problems and solutions are as follows:

Blank pages print   Verify that there is toner in the cartridge. If it's an old cartridge, you can often shake it slightly to free up toner once before replacing. If it's a new cartridge, make sure the sealing tape has been removed from the cartridge prior to placing it in the printer.

WARNING   Be very careful when doing this operation. Someone who has asthma or is sensitive to microfine particles could be adversely affected by the toner.

Dark spots print   The most likely culprit is too much toner. Run blank pages through the printer to clean it.

Garbled pages print   Make sure you're using the right printer driver in your application.

Print-quality problems   See if your printer has the ability to turn Resolution Enhancement Technology (RET) on and off. This is what allows the printer to use partial-size dots for images that are rounded. If it's turned off, turn it back on.

Preventive maintenance, in addition to the ozone filter, includes the following:

- Never reuse paper that has been through the printer once. Although it may look blank, you're repeating the charging and fusing process on a piece of paper that most likely has *something* already on it.

- Change the toner when needed. You should recycle; most toner manufacturers participate in a recycling program of some type. The toner cartridge should never be exposed to light for longer than a few minutes; it usually comes sealed in a black plastic light-resistant bag.

- Clean any toner that accidentally spills into the printer with a dry, lint-free cloth. Bear in mind that spilled toner in the paper path should clear after you run a few blank pages through. If toner gets on your clothes, wipe them with a dry cloth and wash them with cold water (hot water works like the fusing process to set them into the material).

- Clean any paper shreds/dust/dander that get deposited in the printer. Pressurized air is the most effective method of removal.
- Keep the drum in good working order. If it develops lines, replace it.

Troubleshooting Scanners

There are three typical problems that occur with scanners. This section looks at each of them.

Scanner won't turn on   Many times when you go to power up the scanner it won't turn on. The simplest explanation is that the power cord has become unplugged. Check that both ends of the power cord for the scanner are plugged in correctly. You should also check any other cables connected to it to make sure they are secure. Disconnect and reconnect the power and this will usually correct the problem.

Strange noises from the scanner   Most scanners make strange noises during operation. While some sound like a buzzing sound, others can sound like fingernails on a chalkboard. The scanner will make noise when first turned on (as it does internal calibration) and during operation. These noises are normal and not a sign of problems.

Scanner won't scan   Cycling the scanner—disconnecting the power and other cords, then reconnecting them—will often solve the problem. If it does not, you should examine the scanner for visible problems with it: a scanning head lock is included on many scanners for use only during shipping, but someone could have accidentally switched a working scanner back to the lock position.

Exam Essentials

Know the common printing problems listed.   Understand the most common problems that occur in an environment.

Know the tools that can help you fix common problem types.   Each tool has its own purpose and can be essential in trying to solve a particular type of problem. Be familiar with the most likely repair options for each common problem.

Printer/Scanner Preventative Maintenance

Keeping printers and scanners working well can save you both time and money. As with an automobile or any other major purchase, a little routine—preventative—maintenance can go a long way toward extending the life of the item.

Critical Information

To keep your printers and scanners working efficiently and extend their life as much as possible, you should start by creating a log of scheduled maintenance as outlined by the vendor's guidelines and then make certain this is adhered to. For many printers, the scheduled maintenance includes installing maintenance kits. Maintenance kits typically include a fuser, transfer roller, pick-up rollers (for the trays), separation rollers, and feed rollers.

After installing the maintenance kit, you need to reset the maintenance counter as explained in the vendor's documentation.

Pay a great deal of attention to the ambient surroundings of the printers/scanners, as well. High temperature, high humidity, and high levels of dust/debris can negatively affect the life of the printer and the quality of print jobs.

Last, always make certain you use recommended supplies. It may be cheaper to buy off-brand supplies that aren't intended for your equipment, but you're taking a gamble with shortening the life or your printer and decreasing the quality of your output.

Exam Essentials

Know the importance of running scheduled maintenance.   Scheduled maintenance can prolong the life of your equipment and help ensure that your output continues to live up to the quality you expect.

Understand the importance of a suitable environment.   If you want your equipment to last as long as possible and deliver quality, you should pay attention to the environment in which you place it.

Review Questions

1. What is used in Windows to add a printer to a client?

2. How many characters can a printer name include?

3. You have shared a printer, but you do not want it to be seen by all users. What character can you use to "hide" it?

4. What protocol is needed for Internet printing?

5. Which tab on a print server's Properties provides the location of the spooler?

6. What type of support allows the printer to send unsolicited messages (such as out of paper, low on toner, and so on) to the workstation?

7. What is the range of number that can be used for printer priority?

8. True or false: By default, Windows does not separate print jobs or use a separator page.

9. What is the term used for a single logical printer that prints to more than one printing device?

10. It you choose to allow the computer to use a network scanner, what must you configure because it is not allowed by default?

Answers to Review Questions

1. The Add Printer Wizard is used in Windows to add a printer to a client.

2. The printer name can contain up to 32 characters.

3. You can place a dollar sign ($) at the end of the name to prevent it from being visible to all other users even though you may choose to share it.

4. Internet printing is made possible by Internet Printing Protocol (IPP).

5. The Advanced tab provides the location of the spooler and an assortment of logging and notification options.

6. Bidirectional support allows the printer to send unsolicited messages (such as out of paper, low on toner, and so on) to the workstation.

7. The printer priority range is from 1–99.

8. True. By default, Windows does not separate print jobs or use a separator page.

9. A printer pool is a single logical printer that prints to more than one printing device.

10. If you choose to use a network scanner, you must choose to configure Windows Firewall to allow the computer to use a scanner on the network (with Windows XP, it is not allowed by default).

Chapter

13

Networks

COMPTIA A+ IT TECHNICIAN EXAM OBJECTIVES COVERED IN THIS CHAPTER:

✓ **5.1 Identify the fundamental principles of networks**

- Identify names, purposes, and characteristics of basic network protocols and terminologies, for example:
  - ISP
  - TCP / IP (e.g., gateway, subnet mask, DNS, WINS, static and automatic address assignment)
  - IPX / SPX (NWLink)
  - NETBEUI / NETBIOS
  - SMTP
  - IMAP
  - HTML
  - HTTP
  - HTTPS
  - SSL
  - Telnet
  - FTP
  - DNS

- Identify names, purposes, and characteristics of technologies for establishing connectivity, for example:
  - Dial-up networking
  - Broadband (e.g., DSL, cable, satellite)
  - ISDN networking
  - Wireless (all 802.11)
  - LAN / WAN
  - Infrared
  - Bluetooth
  - Cellular
  - VoIP

✓ **5.2 Install, configure, optimize, and upgrade networks**

- Install and configure browsers
- Enable / disable script support
- Configure proxy and security settings
- Establish network connectivity
- Install and configure network cards
- Obtain a connection
- Configure client options (e.g., Microsoft, Novell) and network options (e.g., domain, workgroup, tree)
- Configure network options
- Demonstrate the ability to share network resources
- Models
- Configure permissions
- Capacities / limitations for sharing for each operating system

✓ **5.3 Use tools and diagnostic procedures to troubleshoot network problems**

- Identify names, purposes, and characteristics of tools, for example:
  - Command line tools (e.g., IPCONFIG.EXE, PING.EXE, TRACERT.EXE, NSLOOKUP.EXE)
  - Cable testing device
- Diagnose and troubleshoot basic network issue, for example:
  - Driver / network interface
  - Protocol configuration
  - TCP / IP (e.g., gateway, subnet mask, DNS, WINS, static and automatic address assignment)
  - IPX / SPX (NWLink)
  - Permissions
  - Firewall configuration
  - Electrical interference

✓ **5.4 Perform preventative maintenance of networks, including securing and protecting network cabling**

COMPTIA A+ REMOTE SUPPORT TECHNICIAN EXAM OBJECTIVES COVERED IN THIS CHAPTER:

✓ **4.1 Identify the fundamental principles of networks**

- Identify names, purposes, and characteristics of the basic network protocols and terminologies, for example:
  - ISP
  - TCP/IP (e.g., Gateway, Subnet mask, DNS, WINS, static and automatic address assignment)
  - IPX/SPX (NWLink)
  - NETBEUI/NETBIOS
  - SMTP
  - IMAP
  - HTML
  - HTTP
  - HTTPS
  - SSL
  - Telnet
  - FTP
  - DNS
- Identify names, purposes, and characteristics of technologies for establishing connectivity, for example:
  - Dial-up networking
  - Broadband (e.g., DSL, cable, satellite)
  - ISDN Networking
  - Wireless
  - LAN/WAN

✓ **4.2 Install, configure, optimize, and upgrade networks**

- Establish network connectivity and share network resources

✓ **4.3 Identify tools, diagnostic procedures, and troubleshooting techniques for networks**

- Identify the names, purposes, and characteristics of command line tools, for example:
  - IPCONFIG.EXE
  - PING.EXE
  - TRACERT.EXE
  - NSLOOKUP.EXE
- Diagnose and troubleshoot basic network issues, for example:
  - Driver/network interface
  - Protocol configuration
  - TCP/IP (e.g., Gateway, Subnet mask, DNS, WINS, static and automatic address assignment)
  - IPX/SPX (NWLink)
  - Permissions
  - Firewall configuration
  - Electrical interference

Although the networking domain constituted 12 percent of the weight of the Essentials exam, it's also 11 percent of the IT Technician and Remote Support Technician exams (it's absent from the Depot Technician exam).

NOTE Some of the material here was also discussed in Chapter 5, which covered the Essentials exam. Every attempt has been made to have no more repetition than necessary.

Fundamental Principles of Networks

For this portion of the exam, you're expected to know the definition and characteristics of topics in two key areas:

- Network protocols/technologies
- Connectivity

Both of these are covered in the section that follows.

Critical Information

It isn't enough to know how the network you currently have works and to know the technologies you're employing. You must also know about the technologies and protocols you *aren't* using so you can evaluate which ones should be incorporated into your environment. It's important to stay atop of new developments in the field and appraise them for suitability to the needs of your organization.

The following definitions are those CompTIA expects you to know in each of the topic areas beneath this objective.

Network Protocols and Technologies

The following protocols and technologies are those you should know for this exam:

DNS   Domain Name Service (DNS) is a network service used in TCP/IP networks that translates host names to IP addresses. The first attempts at this were done using static files called *HOSTS files*. When the systems grew too large for the files to be feasible, the DNS was created to handle it.

Several of these—such as TCP/IP—were discussed at considerable length in Chapter 5.

FTP The File Transfer Protocol (FTP) is both a TCP/IP protocol and software that permits the transferring of files between computer systems. Because FTP has been implemented on numerous types of computer systems, files can be transferred between disparate systems (for example, a personal computer and a minicomputer). It uses ports 20 and 21 by default.

Table 5.2 contains a list of popular top-level domains.

HTML Hypertext Markup Language (HTML) is a set of codes used to format text and graphics that will be displayed in a browser. The codes define how data will be displayed.

HTTP Hypertext Transfer Protocol (HTTP) is the protocol used for communication between a web server and a web browser. It uses port 80 by default.

HTTPS Hypertext Transfer Protocol over Secure Sockets Layer (HTTPS) is a protocol used to make for a secure connection. It uses port 443 by default.

IMAP Internet Message Access Protocol (IMAP) is a protocol with a store-and-forward capability. It can also allow messages to be stored on an e-mail server instead of downloaded to the client. The current version of the protocol is 4 (IMAP4), and the counterpart to it is Post Office Protocol (POP).

IPX/SPX Internetwork Packet Exchange/Sequenced Packet Exchange (IPX/SPX) is a connectionless, routable network protocol based on the Xerox XNS architecture. It's the default protocol for versions of NetWare before NetWare 5. It operates at the Network layer of the Open Systems Interconnection (OSI) model and is responsible for addressing and routing packets to workstations or servers on other networks. The Microsoft transport that is compatible with IPX/SPX is NWLink.

ISP An Internet Service Provider (ISP) is a company that provides direct access to the Internet for home and business computer users.

NetBEUI/NetBIOS Network Basic Input/Output System (NetBIOS), in its most generic form, is the API that Microsoft originally used to allow Windows to utilize networking. NetBIOS Extended User Interface (NetBEUI) expanded on this and is used to transport NetBIOS across a local area network (LAN).

SMTP Simple Mail Transfer Protocol (SMTP) is a protocol for sending e-mail between SMTP servers. Clients typically use either IMAP or POP to access it.

SSL Secure Socket Layer (SSL) is a protocol that secures messages by operating between the Application layer (HTTP) and the Transport layer.

TCP/IP   Transmission Control Protocol/Internet Protocol (TCP/IP) is a suite of networking protocols and applications.

TCP/IP is elaborated on in Chapter 5, and you should reread that material—particularly the discussion on addressing—when studying for the technician exam.

Telnet   Telnet is a protocol that functions at the Application layer of the OSI model, providing terminal-emulation capabilities.

Network Connectivity

The following connectivity technologies are those you should know for this exam:

Again, many of these were discussed in Chapter 5, and you should reread that chapter when studying for this exam.

Bluetooth   Bluetooth is a wireless standard that uses radio waves in the 2.4 to 2.485 GHz range. The most widely used Bluetooth technology (Class 2) is limited to about 35 feet in range, so it is not commonly used except for communications between notebook PCs and PDAs.

Broadband (DSL, cable, satellite)   There are essentially three methods of broadband access (using a single medium for several channels) that CompTIA looks at. Digital Subscriber Line (DSL) employs high-speed connections from telephone switching stations. Cable uses a cable modem and the cable line from providers who used to carry only television signals. Satellite replaces the terrestrial cable with signals through the air. The opposite of broadband is *baseband*—which allows only one signal at a time to be transmitted.

Cellular   Cellular networking is a means of communication utilizing geographic regions known as *cells*. The cells divide the area and handle communications in them by assigning each a separate frequency.

Dial-up networking   One of the first ways of communicating with ISPs and remote networks was through dial-up connections. Although this is still possible, it isn't used much anymore due to limitations on modem speed.

Infrared   Infrared is a type of networking that requires line of sight and is useful for small areas; it isn't used much beyond that. Many printers have infrared (IrDA) capabilities, as do mice and other wireless peripherals.

ISDN   Integrated Services Digital Network (ISDN) is a WAN technology that performs link management and signaling by virtue of packet switching. The original idea behind it was to let existing phone lines carry digital communications by using multiplexing to support multiple channels.

LAN/WAN   A LAN is a network that is geographically confined in a small space. That small space can be only a single room, a floor, a building, and so on. By being confined, it has tighter security and can normally offer higher speeds. A wide area network (WAN) is a collection of two or more LANs, typically connected by routers. The geographic limitation is removed, but WAN speeds are traditionally less than LAN speeds.

VoIP   Voice over IP (VoIP) is also known as IP telephony and Internet telephony. It's the routing of voice traffic over the Internet (it could be across any smaller IP-based network, but generally it's the Internet).

Wireless   Wireless networking is defined by the 802.11 body of standards and was discussed in detail in Chapter 5.

Exam Essentials

Know the definitions for various networking protocols.   You should be familiar with all the protocols and technologies listed in this chapter and able to differentiate between them.

Know the connectivity options.   Be able to discriminate between various options based on definitions given.

Install, Configure, Optimize, and Upgrade Networks

This objective tests your knowledge of browsers, network connectivity, and network resources. It expects you to understand the terms and topics and be able to work with them in the real world.

Critical Information

This objective expects basic knowledge of browsers, with an emphasis on Internet Explorer, as well as network connectivity and network resources. Each of these items is discussed in detail in the sections that follow.

Working with Browsers

A *browser* is any application that lets you interact with software or code. There are many different types of browsers, and although CompTIA uses only that word in the objective, what they really mean is a *web browser*. Web browsers provide an interface for web pages—showing the text, figures, hyperlinks, and other information coded in HTML.

A few web browsers are available, and most are freely distributed. Two of the most popular are Internet Explorer and Mozilla Firefox. Almost every operating system from Windows to Linux ships with a web browser of some type installed, or packaged, with it. If you don't want to use that browser, you can download another and install it according to the instructions supplied by the vendor.

You can configure such things as script support, proxy settings, and other variables directly within the browser. In Internet Explorer, for example, choose Internet Options from the Tools menu, and then choose the Security tab. From here, you can pick a default level of security or customize your own by clicking the Custom Level command button. This opens a myriad of choices, as shown in Figure 13.1.

By choosing the Connections tab, you can configure dial-up and VPN settings, as well as click on LAN Settings to configure proxy settings.

In Mozilla Firefox, choose Preferences from the Edit menu, and then click Advanced to configure similar security information, as shown in Figure 13.2.

FIGURE 13.1   Configure custom security choices in Internet Explorer.

FIGURE 13.2   Configure custom choices in Mozilla Firefox.

From the General tab in Firefox, you can choose Connection Settings and configure proxy values.

Network Connectivity

For network connectivity to occur, there must be a network card and a language shared between the hosts. The network card can be a wired card requiring LAN cabling, or it may be a wireless card. The language can be the TCP/IP protocol (the most popular), IPX/SPX, or any of a number of other possibilities.

To configure a Windows XP client on a new network, choose My Network Places (depending on the Desktop used, it may be on the Desktop or accessible from the Start menu), and then choose Set Up a Home or Small Office Network (or Set Up a Wireless Network for a Home or Small Office, if appropriate) beneath Network Tasks. This starts the Network Setup Wizard shown in Figure 13.3 and walks you through the configuration of the client.

FIGURE 13.3   The Network Setup Wizard walks you through the process of adding an XP client to a network.

Once configured on the network, you can always go to Network Tasks and choose Add a Network Place when needed. Doing so starts the Add Network Place Wizard and allows you to configure Internet connections as well as create shortcuts to websites, FTP sites, and other network locations. If you click View Network Connections, right-click a LAN or high-speed connection, and choose Properties, you can install, uninstall, and change the properties for any available client, service, or protocol, as shown in Figure 13.4.

The Advanced tab allows you to configure Windows Firewall and Internet Connection Sharing parameters.

Different Linux vendors include the same functionality but use different tools. With SUSE Linux, for example, you can start Yet another Setup Tool (YaST) and then choose the options between Network Devices and Network Services to configure the same parameters. Figure 13.5 shows the settings for the network card in SUSE Linux.

FIGURE 13.4   Configure the client, service, and protocol settings in XP.

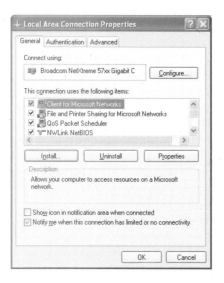

FIGURE 13.5   Configure network-card parameters in SUSE Linux.

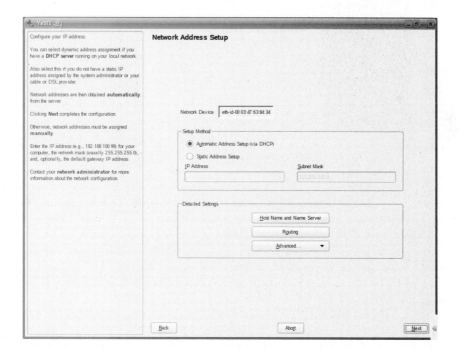

Sharing Network Resources

The real reason for a network is to be able to share resources, whether those resources are printers, files, or something different. In each operating system, sharing is almost as simple as configuring network access.

With the Microsoft Windows operating systems, workgroup members who are to share resources must have the File and Printer Sharing for Microsoft Networks client installed (it need not be installed for those who are only going to access it). You can then choose to share printers by right-clicking them and choosing Share This Printer, as shown in Figure 13.6.

Similarly, to share files or folders, right-click them, choose Properties, and then click the Sharing tab (you can also choose Sharing and Security from the pop-up menu). Doing so offers the choices shown in Figure 13.7.

Once a folder is shared, a hand appears beneath it, and others can access it. Share permissions apply only when a user is accessing a file or folder through the network. Local permissions and attributes are used to protect the file when the user is local.

If you aren't using a workgroup configuration, then files to be shared are typically placed on the server; rights associated with the server operating system can be used to differentiate between users. Table 13.1, for example, lists NTFS directory permissions.

FIGURE 13.6   Configure printer sharing in Windows XP.

FIGURE 13.7   Configure folder sharing in Windows XP.

TABLE 13.1   NTFS Directory Permissions

NTFS Permission	Meaning
Full Control	Gives the user all the other choices and the ability to Change Permission. The user also can take ownership of the directory or any of its contents.
Modify	Combines the Read & Execute permission with the Write permission, and allows the user to delete everything, including the folder.
Read & Execute	Combines the permissions of Read with those of List Folder Contents, and adds the ability to run executables.
List Folder Contents	Known as List in previous versions. Allows the user to view the contents of a directory and to navigate to its subdirectories. It doesn't grant the user access to the files in these directories unless that is specified in file permissions.
Read	Allows the user to navigate the entire directory structure, view the contents of the directory, view the contents of any files in the directory, and see ownership and attributes.
Write	Allows the user to create new entities in the folder, as well as to change ownership, permissions, and attributes.

With Linux, you can choose to copy files/directories to the Public folder (`public_html`) to make them available across the network, and you can share printers in much the same way as with Windows. One key protocol/suite that should be installed on Linux is Samba, to allow Linux and Windows hosts to communicate with each other. Once this is installed, the Linux hosts can generally communicate on a Windows-based network as easily as any other client.

Permissions in Linux are divided into Read, Write, and Execute and are set separately for the owner of the resource, the group the owner belongs to, and everyone else (others). Figure 13.8 shows the permissions for a file in the public folder.

FIGURE 13.8   Configure permissions for shared files in Linux.

Exam Essentials

Know that different browsers exist.   The most popular web browsers are Internet Explorer (IE) and Mozilla Firefox, but you can download any of a number of others and choose to use them as well.

Know how to establish network connectivity.   For a client on a network, you need a network card and a language (protocol) shared between the client and other hosts.

Know how to share resources.   Printers and files are the most commonly shared network resources. You can share them easily with the wizards or other tools.

Network Tools and Diagnostics

This objective tests your knowledge of diagnostic procedures and ability to recognize the right tool to use for the situation. In addition to knowing the purpose of each of the utilities discussed here, you should be able to recognize the output that they provide and be able to identify the tool used just by looking at that output.

Critical Information

This objective expects basic knowledge of network diagnostic tools and utilities. We'll first look at the testing tools, and then list some symptoms of common problems.

Network Tools to Use

The following list of utilities, some of which were also discussed in Chapter 5, constitutes those CompTIA wants you to know for this part of the exam.

> They also expect knowledge of cable-testing devices. This is a broad category of any type of device that can isolate a break or problem with a cable or termination.

IPCONFIG.EXE

With Windows-based operating systems, you can determine the network settings that a *Dynamic Host Configuration Protocol* (DHCP) server has leased to your computer by typing the following command at a command prompt:

```
IPCONFIG /all
```

IPCONFIG (with the /ALL parameter) also gives you full details on the duration of your current lease. You can verify whether a DHCP client has connectivity to a DHCP server by releasing the client's IP address and then attempting to lease an IP address. You can conduct this test by typing the following sequence of commands from the DHCP client at a command prompt:

```
IPCONFIG /release
IPCONFIG /renew
```

This is one of the first tools to use when experiencing problems accessing resources, because it will show you whether an address has been issued to the machine. If the address displayed falls in the 169.254.x.x category, then the client was unable to reach the DHCP server and has defaulted to Automatic Private IP Addressing (APIPA), which will prevent it from communicating outside of its subnet, if not altogether.

> In the Linux world, a utility similar to IPCONFIG is IFCONFIG.

NSLOOKUP.EXE

NSLOOKUP is a command-line utility that enables you to verify entries on a DNS server. You can use NSLOOKUP in two modes: interactive and noninteractive. In interactive mode, you start a session with the DNS server, in which you can make several requests. In noninteractive mode, you specify a command that makes a single query of the DNS server. If you want to make another query, you must type another noninteractive command.

One of the key issues regarding the use of TCP/IP is the ability to resolve a host name to an IP address—an action usually performed by a DNS server.

PING.EXE

PING is one of the most useful commands in the TCP/IP protocol. It sends a series of packets to another system, which in turn sends back a response. This utility can be extremely useful for troubleshooting problems with remote hosts.

The PING command indicates whether the host can be reached and how long it took for the host to send a return packet. On a LAN, the time is indicated as less than 10 milliseconds. Across WAN links, however, this value can be much greater.

TRACERT.EXE

TRACERT is a command-line utility that enables you to verify the route to a remote host. Execute the command TRACERT *hostname*, where *hostname* is the computer name or IP address of the computer whose route you want to trace. TRACERT returns the different IP addresses the packet was routed through to reach the final destination. The results also include the number of hops needed to reach the destination. If you execute the TRACERT command without any options, you see a help file that describes all the TRACERT switches.

The TRACERT utility determines the intermediary steps involved in communicating with another IP host. It provides a road map of all the routing an IP packet takes to get from host A to host B.

As with the PING command, TRACERT returns the amount of time required for each routing hop.

Network Troubleshooting

The following common network problems and their symptoms are those CompTIA wants you to know for this part of the exam:

DNS problems   Issues with DNS not properly working or configured often manifest themselves as a host being unable to communicate using host names (Fully Qualified Domain Names [FQDNs]) but still able to communicate if IP addresses are used.

Driver problems   Hardware devices use drivers to communicate. With the release of new sets of files, you can change drivers, fix related problems, or add functionality that is presently lacking. Problems with drivers can usually be identified by an inability to perform functions that should be done.

Electrical interference problems   Electromagnetic interference (EMI) will degrade network performance. This can be identified by the poor operation present. Be sure to run cables around (not over) ballasts and other items that can cause EMI.

Firewall configuration problems   Issues with firewalls can prevent access to data. By default, once firewalls are enabled, they tend to limit as much as possible; you must configure them to let through the traffic that you want to pass.

Gateway problems   A gateway allows traffic out of the network. If the gateway isn't configured properly, the hosts will have no difficulty communicating on the network, but they will be unable to communicate beyond the LAN.

IPX/SPX (NWLink) problems   IPX/SPX uses frames—a concept that doesn't exist with TCP/IP. Issues with IPX/SPX typically involve not selecting the correct frame type. It's important that all hosts using IPX/SPX agree on the frame type. With Windows XP, you can choose Auto Detect or one of the other four choices (802.2, 802.3, Ethernet II, and SNAP).

Network interface problems   If there are problems with the network card, you usually won't be able to communicate at all. Check the card for a status light(s), and verify that it's on. Blinking typically indicates link activity, and a solid light can indicate that all is working well. A light that isn't on indicates that there is no activity and the card should be replaced.

Permission problems   Issues with permissions prevent users from accessing resources. Make sure the users or groups have the appropriate permissions to be able to use the resource as intended.

Static and automatic address assignment problems   If DHCP is used to issue automatic addresses, you must make sure the host can be reached and has enough addresses in its scope to be able to service all clients. If you're using static addresses, one of the most common problems is issuing the same address to two clients, which causes both to be unable to communicate. Every host on the network must have a unique IP address.

Subnet mask problems   Problems with subnet masks (incorrect values) prevent the client from being able to communicate with other hosts on the network. A common issue is leaving the default value and forgetting to set it to a value your network is using.

WINS problems   Windows Internet Naming Service (WINS) provides name resolution for Microsoft networks. If your network uses WINS for name resolution, your computer needs to be configured with the IP address of a WINS server. (The IP address of a secondary WINS server can also be specified.) Although host names (and thus DNS) are understood on *all* operating systems running TCP/IP, NetBIOS names (and thus WINS) are understood only in the world of Microsoft operating systems. Eventually, WINS will be completely phased out in favor of DNS.

Exam Essentials

Know which utilities can be used for troubleshooting.   The objectives include four utilities that work in the Windows world, and you should know each of them.

Know common symptoms of network problems.   Review the list given in this chapter, and make sure you know common issues and problems and how they manifest themselves.

Preventative Network Maintenance

This objective wants you to appreciate the need to secure and protect network cabling.

Critical Information

A number of different types of cabling can be used in setting up a network. Each has its own benefits and susceptibilities, as examined in Chapter 5. You should know that regardless of the type of cabling you employ, you should protect it the best you can.

Protecting the cabling entails running it in such a way as to prevent it from being damaged (or degraded) by its environment and making sure it isn't accessible to those wishing to harm your network. It's fairly easy to tap into a 10BaseT cable without being detected, but it's much harder to do so with fiber cabling. Likewise, it can be easy to tap in to a wireless network; you'll want to make it as difficult as possible for those you don't want on the network.

In addition to protecting the cabling, you can secure the network by using firewalls, strong authentication, and a great deal of common sense when establishing the rules of the network.

CompTIA offers an entire certification on network security. It's the Security+ exam, and *CompTIA Security+ Study Guide, Third Edition* (Wiley, 2006) can help you prepare for it.

Exam Essentials

Know the importance of protecting your network.   You can protect your data by securing and protecting the cabling and the network to keep those who should not be accessing it from doing so.

Review Questions

1. Which network service is used in TCP/IP networks to translate host names to IP addresses?

2. What name translation service works only with Windows-based hosts?

3. Which port does HTTPS use by default?

4. What does IPX/SPX use that must be agreed on by all hosts on the network?

5. What is NETBEUI an acronym for?

6. What protocol in TCP/IP transfers mail between servers?

7. Which two protocols can clients use to access e-mail on servers?

8. What are two popular web browsers?

9. For a Windows-based client to be able to share files, what must be installed?

10. Which NTFS directory permission allows the user to navigate the entire directory structure, view the contents of the directory, view the contents of any files in the directory, and see ownership and attributes?

Answers to Review Questions

1.   DNS is the network service used in TCP/IP networks to translate host names to IP addresses.

2.   Windows Internet Naming Service (WINS) is similar to DNS, but it works only with Windows-based hosts.

3.   HTTPS uses port 443 by default.

4.   IPX/SPX uses frames. The frame type needs to be agreed on by all hosts on the network.

5.   NetBIOS Extended User Interface

6.   Simple Mail Transfer Protocol (SMTP) is used to send mail between servers.

7.   Post Office Protocol (POP) and Internet Message Access Protocol (IMAP) can be used by clients to access e-mail.

8.   Internet Explorer and Mozilla Firefox are both popular web browsers.

9.   The File and Printer Sharing for Microsoft Networks client must be installed.

10. The Read permission allows the user to navigate the entire directory structure, view the contents of the directory, view the contents of any files in the directory, and see ownership and attributes.

Chapter

14

Security

COMPTIA A+ 220-602 EXAM OBJECTIVES COVERED IN THIS CHAPTER:

✓ **6.1 Identify the fundamentals and principles of security**

- Identify the purposes and characteristics of access control, for example:
- Access to operating system (e.g., accounts such as user, admin, and guest. Groups, permission actions, types and levels), components, restricted spaces
- Identify the purposes and characteristics of auditing and event logging

✓ **6.2 Install, configure, upgrade, and optimize security**

- Install and configure software, wireless and data security, for example:
    - Authentication technologies
    - Software firewalls
    - Auditing and event logging (enable/disable only)
    - Wireless client configuration
    - Unused wireless connections
    - Data access (e.g., permissions, basic local security policy)
    - File systems (converting from FAT32 to NTFS only)

✓ **6.3 Identify tools, diagnostic procedures, and troubleshooting techniques for security**

- Diagnose and troubleshoot software and data security issues for example:
    - Software firewall issues
    - Wireless client configuration issues
    - Data access issues (e.g., permissions, security policies)
    - Encryption and encryption technology issues

✓ **6.4 Perform preventative maintenance for security**

- Recognize social engineering and address social engineering situations

COMPTIA A+ 220-603 EXAM OBJECTIVES COVERED IN THIS CHAPTER:

✓ **5.1 Identify the fundamental principles of security**

- Identify the names, purposes, and characteristics of access control and permissions
- Accounts including user, admin, and guest
- Groups
- Permission levels, types (e.g., file systems and shared), and actions (e.g., read, write, change, and execute)

✓ **5.2 Install, configure, optimizing, and upgrade security**

- Install and configure hardware, software, wireless and data security, for example:
  - Smart card readers
  - Key fobs
  - Biometric devices
  - Authentication technologies
  - Software firewalls
  - Auditing and event logging (enable/disable only)
  - Wireless client configuration
  - Unused wireless connections
  - Data access (e.g., permissions, security policies)
  - Encryption and encryption technologies

✓ **5.3 Identify tools, diagnostic procedures, and troubleshooting techniques for security issues**

- Diagnose and troubleshoot software and data security issues, for example:
  - Software firewall issues
  - Wireless client configuration issues
  - Data access issues (e.g., permissions, security policies)
  - Encryption and encryption technology issues

✓ **5.4 Perform preventative maintenance for security**

- Recognize social engineering and address social engineering situations

COMPTIA A+ 220-604 EXAM OBJECTIVES COVERED IN THIS CHAPTER:

✓ **4.1 Identify the names, purposes, and characteristics of physical security devices and processes**

- Control access to PCs, servers, laptops, and restricted spaces
- Hardware
- Operating systems

✓ **4.2 Install hardware security**

- Smart-card readers
- Key fobs
- Biometric devices

This domain was given a weight of 11 percent on the A+ Essentials exam. It appears on the 220-602 (IT Technician) exam, where its weight is 8 percent; on the 220-603 (Remote Support Technician) exam, where it's elevated to 15 percent of the exam weight; and on the 220-604 (Depot Technician Exam), where it's lowered to 5 percent of the exam weight. In other words, no matter which elective you take, you'll be tested on this topic again.

There is a fair amount of overlap between these objectives and the ones you needed to know for the Essentials Exam. Rather than repeating that information verbatim, the focus here is on the implementation of security in the operating systems.

 It's highly recommended that you read Chapter 6 in addition to this chapter as you study for your technician exam.

Identifying the Fundamental Principles of Security

Hardening is the process of reducing or eliminating weaknesses, securing services, and attempting to make your environment immune to attacks. Typically, when you install operating systems, applications, and network products, the defaults from the manufacturer are to make the product as simple to use as possible and allow it to work with your existing environment as effortlessly as possible. That isn't always the best scenario when it comes to security.

This objective expects you to know how to create a baseline for security and restrict access to data and components.

Critical Information

You want to make certain that your systems, and the data within them, are kept as secure as possible. The security prevents others from changing the data, destroying it, or inadvertently harming it.

Security Baselines

One of the first steps in developing a secure environment is to develop a baseline of your organization's minimum security needs. A *security baseline* defines the level of security that will be implemented and maintained. You can choose to set a low baseline by implementing next to no security, or a high baseline that doesn't allow users to make any changes at all to the network or their systems. In practicality, most implementations fall between the two extremes; you must determine what is best for your organization.

The baseline provides the input needed to design, implement, and support a secure network. Developing the baseline includes gathering data on the specific security implementation of the systems with which you'll be working.

One of the newest standards for security is *Common Criteria (CC)*. This document is a joint effort between Canada, France, Germany, the Netherlands, the United Kingdom, and the United States. The standard outlines a comprehensive set of evaluation criteria, broken down into seven *Evaluation Assurance Levels (EAL)*. EAL 1 to EAL 7 are discussed here:

EAL 1   EAL 1 is primarily used where the user wants assurance that the system will operate correctly, but threats to security aren't viewed as serious.

EAL 2   EAL 2 requires product developers to use good design practices. Security isn't considered a high priority in EAL 2 certification.

EAL 3   EAL 3 requires conscientious development efforts to provide moderate levels of security.

EAL 4   EAL 4 requires positive security engineering based on good commercial development practices. It's anticipated that EAL 4 will be the common benchmark for commercial systems.

EAL 5   EAL 5 is intended to ensure that security engineering has been implemented in a product from the early design phases. It's intended for high levels of security assurance. The EAL documentation indicates that special design considerations will mostly likely be required to achieve this level of certification.

EAL 6   EAL 6 provides high levels of assurance of specialized security engineering. This certification indicates high levels of protection against significant risks. These systems will be highly secure from penetration attackers.

EAL 7   EAL 7 is intended for extremely high levels of security. The certification requires extensive testing, measurement, and complete independent testing of every component.

EAL certification has replaced the Trusted Computer Systems Evaluation Criteria (TCSEC) system for certification. The recommended level of certification for commercial systems is EAL 4.

Currently, only a few operating systems have been approved at the EAL 4 level, and even though one may be, that doesn't mean your own individual implementation of it is functioning at that level. If your implementation doesn't use the available security measures, then you're operating below that level. The network is only as strong as its weakest component. If users can install software, delete files, and change configurations, then these actions can be done within software programs such as viruses and malware as well.

Hardening the OS and NOS

As we just stated, any network is only as strong as its weakest component. Sometimes, the most obvious components are overlooked, and it's your job as a security administrator to make certain that doesn't happen. You must make sure the operating systems running on the workstations and on the network servers are as secure as they can be.

Hardening an operating system (OS) or network operating system (NOS) refers to the process of making the environment more secure from attacks and intruders. This section discusses hardening an OS and the methods of keeping it hardened as new threats emerge. This section will also discuss some of the vulnerabilities of the more popular operating systems and what can be done to harden those OSs.

Hardening Microsoft Windows 2000

Windows 2000 entered the market at the millennium. It includes workstation and several server versions. The market has embraced these products, and they offer reasonable security when updated. Windows 2000 provides a Windows Update icon on the Start menu; this icon allows you to connect to the Microsoft website and automatically download and install updates. A large number of security updates are available for Windows 2000—make sure they're applied.

In the Windows environment, the Services manager or applet is one of the primary methods (along with policies) used to disable a service.

The server and workstation products operate in a manner similar to Windows NT 4. These products run into the most security-related problems when they're bundled with products that Microsoft has included with them. Some of the more attack-prone products include Internet Information Server (IIS), FTP, and other common web technologies. Make sure these products are disabled if they aren't needed, and keep them up-to-date with the most recent security and service packs.

Many security updates have been issued for Windows 2000. The Microsoft TechNet and Security websites provide tools, whitepapers, and materials to help secure Windows 2000 systems.

You can find the Microsoft TechNet website at http://technet.microsoft.com/default.aspx. The Microsoft security website is at http://www.microsoft.com/security/.

Windows 2000 includes extensive system logging, reporting, and monitoring tools. These tools help make the job of monitoring security fairly easy. In addition, Windows 2000 provides a great deal of flexibility in managing groups of users, security attributes, and access control to the environment.

The Event Viewer is the major tool for reviewing logs in Windows 2000. Figure 14.1 shows a sample Event Viewer log. A number of different types of events can be logged using Event Viewer, and administrators can configure the level of events that are logged.

Another important security tool is Performance Monitor. As an administrator of a Windows 2000 network, you must know how to use Performance Monitor. This tool can be a lifesaver when you're troubleshooting problems and looking for resource-related issues.

Windows 2000 servers can run a technology called *Active Directory (AD)*, which lets you control security configuration options of Windows 2000 systems in a network. Unfortunately, the full power of AD doesn't work unless all the systems in the network are running Windows 2000 or higher.

FIGURE 14.1   Event Viewer log of a Windows 2000 system

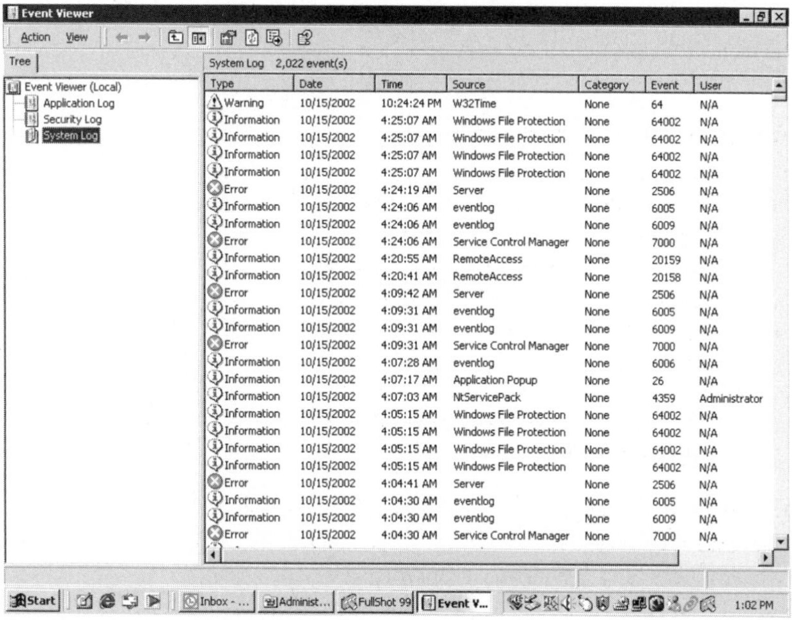

Hardening Microsoft Windows XP

Windows XP functions as a replacement for both the Windows 9x family and Windows 2000 Professional. There are multiple versions of Windows XP, including the Home, Media Center, and Professional editions.

The Windows XP Home edition was intended specifically to replace Windows 9x clients and could be installed either as an upgrade from Windows 9x or as a fresh installation on new systems. Media Center adds entertaining options (such as a remote control for TV), and Windows XP Professional is designed for the corporate environment. Windows XP Professional has the ability to take advantage of the security possible from Windows 200x servers running Active Directory.

With Microsoft's increased emphasis on security, it's reasonable to expect that the company will be working hard to make this product secure. At the time of this writing, the second service pack for XP is available. The service packs fix minor security openings within the operating system, but nothing substantial has been reported as a weakness with XP.

Hardening Windows Server 2003

The update for Microsoft's Windows 2000 Server line of products is Windows Server 2003, which is available in four editions:

- Web edition
- Standard edition

- Enterprise edition
- Datacenter edition

This product introduced the following features to the Microsoft server line:

- Internet connection firewall (now called the Windows Firewall)
- Secure authentication (locally and remotely)
- Wireless connections
- Software restriction policies
- Secure web server (IIS 6)
- Encryption and cryptography enhancements
- Improved security in VPN connections
- Public key infrastructure (PKI) and X.509 certificate support

In short, the goal was to make a product that is both secure and flexible.

Hardening Unix/Linux

The Unix environment and its derivatives are some of the most-installed server products in the history of the computer industry. Over a dozen different versions of Unix are available; the most popular is a free version derivative called *Linux*.

Unix was created in the 1970s. The product designers took an open-systems approach, meaning that the entire source code for the operating system was readily available for most versions. This open source philosophy has allowed tens of thousands of programmers, computer scientists, and systems developers to tinker with and improve the product.

Linux and Unix, when properly configured, provide a high level of security. The major challenge with the Unix environment is configuring it properly.

Unix includes the capacity to handle and run almost every protocol, service, and capability designed. You should turn off most of the services when they aren't needed, by running a script during system startup. The script will configure the protocols, and it will determine which services are started.

All Unix security is handled at the file level. Files and directories need to be established properly in order to ensure correct access permissions. The file structure is hierarchical by nature, and when a file folder access level is set, all subordinate file folders usually inherit this access. This inheritance of security is established by the systems administrator or by a user who knows how to adjust directory permissions.

Keeping patches and updates current is essential in the Unix environment. You can accomplish this by regularly visiting the developer's website for the version/flavor you're using, and downloading the latest fixes.

Linux also provides a great deal of activity logging. These logs are essential in establishing patterns of intrusion.

An additional method of securing Linux systems is accomplished by adding *TCP wrappers*, which are low-level logging packages designed for Unix systems. Wrappers provide additional detailed logging on activity using a specific protocol. Each protocol or port must have a wrapper installed for it. The wrappers then record activities and deny access to the service or server.

As an administrator of a Unix or Linux network, you're confronted with a large number of configuration files and variables that you must work with in order to keep all hosts communicating properly.

Hardening Novell NetWare

Novell was one of the first companies to introduce a NOS for desktop computers, called NetWare. Early versions of NetWare provided the ability to connect PCs into primitive but effective LANs. The most recent version of NetWare, version 6.5, includes file sharing, print sharing, support for most clients, and fairly tight security.

NetWare functions as a server product. The server has its own NOS. The NetWare software also includes client applications for a number of different types of systems, including Macintoshes and PCs. You can extend the server services by adding NetWare Loadable Modules (NLMs) to the server. These modules allow executable code to be patched or inserted into the OS.

NetWare version 6.x is primarily susceptible to denial of service (DoS) types of attacks, as opposed to exploitation and other attacks. NetWare security is accomplished through a combination of access controls, user rights, security rights, and authentication.

> The heart of NetWare security is the NetWare Directory Service (NDS) or eDirectory (for newer Novell implementations). NDS and eDirectory maintain information about rights, access, and usage on a NetWare-based network.

A number of additional capabilities make NetWare a product worth evaluating in implementation. These include e-commerce products, document retrieval, and enhanced network printing.

> Prior to version 5, NetWare defaulted to the proprietary IPX/SPX protocol for networking. All newer versions of NetWare default to TCP/IP.

Hardening Apple Macintosh

Macintosh systems seem to be most the most vulnerable to physical access attacks targeted through the console. The network implementations are as secure as any of the other systems discussed in this chapter.

Macintosh security breaks down in its access control and authentication systems. Macintosh uses a simple 32-bit password encryption scheme that is relatively easy to crack. The password file is located in the Preference folder; if this file is shared or is part of a network share, it may be vulnerable to decryption.

Macintosh systems also have several proprietary network protocols that aren't intended for routing. Recently, Macintosh systems have implemented TCP/IP networking as an integral part of the OS.

Working with Access Control Lists

Access Control Lists (ACLs) enable devices in your network to ignore requests from specified users or systems, or to grant them certain network capabilities. You may find that a certain IP address is constantly scanning your network, and thus you can block this IP address from your network. If you block it at the router, the IP address will automatically be rejected any time it attempts to utilize your network.

ACLs allow a stronger set of access controls to be established in your network. The basic process of ACL control lets the administrator design and adapt the network to deal with specific security threats.

General Rules

You should adhere to a number of general rules, regardless of which OSs are employed on your servers and clients. Among those rules are the following:

- Limit access to the OS to only those who need it. As silly as it may sound, every user should be a user who has to access the system. This means that every user has a unique username and password that are shared with no one else. Don't allow users to use guest accounts or admin accounts (regardless of whether your OS calls them admin, root, supervisor, and so on).

- Not only do you require users to have unique access, but you limit that access to only what they need access to. In other words, you start out assuming they need access to nothing, and then you back off slowly from that position. It's always better to have a user with too little permission, and whose settings you have to tweak a bit, than to have one with too much permission who "accidentally" deletes important files.

- Trying to manage individual users becomes more of a nightmare as the size of the systems increases. For that reason, management should be done (as much as possible) by groups. Users with similar traits, job duties, and so on, are added to groups, and the groups are assigned the permissions the users need. If a user needs access to more than what a specific group offers, you make them a member of multiple groups—don't try to tweak their settings individually.

- All administrative tools, utilities, and so on, should be safely guarded behind secure rights and permissions. You should regularly check to see who has used such tools (see the discussion of auditing in the next section) and make sure they aren't being used by users who shouldn't be able to do so.

- Control permissions to resources as granularly as possible. The next objective discusses permissions and ACLs as they apply to different OSs. Know the ones that exist in your environment and how to use them effectively.

Auditing and Logging

Most systems generate *security logs* and *audit files* of activity on the system. These files do absolutely no good if they aren't periodically reviewed for unusual events. Many web servers provide message auditing, as do logon, system, and application servers.

The amount of information these files contain can be overwhelming. You should establish a procedure to review them on a regular basis. A rule of thumb is to never start auditing by trying to record everything, because the sheer volume of the entries will make the data unusable. Approach auditing from the opposite perspective, and begin auditing only a few key things; then, expand the audits as you find you need more data.

These files may also be susceptible to access or modification attacks. The files often contain critical systems information, including resource sharing, security status, and so on. An attacker may be able to use this information to gather more detailed data about your network.

In an access attack, these files can be deleted, modified, and scrambled to prevent systems administrators from knowing what happened in the system. A logic bomb could, for example, delete these files when it completes. Administrators might know that something happened, but they would get no clues or assistance from the log and audit files.

You should consider periodically inspecting systems to see what software is installed and whether passwords are posted on sticky notes on monitors or keyboards. A good way to do this without attracting attention is to clean all the monitor faces. While you're cleaning the monitors, you can also verify that physical security is being upheld. If you notice a password on a sticky note, you can "accidentally" forget to put it back. You should also notify that user that this is an unsafe practice and not to continue it.

 Under all conditions, you should always work within the guidelines established by your company.

You should also consider obtaining a vulnerability scanner and running it across your network. A *vulnerability scanner* is a software application that checks your network for any known security holes; it's better to run one on your own network before someone outside the organization runs it against you. One of the best-known vulnerability scanners is Security Administrator's Integrated Network Tool (SAINT).

Exam Essentials

Know the purpose and characteristics of access control.   The purpose of access control is to limit who can access what resources on a system. The characteristics depend on the type of implementation utilized. You should always harden your systems to make them as secure as possible.

Know the purpose and characteristics of auditing and logging.   Log files are created to hold entries about the operations that take place on the system. Auditing is merely viewing those log files. There is often a fair amount of granularity in choosing what you want to allow into a log—the danger in recording too much information is that it can overwhelm you when you examine it.

Installing, Configuring, Optimizing, and Upgrading Security

The topics beneath this objective focus on wireless security—which was fully covered in Chapter 6—and data access/filesystems, as well as the need to keep the system current. To avoid repetition, only the new material for this objective is covered here.

Critical Information

The previous objective discussed the need to harden OSs. This objective looks at the issue from the view of the filesystem and the need to keep the system current.

Hardening Filesystems

Several filesystems are involved in the OSs we've discussed, and they have a high level of interoperability between them—from a network perspective, that is. Through the years, the different vendors have implemented their own sets of file standards. Some of the more common filesystems include the following:

Microsoft FAT   Microsoft's earliest filesystem was referred to as File Allocation Table (FAT). FAT is designed for relatively small disk drives. It was upgraded first to FAT16 and finally to FAT32. FAT32 allows large disk systems to be used on Windows systems. FAT allows only two types of protection: share-level and user-level access privileges. If a user has write or change access to a drive or directory, they have access to any file in that directory. This is very unsecure in an Internet environment.

Microsoft NTFS   The New Technology File System (NTFS) was introduced with Windows NT to address security problems. Before Windows NT was released, it had become apparent to Microsoft that a new filesystem was needed to handle growing disk sizes, security concerns, and the need for more stability. NTFS was created to address those issues.

Although FAT was relatively stable if the systems that were controlling it kept running, it didn't do well when the power went out or the system crashed unexpectedly. One of the benefits of NTFS was a transaction tracking system, which made it possible for Windows NT to back out of any disk operations that were in progress when Windows NT crashed or lost power.

With NTFS, files, directories, and volumes can each have their own security. NTFS's security is flexible and built in. Not only does NTFS track security in ACLs, which can hold permissions for local users and groups, but each entry in the ACL can specify what type of access is given—such as Read-Only, Change, or Full Control. This allows a great deal of flexibility in setting up a network. In addition, special file-encryption programs were developed to encrypt data while it was stored on the hard disk.

Microsoft strongly recommends that all network shares be established using NTFS. Several current OSs from Microsoft support both FAT32 and NTFS. It's possible to convert from FAT32 to NTFS without losing data, but you can't do the operation in reverse (you would need to reformat the drive and install the data again from a backup tape).

Novell NetWare Storage Service   Novell, like Microsoft, implemented a proprietary file structure called NetWare File System. This system allows complete control of every file resource on a NetWare server. The NetWare File System was upgraded to NetWare Storage Service (NSS) in version 6. NSS provides higher performance and larger file storage capacities than the NetWare File System. NSS, like its predecessor, uses the NDS or eDirectory to provide authentication for all access.

Unix filesystem   The Unix filesystem is completely hierarchical. Each file, filesystem, and subdirectory has complete granularity of access control. The three primary attributes in a Unix file or directory are Read, Write, and Execute. The ability to create these capabilities individually, as well as to establish inheritance to subdirectories, gives Unix the highest level of security available for commercial systems. The major difficulty with Unix is that establishing these access-control hierarchies can be time-consuming when the system is initially configured. Figure 14.2 illustrates this hierarchical file structure. Most current OSs have embraced this method of file organization.

FIGURE 14.2   Hierarchical file structure used in Unix and other OSs

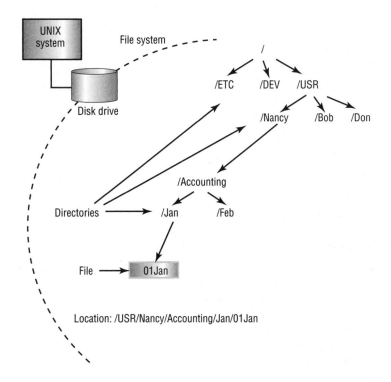

Unix Network Filesystems   Network File System (NFS) is a Unix protocol that allows systems to mount filesystems from remote locations. This ability lets a client system view the server or remote desktop storage as a part of the local client. NFS, although functional, is difficult to secure. The discussion of this process is beyond the scope of this book; the major issue lies in Unix's inherent trust of authentication processes. NFS was originally implemented by Sun Microsystems, and it has become a standard protocol in Unix environments.

Apple File Sharing   Apple File Sharing (AFS) was intended to provide simple networking for Apple Macintosh systems. This system used a proprietary network protocol called *AppleTalk*. An AppleTalk network isn't routed through the Internet and isn't considered secure. AFS allows the file owner to establish password and access privileges. This process is similar to the Unix filesystem. OS X, the newest version of the Macintosh OS, has more fully implemented a filesystem based on the Unix model. In general, Apple networking is considered as secure as the other implementations discussed in the section. The major weakness of the OS involves physical control of the systems.

Each of these filesystem implementations requires careful consideration when you're implementing it in a network. You must evaluate the filesystems' individual capabilities, limitations, and vulnerabilities when you're choosing which protocols or systems to implement.

Most OS providers support multiple protocols and methods. Turn off any protocols that aren't needed, because each protocol or filesystem running on a workstation or server increases your vulnerability and exposure to attack, data loss, or DoS attacks.

If at all possible, don't share the root directories of a disk drive. Doing so allows access to system files, passwords, and other sensitive information. Establish shares off hard drives that don't contain system files.

Make sure you periodically review the manufacturers' support websites and other support resources that are available to apply current updates and security patches to your systems. Doing this on a regular basis will lower your exposure to security risks.

Updating Your Operating System

OS manufacturers typically provide product updates. For example, Microsoft provides a series of regular updates for Windows 2000 (a proprietary system) and other applications. However, in the case of public source systems (such as Linux), the updates may come from a newsgroup, the manufacturer of the version you're using, or a user community.

In both cases, public and private, updates help keep OSs up to the most current revision level. Researching updates is important; when possible, so is getting feedback from other users before you install an update. In a number of cases, a service pack or update has rendered a system unusable. Make sure your system is backed up before you install updates.

Make sure you test updates on test systems before you implement them on production systems.

Three different types of updates are discussed here: hotfixes, service packs, and patches.

Hotfixes

Hotfixes are used to make repairs to a system during normal operation, even though they may require a reboot. A hotfix may entail moving data from a bad spot on the disk and remapping the data to a new sector. Doing so prevents data loss and loss of service. This type of repair may also involve reallocating a block of memory if, for example, a memory problem occurred. This allows the system to continue normal operations until a permanent repair can be made. Microsoft refers to a bug fix as a *hotfix*. This involves the replacement of files with an updated version.

Service Packs

A *service pack* is a comprehensive set of fixes consolidated into a single product. A service pack may be used to address a large number of bugs or to introduce new capabilities in an OS. When installed, a service pack usually contains a number of file replacements.

Make sure you check related websites to verify that the service pack works properly. Sometimes a manufacturer releases a service pack before it has been thoroughly tested. An untested service pack can cause extreme instability in an OS or, even worse, render it inoperable.

Patches

A *patch* is a temporary or quick fix to a program. Patches may be used to temporarily bypass a set of instructions that have malfunctioned. Several OS manufacturers issue patches that can be either manually applied or applied using a disk file to fix a program.

When you're working with customer support on a technical problem with an OS or applications product, customer service may have you go into the code and make alterations to the binary files that run on your system. Double-check each change to prevent catastrophic failures due to improperly entered code.

When more data is known about the problem, a service pack or hotfix may be issued to fix the problem on a larger scale. Patching is becoming less common, because most OS manufacturers would rather release a new version of the code than patch it.

General Rules

As with the first objective, there are a number of general rules to adhere to, regardless of which OSs are employed on your servers and clients. Among those rules for this objective are the following:

- Know the authentication possibilities for the OSs you use, and know what each allows. In addition to those that come standard with the OS, you can also employ add-on devices such as biometric scanners to increase the security of the authentication process.

- Understand that firewalls can be software- or hardware-based, and are usually some combination of the two. Software-only firewalls are usually limited to home use and provide the line of defense preventing outside users from gaining access to the home computer.

- Event logging is used to record events and provide a trail that can be followed to determine what was done. Auditing involves looking at the logs and finding problems.

- Wireless clients can be configured to access the network the same as wired clients, but wireless security is a touchy issue. There are protocols that you can use to add security, but it's still difficult to secure a wireless network the same way you can secure a wired one. Unused wireless connections are the same as leaving a security door open.

- Data access can be limited a number of different ways—permissions to the data and basic local security policies are two universal methods that should be used regardless of the OS you're employing.

- The filesystem you're using can determine what permissions you have available to assign to resources. NTFS offers a great deal of granularity in terms of permissions, whereas FAT32 offers few choices. You can convert from FAT32 to NTFS without data loss by using the `convert` utility.

- To increase the level of authentication, you can employ biometrics, key fobs, and smart cards. Smart-card readers may be contact-based (you have to insert the card) or contact-less (the card is read when it's in proximity to the reader). Key fobs are often used to provide a randomly generated number that you can enter for authentication, and biometric devices identify the user by some physical aspect (such as a thumb print).

While key fobs are often thought of as generating random numbers, the term is also used for many small devices that allow for keyless entry into buildings or vehicles. While those only require proximity and a clear line of sight, when it comes to true security, you want something that also incorporates a challenge/response to authenticate the user.

Exam Essentials

Know the concepts of data security.   You should know that it's imperative to keep the system up-to-date and to install all relevant upgrades as they become available. You should also understand the importance of using a secure filesystem.

Identifying Tools, Diagnostic Procedures, and Troubleshooting Techniques for Security

The majority of this objective closely mirrors the previous objectives. One area of focus not touched on heavily elsewhere is security policies, so it's discussed here.

Critical Information

One of the most wide-sweeping administrative features that Windows 200x offers over its predecessors and other OSs is that of *Group Policy*. A part of IntelliMirror, the Group Policy feature enables administrators to control desktop settings, utilize scripts, perform Internet Explorer maintenance, roll out software, redirect folders, and so forth. All of these features can be an administrator's dream in supporting LAN users.

Consider this analogy: When you connect a television set to the subscription cable coming through the living-room wall, you get all the channels to which you subscribe. If you pay an extra $50 per month (depending on where you live), you can get close to 100 channels, including a handful of premium channels.

When you turn on the television, you're free to watch any of the channels—regardless of whether the content is questionable or racy. And when you're gone, your children are free to do the same. Enter the V-chip. Before leaving your children alone with the television, you enable the V-chip. The V-chip lets you (the "administrator") restrict access to stations that air questionable or racy programming.

How is this example analogous to an OS? On Windows 2000 Professional, for example, users can do just about anything they want. They can delete programs and never be able to run them again; they can send huge graphics files to a tiny printer that can print only one page every 30 minutes; they can delete the Registry and never be able to use the system again; and so forth. Enter Group Policy.

Group Policy places restrictions on what a user/computer is allowed to do. It takes away liberties that were otherwise there; therefore, they are never implemented for the benefit of the user (restrictions don't equal benefits) but are always there to simplify administration for the administrator.

From an administrator's standpoint, if you take away the ability to add new software, then you don't have to worry about supporting nontested applications. If you remove the ability to delete installed printers (accidentally, of course), then you don't have to waste an hour reinstalling the printer. By reducing what users can do, you reduce what you must support, and you also reduce the overall administrative cost of supporting the network/computer/user.

Before going any further, it's important to differentiate between roaming users and mobile users, because the two are often confused. As the name implies, *roaming users* are users who roam throughout the LAN. One example is a secretary in a secretarial pool. On Monday, the secretary may be working in Accounting, on Tuesday in Human Resources, and for the remainder of the week in Marketing. Within each department, the secretary has a different computer but is still on the same LAN. By placing the secretary's profile on the network and configuring them as a roaming user, you give them the same desktop and access to all resources regardless of where the secretary works on any given day. Not only that, but the same Group Policy applies (and is routinely refreshed), to prevent the secretary from permanently deleting software that has been assigned, changing the desktop, and so on.

An example of a *mobile user,* on the other hand, is a salesperson who is in the field calling on customers. In their possession is a $6,000 laptop capable of doing everything shy of changing the oil of the company car. Whenever the salesperson has a problem with the computer, they call from 3,000 miles away and begin the conversation with, "It did it again." You not only have no idea to whom you're talking, you have no idea what "it" refers to.

In short, roaming users use different computers within the same LAN, whereas mobile users use the same workstation but don't connect to the LAN. Because you can't force mobile users to connect to a server on your LAN each time they boot (and when they do, it's over slow connections), you're less able to enforce administrative restrictions—such as Group Policies. However, it isn't impossible to apply administrative restrictions to mobile users. System Policies (used in Windows 9x) are the predecessors of Group Policies. They're restricted to governing Registry settings only, whereas Group Policies exceed that functionality.

In the absence of a regular connection to the LAN (and, therefore, to Active Directory), there are a number of Group Policy restrictions that you can't enforce or utilize. Therefore, it's always in the best interest of the administrators to have the systems connect to the network (and require them to do so) whenever possible. The following is a list of restrictions that can't be enforced without such a connection:

Assigning and publishing software   The Software Installation extension enables you to centrally manage software. You can publish software to users and assign software to computers.

Folder redirection   The Folder Redirection extension lets you reroute special Windows 2000 folders—including My Documents, Application Data, Desktop, and the Start Menu—from the user profile location to elsewhere on the network.

Remote installation   The Remote Installation Services (RIS) extension enables you to control the Remote Operating System Installation component, as displayed to the client computers.

Roaming profiles   By placing the user's profile on the server, they can have the same desktop regardless of which computer they use on a given day.

In addition to these, you can place all the other settings directly on the mobile computer—making them local policies. Local policies can apply to the following:

Administrative templates   The administrative templates consist mostly of the Registry restrictions that existed in System Policies. They let you manage the Registry settings that control the desktop, including applications and OS components.

Scripts   Scripts enable you to automate user logon and logoff.

Security settings   The Security Settings extension lets you define security options (local, domain, and network) for users within the scope of a Group Policy object, including Account Policy, encryption, and so forth.

Creating the Local Policy

You can create a local policy on a computer by using the Group Policy Editor. You can start the Group Policy Editor in one of the following two ways:

- Choose Start ➢ Run, and then enter **gpedit.msc**.

- Choose Start ➢ Run, and then enter **MMC**. In the MMC console, choose Console ➢ Open, and then select GPEDIT.MSC from the System32 directory.

When opened, a local policy has two primary divisions: Computer Configuration and User Configuration. The settings you configure beneath Computer Configuration apply to the computer, regardless of who is using it. Conversely, the settings you configure beneath User Configuration apply only if the specified user is logged on. Each of the primary divisions can be useful for certain circumstances. Note that the Computer Configuration settings are applied whenever the computer is on, whereas the User Configuration settings are applied only when the user logs on.

The following options are available under the Computer Configuration setting:

Software Settings   These settings typically are empty on a new system.

Administrative Templates   These settings are those administrators commonly want to apply.

Windows Settings   The Windows Settings are further divided:

Scripts   Scripts are divided into Startup and Shutdown, both of which enable you to configure items (.EXE, .CMD, .BAT, and other files) to run when a computer starts and stops. Although your implementation may differ, for the most part, little here is pertinent to the mobile user.

Security Settings   Security Settings are divided into Account Policies, Local Policies, Public Key Policies, and IP Security Policies on the local machine.

The following sections examine some of the Security Settings choices.

Account Policies

Account Policies further divides into Password Policy and Account Lockout Policy. The following seven choices are available under Password Policy, and the majority of them were previously in the Account Policy menu of User Manager on Windows NT Workstation:

Enforce Password History   This allows you to require unique passwords for a certain number of iterations. The default number is 0, but it can go as high as 24.

Maximum Password Age   The default is 42 days, but values range from 0 to 999.

Minimum Password Age   The default is 0 days, but values range to 999.

Minimum Password Length   The default is 0 characters (meaning no passwords are required), but you can specify a number up to 14.

Passwords Must Meet Complexity Requirements of the Installed Password Filter   The default is disabled.

Store Password Using Reversible Encryption for All Users in the Domain   The default is disabled.

User Must Logon to Change the Password   The default is disabled, thus allowing a user with an expired password to specify a new password during the logon process.

Because the likelihood of laptops being stolen always exists, it's strongly encouraged that you use good password policies for this audience. Here's an example:

- Enforce Password History: 8 passwords remembered
- Maximum Password Age: 42 days
- Minimum Password Age: 3 days
- Minimum Password Length: 6 to 8 characters

Leave the other three settings disabled.

Account Lockout Policy

The Account Lockout Policy setting divides into the following three values:

Account Lockout Counter   This is the number of invalid attempts before lockout occurs. The default is 0 (meaning the feature is turned off). Invalid attempt numbers range from 1 to 999.

A number greater than 0 changes the values of the following two options to 30 minutes; otherwise, they are "not defined."

Account Lockout Duration This is a number of minutes ranging from 1 to 99999. A value of 0 is also allowed here and signifies that the account never unlocks itself—administrator interaction is always required.

Reset Account Lockout Counter After This is a number of minutes, ranging from 1 to 99999.

When you're working with a mobile workforce, you must weigh the choice of users calling you in the middle of the night when they've forgotten their password against keeping the system from being entered if the wrong user picks up the laptop. A good recommendation is to use a lockout after five attempts for a period of time between 30 and 60 minutes.

Local Policies

The Local Policies section divides into three subsections: Audit Policy, User Rights Assignment, and Security Options. The Audit Policy section contains nine settings, the default value for each being "No auditing." Valid options are Success and/or Failure. The Audit Account Logon Events entry is the one you should consider turning on for mobile users to see how often they log in and out of their machines.

When auditing is turned on for an event, the entries are logged in the Security log file.

The User Rights Assignment subsection of Local Policies is where the meat of the old System Policies come into play. User Rights Assignment has 34 options, most of which are self-explanatory. Also shown in the list that follows are the defaults for who can perform these actions; "not defined" indicates that no one is specified for this operation.

The list of rights and default permissions includes the following:

- Access this Computer from the Network: Everyone, Administrators, Power Users
- Act as Part of the Operating System: [blank]
- Add Workstations to Domain: [blank]
- Backup Files and Directories: Administrators, Backup Operators
- Bypass Traverse Checking: Everyone
- Change the System Time: Administrators, Power Users
- Create a Pagefile: Administrators
- Create a Token Object: [blank]
- Create Permanent Shared Objects: [blank]
- Debug Programs: Administrators
- Deny Access to this Computer from the Network: [blank]
- Deny Logon as a Batch Job: [blank]
- Deny Logon as a Service: [blank]

- Deny Logon Locally: [blank]

- Enable Computer and User Accounts to Be Trusted for Delegation: [blank]

- Force Shutdown from a Remote System: Administrators, Power Users

- Generate Security Audits: [blank]

- Increase Quotas: Administrators

- Increase Scheduling Priority: Administrators, Power Users

- Load and Unload Device Drivers: Administrators

- Lock Pages in Memory: [blank]

- Log On as a Batch Job: Administrator

- Log On as a Service: [blank]

- Log On Locally: Everyone, Administrators, Users, Guests, Power Users, Backup Operators

- Manage Auditing and Security Log: Administrators

- Modify Firmware Environment Values: Administrators

- Profile Single Process: Administrators, Power Users

- Profile System Performance: Administrators

- Remove Computer from Docking Station: [blank]

- Replace a Process Level Token: [blank]

- Restore Files and Directories: Administrators, Backup Operators

- Shut Down the System: Everyone, Administrators, Users, Power Users, Backup Operators

- Synchronize Directory Service Data: [blank]

- Take Ownership of Files or Other Objects: Administrators

This is the default list. You can add groups and users, but you can't remove them. (This functionality isn't needed.) If you want to "remove" users or groups from the list, uncheck the box granting them access. If your mobile users need to be able to install, delete, and modify their environment, make them a member of the Power Users group.

The Security Options section includes 38 options, which, for the most part, are Registry keys. The default for each is "Not defined"; the two definitions that can be assigned are Enabled and Disabled, or a physical number (as with the number of previous logons to cache).

General Rules

As with the first two objectives, you should adhere to a number of general rules, regardless of which OSs are employed on your servers and clients. Among those rules for this objective are the following:

- Software-only firewalls are typically suitable only for home use. They protect the computer they're running on but require resources from that computer (which could potentially slow down the user using the computer and other applications sharing the computer).

- Wireless networks need to be carefully configured to allow access to legitimate clients and only the legitimate network clients.

- Data access and encryption can work together. You should be able to limit access to only those eyes that need to see the data, but encrypting data helps to keep it secure if it does fall in to the wrong hands.

Exam Essentials

Diagnose and troubleshoot software and data security issues. It's important to know the reason why policies exist and the types of possibilities they offer to an administrator. What were once called System Policies have now become Group Policies in the Microsoft world. They let you lock down workstations and prevent users from making changes you don't want to allow.

Performing Preventative Maintenance for Security

Overlook the name of this objective—it focuses on only one area: social engineering. This objective tests your knowledge of that topic, and only that topic.

Critical Information

Social engineering attacks can develop very subtly. They're also hard to detect. Let's look at some classic social engineering attacks:

- Someone enters your building wearing a white lab jacket with a logo on it. He also has a toolkit. He approaches the receptionist and identifies himself as a copier repairman from a major local copier company. He indicates that he's here to do preventive service on your copier. In most cases, the receptionist will let him pass and tell him where the copier is. Once the "technician" is out of sight, the receptionist probably won't give him a second thought. Your organization has just been the victim of a social engineering attack. The attacker has now penetrated your first and possibly even your second layer of security. In many offices, including security-oriented offices, this individual will have access to the entire organization and will be able to pass freely anywhere he wants. This attack didn't take any particular talent or skill other than the ability to look like a copier repairman. Impersonation can go a long way in allowing access to a building or network.

- The next example is a true situation; it happened at a high-security government installation. Access to the facility required passing through a series of manned checkpoints. Professionally trained and competent security personnel manned these checkpoints. An employee decided to play a joke on the security department: He took an old employee badge, cut his picture out of it, and pasted in a picture of Mickey Mouse. He was able to gain access to the facility for two weeks before he was caught.

Social engineering attacks like these are easy to accomplish in most organizations. Even if your organization uses biometric devices, magnetic card strips, or other electronic measures, social engineering attacks are still relatively simple. A favorite method of gaining entry to electronically locked systems is to follow someone through the door they just unlocked, a process known as *tailgating*. Many people don't think twice about this event—it happens all the time.

Famed hacker Kevin Mitnick wrote a book called *The Art of Deception: Controlling the Human Element of Security*, in which 14 of the 16 chapters are devoted to social engineering scenarios that have been played out. If nothing else, the fact that one of the most notorious hackers—who could write on any security subject he wants—chose to write a book on social engineering should emphasize the importance of the topic to you.

As an administrator, one of your responsibilities is to educate users to not fall prey to social engineering attacks. They should know the security procedures that are in place and follow them to a tee. You should also have a high level of confidence that the correct procedures are in place, and one of the best ways to obtain that confidence is to check your users on occasion.

Preventing social engineering attacks involves more than just training about how to detect and prevent them. It also involves making sure that people stay alert. One form of social engineering is known as *shoulder surfing*, and it involves nothing more than watching someone when they enter their username/password/sensitive data.

Social engineering is easy to do, even with all of today's technology at our disposal. Education is the one key that can help.

Don't overlook the most common personal motivator of all: greed. It may surprise you, but people can be bribed to give away information. If someone gives out the keys, you won't necessarily know it has occurred. Those keys can be literal (the keys to the back door) or figurative (the keys to decrypt messages).

It's often comforting to think that we can't be bought. We look to our morals and standards and think that we're above being bribed. The truth of the matter, though, is that almost everyone has a price. Your price may be so high that for all practical purposes you don't have a price, but can the same be said for the other administrators in your company?

The movie and book *The Falcon and the Snowman* detailed the accounts of two young men, Christopher Boyce and Daulton Lee, who sold sensitive United State codes to the Russians for several years. The damage they did to U.S. security efforts was incalculable. In another case, U.S. Navy Petty Officer John Walker sold the Russians electronic key sets that gave them access to communications between the U.S. Navy and the nuclear submarine fleet in the Atlantic. Later, he sold information and keys for ground forces in Vietnam. His actions cost the U.S. Army countless lives. During the height of his activities, he recruited family members and others to gather this information for him.

Social engineering can have a hugely damaging effect on a security system, as the preceding note illustrates.

Exam Essentials

Know how social engineering works.   Social engineering is the process by which intruders gain access to your facilities, your network, and even to your employees by exploiting the generally trusting nature of people.

Review Questions

1. What is hardening?

2. What does a security baseline define?

3. How many EAL levels does Common Criteria define?

4. Which EAL level is it anticipated will be the common benchmark for commercial systems?

5. What is the major tool for reviewing logs in Windows 200*x*?

6. Which Windows 2000*x* tool can be a lifesaver when you're troubleshooting problems and looking for resource-related issues?

7. How many service packs are available for Windows XP?

8. True or false: All Unix security is handled at the file level.

9. What filesystem can FAT32 be upgraded to—without loss of data—in many current Microsoft operating systems?

10. What is the default value for the Account Lockout Counter in Group Policy?

Answers to Review Questions

1. Hardening is the process of reducing or eliminating weaknesses, securing services, and attempting to make your environment immune to attacks.

2. A security baseline defines the level of security that will be implemented and maintained.

3. Common Criteria (CC) defines seven EALs (Evaluation Assurance Levels).

4. It's anticipated that EAL 4 will be the common benchmark for commercial systems.

5. The Event Viewer is the major tool for reviewing logs in Windows 200*x*.

6. Performance Monitor can be a lifesaver when you're troubleshooting problems and looking for resource-related issues.

7. At the time of this writing, two service packs are available for Windows XP.

8. True. All Unix security is handled at the file level.

9. FAT32 can be upgraded to NTFS without data loss through the use of the convert utility.

10. Account Lockout Counter is the number of invalid attempts it takes before lockout occurs. The default is 0.

Chapter 15

Safety and Environmental Issues

COMPTIA A+ IT TECHNICIAN EXAM OBJECTIVE COVERED IN THIS CHAPTER:

✓ 7.1 Identify potential hazards and proper safety procedures, including power supply, display devices, and environment (e.g., trip, liquid, situational, atmospheric hazards, and high-voltage and moving equipment)

COMPTIA A+ DEPOT TECHNICIAN EXAM OBJECTIVE COVERED IN THIS CHAPTER:

✓ 5.1 Identify potential hazards and proper safety procedures, including power supply, display devices, and environment (e.g., trip, liquid, situational, atmospheric hazards, and high-voltage and moving equipment)

The inclusion of this domain in the elective exam is a first for CompTIA. The topics have always been tested in the core, but they have been isolated there. Now, the domain and its single objective appear on the 220-602 elective (where its weight is 5 percent) and the 220-604 elective (where its weight is 10 percent); it doesn't appear on the 220-603 elective exam's domains/objectives.

There is a fair amount of overlap between the material in this chapter and that in Chapter 7 because overlap exists in the objectives: The single objective here combines portions of 7.2 and 7.3 of the Essentials exam that was covered there.

Hazards and Safety Procedures

This objective requires you to know the potential safety hazards that exist when working with computer elements, and the safety procedures you should follow to lessen their likelihood.

Critical Information

Many parts of a computer, including monitors and printers, can pose a danger if handled carelessly. All electrical equipment has the potential to overheat and cause problems if not carefully monitored. Because technical devices contain capacitors, power supplies, and other elements, only trained individuals should work with sensitive equipment.

Power Supply Safety

Although it's possible to work on a power supply, doing so is *not* recommended except by a highly trained repairperson. Because power supplies contain capacitors that can hold deadly charges after they have been unplugged, it's dangerous to open the case of a power supply or attempt to work with it. As we pointed out in Chapter 7, given the cost of a power supply, it's generally cheaper (and much safer) to replace it than to do any work on it.

The number of volts in a power source represents its potential to do work, but volts don't do anything by themselves. *Current* (amperage, or amps) is the force behind the work being done by electricity. Most computer power supplies include more that one volt setting so they can work in other countries. Figure 15.1 shows the setting switch on a sample computer.

FIGURE 15.1   Choose the proper volt setting.

It's important to make sure this switch is set correctly for your country before you plug in a new system, and it's also important to make sure this setting doesn't get changed when you're performing maintenance on the computer.

Display Device Safety

Other than the power supply, one of the most dangerous components to try to repair is the monitor, or cathode ray tube (CRT). We recommend that you *not* try to repair monitors. To avoid the extremely hazardous environment contained inside the monitor—it can retain a high-voltage charge for hours after it's been turned off—take it to a certified monitor technician or television repair shop. The repair shop or certified technician will know and understand the proper procedures to discharge the monitor, which involves attaching a resistor to the flyback transformer's charging capacitor to release the high-voltage electrical charge that builds up during use. They can also determine whether the monitor can be repaired or needs to be replaced. Remember, the monitor works in its own extremely protective environment (the monitor case) and may not respond well to your desire to try to open it. The CRT is vacuum sealed. Be extremely careful when handling it—if you break the glass, the CRT will implode, which can send glass in any direction.

Even though we recommend not repairing monitors, the A+ exam does test your knowledge of the safety practices to use when you need to do so. If you have to open a monitor, you must first discharge the high-voltage charge on it using a high-voltage probe. This probe has a very large needle, a gauge that indicates volts, and a wire with an alligator clip. Attach the alligator clip to a ground (usually the round pin on the power cord). Slip the probe needle under the high-voltage cup on the monitor. You will see the gauge spike to around 15,000 volts and slowly reduce to zero. When it reaches zero, you may remove the high-voltage probe and service the monitor's high-voltage components.

Environmental Safety

This catch-all topic includes electrical tripping, working with liquids, being aware of atmospheric hazards, high voltage, and moving equipment. Each of these items is examined separately in the discussion that follows.

Electrical Tripping

Tripping occurs when the breaker on a device such as a power supply, surge protector, or UPS turns off the device because it received a spike. If the device is a UPS, when the tripping happens, the components plugged in to the UPS should go to battery instead of pulling power through the line. Under most circumstances, the breaker is reset and operations continue as normal. Figure 15.2 shows a surge-protector power strip, with the trip button to reset at the top.

FIGURE 15.2   The reset button on a surge-protector power strip

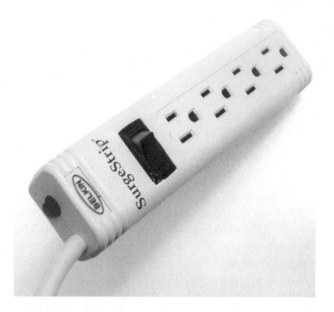

Nuisance tripping is the phrase used if tripping occurs often and isn't a result of a serious condition. If this continues, you should isolate the cause and correct it, even if it means replacing the device that continues to trip.

Surge protectors, either standalone or built into the UPS, can help reduce the number of nuisance trips. If your UPS doesn't have a surge protector, you should add one to the outlet before the UPS in order to keep the UPS from being damaged if it receives a strong surge. Figure 15.3 shows an example of a simple surge protector for a home computer.

All units are rated by Underwriters Laboratories (UL) for performance. One thing you should never do is plug a UPS or computer equipment into a Ground Fault Circuit Interrupter (GFCI) receptacle. These receptacles are intended for use in wet areas, and they trip very easily.

WARNING   Don't confuse a GFCI receptacle with an isolated ground receptacle. Isolated ground receptacles are identifiable by orange outlets and should be used for computer equipment to avoid their picking up a surge passed to the ground by any other device.

FIGURE 15.3   A simple surge protector

Working with Liquids

As a rule of thumb, liquids and computers don't mix and should be kept as far apart from each other as two male Siamese fighting fish. Liquid provides a great conductor between electrical components if spilled and can quickly fry a system. This refers not only to the soda an office worker carries in a cup to their cubicle, but also to the venting of the air-conditioning unit in the server room. If it's improperly draining or plumbed, it could cause serious damage to the equipment in its vicinity.

The exception to the liquid rule is cleaning alcohol. Isopropyl alcohol is commonly used for cleaning some components. You can find special-purpose cleaners in computer stores for cleaning specific items; if you use one, consult a material safety data sheet (MSDS) for the product or consult the manufacturer to find out whether any special handling and disposal is required.

Atmospheric Hazards

One of the most harmful atmospheric hazards to a computer is dust. Dust, dirt, hair, and other airborne contaminants can get pulled into computers and build up inside. Because computer fans work by pulling air through the computer (usually sucking it in through the case and then pushing it out the power supply), it's easy for these items to enter and then become stuck. Every item in the computer builds up heat, and these particles are no exception. As they build up, they hinder the fan's ability to perform its function, and the components get hotter than they would otherwise. Figure 15.4 shows the inside of a system in use for only six months in an area with carpeting and other dusty surroundings.

FIGURE 15.4   Dust builds up inside the system.

The heat that builds up can lead to *chip creep* and other conditions. Heating the pins too much causes expansion and keeps them seated tighter, but heating them too far and then cooling them repeatedly (at shutdown) causes the chips to gradually "creep" out of the sockets.

You can remove dust and debris from inside computers with compressed air blown in short bursts. The short bursts are useful in preventing the dust from flying too far out and entering another machine, as well as in preventing the can from releasing the air in liquid form. Compressed air cans should be held 2–3 inches from the system and always used upright so the content is released as a gas. If the can becomes cold to the touch, discontinue using it until it heats back to room temperature.

It's possible to use an air compressor instead of compressed-air cans when you need a lot of air. If you take this approach, make sure you keep the pounds per square inch (PSI) at or below 40, and include measures on the air compressor to remove moisture.

Dust can build up not just within the computer but also in crevices on the outside. Figure 15.5 shows USB ports on the back of a system that have become a haven for small dust particles. These ports need to be blown out with compressed air before being used, or else degradation with the device connected to them could occur.

FIGURE 15.5   Dust collects in unused ports as well.

Relative humidity should be maintained at around 50 percent for optimal operations. Be careful not to increase the humidity too far, to the point where moisture starts to condense on the equipment! Also use antistatic spray, which is available commercially, to reduce static buildup on clothing and carpets. In a pinch, a solution of diluted fabric softener sprayed on these items will do the same thing.

At the very least, be mindful of the dangers of electrostatic discharge (ESD) and take steps to reduce its effects. Beyond that, you should educate yourself about those effects so you know when ESD is becoming a major problem.

Working with High Voltage

Two computer devices have the potential to carry high voltages: the monitor and the power supply. The power supply converts AC current into DC current, and the capacitor associated with it holds 120 volts for quite a while.

The monitor uses a lot of power as it directs electrons on the screen via a strong magnet. The electrons and magnet require a considerable amount of voltage in order to be able to do their task. Like power supplies, monitors have the ability to hold their charge a long time after the power has been disconnected.

You should never open a power supply or a monitor for the reasons discussed here. The risk of electrocution with these two devices is significant.

If you question the presence of electricity, or the voltage of it, use a voltmeter. Figure 15.6 shows a simple voltmeter capable of working with both AC and DC currents.

Moving Equipment

When my first child was born, I left the hospital with her strapped securely in the child seat, surrounded by pillows and grandparents, with no possibility of moving an inch. I drove home—all 20 miles—at a speed that never exceeded 30 miles per hour. If she so much as yawned, I immediately looked to see what was going on and whether I needed to stop the car and make some adjustments.

Less than a year after the ride home, I was helping relocate a call center from one part of a busy city to another. Another technician and I were overseeing the work, and the company brought in inmates from a prison to help with heavy lifting. Needless to say, most of them didn't have a great deal of incentive to make sure the equipment was treated well. My partner slapped a mini-tower on a cart and went racing through the parking lot as if he were in a campus bed race. Once he reached the moving truck, he grabbed the tower in a bear hug and tossed it in, but not far enough back—its weight caused it to tip off the ledge and break into little pieces all over the parking lot. That is the way to lose a customer as well as data and any profit that could have been made on the project.

The first example is the one to follow when moving computer equipment—treat every piece you move as if it's your first child. One of the easiest ways to damage equipment is to move it with abandon. Take care to disconnect all cables and move the equipment in such a way as to do no harm.

Every cable should be carefully labeled and each component carefully stowed in a container that will protect it during the move. The move may take longer than you would like, but this approach can save you significant time and expense over having to re-create a system—even one as small as a user's workstation—from scratch.

FIGURE 15.6 A simple voltmeter

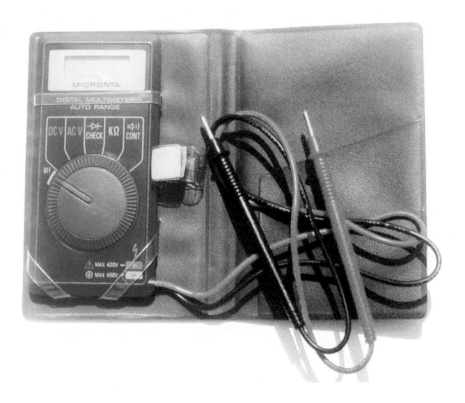

Exam Essentials

Know the safety procedures to follow when working with computers. Be careful when moving computers or working around any electrical components. Know that liquids and computers don't mix, and keep the systems as clean and dust-free as possible to ensure optimal operation.

Review Questions

1. What part of a computer should you never attempt to repair?

2. What electrical item stores current?

3. How far away from a component should you hold a can of compressed air when using it?

4. What is chip creep?

5. What is tripping?

6. What is nuisance tripping?

7. What organization rates surge protectors and UPSs?

8. How are isolated ground receptacles identified visually?

9. If you use an air compressor to clean out dust in a system, what is the maximum PSI that should be used?

10. What can be used to check for the presence of current?

Answers to Review Questions

1. The power supply. The stored electricity can electrocute you.

2. Capacitors. They are used with power supplies and monitors.

3. 2–3 inches.

4. When chips and boards get hot inside a computer and then cool enough to begin working their way out of their sockets.

5. Tripping is a condition that occurs when the breaker on a device such as a power supply, surge protector, or UPS turns it off because it received a spike.

6. Nuisance tripping means the tripping occurs often and isn't a result of a serious condition.

7. All units are rated by Underwriters Laboratories (UL) for performance.

8. Isolated ground receptacles are identifiable by orange outlets.

9. The maximum PSI should be 40.

10. A voltmeter can be used to check for the presence of current.

Chapter 16

Professionalism and Communication

COMPTIA A+ 220-602 EXAM OBJECTIVES COVERED IN THIS CHAPTER:

✓ **8.1 Use good communication skills, including listening and tact / discretion, when communicating with customers and colleagues**

  ▪ Use clear, concise, and direct statements

  ▪ Allow the customer to complete statements – avoid interrupting

  ▪ Clarify customer statements – ask pertinent questions

  ▪ Avoid using jargon, abbreviations, and acronyms

  ▪ Listen to customers

✓ **8.2 Use job-related professional behavior, including notation of privacy, confidentiality, and respect for the customer and customers' property**

  ▪ Behavior

    ▪ Maintain a positive attitude and tone of voice

    ▪ Avoid arguing with customers and / or becoming defensive

    ▪ Do not minimize customers' problems

    ▪ Avoid being judgmental and / or insulting or calling the customer names

    ▪ Avoid distractions and / or interruptions when talking with customers

  ▪ Property

    ▪ Telephone, laptop, desktop computer, printer, monitor, etc.

COMPTIA A+ 220-603 EXAM OBJECTIVES COVERED IN THIS CHAPTER:

✓ **6.1 Use good communication skills, including listening and tact / discretion, when communicating with customers and colleagues**

- Use clear, concise, and direct statements
- Allow the customer to complete statements – avoid interrupting
- Clarify customer statements – ask pertinent questions
- Avoid using jargon, abbreviations, and acronyms
- Listen to customers

✓ **6.2 Use job-related professional behavior, including notation of privacy, confidentiality, and respect for the customer and customers' property**

- Behavior
  - Maintain a positive attitude and tone of voice
  - Avoid arguing with customers and / or becoming defensive
  - Do not minimize customers' problems
  - Avoid being judgmental and / or insulting or calling the customer names
  - Avoid distractions and / or interruptions when talking with customers
- Property
  - Telephone, laptop, desktop computer, printer, monitor, etc.

This domain—and both of its objectives, almost word for word—appear on the A+ Essentials exam, where it's given a weight of 5 percent of the total exam. It appears on the IT Technician exam (where its weight has jumped to 15 percent) and on the Remote Support Technician exam (where it's all the way up to 20 percent of the exam weight). The topic is absent from the Depot Technician elective's domains/objectives primarily because Depot Technicians have little, if any, customer interaction.

Because the objectives are exactly the same as they are for the core exam, there is overlap between the material in this chapter and that in Chapter 8. Instead of repeating that information verbatim, however, we'll expand on that material a bit and look at it in a different way.

Use Good Communication Skills

Marriages disintegrate when couples don't communicate effectively, or so many of the experts proclaim. Communication is ranked as one of the most important skills needed in order to make a marriage, or any similar partnership, work. The same can be said for business partnerships—it's important to make certain you're listening to your customers, whether they're truly customers in the traditional sense of the word, or whether they're internal users you have to support. The same can also be said of managers and vendors—you need to listen do their concerns and information and then make sure you understand them before beginning a project.

Similarly, you need to make certain the parties in question understand what you're saying to them. It isn't acceptable to resort to the, "But I told you ..." excuse when a customer/partner isn't pleased with the results. Making certain they understand what you're telling them is as important as making certain you understand what they're telling you.

Critical Information

When computers communicate across a network, they search for a common protocol. The protocol is the language that is used, and it isn't uncommon to have more than one protocol bound to a network adapter card.

Consider a scenario in which a server has TCP/IP as its one and only network protocol, and a laptop has NetWare Link (NWLINK) as its first binding and TCP/IP as its second. The laptop will first try to communicate to the server using NWLINK. When that fails, it will try by using TCP/IP. The laptop and server will find that they have a common language (protocol) between them and begin to communicate. The data sent and received by the laptop will be formatted differently than if it were using NWLINK, and it will adapt to that.

To carry the analogy from hardware components to individuals, you must be that laptop. You must be able to adapt your level of communication to fit the individuals you're talking with. If you're discussing issues with another administrator, spouting acronyms one after the other acts as shorthand and is perfectly acceptable. On the other hand, if you're talking with the receptionist and trying to diagnose problems she is encountering, you have to step down your language to the point that you're able to effectively communicate with her.

 One of the best ways to become proficient in this type of communication is to pretend that you aren't the expert and are instead a novice about computers. None of us are experts in every field, so think of the area where you're weak— auto repair, home repair, and so on—and imagine how you would want a professional in that area to discourse with you.

Communication, and problems that can occur with it, isn't isolated to the IT world. Almost every profession stresses the importance of good communication. For example, Sarah Fenson and Jamie Walters—the founder and the chief vision and strategy officer for Ivy Sea, Inc.—wrote an article for *Inc.* on steps to smoother conversations (`http://www.inc.com/articles/2000/08/20000.html`) that included this advice:

- Don't take another person's reaction or anger personally, even if they lash out at you in what seems a personal manner.

- You don't have to have all the answers. It's OK to say, "I don't know."

- Respond (facts and feelings); don't react (feelings)—e.g., "Tell me more about your concern" or "I understand your frustration" instead of "Hey, I'm just doing my job" or "It's not my job."

- Understand that people want to feel heard more than they care about whether you agree with them.

- Remember that what someone says and what we hear can be amazingly different!

- Acknowledge inconvenience or frustration and offer a timeline, particularly if you need someone else's cooperation or your activities will affect them.

- Look for common ground instead of focusing solely on differences.

- Remember that change is stressful for most people, particularly if your activities affect them in a way that they aren't scheduling or controlling.

- Work to keep a positive mental focus.

- Understand that most people, including you, have a unique, often self-serving agenda.

The Federal Emergency Management Agency (FEMA) has a 158-page PDF online (`http://www.training.fema.gov/EMIWeb/downloads/IS242.pdf`) that offers these tidbits:

- The average worker spends 50 percent of his or her time communicating.

- Business success is 85 percent dependent on effective communication and interpersonal skills.

- Forty-five percent of time spent communicating is listening.
- One-fourth of all workplace mistakes are the result of poor communication.
- A remarkable 75 percent of communication is nonverbal.

The six steps they offer for active listening are as follows:

1. Decide to listen, and concentrate on the speaker.
2. Use your imagination, and enter the speaker's situation.
3. Observe the speaker's vocal inflection, enthusiasm or lack of it, and style of delivery.
4. Listen without interruption.
5. Use paraphrasing or clarifying questions to confirm that you received the intended message.
6. Provide feedback to the speaker.

FEMA also recommends that you make eye contact with the person and adjust your body posture to suggest that you're listening. You should give verbal acknowledgement that you're listening, and avoid distractions that may be present. Barriers, or roadblocks, to effective communication include the following:

- Emotional interference
- Defensiveness
- Hearing only facts and not feelings
- Not seeking clarification
- Hearing what is expected instead of what is said
- Stereotyping
- The halo effect (being influenced by some loosely associated factor)
- Automatic dismissal ("We've never done it that way before")
- Resistance to change

Nonverbal communication, also known as *body language*, can include cues that you're communicating effectively or poorly. This can include things like

- Gestures
- Facial expression
- Posture, gaze, and gait
- Vocal cue, such as volume, pitch, or even silence
- Physical appearance, including hairstyle and clothing

All of these items work together to affect the message that is being communicated, whether you're conscious of them at the time or not. The fact that communication is such an important topic in so many other fields should indicate to you its weight in IT as well.

For more information on nonverbal cues, read "Show Me What You Mean: Nonverbal Communication Theory and Application," located at http:// www.asha.org/about/publications/leader-online/archives/2003/q4/ f031216a.htm.

Exam Essentials

Use good communication skills.   Not only must you listen to the party you're communicating with, but you must make certain that you understand them and they understand you. Effective communication is a necessity in the IT world, as it is in many other fields.

Respecting the Customer

It isn't enough to hear the customer and communicate with them—you must also respect them and treat them as well as you would hope another would treat you. This objective tests your knowledge of what is—and isn't—respect for the customer and the customer's property.

Critical Information

The Customer Respect Group, http://www.customerrespect.com, measures the behavior of corporations and the respect they give to customers through their websites. Such items as privacy, responsiveness, attitude, simplicity, transparency, and business principles are combined to create a Customer Respect Index (CRI) ranking. The items they rank in the online world are just as important in the offline world. These items can be interpreted as follows:

Privacy   Do you safeguard all data about, and belonging to, the customer as if it were your own Social Security number (or country-specific identification)?

Responsiveness   How quick—and helpful—are you when a problem first crops up? Do you have a one-hour response time, or is it more like a day or week?

Attitude   Do you make the customer your top priority, or do you tend to their problems while also talking to the realtor on your cell phone about the need to start getting more offers on your house?

Simplicity   Is it easy for customers to get ahold of you? Can they contact you and others working with you without difficulty? Is it easy for them to work with your website, your order forms, and your programs?

Transparency   Are the policies you adhere to (typically those set by the company you work for) open and honest? Do you treat the policies and the customers with integrity?

Business principles   What are the values you place on the customer relationship?

Respecting the customer shouldn't be thought of as rocket science. All you need to do—for this exam, and in the real world—is think of how you would want someone to treat you. Two examples of respecting the customer from my own experience follow:

- My wife and I were in an unknown part of Chicago without ready access to a vehicle, when we started to get hungry. Traditionally, I am a meat-and-potato man and rarely take chances on anything else. There were no establishments of that type around, however, and we wound up in an Asian grill. Expecting not to like the buffet, I ordered a side of lettuce wraps, two buffets, and drinks. As it turned out, I liked the buffet a great deal and went back many times. We also liked the drinks and got several of those. Everything was great, except they forgot to bring the lettuce wraps. I dismissed it and made a mental note to remind the waiter when he brought the bill and have him deduct them from the total. Instead, the manager brought the bill when we were finished eating; he had scribbled on it, "No charge." When I asked him why, he apologized that no one brought the wraps and said he hoped we would come back again another time. I was beside myself with disbelief, thanked him profusely, and as a result have told many people about the best place in Chicago I know of to eat.

- While driving home one night, a dashboard light came on reading "Low tire pressure." Upon inspection, I could hear the right rear tire hissing. I drove to a tire store and explained the situation. I have used this same tire store over the past 14 years for tires, oil changes, exhaust, maintenance, and a number of other things on the vehicles I've owned. The manager came out and said they found a nail in the tire, which they removed; they then patched the tire and charged me $13. I was delighted—expecting the repair to cost me much more—paid my money and went on my way. The next morning, I woke up to find the right rear tire completely flat. I cancelled the morning's appointment, filled the tire with an air compressor, and drove back to the tire store. After a short while, the manager came out and told me that they found another nail in that tire; they were going to eat the $13 on this one, but it had better not happen again. I could not believe the insinuation—that I was driving about looking for nails to hit with that one tire just so I could spend my morning taking them for $13! Instead of offering the possibility that they had overlooked a nail last night and apologizing for the inconvenience, or anything of that sort, they shifted the responsibility to me. Needless to say, I have not been back since, and all of my repair business is now done elsewhere.

These two examples illustrate two different approaches to respecting the customer. In the first example, the customer is well respected and treated better than they ever expected. In the second example, the customer isn't respected at all and is treated as an inconvenience. Given the lifetime value of the customer, it's always better to respect them—and retain them—than to offhandedly dismiss them.

One last area to consider that directly relates to this topic is that of ethics. *Ethics* is the application of morality to situations. Although there are different schools of thought, one of the most popular areas of study is known as *normative ethics*, which focuses on what is normal or practical (right versus wrong, and so on). Regardless of religion, culture, and other influences, there are generally accepted beliefs that some things are wrong (stealing, murder, and so on) and some things are right (such as the Golden Rule). You should always attempt to be ethical in everything you do, because it reflects not only on your character but also on the company for which you work.

Treat the customer's property as if it has value, and you'll win their respect. What may look worthless to you, or may seem inconsequential, can be of great intrinsic value to them. Their property includes the system you're working on (laptop/desktop computer, monitor, peripherals, and so on) as well as other items associated with their business, including their time. Don't use their telephone to make personal calls or unnecessarily call other customers while you're at this site. Don't use their printers or other equipment unless it's in a role associated with the problem you've been summoned to fix.

Exam Essentials

Use job-related professional behavior. Treat your customers with respect. Let them know that you value them and are dealing with them in an ethical manner.

Review Questions

1. True or false: It is OK to say to a customer, "I don't know."

2. True or false: Communication is a critical component of any relationship, even one between a customer and a vendor.

3. True or false: You should react to a customer rather than respond.

4. True or false: People want to feel heard more than they care about whether you agree with them.

5. True or false: You should focus solely on differences rather than wasting time looking for common ground.

6. What percent of time per day does the average worker spend communicating?

7. What percent of time spent communicating is listening?

8. What fraction of all workplace mistakes are the result of poor communication?

9. What is the halo effect?

10. Gestures, facial expressions, posture, gaze, and gait and all forms of what?

Answers to Review Questions

1. True. Honesty is a trait that is highly valued, and there is no shame in admitting that you do not know something. The key is to not leave it at that, but to follow up with the offer to find out.

2. True. Communication is a critical component of any relationship, even one between a customer and a vendor.

3. False. Responding includes facts and feelings, whereas reacting focuses on feelings.

4. True. People want to feel heard more than they care about whether you agree with them.

5. False. Look for common ground instead of focusing solely on differences.

6. The average worker spends 50 percent of their time communicating.

7. Forty-five percent of time spent communicating is listening.

8. One-fourth of all workplace mistakes are the result of poor communication.

9. The halo effect is when you are influenced by something other than the item you should be focusing on—usually it is a loosely associated factor.

10. Gestures, facial expressions, posture, gaze, and gait and all forms of nonverbal communication.

Index

Note to the reader: Throughout this index **boldfaced** page numbers indicate primary discussions of a topic. *Italicized* page numbers indicate illustrations.

Symbols and Numbers

A

G

H

J

U

Wiley Publishing, Inc.
End-User License Agreement

READ THIS. You should carefully read these terms and conditions before opening the software packet(s) included with this book "Book". This is a license agreement "Agreement" between you and Wiley Publishing, Inc. "WPI". By opening the accompanying software packet(s), you acknowledge that you have read and accept the following terms and conditions. If you do not agree and do not want to be bound by such terms and conditions, promptly return the Book and the unopened software packet(s) to the place you obtained them for a full refund.

1. License Grant. WPI grants to you (either an individual or entity) a nonexclusive license to use one copy of the enclosed software program(s) (collectively, the "Software," solely for your own personal or business purposes on a single computer (whether a standard computer or a workstation component of a multi-user network). The Software is in use on a computer when it is loaded into temporary memory (RAM) or installed into permanent memory (hard disk, CD-ROM, or other storage device). WPI reserves all rights not expressly granted herein.

2. Ownership. WPI is the owner of all right, title, and interest, including copyright, in and to the compilation of the Software recorded on the physical packet included with this Book "Software Media". Copyright to the individual programs recorded on the Software Media is owned by the author or other authorized copyright owner of each program. Ownership of the Software and all proprietary rights relating thereto remain with WPI and its licensers.

3. Restrictions On Use and Transfer.

(a) You may only (i) make one copy of the Software for backup or archival purposes, or (ii) transfer the Software to a single hard disk, provided that you keep the original for backup or archival purposes. You may not (i) rent or lease the Software, (ii) copy or reproduce the Software through a LAN or other network system or through any computer subscriber system or bulletin-board system, or (iii) modify, adapt, or create derivative works based on the Software.

(b) You may not reverse engineer, decompile, or disassemble the Software. You may transfer the Software and user documentation on a permanent basis, provided that the transferee agrees to accept the terms and conditions of this Agreement and you retain no copies. If the Software is an update or has been updated, any transfer must include the most recent update and all prior versions.

4. Restrictions on Use of Individual Programs. You must follow the individual requirements and restrictions detailed for each individual program in the About the CD-ROM appendix of this Book or on the Software Media. These limitations are also contained in the individual license agreements recorded on the Software Media. These limitations may include a requirement that after using the program for a specified period of time, the user must pay a registration fee or discontinue use. By opening the Software packet(s), you will be agreeing to abide by the licenses and restrictions for these individual programs that are detailed in the About the CD-ROM appendix and/or on the Software Media. None of the material on this Software Media or listed in this Book may ever be redistributed, in original or modified form, for commercial purposes.

5. Limited Warranty.

(a) WPI warrants that the Software and Software Media are free from defects in materials and workmanship under normal use for a period of sixty (60) days from the date of purchase of this Book. If WPI receives notification within the warranty period of defects in materials or workmanship, WPI will replace the defective Software Media.

(b) WPI AND THE AUTHOR(S) OF THE BOOK DISCLAIM ALL OTHER WARRANTIES, EXPRESS OR IMPLIED, INCLUDING WITHOUT LIMITATION IMPLIED WARRANTIES OF MERCHANTABILITY AND FITNESS FOR A PARTICULAR PURPOSE, WITH RESPECT TO THE SOFTWARE, THE PROGRAMS, THE SOURCE CODE CONTAINED THEREIN, AND/OR THE TECHNIQUES DESCRIBED IN THIS BOOK. WPI DOES NOT WARRANT THAT THE FUNCTIONS CONTAINED IN THE SOFTWARE WILL MEET YOUR REQUIREMENTS OR THAT THE OPERATION OF THE SOFTWARE WILL BE ERROR FREE.

(c) This limited warranty gives you specific legal rights, and you may have other rights that vary from jurisdiction to jurisdiction.

6. Remedies.

(a) WPI's entire liability and your exclusive remedy for defects in materials and workmanship shall be limited to replacement of the Software Media, which may be returned to WPI with a copy of your receipt at the following address: Software Media Fulfillment Department, Attn.: *CompTIA A+ Complete Fast Pass*, Wiley Publishing, Inc., 10475 Crosspoint Blvd., Indianapolis, IN 46256, or call 1-800-762-2974. Please allow four to six weeks for delivery. This Limited Warranty is void if failure of the Software Media has resulted from accident, abuse, or misapplication. Any replacement Software Media will be warranted for the remainder of the original warranty period or thirty (30) days, whichever is longer.

(b) In no event shall WPI or the author be liable for any damages whatsoever (including without limitation damages for loss of business profits, business interruption, loss of business information, or any other pecuniary loss) arising from the use of or inability to use the Book or the Software, even if WPI has been advised of the possibility of such damages.

(c) Because some jurisdictions do not allow the exclusion or limitation of liability for consequential or incidental damages, the above limitation or exclusion may not apply to you.

7. U.S. Government Restricted Rights. Use, duplication, or disclosure of the Software for or on behalf of the United States of America, its agencies and/or instrumentalities "U.S. Government" is subject to restrictions as stated in paragraph (c)(1)(ii) of the Rights in Technical Data and Computer Software clause of DFARS 252.227-7013, or subparagraphs (c) (1) and (2) of the Commercial Computer Software - Restricted Rights clause at FAR 52.227-19, and in similar clauses in the NASA FAR supplement, as applicable.

8. General. This Agreement constitutes the entire understanding of the parties and revokes and supersedes all prior agreements, oral or written, between them and may not be modified or amended except in a writing signed by both parties hereto that specifically refers to this Agreement. This Agreement shall take precedence over any other documents that may be in conflict herewith. If any one or more provisions contained in this Agreement are held by any court or tribunal to be invalid, illegal, or otherwise unenforceable, each and every other provision shall remain in full force and effect.

The Best CompTIA A+ Quick Reference Book/CD Combo Available!

Brush up on key A+ topics with hundreds of challenging review questions!

- Four bonus exams—one for each of the four A+ exams—available only on the CD. Each question includes a detailed explanation.

- Four sets of flash card questions—one for A+ Essentials, one for A+ IT Technician, one for Remote Support Technician, and one for Depot Technician.

- Glossary of key terms for instant reference.

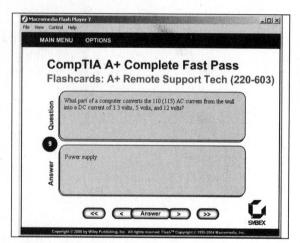

Use the Glossary for instance reference!

- Focus on the important topics, and zero in on the terms you need to know to pass the exam.

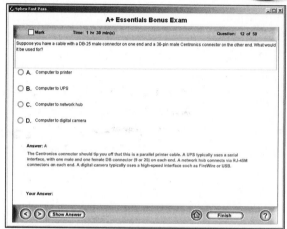

Reinforce understanding of key topics with flash cards for your PC, Pocket PC, or Palm handheld!

- Contains over 150 flash card questions.

- Runs on multiple platforms for usability and portability.

- Quiz yourself anytime, anywhere!